The Golden Age of the American Essay

Edited by Phillip Lopate

Phillip Lopate is the author of *To Show and to Tell: The Craft of Literary Nonfiction* and four essay collections: *Bachelorhood, Against Joie de Vivre, Portrait of My Body,* and *Portrait Inside My Head.* He is the editor of the anthologies *The Glorious American Essay, The Art of the Personal Essay, Writing New York,* and *American Movie Critics.* He was awarded a John Simon Guggenheim Fellowship, a Cullman Center Fellowship, two National Endowment for the Arts grants, and two New York Foundation for the Arts grants. He is a professor of writing at Columbia University's nonfiction MFA program and lives in Brooklyn, New York.

The
Golden Age
of the
American Essay

The Golden Age of the American Essay

1945–1970

Edited and with an introduction by Phillip Lopate

ANCHOR BOOKS
A DIVISION OF PENGUIN RANDOM HOUSE LLC
NEW YORK

AN ANCHOR BOOKS ORIGINAL, APRIL 2021

Introduction, headnotes, and compilation copyright © 2021 by Phillip Lopate

All rights reserved. Published in the United States by Anchor Books, a division of Penguin Random House LLC, New York, and distributed in Canada by Penguin Random House Canada Limited, Toronto.

Anchor Books and colophon are registered trademarks of Penguin Random House LLC.

Pages 515–19 constitute an extension of this copyright page.

The Cataloging-in-Publication Data is on file at the Library of Congress.

Anchor Books Trade Paperback ISBN: 978-0-525-56733-2
eBook ISBN: 978-0-593-31281-0

Book design by Nicholas Alguire

www.anchorbooks.com

Printed in the United States of America
10 9 8 7 6 5 4 3 2 1

CONTENTS

INTRODUCTION

There are certain historical periods when the essay suddenly comes to the fore, and is popular and talked about and relevant, before sinking back into a more typical commercially wan state. The twenty-five years that followed the end of World War II (1945–1970) were an exceptionally fertile period for American essays. One would have to go back to the mid-nineteenth-century American Renaissance of Emerson, Thoreau, Melville, and Margaret Fuller to find a comparable flowering.

Just to give some idea of the range and talent of the essayists in that era: there were masters of the form such as James Baldwin, E. B. White, Elizabeth Hardwick, Susan Sontag, and Edmund Wilson; critics in literature, film, painting, and dance such as Lionel Trilling, Leslie Fiedler, Robert Warshow, Clement Greenberg, Harold Rosenberg, Edwin Denby, James Agee, Manny Farber, Parker Tyler, Pauline Kael, and Irving Howe; policy pundits and diplomats such as Walter Lippmann and George F. Kennan; theologians on the order of Paul Tillich and Reinhold Niebuhr; novelists who moonlighted as essayists, including Norman Mailer, Mary McCarthy, Ralph Ellison, Saul Bellow, Philip Roth, John Updike, Flannery O'Connor, and Gore Vidal; poet-essayists like Randall Jarrell; social scientists and historians, including Robert K. Merton, Margaret Mead, Erving Goffman, Richard Hofstadter, and David Riesman; nature and science writers like Loren Eiseley, Rachel Carson, Edward Hoagland, Annie Dillard, and Lewis Thomas; the food writers M. F. K. Fisher and A. J. Liebling; and New Journalists Joan Didion, Tom Wolfe, Gay Talese, and Seymour Krim.

Why should this proliferation of the essay have occurred at

this particular moment? One could offer several explanations. At war's end, the United States was positioned as the dominant world power, which gave its writers a responsibility to reflect and criticize, with the vanity or expectation that the world would listen. The presence of European émigré thinkers who had fled fascism, such as Hannah Arendt, Theodor Adorno, Nicola Chiaromonte, and Thomas Mann, had raised the intellectual bar and invited a more cosmopolitan perspective, and a wish to emulate that sophisticated continental discourse. The figure of the public intellectual, who would be expected to transmit and explain complex ideas, was in ascension. The general public was willing to take instruction from learned commentators without bristling; for example, poets John Ciardi and Kenneth Rexroth introduced their readers to masterpieces of world literature in their periodical columns. In tandem was the proliferation of weeklies, little magazines, and quarterlies that welcomed such voices, such as *Partisan Review*, *Commentary*, *The Paris Review*, *Saturday Review*, *The New York Review of Books*, *The New Leader*, *The Hudson Review*, *The Village Voice*, and *The New Yorker*. Even established mass-market journals like *Esquire*, *Harper's*, *Vogue*, and *Playboy*, not to mention newspapers, all romanced the essay for a while. The astounding growth of American universities and colleges in the postwar era nourished academic disciplines and provided freelance writers and scholars with a living, with the proviso that they "publish or perish."

Meanwhile, the tensions that rippled through the postwar era and beyond cried out for interpretation and commentary. There was the Cold War with the Soviet Union and its side effect, McCarthyism, which elicited heated debate when it did not provoke silence and fear; the armed conflicts in Korea and Vietnam, and the nuclear threat hovering over everyone; the enduring problems of racism, sexism, poverty, and ecological degradation; the clash between puritanical family values and sexual freedom—all of which spawned the civil rights movement, women's liberation, and the environmental, gay rights, and antiwar movements, and their attendant essayistic formulations.

But let's go back to the start of the postwar era and try to disentangle these strands. The jubilation that followed the defeat of the Axis powers was widespread. As Anatole Broyard described it in *Kafka Was the Rage*: "Nineteen forty-six was a good time—perhaps the best time—in the twentieth century. The war was over, the Depression had ended, and everyone was rediscovering the simple pleasures. A war is like an illness and when it's over you think you've never felt so well. There's a terrific sense of coming back, of repossessing your life." There was also newfound pride in the nation's position: the twentieth century was dubbed "the American Century" and New York City, home to the newly established United Nations, referred to as "the capital of the world."

It's odd, in retrospect, to consider how short-lived that era of good feeling was. It fell swiftly to anxiety. By 1948 the threat of an expansionist Soviet Union had given rise to the House Un-American Activities Committee hearings, intended to ferret out Communists or fellow travelers in the Hollywood community, and Senator Joseph McCarthy's probes of alleged spies in the federal government soon followed. The Republican Party, which had been locked out of power during Franklin Roosevelt and Harry Truman's combined five terms of office, saw anti-Communism as both a patriotic issue and an opportunity to begin to roll back the New Deal's social programs. The anti-Stalinist Left was torn between acknowledging the Soviet Union's threat and deploring wholesale attacks on radicals' speech.

Some of the anxiety and malaise that took hold of the country can be seen as a hangover from the tragedies surrounding World War II. Norman Mailer put it this way in his 1957 essay "The White Negro": "Probably, we will never be able to determine the psychic havoc of the concentration camp and the atomic bomb upon the unconscious mind of almost everyone in those years. . . . The Second World War presented a mirror to the human condition which blinded everyone who looked into it. For if tens of millions were killed in concentration camps . . . if society was so murderous, then who could ignore the most hideous of questions about his own nature? Worse. One could hardly maintain the courage to be individual, to speak with one's own voice, for the years in which one could complacently accept oneself as part of an elite by being a radical were forever gone. A man knew that when he dissented, he gave a note upon his life which could be called in any year of overt crisis. No wonder then that these have been years of conformity and depression. A stench of fear has come out of every pore of American life, and we suffer from a collective failure of nerve."

For Mailer, there were only two choices: the meek Organization Man, and the existential outlaw-hipster living in the margins of society. The 1950s, especially during General Eisenhower's two terms as president, 1953–1961, have been called "the Age of Conformity," to quote the title of Irving Howe's essay. I think that the era's level of conformity can be overstated: there were many contrarian and critical voices at the time among the nation's essayists. Certainly, however, the collapse of the Old Left, not just because of McCarthyite persecution of members of the Communist Party but also because of an increasing awareness of Stalin's murderous regime, meant that Soviet-style Marxism came to be seen as "the God that failed." That left most American writers and intellectuals pretty much in agreement, united behind a liberal consensus. Call it a collective failure of nerve or a realistic adjustment, as you wish. In any case, Lionel Trilling, in the introduction to his book *The Liberal Imagination*, went so far as to say: "In the United States at this time liberalism is not only the dominant but even the sole intellectual tradition. This does not mean, of course, that there is no impulse to conservatism or to reaction. Such impulses are certainly very strong, perhaps even stronger than most of us know. But the conservative impulse and the reactionary impulse do not, with some isolated and some ecclesiastical exceptions, express themselves in ideas but only in action or in irritable mental gestures which seek to resemble ideas."

Before considering whether Trilling was correct in saying this, or for how long it would continue to be correct, let us remember he was writing it in 1950, before the word "liberal" was attacked and disparaged by both Left and Right. There is also the problem of what exactly is meant by "liberalism." As Stefan Collini has written, "the term has been thrown around in such various and contested ways that it has become more or less unusable unless one specifies temporal and geographical boundaries quite closely." Collini points out that in the United Kingdom, "liberal" is associated with free-trade economics, whereas in the United States it is often applied to "progressive and redistributive policies." I am using it here in the sense of advocating progressive reform, not revolution. One such tenet of that progressive ideology was advocating for pluralism and difference, for ensuring the rights of all minority groups and equal access to the goods of society.

The defeat of the Nazis positioned America in the postwar era as a potential beacon of tolerance. It seemed an auspicious moment to complete the project of American democracy by rooting out inequalities and arriving at a benign acceptance of all who comprised "the Family of Man" (to cite the title of a popular fifties photography exhibit). Message films of the day, such as *Gentleman's Agreement*, *Crossfire*, and *Home of the Brave*, sought to point out the absurdity and perniciousness of anti-Semitism and racism. The sociologist Robert K. Merton, who invented the "self-fulfilling prophecy" concept in a 1948 essay of the same name, demonstrated the illogic of racial and religious bias. Mary McCarthy's depiction of the bigoted colonel in her essay "Artists in Uniform" did the same by way of personal narrative. These were all instances of what I am calling the liberal consensus.

It could even be argued that there is a symbiotic relationship between essayism—the practice or ideology of essay writing—and liberalism. My point is not to defend liberalism as a political philosophy but simply to show a mutually beneficial overlap between *its* temperament and that of the essay. Some attributes with which essays are often associated include skepticism, self-skepticism or thinking against oneself, open-ended speculation, freedom, adaptability, avoidance of system, and refusal of dogmatism. The essay seeks out the middle way. The impulse toward moderation goes all the way back to Montaigne, whom Trilling cited as the ideal for the liberal critic and who was always staking out equanimity and avoidance of extremes. As was Emerson, who said, "I think I have not the common degree of sympathy with dark, turbid, mournful, passionate natures. . . . Very hard it is to keep the middle point. It is a very narrow line." To quote

William H. Gass: "this lack of fanaticism, this geniality in the thinker, this sense of the social proprieties involved (the essay can be polemical but never pushy) are evidence of how fully aware the author is of the proper etiquette for meeting minds. . . . If there is too much earnestness, too great a need to persuade, a want of correct convictions in the reader is implied, and therefore an *absence of community*." Theodor Adorno, who declared that "the innermost form of the essay is heresy," nevertheless insisted that "the essay does not strive for closed, deductive, or inductive, construction. . . . The essay . . . proceeds so to speak methodically unmethodically."

One of the potential weaknesses of liberalism, according to Trilling, is that in the interests of "a general enlargement and freedom and rational direction of human life," it privileges the mind at the expense of the emotions and does not make enough allowance for dark, demonic, terrible, and mystical forces. In this way, too, I see a connection between liberalism and essayism. I suspect that the modern essay, unlike other modernist literature, shies away from the unconscious, the irrational, the violent or emotionally raw, and seems more at home in the appeal to common sense. Even those pleasurably perverse, cranky essays that seek to undermine an apparent good or defend an ostensible evil do so by employing a measured irony that allows the reader to glimpse both sides. Even writers such as Irving Howe and Susan Sontag who identified themselves as radicals wrote essays in a traditionally thoughtful, even-tempered, and persuasive manner, rather than an aesthetically avant-garde or emotionally extreme one.

Irving Howe, in his essay "This Age of Conformity," was very wary of the liberal consensus, finding it too smug, cautious, and protective of the status quo. He thought that intellectuals had been bought off by employment in the "mass culture industries and the academy" and were losing their critical independence. "We have all," he wrote, "even the handful who still try to retain a glower of criticism, become responsible and moderate." He also disagreed with Trilling's optimistic view that there had been an overall improvement in the cultural standards of America, through the spread of higher education, paperbacks, and highbrow tips in periodicals. Howe saw a dilution and vulgarization: "It seems to me that, thus far at least, in the encounter between high and middle culture, the latter has come off by far the better." He was not alone. During the fifties and early sixties, many essayists regarded themselves as gatekeepers, guardians of standards that they warned were being eroded by the barbarian middlebrows. Randall Jarrell, in his essay "The Sad Heart at the Supermarket," discerned what he saw as pop culture's vampiric relation to high culture, one that pandered to the lowest common denominator. So did Dwight Macdonald in his screeds against the middlebrow. In Macdonald's words: "It is sometimes called 'Popular Culture,' but I think 'Mass Culture' a more accurate term, since its distinctive mark is that it is solely and directly an article for mass consumption, like chewing gum." Consumerism, driven by Madison Avenue ad agencies, was seen as inducing a hypnotized sheeplike populace. Robert Warshow worried in an essay that his son might become too attached to comic books. Harold Rosenberg not only dissected mass culture's dependence on intellectuals but took potshots at Warshow, Trilling, and Edmund Wilson.

It was common practice then for public intellectuals to criticize each other, like members of a quarreling family. If that made for some nasty competitiveness, it also showed that ideas were taken seriously enough to be tested in written debate. This was particularly true for the group that was centered around *Partisan Review*, the New York Intellectuals. Their approach was shrewdly anatomized by Irving Howe, himself one of them: "In their published work during these years, the New York intellectuals developed a characteristic style of exposition and polemic. With some admiration and a bit of irony, let us call it the style of brilliance. The kind of essay they wrote was likely to be wide-ranging in reference, melding notions about literature and politics, sometimes announcing itself as a study of a writer or literary group but usually taut with a pressure to 'go beyond' its subject, toward some encompassing moral or social observation. It is a kind of writing highly self-conscious in mode, with an unashamed vibration of bravura. Nervous, strewn with knotty or flashy phrases, impatient with transitions and other concessions to dullness, calling attention to itself as a form or at least an outcry, fond of rapid twists, taking pleasure in dispute, dialectic, dazzle—such, at its best or most noticeable, was the essay cultivated by the New York writers."

One thing to observe about the essays that dominated the postwar era on into the mid-1960s was the prevalence of a formal intellectual tone. Regardless of how their positions may have differed or how much they lambasted each other, they were all writing to show off their intelligence and learning. Though bristling with intended charisma, they still seemed attached to the impersonal ideal that T. S. Eliot had advocated in his famous essay "Tradition and the Individual Talent." Seymour Krim, a late arrival on the scene, described how difficult it could be for a young aspiring critic to adopt the approved manner: "For people of my age and bent . . . the whole *PR* [*Partisan Review*] phenomenon along with the *Kenyon Review*, the *Sewanee*, the *Hudson Review* . . . and all the others unfertilized into being by the Anglo-Protestant New Critical chill was a very bad, inhibiting, distorting, freakish influence. It made us ashamed to be what we were and the cruel acid of its standards tore through our writing and scarred our lives as well; in our prose we had to put on Englishy airs, affect all sorts of impressive scholarship and social register unnaturalness and in general contort ourselves into literary pretzels in order to slip through their narrow transoms and get into their pages."

In the sixties, that high formal tone of Trilling or Gore Vidal that had signified quality in American nonfiction prose began to break down. Brasher vernacular voices emerged first among the New Journalists: Tom Wolfe, Hunter S. Thompson, and Krim himself (who took inspiration from the Beats' Jack Kerouac) put forward a flashy, no-holds-barred, jazzy, sometimes stream-of-consciousness style and an insistent way of inserting themselves as protagonists into the reported story. Even the more elegant New Journalism prose stylists, such as Joan Didion and Norman Mailer, proceeded from more subjective autobiographical assumptions. It would not be long before the essay genre itself became dominated by the personal essay. This shift away from the impersonal was in line with a growing distaste for the all-knowing authority of the public intellectual, who was perceived as academic or elitist.

Another outcropping of more casual, unbuttoned essay prose came from pop culture criticism. The staying power and inherent vitality of popular culture had outlasted the snobbish disdain of the gatekeepers and caused writers everywhere, even in the academy, to take it more seriously. In step with the sixties' explosion of youth culture and the antiwar movement, pop culture was looked to as a source of rebellious energy, a weapon against the staid establishment. Susan Sontag expressed approval of the Beatles, rock 'n' roll, and science fiction movies: the kids were all right. (Thirty years later, she had second thoughts: "To laud work condescended to then as 'popular' culture did not mean to conspire in the repudiation of high culture and its complexities. . . . What I didn't understand . . . was that seriousness itself was in the early stages of losing credibility in the culture at large, and that some of the more transgressive art I was enjoying would reinforce frivolous, merely consumerist transgressions.") In retrospect, you might say it was a trade-off: essayists no longer felt obliged to demonstrate their intellectual bona fides, which unleashed a new vitality into their prose even as it cut them off from a conversation with the ancestral traditions of the form.

Throughout history, essayists have conversed with each other in dialogues that might span decades or centuries. Montaigne quoted Seneca, Plutarch, and Cicero; William Hazlitt wrote an appreciation of Montaigne; Virginia Woolf wrote about Hazlitt and Montaigne, and so on. The essay tradition has been a linked conversation, an invitation to form friendship with the reader and to affirm or joust with one's fellow essayists. So Susan Sontag wrote a beautiful eulogy to Paul Goodman about their failed friendship; James Baldwin wrote a searching analysis of his relationship with Richard Wright, which shifted from mentor to peer to one of ruefully alienated affection.

Minorities were drawn to the essay form as a useful way to define and refine group identity, to embrace or situate oneself at a distance from the tribe. Gerald Early has shrewdly analyzed this linkage: "It is not surprising that many black writers have been attracted to the essay as a literary form since the essay is the most

exploitable mode of the confession and the polemic, the two vari-
ants of the essay that black writers have mostly used. (Few black
writers have written what might be strictly called *belles lettres*–
style essays.) The conditions under which many black writers
felt they had to write (and live), and their coming to terms with
these conditions, have constituted their most driving intellectual
obsession. Thus, the black essay has been, in truth, a political
provocation and a flawed example, if not a full representation, of
a philosophical rumination even if the work itself was sometimes
entangled in a wealth of sociological detail. Black writers could
not help but see their writing as political, since they saw their
condition in these terms and their writing and their *condition*
have been largely inseparable." Early goes on to say that much
of this writing had been done by a bourgeois elite, who were
often driven out of guilt to romanticize "the poverty culture of
lower- or under-class blacks," and who found themselves caught
between speaking for the African American experience but often
not to the majority of blacks. This may partly explain the prose
styles of James Baldwin, Ralph Ellison, or Albert Murray, who
incorporated rhetorical Anglicisms, qualifying interjections, and
ornate syntax—all of which was expected of essayists—while
adding gritty, colloquial tonalities from the blues and the street.

The civil rights movement was given its most direct articulation by Reverend Martin Luther King, Jr., in his famous "Letter
from Birmingham Jail" and his "I Have a Dream" and anti–
Vietnam War speeches. Though these may have taken shape
initially as speeches or letters, they were in fact essays in the classical sense, circling their subject matter with complexity, doubt,
and interrogation. James Baldwin passionately articulated the
anger, sorrow, and disappointment of African Americans and
their despair at the poor condition of ghetto neighborhoods, at
the same time as he put forward a self-portrait of stunning speci-
ficity. Meanwhile, Ralph Ellison and his friend and fellow Harlem writer Albert Murray took friendly issue with Baldwin for
overstressing the miseries of blacks in America and leaving out
their joy, humor, creativity, and resilience.

Increasingly during this period, women came to the fore as
essayists. They had long been underrepresented on publishers'

lists. Now they emerged as celebrated spokespersons for both gender and region. There were Southerners such as Flannery O'Connor and Elizabeth Hardwick, and a number of West Coast women—Mary McCarthy, Susan Sontag, Joan Didion—who moved east to claim their seat at Gotham's table while expressing irritation at the smug provinciality of the New York intelligentsia. When the women's movement caught fire in the 1970s, feminism was given ideological shape and urgent witness by essayists such as Adrienne Rich, Audre Lorde, Vivian Gornick, and Andrea Dworkin. Earlier, Rachel Carson sounded the alarm about chemical pollution in her seminal book *Silent Spring*, and a whole generation of environmental essayists followed her lead.

Essays got talked about, as they still do. George F. Kennan's "The Sources of Soviet Conduct," Norman Mailer's "The White Negro," Leslie Fiedler's "Come Back to the Raft Ag'in, Huck Honey!," James Baldwin's essays in *The Fire Next Time*, Susan Sontag's "Notes on Camp," Joan Didion's "Slouching Towards Bethlehem," and many others were staples of dinner party conversation. As James Wolcott has stated, "essays can make news, excite the chattering classes, provoke op-eds, catch a cultural phenomenon in a butterfly net, clear away the deadwood of received opinion or simply make the reader privy to the writer's thought processes and preoccupations."

Not surprisingly, many of the era's novelists took a crack at essay writing, especially when magazines enticed them with big paydays, sending them off to report on political conventions or sporting events. Some, including Ralph Ellison, Philip Roth, Flannery O'Connor, and William Styron, proved equally adept at both forms. Saul Bellow never put his full energies into essay writing, electing to save them for his essayistic fiction. Since essays have never enjoyed the same status as novels, writers who practiced both forms understandably preferred to be regarded primarily as novelists. That being said, it would seem that more than a few—James Baldwin, Joan Didion, Susan Sontag, Mary McCarthy, Gore Vidal, Norman Mailer—did their most lasting work in essays and extended nonfiction. The most lively, memorable, believable characters they created on the page were their essayistic I-narrators: Jimmy, Joan, Susan, Mary, Gore, Aquarius. Whether this outcome was because the novel had temporarily reached an impasse between played-out realism and overly tricky postmodernism, or because the turmoil of those postwar years and beyond was better suited to a form that encouraged quick response, the essay was having one of its moments.

The essays I have chosen for this anthology are by no means the only significant ones to have been written during the years covered. I could have easily filled several volumes with representative samples, but page limitations prevailed. What I've tried to do is to convey the quality, range, and variety of essays in the postwar period and beyond, the way the form was taken up in every field and discipline, and how it reflected the historical times, both the noisy overt issues and the quieter undercurrents. Sometimes I have chosen the canonical essay of an author; at other times I have opted for a lesser-known work that seems equally provocative, flavorful, or poignant.

I was born in 1943, right before the end of World War II, and so I cannot claim to remember the war years, but I have a sort of in-utero identification with that period. Being something of a Freudian, I could even ascribe my sympathetic interest in those years to an oedipal desire to insert myself in the midst of my then-young parents. By 1950 I was seven years old and starting to come into consciousness about the surrounding world. I entered college in 1960, graduated in 1964, protested the Vietnam War in 1968, and shortly after began dual careers as a writer and a teacher. I have elected to end this anthology's chronology, somewhat arbitrarily, at 1970 with Joan Didion's fine essay "On the Morning After the Sixties," which brings down the curtain on that era.

I am well aware that there is something suspect about the whole notion of a "golden age," which invites the sentimentality of fuddy-duddies who can't seem to feel comfortable in the present and who discount the value of youthful creativity. As it happens, we are again going through a thriving period for the essay. I hope to show my openness to these new achievements in a subsequent anthology, which will be dedicated to the contemporary, twenty-first-century essay. Meanwhile, it has been an utter joy to hang out again in what is to me a special chunk of time, reading about these years and retrospectively reliving them through the spirited accounts and reflections of the essayists in this collection.

The
Golden Age
of the
American Essay

James Agee (1909–1955) is today celebrated most for his singular, rhapsodic study of Southern sharecroppers, Let Us Now Praise Famous Men, *and his achingly beautiful, posthumously published novel* A Death in the Family. *But he also had an extensive journalistic career writing for Henry Luce's publications* Time, Life, *and* Fortune—*as a film critic, reporter, and commentator. Luce called on Agee to bring a high literary style to topical events, such as reflecting on the death of President Franklin Delano Roosevelt. When the country found itself at peace at the end of World War II, it was Agee's task to sum up the national mood in a list essay, one that would honor the range, variety, and complexity of life at a key historical moment.*

THE NATION: DEMOCRATIC VISTAS

Out on the Montana range, rattlesnakes were unusually plentiful, and the old men predicted a long warm fall and a short easy winter.

In Chatsworth, Illinois, First Lieut. Billie Wither, an Army nurse, made Page One of the weekly *Plaindealer* when she got back home: "She has seen much front-line active duty in the European sector, including Italy and Germany. She was able to see the Alps in all their beauty and says Switzerland, especially, is beautiful."

In Manhattan, a nobly decorated veteran of the Pacific was passed along by a junior executive, who was unfavorably impressed by his willingness to take "anything," to a junior executive who told him, kindly, "You know, I don't think this is exactly the job for you." Upon hearing this, the young hero burst into tears.

Happy days, more or less, were here again. Despite prodigious achievements at home & abroad, the nation had not been essentially changed by war. Now, returning to peace rather than struggling through to it nine-tenths dead, the United States was more like itself than ever—in a world which would never again be remotely the same.

Butter pats were served again at Schrafft's and Henrici's; cases against cigaret blackmarketers were dropped. Along the highways, in whatever cars they had, people were blowing out tires and bumping into each other again; the city traffic tie-ups were something awful. Other moral equivalents to war were the fall's football games—which drew record crowds—and a shooting season so trigger-happy that Colorado's game department recommended manslaughter laws for hunters.

Army deaths were totaled 216,966, the Navy's 55,896; the National Safety Council announced that on the home front, since Pearl Harbor, 355,000 had been killed through accident, and 36,000,000 injured.

The great hit songs of the season were "Till the End of Time," "I'll Buy That Dream," "On the Atchison, Topeka & the Santa Fe." Bestselling novels were *The Black Rose* and *Forever Amber*. A big movie hit was *Love Letters*, a romance about amnesia. A psychologist claimed that Superman provided a beneficent Aristotelian catharsis; a Jesuit saw in him a fascist archetype. Young girls tried to look like Bacall with a dash of Hepburn. Their elders went in for cosmetics with manic names like Fatal Apple and Havoc. They also favored detachable daintiness features and phantom crotches. In ads as expressive as dreams, fathers forfeited their children's love because of denture breath, and women exclaimed: "Don't expect me to marry you with a mouthful of cavities!"

A Navy doctor, soon to come home, wrote warning his wife rather sadly that he had gotten bald and heavy. She wrote back gently: "You will find, that three years has done quite a bit to me, too."

A partially paralyzed ex–defense worker gave his six-year-old daughter a doll, his nine-year-old son a pack of cards, told them to shut their eyes because more was coming, and shot them through their heads.

The war was over. The postwar world was born. Everywhere the returning traveler saw signs of change, signs of no change at all, signs of change but too fast, signs of change but not fast enough: signs by the millions.

In Seattle a twenty-five-year-old veteran was sore about the skimpiness of his civilian shirttails. All over the United States, businessmen read a brochure: "Among Convention Leaders Who Know—It's Chicago 81 to 65." In New Haven a CIOrganizer told ralliers: "We want full employment and if free enterprise must go, let it go. The manufacturers want to return to normalcy—the normalcy of no labor movement."

In the window of a gas station–soda fountain in McFarland, California (pop. 605), appeared a wobbly handmade sign: "Colored Trade Not Solisited at Fountain."

In New Orleans white housewives, proud for the first time in their lives of doing their own housework, said "those niggers all want $12 or $15 a week and they're no good at that." The editor of the Laurel, Mississippi, *Leader-Call* listened to servicemen on a train en route to mustering-out camp, talking of sports, and home, and their tremendous desire to get back to the joys of civilian life. He wrote: "I wonder if they aren't going to get a great jolt."

In Kansas City, which calls itself the heart of America, a veteran of the Pacific observed: "Over there in the line we talked about life and death, and who was going to get it next. So what happens when I get home? I no more get into the house the old man begins to tell me about his God-damned lawn mower."

A twelve-year-old delinquent phoned home at three a.m.: "Mom! Guess where I am? In jail again."

At the height of a historic, nationwide housing shortage, such classified ads as this were common in the *Star*: "Desperate. No place to go. Veteran, wife and two children need home immediately."

In Davey Markowitz's place two veterans, former friends and schoolmates, met for the first time in four years. The ex-sergeant gave his boyhood friend, an ex-lieutenant, only a perfunctory greeting: "I hate lieutenants," he snarled.

Over in Byers, Kansas, Wayne Fisk came back from the Navy and said that a long rest would sure look good to him. But a day of loafing was enough. So while he was resting he painted his father's house.

In its own quiet way, it was a period as madly chaotic in the relatively unscathed United States as in the shattered rest of the world. Nobody seemed able to see much beyond the end of his nose. Business tossed on the greatest wave of labor unrest since the middle thirties. In vast numbers ex–war workers, some unwilling and some unable to live on reduced postwar wages, floated along on war savings or on unemployment compensation while, in vast numbers, jobs went begging. Veterans too wanted time to rest up and to enjoy themselves and to get readjusted, and they didn't want to be hurried about it either. Many were jealous of the high wages paid in wartime and paid no longer; many others, who took back their old jobs, left them within a few weeks.

Everywhere, people had expected an immediate, dreamlike postwar flow of the autos and refrigerators and radios and washing machines and farm machines and nylons and plumbing and good clothes which had been promised all through the war to the most machine-dependent and comfort-loving of nations. Everywhere, such hopes were sorely disappointed.

Underneath all the pleasure-bending, elbow-bending and tongue-bending (reflected perhaps—and perhaps not—in increased church attendance) lay a more mature awareness, a profound, bewildered foreboding, a tragic and justified uneasiness, a still more disturbing fatalism. Many Americans assumed that the nation's interracial troubles were barely beginning; that another great depression and another great war were dead certainties; that the next opponent was Russia; that nothing whatever could be done about such matters.

Almost without exception Americans realized that they might not like the neighbors but they had to live with them. Almost without exception they talked a good deal about the atomic bomb; many had it on their minds even more than they talked about it. But almost without exception they were so thoroughly absorbed in immediate troubles, pleasures, hopes, angers and disappointments—and perhaps so essentially far-gone in the basic kind of hope which holds human beings upright—that they were virtually incapable of even trying to take fate into their own hands.

The general attitude about atomic control got no farther than the first primitive reflex of greed and terror; the unkeepable secret must be kept. The general attitude toward racial problems was most sadly expressed by the more thoughtful Southerners, who said they only wished they could spend the next few years where there weren't any Negroes. The general attitude toward Europe was in the first place insufficiently informed, in the second place wearily or even scornfully indifferent.

Isolationism, in its old, simple, scarehead sense, was somewhere near being a thing of the past. But unconscious isolationism, far more insidious, was an all-powerful and increasing phenomenon of the present and future. If civilization, or time itself in the provincial, planetary sense, was to last more than another few decades, the responsibility rested chiefly on the American people. But for wholly understandable, nonetheless tragic reasons, the American people were not very responsible toward any major responsibility. If this troubled season was any indication, they would be too busy trying to buy that wholly unpurchasable dream.

Reinhold Niebuhr (1892–1971) was a Protestant theologian and minister whose voluminous writings, including The Nature and Destiny of Man *(two volumes), assessed the role of Christianity in a secular age. Advocating what he termed "Christian realism," he remained skeptical of utopian ideologies about the goodness of man that downplayed the persistence of evil. "Reinhold Niebuhr remains the great illuminator of the dark conundrums of human nature, history and public policy," wrote Arthur Schlesinger, Jr. His teachings on social justice had a profound impact on Martin Luther King, Jr. "Humor and Faith" began as a sermon and was expanded into essay form.*

HUMOR AND FAITH

He that sitteth in the heavens shall laugh: the Lord shall have them in derision.

Ps. 2:4

This word of the Second Psalm is one of three instances in the Bible in which laughter is attributed to God. God is not frequently thought of as possessing a sense of humor, though that quality would have to be attributed to perfect personality. There are critics of religion who regard it as deficient in the sense of humor, and they can point to the fact that there is little laughter in the Bible. Why is it that Scriptural literature, though filled with rejoicings and songs of praise, is not particularly distinguished for the expression of laughter? There are many sayings of Jesus which betray a touch of ironic humor; but on the whole one must agree with the critics who do not find much humor or laughter in the Bible.

This supposed defect will, however, appear less remarkable if the relation of humor to faith is understood. Humor is, in fact, a prelude to faith; and laughter is the beginning of prayer. Laughter must be heard in the outer courts of religion, and the echoes of it should resound in the sanctuary; but there is no laughter in the holy of holies, laughter is swallowed up in prayer and humor fulfilled by faith.

Humor, Faith, and Incongruity

The intimate relation between humor and faith is derived from the fact that both deal with the incongruities of our existence. Humor is concerned with the immediate incongruities of life and faith with the ultimate ones. Both humor and faith are expressions of the freedom of the human spirit, of its capacity to stand outside of life, and itself, and view the whole scene. But any view of the whole immediately creates the problem of how the incongruities of life are to be dealt with; for the effort to understand the life, our place in it, confronts us with inconsistencies and incongruities which do not fit into any neat picture of the whole. Laughter is our reaction to immediate incongruities and those which do not affect us essentially. Faith is the only possible response to the ultimate incongruities of existence which threaten the very meaning of our life.

We laugh at what? At the sight of a fool upon the throne of the king; or the proud man suffering from some indignity; or the child introducing its irrelevancies into the conversation of the mature. We laugh at the juxtaposition of things which do not fit together. A boy slipping on the ice is not funny. Slipping on the ice is funny only if it happens to one whose dignity is upset. A favorite device of dramatists, who have no other resources of humor, is to introduce some irrelevant interest into the central theme of the drama by way of the conversation of maid or butler. If this irrelevance is to be really funny, however, it must have some more profound relation to the theme than the conversor intended. This is to say that humor manages to resolve incongruities by the discovery of another level of congruity. We laugh at the proud man slipping on the ice, not merely because the contrast between his dignity and his undignified plight strikes us as funny; but because we feel that his discomfiture is a poetically just rebuke of his dignity. Thus we deal with immediate incongruities, in which we are not too seriously involved and which open no gap in the coherence of life in such a way as to threaten us essentially.

But there are profound incongruities which contain such a threat. Man's very position in the universe is incongruous. That is the problem of faith, and not of humor. Man is so great and yet so small, so significant and yet so insignificant. "On the one hand," says Edward Bellamy, "is the personal life of man, an atom, a grain of sand on a boundless shore, a bubble of a foam flecked ocean, a life bearing a proportion to the mass of past, present and future, so infinitesimal as to defy the imagination. On the other hand is a certain other life, as it were a spark of the universal life, insatiable in aspiration, greedy of infinity, asserting solidarity with all things and all existence, even while subject to the limitations of space and time."* That is the contrast.

When man surveys the world he seems to be the very center of it; and his mind appears to be the unifying power which makes sense out of the whole. But this same man, reduced to the limits of his animal existence, is a little animalcule, preserving a precarious moment of existence within the vastness of space and time. There is a profound incongruity between the "inner" and the "outer" world, or between the world as viewed from man's perspective, and the man in the world as viewed from a more ultimate perspective. The incongruity becomes even more profound when it is considered that it is the same man who assumes the ultimate perspective from which he finds himself so insignificant.

Philosophers seek to overcome this basic incongruity by reducing one world to the dimension of the other; or raising one perspective to the height of the other. But neither a purely naturalistic nor a consistently idealistic system of philosophy is ever com-

---

* In *The Religion of Solidarity*.

pletely plausible. There are ultimate incongruities of life which can be resolved by faith but not by reason. Reason can look at them only from one standpoint or another, thereby denying the incongruities which it seeks to solve. They are also too profound to be resolved or dealt with by laughter. If laughter seeks to deal with the ultimate issues of life it turns into a bitter humor. This means that it has been overwhelmed by the incongruity. Laughter is thus not merely a vestibule to faith but also a "no-man's-land" between faith and despair. We laugh cheerfully at the incongruities on the surface of life; but if we have no other resource but humor to deal with those which reach below the surface, our laughter becomes an expression of our sense of the meaninglessness of life.

Laughter and Human Judgment

Laughter is a sane and healthful response to the innocent foibles of men; and even to some which are not innocent. All men betray moods and affectations, conceits and idiosyncrasies, which could become the source of great annoyance to us if we took them too seriously. It is better to laugh at them. A sense of humor is indispensable to men of affairs who have the duty of organizing their fellowmen in common endeavors. It reduces the frictions of life and makes the foibles of men tolerable. There is, in the laughter with which we observe and greet the foibles of others, a nice mixture of mercy and judgment, of censure and forbearance. We would not laugh if we regarded these foibles as altogether fitting and proper. There is judgment, therefore, in our laughter. But we also prove by the laughter that we do not take the annoyance too seriously. However, if our fellows commit a serious offense against the common good, laughter no longer avails. If we continue to indulge in it, the element of forbearance is completely eliminated from it. Laughter against real evil is bitter. Such bitter laughter of derision has its uses as an instrument of condemnation. But there is no power in it to deter the evil against which it is directed.

There were those who thought that we could laugh Mussolini and Hitler out of court. Laughter has sometimes contributed to the loss of prestige of dying oligarchies and social systems. Thus Cervantes's *Don Quixote* contributed to the decline of feudalism, and Boccaccio's *Decameron* helped to signal the decay of medieval asceticism. But laughter alone never destroys a great seat of power and authority in history. Its efficacy is limited to preserving the self-respect of the slave against the master. It does not extend to the destruction of slavery. Thus all the victims of tyranny availed themselves of the weapon of wit to preserve their sense of personal self-respect. Laughter provided them with a little private world in which they could transvalue the values of the tyrant, and reduce his pompous power to the level of the ridiculous. Yet there is evidence that the most insufferable forms of tyranny (as in the concentration camps, for instance) could not be ameliorated by laughter.

Laughter may turn to bitterness when it faces serious evil, partly because it senses its impotence. But, in any case, serious evil must be seriously dealt with. The bitterness of derision is serious enough; but where is the resource of forgiveness to come from? It was present in the original forbearance of laughter; but it cannot be brought back into the bitterness of derision. The contradiction between judgment and mercy cannot be resolved by humor but only by vicarious pain.

Thus we laugh at our children when they betray the jealous conceits of childhood. These are the first buds of sin which grow in the soil of the original sin of our common humanity. But when sin has conceived and brought forth its full fruit, our laughter is too ambiguous to deal with the child's offense; or if it is not ambiguous it becomes too bitter. If we retain the original forbearance of laughter in our judgment it turns into harmful indulgence. Parental judgment is always confronted with the necessity of relating rigorous judgment creatively to the goodness of mercy. That relation can be achieved only as the parent himself suffers under the judgments which are exacted. Not humor but the cross is the meeting point of justice and mercy, once both judgment and mercy have become explicit. Laughter can express both together, when neither is fully defined. But, when it becomes necessary to define each explicitly, laughter can no longer contain them both. Mercy is expelled and only bitterness remains.

Laughter and Divine Judgment

What is true of our judgments of each other is true of the judgment of God. In the word of our text, God is pictured laughing at man and having him in derision because of the vanity of man's imagination and pretensions. There is no suggestion of a provisional geniality in this divine laughter. Derisiveness is pure judgment. It is not possible to resolve the contradiction between mercy and judgment, on the level of the divine, through humor; because the divine judgment is ultimate judgment. That contradiction, which remains an unsolved mystery in the Old Testament, is resolved only as God is revealed in Christ. There is no humor but suffering in that revelation. There is, as we have observed, a good deal of ironic humor in the sayings of Christ. But there is no humor in the scene of Christ upon the Cross. The only humor on Calvary is the derisive laughter of those who cried, "He saved others; himself he can not save. . . . If he be the son of God let him come down from the cross" (Matt. 27:42); and the ironic inscription on the cross, ordered by Pilate: "The King of the Jews." These ironic and derisive observations were the natural reactions of common sense to dimensions of revelation which transcend common sense. Since they could not be comprehended by faith, they prompted ironic laughter.

There is no humor in the cross because the justice and the mercy of God are fully revealed in it. In that revelation, God's justice is made the more terrible because the sin of man is disclosed in its full dimension. It is a rebellion against God from which God Himself suffers. God cannot remit the consequences of sin; yet He does show mercy by taking the consequences upon and into Himself. This is the main burden of the disclosure of God in Christ. This is the final clue to the mystery of the divine character.

Mercy and justice are provisionally contained in laughter; and the contradiction between them is tentatively resolved in the sense of humor. But the final resolution of justice, fully developed, and of mercy, fully matured, is possible only when the sharp edge of justice is turned upon the executor of judgment without being blunted. This painful experience of vicarious suffering is far removed from laughter. Only an echo of the sense of humor remains in it. The echo is the recognition in the sense of humor that judgment and mercy belong together, even though they seem to be contradictory. But there is no knowledge in the sense of humor of how the two are related to each other and how the contradiction between them is to be resolved.

Laughter at the Self

The sense of humor is even more important provisionally in dealing with our own sins than in dealing with the sins of others. Humor is a proof of the capacity of the self to gain a vantage point from which it is able to look at itself. The sense of humor is thus a by-product of self-transcendence. People with a sense of humor do not take themselves too seriously. They are able to "stand off" from themselves, see themselves in perspective, and recognize the ludicrous and absurd aspects of their pretensions. All of us ought to be ready to laugh at ourselves because all of us are a little funny in our foibles, conceits and pretensions. What is funny about us is precisely that we take ourselves too seriously. We are rather insignificant little bundles of energy and vitality in a vast organization of life. But we pretend that we are the very center of this organization. This pretension is ludicrous; and its absurdity increases with our lack of awareness of it. The less we are able to laugh at ourselves the more it becomes necessary and inevitable that others laugh at us.

It is significant that little children are really very sober, though they freely indulge in a laughter which expresses a pure animal joy of existence. But they do not develop the capacity of real humor until the fifth or sixth year, at which time they may be able to laugh at themselves and at others. At about this age their intense preoccupation with self and with an immediate task at hand is partly mitigated. The sense of humor grows, in other words, with the capacity of self-transcendence. If we can gain some perspective upon our own self we are bound to find the self's pretensions a little funny.

This means that the ability to laugh at oneself is the prelude to the sense of contrition. Laughter is a vestibule to the temple of confession. But laughter is not able to deal with the problem of the sins of the self in any ultimate way. If we become fully conscious of the tragedy of sin we recognize that our preoccupation with self, our exorbitant demands upon life, our insistence that we receive more attention than our needs deserve, affect our neighbors harmfully and defraud them of their rightful due. If we recognize the real evil of sin, laughter cannot deal with the problem. If we continue to laugh after having recognized the depth of evil, our laughter becomes the instrument of irresponsibility. Laughter is thus not only the vestibule of the temple of confession but the no-man's-land between cynicism and contrition. Laughter may express a mood which takes neither the self nor life seriously. If we take life seriously but ourselves not too seriously, we cease to laugh. The contradiction in man between "the good that he would and does not do, and the evil that he would not do, and does" (see Rom. 7:15–20) is no laughing matter.

There is furthermore another dimension in genuine contrition which laughter does not contain. It is the awareness of being judged from beyond ourselves. There is something more than self-judgment in genuine contrition. "For me it is a small thing to be judged of men," declares St. Paul, "neither judge I myself; for I know nothing against myself; he who judges me is the Lord" (1 Cor. 4:3–4). In an ultimate sense the self never knows anything against itself. The self of today may judge the self's action of yesterday as evil. But that means that the self of today is the good self. We are within depths of mystery which are never completely fathomed. Man is a spirit; and among the qualities of his spirit are the capacity to regard himself and the world; and to speculate on the meaning of the whole. This man is, when he is the observer, the very center of the universe. Yet the same man "brings his years to an end like a tale that is told" (Ps. 90:9). This man groweth up like grass in the morning which in the evening is cut down and withereth. The brevity of human existence is the most vivid expression and climax of human weakness.

The incongruity of man's greatness and weakness, of his mortality and immortality, is the source of his temptation to evil. Some men seek to escape from their greatness to their weakness; they try to deny the freedom of their spirit in order to achieve the serenity of nature. Some men seek to escape from their weakness to their greatness. But these simple methods of escape are unavailing. The effort to escape into the weakness of nature leads not to the desired serenity but to sensuality. The effort to escape from weakness to greatness leads not to the security but to the evils of greed and lust for power, or to the opposite evils of a spirituality which denies the creaturely limitations of human existence.

The philosophies of the ages have sought to bridge the chasm between the inner and the outer world, between the world of thought in which man is so great and the world of physical extension in which man is so small and impotent. But philosophy cannot bridge the chasm. It can only pretend to do so by reducing one world to the dimensions of the other. Thus naturalists, materialists, mechanists, and all philosophers, who view the world as primarily a system of physical relationships, construct a universe of meaning from which man is the full dimension of spirit and can find no home. The idealistic philosophers, on the other hand, construct a world of rational coherence in which mind is the very stuff of order, the very foundation of existence. But their systems do not do justice to the large areas of chaos in the world; and they fail to give an adequate account of man himself, who is something less, as well as something more, than mind.

Humor and Incongruity

The sense of humor is, in many respects, a more adequate resource for the incongruities of life than the spirit of philosophy. If we are able to laugh at the curious quirks of fortune, in which the system of order and meaning which each life constructs within and around itself is invaded, we at least do not make the mistake of prematurely reducing the irrational to a nice system. Things "happen" to us. We make our plans for a career, and sickness frustrates us. We plan our life, and war reduces all plans to chaos. The storms and furies of the world of nature, which can so easily reduce our private schemes to confusion, do of course have their own laws. They "happen" according to a discernible system of causality. There is no question about the fact that there are systems of order in the world. But it is not so easy to discern a total system of order and meaning which will comprehend the various levels of existence in an orderly whole.

To meet the disappointments and frustrations of life, the irrationalities and contingencies with laughter, is a high form of wisdom. Such laughter does not obscure or defy the dark irrationality. It merely yields to it without too much emotion and friction. A humorous acceptance of fate is really the expression of a high form of self-detachment. If men do not take themselves too seriously, if they have some sense of the precarious nature of the human enterprise, they prove that they are looking at the whole drama of life not merely from the circumscribed point of their own interests but from some further and higher vantage point. One thinks for instance of the profound wisdom which underlies the capacity of laughter in the Negro people. Confronted with the cruelties of slavery, and socially too impotent to throw off the yoke, they learned to make their unpalatable situation more sufferable by laughter. There was of course a deep pathos mixed with the humor, a proof of the fact that laughter had reached its very limit.

Laughter in the Face of Evil and Death

There is indeed a limit to laughter in dealing with life's frustrations. We can laugh at all of life's surface irrationalities. We preserve our sanity the more surely if we do not try to reduce the whole crazy-quilt of events in which we move to a premature and illusory order. But the ultimate incongruities of human existence cannot be "laughed off." We cannot laugh at death. We do try of course.

A war era is particularly fruitful of *Galgenhumor* (gallows humor). Soldiers are known on occasion to engage in hysterical laughter when nerves are tense before the battle. They speak facetiously of the possible dire fate which might befall this or that man of the company. "Sergeant," a soldier is reported to have said before a recent battle, "don't let this little fellow go into battle before me. He isn't big enough to stop the bullet meant for me." The joke was received with uproarious good humor by the assembled comrades. But when the "little fellow" died in battle the next day, everyone felt a little ashamed of the joke. At any rate it was quite inadequate to deal with the depth and breadth of the problem of death.

If we persist in laughter when dealing with the final problem of human existence, when we turn life into a comedy we also reduce it to meaninglessness. That is why laughter, when pressed to solve the ultimate issue, turns into a vehicle of bitterness rather than joy. To laugh at life in the ultimate sense means to scorn it. There is a note of derision in that laughter and an element of despair in that derision.

Just as laughter is the "no-man's-land" between cynicism and contrition when we deal with the incongruous element of evil in our own soul, so is it also the area between despair and faith when dealing with evil and incongruity in the world about us. Our provisional amusement with the irrational and unpredictable fortunes which invade the order and purpose of our life must move either toward bitterness or faith, when we consider not this or that frustration and this or that contingent event, but when we are forced to face the issue of the basic incongruity of death.

Either we have a faith from the standpoint of which we are able to say, "I am persuaded, that neither death, nor life . . . shall be able to separate us from the love of God, which is in Christ Jesus our Lord" (Rom. 8:38–39), or we are overwhelmed by the incongruity of death and are forced to say with Ecclesiastes: "I said in mine heart concerning the estate of the sons of men . . . that they might see that they themselves are beasts. For that which befalleth the sons of men befalleth beasts; . . . as the one dieth, so dieth the other; yea, they all have one breath; so that a man hath no preeminence above a beast; for all is vanity" (Eccles. 3:18–19).

The final problem of human existence is derived from the fact that in one context and from one perspective man has no preeminence above the beast; and yet from another perspective his preeminence is very great. No beast comes to the melancholy conclusion that "all is vanity"; for the purposes of its life do not outrun its power, and death does not therefore invade its life as an irrelevance. Furthermore it has no prevision of its own end and is therefore not tempted to melancholy. Man's melancholy over the prospect of death is the proof of his partial transcendence over the natural process which ends in death. But this is only a partial transcendence and man's power is not great enough to secure his own immortality.

This problem of man, so perfectly and finally symbolized in the fact of death, can be solved neither by proving that he has no preeminence above the beast, nor yet proving that his pre-eminence is a guarantee that death has no final dominion over him. Man is both great and small, both strong and weak, both involved in and free of the limits of nature; and he is a unity of strength and weakness of spirit and creatureliness. There is therefore no possibility of man extricating himself by his own power from the predicament of his amphibious state.

Faith and the Limitations of Laughter

The Christian faith declares that the ultimate order and meaning of the world lies in the power and wisdom of God, who is both Lord of the whole world of creation and the father of human spirits. It believes that the incongruities of human existence are finally overcome by the power and the love of God, and that the love which Christ revealed is finally sufficient to overcome the contradiction of death.

This faith is not some vestigial remnant of a credulous and pre-scientific age with which "scientific" generations may dispense. There is no power in any science or philosophy, whether in a pre- or post-scientific age, to leap the chasm of incongruity by pure thought. Thought which begins on one side of the chasm can do no more than deny the reality on the other side. It seeks either to prove that death is no reality because spirit is eternal, or that spirit is not eternal because death is a reality. But the real situation is that man, as a part of the natural world, brings his years to an end like a tale that is told; and that man as a free spirit finds the brevity of his years incongruous and death an irrationality; and that man as a unity of body and spirit can neither by taking thought reduce the dimension of his life to the limit of nature, nor yet raise it to the dimension of pure spirit. Either his incomplete and frustrated life is completed by a power greater than his own, or it is not completed.

Faith is therefore the final triumph over incongruity, the final assertion of the meaningfulness of existence. There is no other triumph and will be none, no matter how much human knowledge is enlarged. Faith is the final assertion of the freedom of the human spirit, but also the final acceptance of the weakness of man and the final solution for the problem of life through the disavowal of any final solutions in the power of man.

Insofar as the sense of humor is a recognition of incongruity, it is more profound than any philosophy which seeks to devour incongruity in reason. But the sense of humor remains healthy only when it deals with immediate issues and faces the obvious and surface irrationalities. It must move toward faith or sink into despair when the ultimate issues are raised.

That is why there is laughter in the vestibule of the temple, the echo of laughter in the temple itself, but only faith and prayer, and no laughter, in the holy of holies.

George F. Kennan (1904–2005) was stationed as a diplomat in Moscow, an experience that prompted him to write the famous "Long Telegram," advising the Truman administration against expecting any friendship with Soviet Russia. Soon after, he turned that document into an essay, "The Sources of Soviet Conduct," advocating "containment of Russian expansive tendencies." That piece, published in Foreign Affairs *and anonymously signed X, is said to have hastened the start of the Cold War, though Kennan (quickly unmasked as its author) always insisted he meant the United States should try to win over nonaligned countries by economic and diplomatic means, democracy setting an attractive example, rather than engaging the Soviets militarily. Attacked at the time by progressives because of its Cold War thinking, it now seems farsightedly realistic in predicting Russia's ongoing efforts to manipulate U.S. policy. Kennan, who lived to be a hundred and to advocate against the nuclear arms race and for future rapprochement with Russia, was a gifted essayist and memoirist, with classical gravitas.*

THE SOURCES
OF SOVIET CONDUCT

Part I

The political personality of Soviet power as we know it today is the product of ideology and circumstances: ideology inherited by the present Soviet leaders from the movement in which they had their political origin, and circumstances of the power which they now have exercised for nearly three decades in Russia. There can be few tasks of psychological analysis more difficult than to try to trace the interaction of these two forces and the relative role of each in the determination of official Soviet conduct. Yet the attempt must be made if that conduct is to be understood and effectively countered.

It is difficult to summarize the set of ideological concepts with which the Soviet leaders came into power. Marxian ideology, in its Russian-Communist projection, has always been in process of subtle evolution. The materials on which it bases itself are extensive and complex. But the outstanding features of Communist thought as it existed in 1916 may perhaps be summarized as follows: (a) that the central factor in the life of man, the factor which determines the character of public life and the "physiognomy of society," is the system by which material goods are produced and exchanged; (b) that the capitalist system of production is a nefarious one which inevitably leads to the exploitation of the working class by the capital-owning class and is incapable of developing adequately the economic resources of society or of distributing fairly the material goods produced by human labor; (c) that capitalism contains the seeds of its own destruction and must, in view of the inability of the capital-owning class to adjust itself to economic change, result eventually and inescapably in a revolutionary transfer of power to the working class; and (d) that imperialism, the final phase of capitalism, leads directly to war and revolution.

The rest may be outlined in Lenin's own words: "Unevenness of economic and political development is the inflexible law of capitalism. It follows from this that the victory of Socialism may come originally in a few capitalist countries or even in a single capitalist country. The victorious proletariat of that country, having expropriated the capitalists and having organized Socialist production at home, would rise against the remaining capitalist world, drawing to itself in the process the oppressed classes of other countries." It must be noted that there was no assumption that capitalism would perish without proletarian revolution. A final push was needed from a revolutionary proletariat movement in order to tip over the tottering structure. But it was regarded as inevitable that sooner or later that push be given.

For fifty years prior to the outbreak of the Revolution, this pattern of thought had exercised great fascination for the members of the Russian revolutionary movement. Frustrated, discontented, hopeless of finding self-expression—or too impatient to seek it—in the confining limits of the Tsarist political system, yet lacking wide popular support or their choice of bloody revolution as a means of social betterment, these revolutionists found in Marxist theory a highly convenient rationalization for their own instinctive desires. It afforded pseudo-scientific justification for their impatience, for their categoric denial of all value in the Tsarist system, for their yearning for power and revenge and for their inclination to cut corners in the pursuit of it. It is therefore no wonder that they had come to believe implicitly in the truth and soundness of the Marxist-Leninist teachings, so congenial to their own impulses and emotions. Their sincerity need not be impugned. This is a phenomenon as old as human nature itself. It has never been more aptly described than by Edward Gibbon, who wrote in *The Decline and Fall of the Roman Empire*: "From enthusiasm to imposture the step is perilous and slippery; the demon of Socrates affords a memorable instance of how a wise man may deceive himself, how a good man may deceive others, how the conscience may slumber in a mixed and middle state between self-illusion and voluntary fraud." And it was with this set of conceptions that the members of the Bolshevik Party entered into power.

Now it must be noted that through all the years of preparation for revolution, the attention of these men, as indeed of Marx himself, had been centered less on the future form which Socialism would take than on the necessary overthrow of rival power which, in their view, had to precede the introduction of Socialism. Their views, therefore, on the positive program to be put into effect, once power was attained, were for the most part nebulous, visionary and impractical. Beyond the nationalization of industry and the expropriation of large private capital holdings there was no agreed program. The treatment of the peasantry, which, according to the Marxist formulation was not of the proletariat, had always been a vague spot in the pattern of Communist thought; and it remained an object of controversy and vacillation for the first ten years of Communist power.

The circumstances of the immediate post-revolution period— the existence in Russia of civil war and foreign intervention, together with the obvious fact that the Communists represented only a tiny minority of the Russian people—made the establishment of dictatorial power a necessity. The experiment with "war Communism" and the abrupt attempt to eliminate private production and trade had unfortunate economic consequences and caused further bitterness against the new revolutionary regime. While the temporary relaxation of the effort to communize Russia, represented by the New Economic Policy, alleviated some of this economic distress and thereby served its purpose, it also made it evident that the "capitalistic sector of society" was still prepared to profit at once from any relaxation of governmental pressure, and would, if permitted to continue to exist, always constitute a powerful opposing element to the Soviet regime and a serious rival for influence in the country. Somewhat the same situation prevailed with respect to the individual peasant who, in his own small way, was also a private producer.

Lenin, had he lived, might have proved a great enough man to reconcile these conflicting forces to the ultimate benefit of Russian society, though this is questionable. But be that as it may, Stalin, and those whom he led in the struggle for succession to Lenin's position of leadership, were not the men to tolerate rival political forces in the sphere of power which they coveted. Their sense of insecurity was too great. Their particular brand of fanaticism, unmodified by any of the Anglo-Saxon traditions of compromise, was too fierce and too jealous to envisage any permanent sharing of power. From the Russian-Asiatic world out of which they had emerged they carried with them a skepticism as to the possibilities of permanent and peaceful coexistence of rival forces. Easily persuaded of their own doctrinaire "rightness," they insisted on the submission or destruction of all competing power. Outside the Communist Party, Russian society was to have no rigidity. There were to be no forms of collective human activity or association which would not be dominated by the Party. No other force in Russian society was to be permitted to achieve vitality or integrity. Only the Party was to have structure. All else was to be an amorphous mass.

And within the Party the same principle was to apply. The mass of Party members might go through the motions of election, deliberation, decision and action; but in these motions they were to be animated not by their own individual wills but by the awesome breath of the Party leadership and the overbrooding presence of "the word."

Let it be stressed again that subjectively these men probably did not seek absolutism for its own sake. They doubtless believed—and found it easy to believe—that they alone knew what was good for society and that they would accomplish that good once their power was secure and unchallengeable. But in seeking that security of their own rule they were prepared to recognize no restrictions, either of God or man, on the character of their methods. And until such time as that security might be achieved, they placed far down on their scale of operational priorities the comforts and happiness of the peoples entrusted to their care.

Now the outstanding circumstance concerning the Soviet regime is that down to the present day this process of political consolidation has never been completed and the men in the Kremlin have continued to be predominantly absorbed with the struggle to secure and make absolute the power which they seized in November 1917. They have endeavored to secure it primarily against forces at home, within Soviet society itself. But they have also endeavored to secure it against the outside world. For ideology, as we have seen, taught them that the outside world was hostile and that it was their duty eventually to overthrow the political forces beyond their borders. Then powerful hands of Russian history and tradition reached up to sustain them in this feeling. Finally, their own aggressive intransigence with respect to the outside world began to find its own reaction; and they were soon forced, to use another Gibbonesque phrase, "to chastise the contumacy" which they themselves had provoked. It is an undeniable privilege of every man to prove himself right in the thesis that the world is his enemy; for if he reiterates it frequently enough and makes it the background of his conduct he is bound eventually to be right.

Now it lies in the nature of the mental world of the Soviet leaders, as well as in the character of their ideology, that no opposition to them can be officially recognized as having any merit or justification whatsoever. Such opposition can flow, in theory, only from the hostile and incorrigible forces of dying capitalism. As long as remnants of capitalism were officially recognized as existing in Russia, it was possible to place on them, as an internal element, part of the blame for the maintenance of a dictatorial form of society. But as these remnants were liquidated, little by little, this justification fell away, and when it was indicated officially that they had been finally destroyed, it disappeared altogether. And this fact created one of the most basic of the compulsions which came to act upon the Soviet regime: since capitalism no longer existed in Russia and since it could not be admitted that there could be serious or widespread opposition to the Kremlin springing spontaneously from the liberated masses under its authority, it became necessary to justify the retention of the dictatorship by stressing the menace of capitalism abroad.

This began at an early date. In 1924 Stalin specifically defended the retention of the "organs of suppression," meaning, among others, the army and the secret police, on the ground that "as long as there is a capitalistic encirclement there will be danger of intervention with all the consequences that flow from that danger." In accordance with that theory, and from that time on, all internal opposition forces in Russia have consistently been portrayed as the agents of foreign forces of reaction antagonistic to Soviet power.

By the same token, tremendous emphasis has been placed on the original Communist thesis of a basic antagonism between the capitalist and Socialist worlds. It is clear, from many indications, that this emphasis is not founded in reality. The real facts concerning it have been confused by the existence abroad of genuine resentment provoked by Soviet philosophy and tactics and occasionally by the existence of great centers of military power, notably the Nazi regime in Germany and the Japanese government of the late 1930s, which indeed have aggressive designs against the Soviet Union. But there is ample evidence that the stress laid in Moscow on the menace confronting Soviet society from the world outside its borders is founded not in the realities of foreign antagonism but in the necessity of explaining away the maintenance of dictatorial authority at home.

Now the maintenance of this pattern of Soviet power, namely, the pursuit of unlimited authority domestically, accompanied by the cultivation of the semi-myth of implacable foreign hostility, has gone far to shape the actual machinery of Soviet power as we know it today. Internal organs of administration which did not serve this purpose withered on the vine. Organs which did serve this purpose became vastly swollen. The security of Soviet power came to rest on the iron discipline of the Party, on the severity and ubiquity of the secret police, and on the uncompromising economic monopolism of the state. The "organs of suppression," in which the Soviet leaders had sought security from rival forces, became in large measure the masters of those whom they were designed to serve. Today the major part of the structure of Soviet power is committed to the perfection of the dictatorship and to the maintenance of the concept of Russia as in a state of siege, with the enemy cowering beyond the walls. And the millions of human beings who form that part of the structure of power must defend at all costs this concept of Russia's position, for without it they are themselves superfluous.

As things stand today, the rulers can no longer dream of parting with these organs of suppression. The quest for absolute power, pursued now for nearly three decades with a ruthlessness unparalleled (in scope at least) in modern times, has again produced internally, as it did externally, its own reaction. The excesses of the police apparatus have fanned the potential opposition to the regime into something far greater and more dangerous than it could have been before those excesses began.

But least of all can the rulers dispense with the fiction by which the maintenance of dictatorial power has been defended. For this fiction has been canonized in Soviet philosophy by the excesses already committed in its name; and it is now anchored in the Soviet structure of thought by bonds far greater than those of mere ideology.

Part II

So much for the historical background. What does it spell in terms of the political personality of Soviet power as we know it today?

Of the original ideology, nothing has been officially junked. Belief is maintained in the basic badness of capitalism, in the inevitability of its destruction, in the obligation of the proletariat to assist in that destruction and to take power into its own hands. But stress has come to be laid primarily on those concepts which relate most specifically to the Soviet regime itself: to its position as the sole truly Socialist regime in a dark and misguided world, and to the relationships of power within it.

The first of these concepts is that of the innate antagonism between capitalism and Socialism. We have seen how deeply that concept has become imbedded in foundations of Soviet power. It has profound implications for Russia's conduct as a member of international society. It means that there can never be on Moscow's side any sincere assumption of a community of aims between the Soviet Union and powers which are regarded as capitalist. It must inevitably be assumed in Moscow that the aims of the capitalist world are antagonistic to the Soviet regime, and therefore to the interests of the peoples it controls. If the Soviet government occasionally sets its signature to documents which would indicate the contrary, this is to be regarded as a tactical maneuver permissible in dealing with the enemy (who is without honor) and should be taken in the spirit of *caveat emptor*. Basically, the antagonism remains. It is postulated. And from it flow many of the phenomena which we find disturbing in the Kremlin's conduct of foreign policy: the secretiveness, the lack of frankness, the duplicity, the wary suspiciousness, and the basic unfriendliness of purpose. These phenomena are there to stay, for the foreseeable future. There can be variations of degree and of emphasis. When there is something the Russians want from us, one or the other of these features of their policy may be thrust temporarily into the background; and when that happens there will always be Americans who will leap forward with gleeful announcements that "the Russians have changed," and some who will even try to take credit for having brought about such "changes." But we should not be misled by tactical maneuvers. These characteristics of Soviet policy, like the postulate from which they flow, are basic to the internal nature of Soviet power, and will be with us, whether in the foreground or the background, until the internal nature of Soviet power is changed.

This means we are going to continue for a long time to find the Russians difficult to deal with. It does not mean that they should be considered as embarked upon a do-or-die program to overthrow our society by a given date. The theory of the inevitability of the eventual fall of capitalism has the fortunate connotation that there is no hurry about it. The forces of progress can take their time in preparing the final coup de grâce. Meanwhile, what is vital is that the "Socialist fatherland"—that oasis of power which has already been won for Socialism in the person of the Soviet Union—should be cherished and defended by all good Communists at home and abroad, its fortunes promoted, its enemies badgered and confounded. The promotion of premature, "adventuristic" revolutionary projects abroad which might embarrass Soviet power in any way would be an inexcusable, even a counter-revolutionary act. The cause of Socialism is the support and promotion of Soviet power, as defined in Moscow.

This brings us to the second of the concepts important to contemporary Soviet outlook. That is the infallibility of the Kremlin. The Soviet concept of power, which permits no focal points of organization outside the Party itself, requires that the Party leadership remain in theory the sole repository of truth. For if truth were to be found elsewhere, there would be justification for its expression in organized activity. But it is precisely that which the Kremlin cannot and will not permit.

The leadership of the Communist Party is therefore always

right, and has been always right ever since in 1929 Stalin formalized his personal power by announcing that decisions of the Politburo were being taken unanimously.

On the principle of infallibility there rests the iron discipline of the Communist Party. In fact, the two concepts are mutually self-supporting. Perfect discipline requires recognition of infallibility. Infallibility requires the observance of discipline. And the two go far to determine the behaviorism of the entire Soviet apparatus of power. But their effect cannot be understood unless a third factor be taken into account: namely, the fact that the leadership is at liberty to put forward for tactical purposes any particular thesis which it finds useful to the cause at any particular moment and to require the faithful and unquestioning acceptance of that thesis by the members of the movement as a whole. This means that truth is not a constant but is actually created, for all intents and purposes, by the Soviet leaders themselves. It may vary from week to week, from month to month. It is nothing absolute and immutable—nothing which flows from objective reality. It is only the most recent manifestation of the wisdom of those in whom the ultimate wisdom is supposed to reside, because they represent the logic of history. The accumulative effect of these factors is to give to the whole subordinate apparatus of Soviet power an unshakable stubbornness and steadfastness in its orientation. This orientation can be changed at will by the Kremlin but by no other power. Once a given party line has been laid down on a given issue of current policy, the whole Soviet governmental machine, including the mechanism of diplomacy, moves inexorably along the prescribed path, like a persistent toy automobile wound up and headed in a given direction, stopping only when it meets with some unanswerable force. The individuals who are the components of this machine are unamenable to argument or reason, which comes to them from outside sources. Their whole training has taught them to mistrust and discount the glib persuasiveness of the outside world. Like the white dog before the phonograph, they hear only the "master's voice." And if they are to be called off from the purposes last dictated to them, it is the master who must call them off. Thus the foreign representative cannot hope that his words will make any impression on them. The most that he can hope is that they will be transmitted to those at the top, who are capable of changing the party line. But even those are not likely to be swayed by any normal logic in the words of the bourgeois representative. Since there can be no appeal to common purposes, there can be no appeal to common mental approaches. For this reason, facts speak louder than words to the ears of the Kremlin; and words carry the greatest weight when they have the ring of reflecting, or being backed up by, facts of unchallengeable validity.

But we have seen that the Kremlin is under no ideological compulsion to accomplish its purposes in a hurry. Like the Church, it is dealing in ideological concepts which are of long-term validity, and it can afford to be patient. It has no right to risk the existing achievements of the revolution for the sake of vain baubles of the future. The very teachings of Lenin himself require great caution and flexibility in the pursuit of Communist purposes. Again, these precepts are fortified by the lessons of Russian history: of centuries of obscure battles between nomadic forces over the stretches of a vast unfortified plain. Here caution, circumspection, flexibility and deception are the valuable qualities; and their value finds a natural appreciation in the Russian or the oriental mind. Thus the Kremlin has no compunction about retreating in the face of superior forces. And being under the compulsion of no timetable, it does not get panicky under the necessity for such retreat. Its political action is a fluid stream which moves constantly, wherever it is permitted to move, toward a given goal. Its main concern is to make sure that it has filled every nook and cranny available to it in the basin of world power. But if it finds unassailable barriers in its path, it accepts these philosophically and accommodates itself to them. The main thing is that there should always be pressure, unceasing constant pressure, toward the desired goal. There is no trace of any feeling in Soviet psychology that that goal must be reached at any given time.

These considerations make Soviet diplomacy at once easier and more difficult to deal with than the diplomacy of individual aggressive leaders like Napoleon and Hitler. On the one hand it is more sensitive to contrary force, more ready to yield on individual sectors of the diplomatic front when that force is felt to be too strong, and thus more rational in the logic and rhetoric of power. On the other hand it cannot be easily defeated or discouraged by a single victory on the part of its opponents. And the patient persistence by which it is animated means that it can be effectively countered not by sporadic acts which represent the momentary whims of democratic opinion but only by intelligent long-range policies on the part of Russia's adversaries—policies no less steady in their purpose, and no less variegated and resourceful in their application, than those of the Soviet Union itself.

In these circumstances it is clear that the main element of any United States policy toward the Soviet Union must be that of long-term, patient but firm and vigilant containment of Russian expansive tendencies. It is important to note, however, that such a policy has nothing to do with outward histrionics: with threats or blustering or superfluous gestures of outward "toughness." While the Kremlin is basically flexible in its reaction to political realities, it is by no means unamenable to considerations of prestige. Like almost any other government, it can be placed by tactless and threatening gestures in a position where it cannot afford to yield even though this might be dictated by its sense of realism. The Russian leaders are keen judges of human psychology, and as such they are highly conscious that loss of temper and of self-control is never a source of strength in political affairs. They are quick to exploit such evidences of weakness. For these reasons it is a sine qua non of successful dealing with Russia that the foreign government in question should remain at all times cool and collected and that its demands on Russian policy should be put forward in such a manner as to leave the way open for a compliance not too detrimental to Russian prestige.

Part III

In the light of the above, it will be clearly seen that the Soviet pressure against the free institutions of the western world is something that can be contained by the adroit and vigilant application of counter-force at a series of constantly shifting geographical and political points, corresponding to the shifts and maneuvers of Soviet policy, but which cannot be charmed or talked out of existence. The Russians look forward to a duel of infinite duration, and they see that already they have scored great successes. It must be borne in mind that there was a time when the Communist Party represented far more of a minority in the sphere of Russian national life than Soviet power today represents in the world community.

But if the ideology convinces the rulers of Russia that truth is on their side and that they can therefore afford to wait, those of us on whom that ideology has no claim are free to examine objectively the validity of that premise. The Soviet thesis not only implies complete lack of control by the west over its own economic destiny, it likewise assumes Russian unity, discipline and patience over an infinite period. Let us bring this apocalyptic vision down to earth, and suppose that the western world finds the strength and resourcefulness to contain Soviet power over a period of ten to fifteen years. What does that spell for Russia itself?

The Soviet leaders, taking advantage of the contributions of modern techniques to the arts of despotism, have solved the question of obedience within the confines of their power. Few challenge their authority; and even those who do are unable to make that challenge valid as against the organs of suppression of the state.

The Kremlin has also proved able to accomplish its purpose of building up in Russia, regardless of the interests of the inhabitants, an industrial foundation of heavy metallurgy, which is, to be sure, not yet complete but which is nevertheless continuing to grow and is approaching those of the other major industrial countries. All of this, however, both the maintenance of internal political security and the building of heavy industry, has been carried out at a terrible cost in human life and in human hopes and energies. It has necessitated the use of forced labor on a scale unprecedented in modern times under conditions of peace. It has involved the neglect or abuse of other phases of Soviet economic life, particularly agriculture, consumers' goods production, housing and transportation.

To all that, the war has added its tremendous toll of destruction, death and human exhaustion. In consequence of this, we have in Russia today a population which is physically and spiritually tired. The mass of the people are disillusioned, skeptical and no longer as accessible as they once were to the magical attraction which Soviet power still radiates to its followers abroad. The avidity with which people seized upon the slight respite accorded to the Church for tactical reasons during the war was eloquent testimony to the fact that their capacity for faith and devotion found little expression in the purposes of the regime.

In these circumstances, there are limits to the physical and nervous strength of people themselves. These limits are absolute ones, and are binding even for the cruelest dictatorship, because beyond them people cannot be driven. The forced labor camps and the other agencies of constraint provide temporary means of compelling people to work longer hours than their own volition or mere economic pressure would dictate; but if people survive them at all they become old before their time and must be considered as human casualties to the demands of dictatorship. In either case their best powers are no longer available to society and can no longer be enlisted in the service of the state.

Here only the younger generations can help. The younger generation, despite all vicissitudes and sufferings, is numerous and vigorous; and the Russians are a talented people. But it still remains to be seen what will be the effects on mature performance of the abnormal emotional strains of childhood which Soviet dictatorship created and which were enormously increased by the war. Such things as normal security and placidity of home environment have practically ceased to exist in the Soviet Union outside of the most remote farms and villages. And observers are not yet sure whether that is not going to leave its mark on the overall capacity of the generation now coming into maturity.

In addition to this, we have the fact that Soviet economic development, while it can list certain formidable achievements, has been precariously spotty and uneven. Russian Communists who speak of the "uneven development of capitalism" should blush at the contemplation of their own national economy. Here certain branches of economic life, such as the metallurgical and machine industries, have been pushed out of all proportion to other sectors of economy. Here is a nation striving to become in a short period one of the great industrial nations of the world while it still has no highway network worthy of the name and only a relatively primitive network of railways. Much has been done to increase efficiency of labor and to teach primitive peasants something about the operation of machines. But maintenance is still a crying deficiency of all Soviet economy. Construction is hasty and poor in quality. Depreciation must be enormous. And in vast sectors of economic life it has not yet been possible to instill into labor anything like that general culture of production and technical self-respect which characterizes the skilled worker of the west.

It is difficult to see how these deficiencies can be corrected at an early date by a tired and dispirited population working largely under the shadow of fear and compulsion. And as long as they are not overcome, Russia will remain economically a vulnerable, and in a certain sense an impotent, nation, capable of exporting its enthusiasms and of radiating the strange charm of its primitive political vitality but unable to back up those articles of export by the real evidences of material power and prosperity.

Meanwhile, a great uncertainty hangs over the political life of the Soviet Union. That is the uncertainty involved in the transfer of power from one individual or group of individuals to others.

This is, of course, outstandingly the problem of the personal position of Stalin. We must remember that his succession to Lenin's pinnacle of preeminence in the Communist movement was the only such transfer of individual authority which the Soviet Union has experienced. That transfer took twelve years to consolidate. It cost the lives of millions of people and shook the state to its foundations. The attendant tremors were felt all through the international revolutionary movement, to the disadvantage of the Kremlin itself.

It is always possible that another transfer of preeminent power may take place quietly and inconspicuously, with no repercussions anywhere. But again, it is possible that the questions involved may unleash, to use some of Lenin's words, one of those "incredibly swift transitions" from "delicate deceit" to "wild violence" which characterize Russian history, and may shake Soviet power to its foundations.

But this is not only a question of Stalin himself. There has been, since 1938, a dangerous congealment of political life in the higher circles of Soviet power. The All-Union Congress of Soviets, in theory the supreme body of the Party, is supposed to meet not less often than once in three years. It will soon be eight full years since its last meeting. During this period membership in the Party has numerically doubled. Party mortality during the war was enormous; and today well over half of the Party members are persons who have entered since the last Party congress was held. Meanwhile, the same small group of men has carried on at the top through an amazing series of national vicissitudes. Surely there is some reason why the experiences of the war brought basic political changes to every one of the great governments of the west. Surely the causes of that phenomenon are basic enough to be present somewhere in the obscurity of Soviet political life, as well. And yet no recognition has been given to these causes in Russia.

It must be surmised from this that even within so highly disciplined an organization as the Communist Party there must be a growing divergence in age, outlook and interest between the great mass of Party members, only so recently recruited into the movement, and the little self-perpetuating clique of men at the top, whom most of these Party members have never met, with whom they have never conversed, and with whom they can have no political intimacy.

Who can say whether, in these circumstances, the eventual rejuvenation of the higher spheres of authority (which can only be a matter of time) can take place smoothly and peacefully, or whether rivals in the quest for higher power will not eventually reach down into these politically immature and inexperienced masses in order to find support for their respective claims? If this were ever to happen, strange consequences could flow for the Communist Party: for the membership at large has been exercised only in the practices of iron discipline and obedience and not in the arts of compromise and accommodation. And if disunity were ever to seize and paralyze the Party, the chaos and weakness of Russian society would be revealed in forms beyond description. For we have seen that Soviet power is only concealing an amorphous mass of human beings among whom no independent organizational structure is tolerated. In Russia there is not even such a thing as local government. The present generation of Russians have never known spontaneity of collective action. If, consequently, anything were ever to occur to disrupt the unity and efficacy of the Party as a political instrument, Soviet Russia might be changed overnight from one of the strongest to one of the weakest and most pitiable of national societies.

Thus the future of Soviet power may not be by any means as secure as Russian capacity for self-delusion would make it appear to the men of the Kremlin. That they can quietly and easily turn it over to others remains to be proved. Meanwhile, the hardships of their rule and the vicissitudes of international life have taken a heavy toll of the strength and hopes of the great people on whom their power rests. It is curious to note that the ideological power of Soviet authority is strongest today in areas beyond the frontiers of Russia, beyond the reach of its police power. This phenomenon brings to mind a comparison used by Thomas Mann in his great novel *Buddenbrooks*. Observing that human institutions often show the greatest outward brilliance at a moment when inner decay is in reality farthest advanced, he compared one of those stars whose light shines most brightly on this world when in reality it has long since ceased to exist. And who can say with assurance that the strong light still cast by the Kremlin on the dissatisfied peoples of the western world is not the powerful afterglow of a constellation which is in actuality on the wane? This cannot be proved. And it cannot be disproved. But the possibility remains (and in the opinion of this writer it is a strong one) that Soviet power, like the capitalist world of its conception, bears within it the seeds of its own decay, and that the sprouting of these seeds is well advanced.

Part IV

It is clear that the United States cannot expect in the foreseeable future to enjoy political intimacy with the Soviet regime. It must continue to regard the Soviet Union as a rival, not a partner, in the political arena. It must continue to expect that Soviet policies will reflect no abstract love of peace and stability, no real faith in the possibility of a permanent happy coexistence of the Socialist and capitalist worlds, but rather a cautious, persistent pressure toward the disruption and weakening of all rival influence and rival power.

Balanced against this are the facts that Russia, as opposed to the western world in general, is still by far the weaker party, that Soviet policy is highly flexible, and that Soviet society may well contain deficiencies which will eventually weaken its own total potential. This would of itself warrant the United States entering with reasonable confidence upon a policy of firm containment, designed to confront the Russians with unalterable counter-force at every point where they show signs of encroaching upon the interests of a peaceful and stable world.

But in actuality the possibilities for American policy are by no means limited to holding the line and hoping for the best. It is entirely possible for the United States to influence by its actions the internal developments, both within Russia and throughout the international Communist movement, by which Russian policy is largely determined. This is not only a question of the modest measure of informational activity which this government can conduct in the Soviet Union and elsewhere, although that, too, is important. It is rather a question of the degree to which the United States can create among the peoples of the world generally the impression of a country which knows what it wants, which is coping successfully with the problem of its internal life and with the responsibilities of a World Power, and which has a spiritual vitality capable of holding its own among the major ideological currents of the time. To the extent that such an impression can be created and maintained, the aims of Russian Communism must appear sterile and quixotic, the hopes and enthusiasm of Moscow's supporters must wane, and added strain must be imposed on the Kremlin's foreign policies. For the palsied decrepitude of the capitalist world is the keystone of Communist philosophy. Even the failure of the United States to experience the early economic depression which the ravens of the Red Square have been predicting with such complacent confidence since hostilities ceased would have deep and important repercussions throughout the Communist world.

By the same token, exhibitions of indecision, disunity and internal disintegration within this country have an exhilarating effect on the whole Communist movement. At each evidence of these tendencies, a thrill of hope and excitement goes through the Communist world; a new jauntiness can be noted in the Moscow tread; new groups of foreign supporters climb onto what they can only view as the bandwagon of international politics; and Russian pressure increases all along the line in international affairs.

It would be an exaggeration to say that American behavior unassisted and alone could exercise a power of life and death over the Communist movement and bring about the early fall of Soviet power in Russia. But the United States has it in its power to increase enormously the strains under which Soviet policy must operate, to force upon the Kremlin a far greater degree of moderation and circumspection than it has had to observe in recent years, and in this way to promote tendencies which must eventually find their outlet in either the breakup or the gradual mellowing of Soviet power. For no mystical, Messianic movement—and particularly not that of the Kremlin—can face frustration indefinitely without eventually adjusting itself in one way or another to the logic of that state of affairs.

Thus the decision will really fall in large measure in this country itself. The issue of Soviet-American relations is in essence a test of the overall worth of the United States as a nation among nations. To avoid destruction the United States need only measure up to its own best traditions and prove itself worthy of preservation as a great nation.

Surely, there was never a fairer test of national quality than this. In the light of these circumstances, the thoughtful observer of Russian-American relations will find no cause for complaint in the Kremlin's challenge to American society. He will rather experience a certain gratitude to a Providence which, by providing the American people with this implacable challenge, has made their entire security as a nation dependent on their pulling themselves together and accepting the responsibilities of moral and political leadership that history plainly intended them to bear.

Edmund Wilson (1895–1972) was one of the nation's preeminent critics in the twentieth century. His essays and reviews appeared regularly in magazines such as The New Yorker, Vanity Fair, *and* The New Republic. *Wilson was a tireless reader and researcher, and his wide-ranging curiosity resulted in book-length investigations of such varied subjects as symbolist literature, the Dead Sea Scrolls, the Civil War, the tax code, and the Iroquois. His specialty was the biographical sketch, such as this remembrance of Paul Rosenfeld, which sympathetically chronicled the hard-won achievements and isolating disappointments of the literary life.*

PAUL ROSENFELD: THREE PHASES

The death of Paul Rosenfeld has left me not only shocked at the unexpected loss of a friend, but with a feeling of dismay and disgust at the waste of talent in the United States. Paul, when I first knew him—in 1922 I think—was one of the most exciting critics of the "American Renaissance." I had read, while in the army in France, an essay on Sibelius in *The New Republic*, which had had upon me the exhilarating effect that wartime reading sometimes does; and later, when I was back in New York, a longer study on Richard Strauss, a great musical hero of the time, which brought into the writing itself something of the Straussian brilliance but probed with a very sure hand what was specious and vulgar in Strauss. It was the first really searching criticism that I had ever seen of this composer, and both these essays amazed me. They had a kind of fullness of tone, a richness of vocabulary and imagery, and a freedom of the cultural world that were quite different from the schoolmasterish criticism which had become the norm in the United States. *Musical Portraits*, in 1920, the first book that collected these pieces, seemed at the time absolutely dazzling. Paul told me, when I knew him later, that the point when he had felt his maturity was the moment when he had realized with pride that he could turn out as good an article as Huneker; but actually he much surpassed Huneker, who, useful though he was in his role, always remained a rather harried journalist, trying to produce a maximum of copy in order to get money to go abroad. Paul was a serious writer who was working from New York as a base. One had always had the impression that Huneker came in through the back door at Scribner's in a day when the arts were compelled to give precedence to money and gentility, and that there had been something in Bernard Shaw's prophecy that, if he stayed in the United States, he would never be anything but a "clever slummocker"; and one now heard depressing reports that he was old, poor and ill in Brooklyn. But Paul Rosenfeld seemed the spirit of a new and more fortunate age, whose cosmopolitanism was not self-conscious and which did not have to be on the defensive for its catholic interest in art and life. The portraits of Paul's first book dramatized modern music as no criticism had done before; they brought into range a whole fascinating world, united though international, of personality, poetics, texture, mood. Paul Rosenfeld at that time enjoyed a prestige of the same kind as Mencken's and Brooks's, though it was not so widely felt as the former's.

He had inherited a comfortable income, and he built himself at Westport, Connecticut, a small and attractive house, where he lived alone with his work and entertained his friends. The first time I ever saw him, I had not yet met him. It was in Paris sometime in the summer of 1921, and I was dining alone one night in a favorite Italian restaurant, very clean and rather austere—I remember it as always quiet and filled with a clear twilight—to which I had been taken first by somebody during the war and to which I liked to return, ordering almost always the same meal that I had had when I went there first: ravioli and Asti Spumante. A party of three sat down at the table just across from mine,

and though I had never seen any of them before, I recognized
them soon as Paul Rosenfeld, Sherwood Anderson and Anderson's wife, the sculptress, Tennessee Mitchell. I had heard in
New York that Paul was taking the Andersons to Europe, where
Anderson had never been, and I observed the party with interest and heard snatches of their conversation. Tennessee Mitchell
had the aspect and the manner of a raw-boned prairie woman,
and I was touched by Paul's obvious effort to approximate for
her benefit to a modestly folksy manner. I was reminded of the
incident later when I read in Sherwood Anderson's memoirs that
he had sat in the Tuileries one day—he is here apostrophizing
himself—with "the tears running from your eyes, because you
thought everything around you so beautiful." It was all very typical of the period, and so are my first memories of Paul after I
got to know him in New York. I spent a weekend with him once
at Westport—sometime in 1922—and read him an article I had
just written about T. S. Eliot's *Waste Land* on the occasion of
its getting the *Dial* prize. In the city I had been leading at that
time rather a frenetic life, and I remember what a relief it was
to talk about art with Paul in an atmosphere completely free
from the messy dissipation and emotion that were characteristic of the twenties, and for once to get a good night's sleep in a
house where everything was quiet and simple. I had that night a
delightful dream, which still comes back to me quite distinctly, of
little figures that were really alive though much less than life-size,
dancing with slow grace to an exquisite Mozartian music which
filled me with peace and joy. It was an antidote to the stridencies
of the jazz age, which Paul's spirit had managed to exorcise. He
loathed jazz in all its raw forms and could only accept it trans-
muted by the style of a Stravinsky or a Copland.

With his fair reddish hair and mustache, his pink cheeks and
his limpid brown eyes, his clothes which always followed with
dignity the Brooks-cut college model, his presence, short though
he was, had a certain authority and distinction. It was something
that made Anderson call him the well-dressed man of American prose. He had a knack of turning pretty little speeches and
he was also genuinely considerate in a way that was rare in that
era, but he could be forthright when the occasion demanded,

and, though naturally candid and warm, he would retire—which always amused me—at a suspicion of imposture or imposition, into a skeptical and ironic reserve. He was, I think, the only man I have known of whom it could truly be said that he possessed a Heinesque wit, and I always thought it a pity that his humor, which contributed so much to the pleasure of being with him, should have figured so little in his essays. (Since writing this, however, I have been looking into one of his later books, *An Hour with American Music*, and I see that it is full of *wit*. It was the humor of exaggeration, to which he sometimes gave rein in his talk, that rarely appeared in his work.)

When I got to know Paul better, we sometimes compared notes about our childhood and education. He had gone to school on the Hudson and had afterwards graduated from Yale, and the latter institution, though he seemed to feel a certain respect for it, had rather oppressed him at the time he had been there; but he had been fortunate in being able to escape to spend his summer vacations in Europe. When he had once found out, he told me, that there existed somewhere else an artistic and social and intellectual world larger and more exciting than anything he had known in America, and that he could always go back to it later, he found that he could endure New Haven, to which he was so ill-adapted, without fears of suffocation. He had grown up in uptown New York in a German-Jewish household, and he had never belonged to any church or been trained in any religion; but he had got from his parents a grounding in the classical German culture, musical and literary. When he went to Europe in summer, he loved to visit a German uncle, who was something of a bon vivant. His parents had both died when he was young, and his only close relative was a sister. He never married and, so far as I could see, had no real desire to marry, enjoying the bachelor's life which his moderate means made possible.

His strongest tie was undoubtedly with Stieglitz, toward whom he stood in something like a filial relation; and the group around Stieglitz became for him both family and church. The only traditionally and specifically Jewish trait that ever came, in my intercourse with Paul, as something alien that blocked understanding between us was the quality of his piety toward Stieglitz, whom he accepted and revered as a prophet, unquestioningly obedient to his guidance in the spirit that has been sometimes exemplified by the disciples of Freud and Schoenberg; and his range as a writer on the plastic arts was limited by the exclusiveness of his interest in the work of the Stieglitz group. It was difficult, if not impossible, to persuade him to pay attention to any contemporary American painter who was not a protégé of Stieglitz's, and if Stieglitz had excommunicated a refractory or competitive disciple, Paul Rosenfeld, following the official directive, would condemn him, not merely as an artist but as a reprobate who had somehow committed an unpardonable moral treason. He had the tone of the old-fashioned brother whose sister has fallen to shame, or the member of a Communist sect reacting to the name of a heretic.

For the rest, his affectionate and generous nature had to spend itself mainly in the sympathy that he brought to the troubles of his friends, and in the tireless encouragement of talent. He was tactful and unobtrusive in helping people who needed help, his judgment was usually shrewd and sound, and he did not want thanks in return. His taking the Andersons to Europe is an example that happens to be known of the kind of thing he liked to do, and one has heard of his finding, at a critical time, resources for a now famous composer; but he undoubtedly did more for more people than anyone will ever know.

It has remained in my mind that he was present at the deathbed of Randolph Bourne, desperately feeding him with oxygen in the effort to keep him alive. Bourne had been one of the most remarkable of the group that founded the *Seven Arts*. As a hunchback, he was unfit for the services and thus free to repudiate the war as an able-bodied writer could hardly have done so roundly; and the intellectual light and the moral passion, the mastery of self-expression, that led people to forget his deformity as soon as he began to talk, made his friends of that era feel that he was keeping alive spiritual values that might otherwise have gone by the board. "When he died," Paul wrote, "we knew that perhaps the strongest mind of the entire younger generation in America had gone. . . . We see the size of him plainly in the bitter moments in which we realize how vacant the scene has become in the many fields to which he brought the light of his own clear nature!"

II

Paul later sold his house at Westport and took a little corner apartment in an old and elevatorless house on the west side of Irving Place. There, however, he continued to flourish. He liked to give evening parties which were none the less agreeable for their rather old-fashioned character. What was unusual in the dry twenties was that there was very little liquor served: a highball or two or a little punch; and poets read their poetry and composers played their music. One met Ornstein, Milhaud, Varèse; Cummings, Hart Crane and Marianne Moore; the Stieglitzes and all their group; the Stettheimers, Mumford, Kreymborg. One of the images that remains with me most vividly is the bespectacled figure of Copland, at that period gray-faced and lean, long-nosed and rather unearthly, bending above the keyboard as he chanted in a high, cold and passionate voice a poem of Ezra Pound's— "An Immorality"—for which he had written a setting.

In those days I saw a good deal of Paul in a business as well as in a friendly way, for I was working first on *Vanity Fair*, then on *The New Republic*, and Paul wrote a good deal for both. He grew rather stout at this time, and his style betrayed a tendency toward floridity. He felt afterwards, he told me, that his writing, like so many other things during the Boom, had, to its detriment, become somewhat overinflated. My impression is that when people say they do not like Paul Rosenfeld's style, they are thinking of characteristics that only became really rampant in some of his work of this period, and that they have no real acquaintance with his criticism either before or after. As an editor, I had sometimes to struggle with him over the locutions and vocabulary of his essays, and I am fully aware of his faults. He had spent so much time in Europe and he read so much French and German that he could never quite keep his English distinct from his other languages, and habitually wrote *ignore* as if it meant the same thing as *ignorer* and *genial* as if it meant possessing genius. He had also a way of placing adverbs that used to set my teeth on edge, as did some of these adverbs themselves, such as *doubtlessly* and *oftentimes*. There were moments when he did overwrite, working himself up into a state of exaltation with romantic Germanic abstractions that sounded a little ridiculous in English. But, going back to his essays today, one is not much bothered by this or even necessarily conscious of it. One finds a body of musical criticism that covers the modern field more completely than one had remembered and that stands up, both as writing and as interpretation, so solidly as to make quite unimportant these minor idiosyncrasies and slips.

There is of course an objection to Paul's writing which is based on disapproval on principle of the romantic and impressionistic school that he enthusiastically represented. In the serious literary journals, a new tone had just been set in the twenties by T. S. Eliot's *The Sacred Wood*, which was spare and terse in style, analytical and logical in treatment. Paul Rosenfeld, who lacked the intellectual instruments for dealing with literary ideas (though he was expert at dealing with musical ones), was somewhat less satisfactory—except when writing of certain kinds of poetry that had something in common with music—on the subject of literature than he was on music and painting; but it was very unjust that this fashion should have prejudiced against him the editors of the kind of magazine on which he most depended for a market. The same tendency appeared in the musical world; and the critics—though less, I think, the composers—complained of his lack of scholarship on the technical side of music. To this a writer who is not a musician can only reply that it seems to him that the moment the critic departs from the technical analysis of a score, he is writing impressionistic criticism; and that Berlioz in his essays on Beethoven's symphonies and Debussy when he is putting on record such an opinion as that Edvard Grieg was a bonbon stuffed with snow are just as much impressionistic critics as Paul Rosenfeld ever was. Berlioz and Debussy, of course, were a great deal more literary and programmatic than the generation of Schoenberg and Stravinsky have liked to be thought to be; but I believe that Paul was right in insisting that every valid work of art owes its power to giving expression to some specific human experience and connecting it with some human ideal. For musicians it must of course be profitable to read the kind of score-by-score study that has been made by Albert Berger, for example, of the development of Aaron Copland; but, as a layman who merely listens to music, I do not see that it is easy to dismiss the interpretations given by Paul of the emotional and social content of the more "abstract" modern composers: Schoenberg and Stravinsky, Bartók and Hindemith. It is just here, where the composer invites it least, that Paul's insight most proves his genius.

All those years we talked much of such matters. The kind of writing I did myself aimed at something rather different from his, and he horrified me once by saying that his idea of good prose was something that was laid on like a thick coat of paint; but we had in common a fundamental attitude and invoked a common cultural tradition, which it is easiest to call humanistic: Among the few things that I really look back upon with anything like nostalgia in the confusion and waste of the twenties are such conversations as those with Paul when we would sit in his corner room, beneath his little collection of Hartleys and O'Keeffes and Marins, surrounded by his shelves full of Nietzsche and Wagner, Strindberg, Shaw and Ibsen, Tolstoy and Dostoevsky, Flaubert, Claudel and Proust, Henry James and Poe, and the English poets that he had read at Yale, or walk back and forth at night between my place and his. He liked New York, was a thorough New Yorker, and—except for a few weeks in the summer, when he would visit the Stieglitzes at Lake George and, as Georgia O'Keeffe once told me, take the same walk every afternoon, or for an occasional out-of-town lecture or concert—he rarely ventured to leave the city. He did visit the Andersons in Virginia, and once got as far as New Mexico—when Georgia O'Keeffe was there—and even saw an Indian corn dance; but it was difficult to make him take an interest in any but the most self-consciously aesthetic aspects of American cultural life. I tried again and again to get him to read such writers as Ring Lardner and Mark Twain, but I never had the least success. When I finally resorted to the device of giving him *Huckleberry Finn* as a Christmas present, he obstinately refused to open it, having learned that Henry James had characterized Mark Twain as a writer for immature minds. I told Paul once later on, when the first liveliness of the twenties was spent, that he would not have lived very differently if he had been the leading music critic of Frankfurt, Dresden or Munich; but he protested at once against this. He could never be so free, he said, in Germany—or anywhere else except New York.

III

The depression was disastrous for Paul. His income dwindled almost to nothing; and he was forced to give up Irving Place, moving first to a small apartment on Eleventh Street just off Fifth Avenue, then later to a much less accessible one in the far reaches of West Eleventh Street. The *Dial* suspended publication in 1929; *The New Republic* was in the hands of an editor of whom it might almost be said, as the Nazis said of themselves, that when he heard the word *culture* he reached for his gun. Paul, for the first time in his life, was obliged to resort to real hackwork: little odd jobs and reviews, for which he was not well paid. He developed diabetes and grew thin; and something, I got the impression, went wrong with his personal affairs—though of this I never heard him speak. The staffs and the principal contributors of *The Dial* and *The New Republic*, both non-commercial affairs financed by rich patrons, had been groups of serious writers who had had lunches and dinners together, where plans and current events were discussed, and who had been part of Paul's social life as well as a stimulus to his work. But now, when endowments were drying up, there was a movement toward the political Left, and such groupings and common undertakings as the New York "intellectuals" (so called now rather than "writers" or "artists") continued to go in for in the thirties, were mostly oriented in the direction of Communism. Paul intensely disliked all this, and though one of the great merits of his criticism had been its sure sense of musical personalities as the reflections of their national and social backgrounds, he would indignantly deny at this time that art had anything to do with history. When I argued such questions with him, I found that "the Artist" meant for him a being unique and god-like, and that Paul would not admit for a minute that a philosopher or a scientist or a statesman could achieve an equal creative importance. On one occasion he was somehow persuaded to attend an election rally held by the Communists in Cooper Union, at which there were to be speeches by writers who had announced that they would vote for the Communists and who paid their homage to Communism as a literary restorative and bracer in the vein of the new convert to evangelism or the patent medicine testimonial; but, seated in a conspicuous place in one of the front rows, he attracted unfavorable attention by pointedly refusing to rise when "The International" was sung.

I was deep in Left activities myself, but I always continued to see him and occasionally went to concerts with him. If you dined with him in his apartment, he cooked and served the dinner; and the difficulty was, if you ate out with him in one of the Greenwich Village restaurants, ever to pay back his hospitality, as he invariably snatched the check and insisted on settling it himself. Even now that he had no regular platform, he continued to go to concerts and make notes on his impressions of the music and put them away in his files; and he continued to look for new talent and to acquire new protégés—though he sometimes had fits of gloom in which he would declare that American music was an abomination of desolation. He was sharply unsympathetic with the new tendency of American composers to abandon the abstruse researches into which they had been led by Schoenberg, the high seasoning and classicizing and virtuosity of abbreviation characteristic of Stravinsky and others, and to try to produce a music that could be heard and enjoyed by bigger audiences than those of the Composers' League. He was shocked, almost personally hurt, when Americans whose work he had thought promising did anything for the radio or Hollywood or published popular books. He expressed his views on this general subject in his essay on Kurt Weill and *Gebrauchsmusik*, in which he asserted that all music was useful, since "all works of musical art express essences and ideas and thus, with their symbols of the inner truth of life, provide the best of bases of social relationships," and that there was of course no reason why composers who "deeply felt the spirit and symbols of social rituals" should not provide these rituals with music—so long as the music provided "conveyed an individual interpretation of the meanings of the ritual" and not merely "general and conventional symbols and a sort of collective expression." He concluded: "Let us by all means have *Gebrauchsmusik*. But let it be the work of artists, not of 'revolutionary' academicians." It will be seen that these considered and formulated views were less severe than his instinctive attitude toward the practice of American composers; and I guessed that this attitude was due to his lately having felt himself a little out of things as well as to disappointment at any evidence that other artists cared anything for popular success.

But it worried me to feel, as time went on, that he was beginning to lose his self-confidence. He had put a good deal of work into the writing of what I gathered from his descriptions was a kind of symphonic novel based on a visit he had made to Rome, but he had decided that his whole conception was vitiated by some moral falsity and he withheld it from publication—which seemed to me a morbid symptom. A healthy writer either knows what he is doing or doesn't discover his error till after he has published the book. The persecution of the Jews by Hitler came later to weigh upon Paul and to become overpoweringly identified with the difficulties he was facing at fifty. The times had not brought to fulfillment that creative and enlightened era of which the sun had seemed to be rising in the days when the *Seven Arts* was founded: totalitarian states and class pressures were closing down on the artistic elite. The independent American journalism that had flared up for a while in the twenties had given way to the streamlined commercial kind, and the non-commercial magazines were composed for the most part by this time of second-rate academic papers and the commentaries of Talmudic Marxists. Even *The New Yorker*, more liberal and literate than most of the new magazines, and in its own way quite independent, was unable to find a place for Paul: it, too, had a conventional style, which sometimes ran to insipidity through the solicitous care of the editors to eliminate anything unexpected in the way that their writers expressed themselves. It was primarily a humorous weekly and had a department that exploited the absurdities that appeared in other papers, so that they had to be on their guard against writing that might be thought ridiculous. It was one of the most cruel blows of Paul Rosenfeld's later years that *The New Yorker* would not print his articles after asking him, as he assumed, to act as their regular art critic. Paul's prose, as I knew, had its blemishes, but at its best it would have been hopelessly refractory to *The New Yorker* processing mill. There was at that time not a single periodical which would print the work of a writer simply because he knew his subject and wrote about it well. Paul sometimes showed signs of a fear that he had been made the victim of a boycott; and at others was too ready to blame himself. He said to me once that his inheritance from his grandmother had unfitted him to struggle with the world; that he had thrown up his first and only job—as a reporter on a New York paper—when, finding that the work embarrassed him, he had reflected that he did not need a job to live. Certainly he was unfitted for putting himself over or making terms with editors and publishers; no one ever had less sense of business. He never could understand that writing was a commodity like any other, which, from the moment one lacked a patron, had to be sold in a hard-boiled way; and the world came more and more to divide itself for him into two classes, black and white: the negative forces of darkness that were closing down to crush him and the few pure children of light who survived and could heal and save.

I was distressed by him in these latter days and used to wonder how the circumstances had been combined to undermine so able a man, with the shift in economic conditions, by way of his very virtues even more than by way of his weaknesses. Certainly it was unwise of Paul to have depended as much as he did on the writing of musical criticism. Since he was himself not a musician but a writer, he should not have tied up his talent with the reporting of contemporary concerts. It is impossible for a master of words completely to express himself by merely rendering the effects of some other art; and I have never really understood why Paul did not tackle some bigger subject—a history of American music or a biography of some composer—which would have got him an advance from a publisher and supplied him with a sustaining interest. One might have said the same thing about

Huneker; but it is no great comfort to realize that Paul Rosenfeld, in an age which prided itself on its emergence from the Philistinism of Huneker's, should have burned out in much the same way and been left in the same neglect. The burning-out and the public indifference seem somehow to work together. They are an old and depressing story in the American intellectual world.

When I got back to New York from Europe in the autumn of 1945, I spent with Paul a wonderful evening, which, though I may have seen him once or twice afterwards, has left me with a last lively impression that I am extremely glad to have. He was in very much better spirits than he had been during the years of the war. He had received from a foundation a substantial grant to do a book of literary studies; and it seemed to cheer him up to hear talk about Europe again, now that the war was over and the arts might be expected to revive. I told him about my enthusiasm for Benjamin Britten's opera *Peter Grimes*, which I had heard that summer in London. And both of us were glad to find someone to whom one could express oneself freely about the current state of letters and art. He was angry over his treatment at the hands of one of the highbrow quarterlies, the editor of which had first asked him to be a member of the advisory board and had then refused to print his articles, keeping them, however, for months without letting him know about them. I had had with this same magazine an almost equally annoying experience; and I managed to make Paul laugh by describing to him an essay in which this pedantic editor, in the course of a rigorous analysis of Macbeth's "Out, out, brief candle" speech, conducted in the rigorous spirit of the new "methodological" criticism, had said something like, "We cannot know why Shakespeare has chosen for death the curious adjective *dusty*, but the epithet has a quaint appropriateness that can be felt but hardly explained." We rapidly became so exhilarated, abounding so, as Henry James would say, in our own old sense, affirming our convictions so heartily and making such hilarious fun of the more tiresome of our contemporaries, that we went on till what was for Paul a late hour, walking the autumn streets and stopping off for coffee and beer at Childs' and the Lafayette, almost as if we had been back in the twenties, with the new era of American art just beginning to burst into life between

MacDougal Street and Irving Place. Less than a year later, Paul died of a heart attack as he was coming out of a movie, to which he had gone alone.

And now, despite the miseries of his later years, he remains for me, looking back, one of the only sound features of a landscape that is strewn with distortions and wrecks: a being organically moral on whom one could always rely, with a passion for creative art extinguishable only with life. It has worried me to reflect that the rise in morale I thought I had noted in him when I talked to him last was not, after all, to lead to anything, and to remember how unhappy and insecure, how unrewarded, he was at the end. There are tragedies of untimely death which—coming at the end of a man's work or breaking off his career at a crisis—represent a kind of fulfillment. But one can find no justice in Paul's. His death had no dramatic appropriateness; nor was it preceded, I fear, by any very steady serenity. It had been obvious, in view of the interest that had been stimulated in American music, partly through Paul's own efforts, and of the quantity of books about music that were now getting into type, that it was time for a reprinting of Paul's criticism; and the suggestion had been made to two publishers that an omnibus be brought out. But he had not had even this gratification. One can only reassure oneself by remembering that the work he had done was of the kind that pays for itself, because it is done for love, in the desire to give life away, and because it brings, in the doing, elevation and liberation of spirit. To have had thirty years of such work is not the least enviable of destinies; and Paul's best writing bears on every page his triumph and his justification.

Walter Lippmann (1889–1974) was, during his long writing career, the very model of the public intellectual. His daily columns, periodical essays, and books, with their measured, thoughtful tone, were read respectfully by millions. Seeking a reasonable balance, which landed him frequently in a centrist position, he performed for America the role of the sage, advising statesmen and governing bodies, and warning, like Tocqueville, against the potential tyranny of the majority. His personal dilemma was the tension between being a detached scholar-observer preserving independent integrity and an inside player hoping to influence policy.

THE DILEMMA OF LIBERAL DEMOCRACY: SHOULD THE MAJORITY RULE?

In the oration which Henry Lee delivered in the House of Representatives a few days after Washington's death, he spoke the words that have become so celebrated. Washington, he said, was "everywhere present . . . himself a host, he assuaged our sufferings, limited our privations, and upheld our tottering Republic. . . . First in war, first in peace, first in the hearts of his countrymen, he was second to none in the humble and endearing scenes of private life." Yet in the veneration which has always been given to Washington, must we not add that he has in these later days become separated somehow from the inner life of his countrymen?

The cause of it is not in the legend of his immaculate perfection. Nor is it in any want of flesh and blood in the man himself. The cause is much deeper and it cannot be removed by proving that he was less perfect than his legend, or by popularizing anecdotes of his life and aspects of his character which provide what is called human interest.

The truth of the matter, I believe, is that we are separated not from the man but from his ideas. There is an opposition between what he believed to be the conditions and the first principles of free government and what has come increasingly to be the working belief of the great masses of the people who, in their impact on public affairs, invoke the ideals of democracy.

This opposition appeared while Washington was still alive, and it has been accentuated during the past hundred and fifty years. In our time it has reached its climax and its crisis. If then we wish to understand Washington, and to appreciate the universal importance of his example, what is it that we must do? We must, I believe, refuse to identify the cause of freedom, justice and good government with the rule of the majority.

There lies the root of the matter. Washington believed that the people should rule. But he did not believe that because the people ruled, there would be freedom, justice, and good government. He did not believe that the sovereign people, any more than the royal sovereigns whom they succeeded, could be trusted with absolute power.

He did not deceive himself. As a young man, he had served the royal governor, Dinwiddie. Later on, as commander in chief, he had served the Continental Congress. He had no illusion that the mere transfer of power from a king to the people would ensure free, just, and good government.

He knew, on the contrary, that the new popular sovereign, like its royal predecessors, was subject, as he once said to Edmund Randolph, to "the various passions" which are "the concomitants of fallibility." He did not believe in what has become the prevailing ideology of democracy—that whatever the mass of the people happen to think they want must be accepted as the right. "I am sure," he once wrote to John Jay, "that the mass of citizens in these United States *mean well*, and I firmly believe that they will always *act well*, whenever they can obtain a right understanding of matters: but . . . it is not easy to accomplish this, especially as is the case invariably when the inventors and abettors of pernicious measures are infinitely more industrious in disseminating their poison than the well-disposed part of the community to furnish the antidote."

Thus Washington did not look upon the rise of popular government as the triumphant culmination of the struggle for freedom and justice. He knew that there was no guarantee that the rule of the people would not in its turn be despotic, arbitrary, corrupt, unjust, and unwise. The people, too, had to be restrained. They, too, had to be held to account. They, too, had to be taught. They, too, had to be raised above their habitual conduct. Because their power, when passionately aroused, was overwhelming, it could be fearfully abused.

Though he was an ardent supporter of the new Constitution, he did not believe that any mechanical device, such as the system of checks and balances, would in itself ensure freedom and good government. Least of all did he believe that bad government could be cured by weak government. He had learned from his own hard experience that popular government tends to be weak, and that local and private interests may so divide its authority and may so paralyze its decisions that the time may come when there seems to be no remedy for anarchy except the surrender of freedom to a despot. He knew that in the last analysis there was nothing which could save a nation from this choice between anarchy and tyranny except the restraint imposed by the virtue of its citizens and the wisdom of those leaders whom they are sufficiently enlightened to follow.

This conception of popular government has become obscured by another, which, though it uses many of the same terms and proposes the same ideal ends, is its profound opposite. There the will of a majority of the people is held to be sovereign and supreme. That majority is bound by no laws because it makes the laws. It is itself the final judge, from whom there is no appeal, of what is right and what is wrong. This doctrine has led logically and in practice to the totalitarian state—to that modern form of despotism which does not rest upon hereditary titles or military conquest but springs directly from the mass of the people. For if all power is in the people, if there is no higher law than their will, and if by counting their votes, their will may be ascertained—then the people may entrust all their power to anyone, and the power of the pretender and the usurper is then legitimate. It is not to be challenged since it came originally from the sovereign people.

This is the supreme political heresy of our time. It masquerades as democracy. Though it is widely current among us, here at home at least it is not uncontested. But elsewhere, in many countries, it has led to a fantastic and tragic paradox. We have seen a majority of the people vote away their own right to continue to live by majority rule; we have seen the declared enemies of human freedom allowed to exploit free institutions until they had captured the power to destroy them. We have seen the right of a nation to be independent interpreted to mean that it was independent of all the laws of God and of man.

We, who have seen these things happen, are perhaps prepared, as we could not have been before, to appreciate the significance of the original American idea: that the sovereignty of the people is never absolute, that the people are under the law, and that the people may make no law which does not conform to that higher law which has been gradually revealed to the awakening conscience of mankind. In this, the American doctrine, the will of the people does not, then, determine its own standard of what is right and what is wrong. It is itself accountable to standards superior to its own opinions and its own will. Here the moral order does not stem from the will of the people. The people, like all other rulers, are within the moral order, and they are subject to it.

This American doctrine is also the ancient and central doctrine of civilized mankind. Washington himself lived by and worked in that tradition, and by his achievements and his example he did more than any other to establish it in this new land. We are greatly blessed that such a man was the Father of this country.

Robert Warshow (1917–1955) was a film critic and analyst of popular culture, who died tragically at the age of thirty-seven. His essays, collected in one slim, dazzling book, The Immediate Experience, *frequently appeared in* Commentary *(where he had worked as an editor) and* Partisan Review. *Warshow brought a high moral and intellectual seriousness to subjects previously dismissed as lowbrow, and his synthesis of aesthetics and social commentary was bracingly suggestive.*

THE GANGSTER AS TRAGIC HERO

America, as a social and political organization, is committed to a cheerful view of life. It could not be otherwise. The sense of tragedy is a luxury of aristocratic societies, where the fate of the individual is not conceived of as having a direct and legitimate political importance, being determined by a fixed and supra-political—that is, non-controversial—moral order or fate. Modern equalitarian societies, however, whether democratic or authoritarian in their political forms, always base themselves on the claim that they are making life happier; the avowed function of the modern state, at least in its ultimate terms, is not only to regulate social relations, but also to determine the quality and the possibilities of human life in general. Happiness thus becomes the chief political issue—in a sense, the only political issue—and for that reason it can never be treated as an issue at all. If an American or a Russian is unhappy, it implies a certain reprobation of his society, and therefore, by a logic of which we can all recognize the necessity, it becomes an obligation of citizenship to be cheerful; if the authorities find it necessary, the citizen may even be compelled to make a public display of his cheerfulness on important occasions, just as he may be conscripted into the army in time of war.

Naturally, this civic responsibility rests most strongly upon the organs of mass culture. The individual citizen may still be permitted his private unhappiness so long as it does not take on political significance, the extent of this tolerance being determined by how large an area of private life the society can accommodate. But every production of mass culture is a public act and must conform with accepted notions of the public good. Nobody seriously questions the principle that it is the function of mass culture to maintain public morale, and certainly nobody in the mass audience objects to having his morale maintained.* At a time when the normal condition of the citizen is a state of anxiety, euphoria spreads over our culture like the broad smile of an idiot. In terms of attitudes towards life, there is very little difference between a "happy" movie like *Good News*, which ignores death and suffering, and a "sad" movie like *A Tree Grows in Brooklyn*, which uses death and suffering as incidents in the service of a higher optimism.

But, whatever its effectiveness as a source of consolation and a means of pressure for maintaining "positive" social attitudes, this optimism is fundamentally satisfying to no one, not even to those who would be most disoriented without its support. Even within the area of mass culture, there always exists a current of opposition, seeking to express by whatever means are available to it that sense of desperation and inevitable failure which optimism itself helps to create. Most often, this opposition is confined to rudimentary or semiliterate forms: in mob politics and

---

* In her testimony before the House Committee on Un-American Activities, Mrs. Leila Rogers said that the movie *None but the Lonely Heart* was un-American because it was gloomy. Like so much else that was said during the unhappy investigation of Hollywood, this statement was at once stupid and illuminating. One knew immediately what Mrs. Rogers was talking about; she had simply been insensitive enough to carry her philistinism to its conclusion.

journalism, for example, or in certain kinds of religious enthusiasm. When it does enter the field of art, it is likely to be disguised or attenuated: in an unspecific form of expression like jazz, in the basically harmless nihilism of the Marx Brothers, in the continually reasserted strain of hopelessness that often seems to be the real meaning of the soap opera. The gangster film is remarkable in that it fills the need for disguise (though not sufficiently to avoid arousing uneasiness) without requiring any serious distortion. From its beginnings, it has been a consistent and astonishingly complete presentation of the modern sense of tragedy.*

In its initial character, the gangster film is simply one example of the movies' constant tendency to create fixed dramatic patterns that can be repeated indefinitely with a reasonable expectation of profit. One gangster film follows another as one musical or one Western follows another. But this rigidity is not necessarily opposed to the requirements of art. There have been very successful types of art in the past which developed such specific and detailed conventions as almost to make individual examples of the type interchangeable. This is true, for example, of Elizabethan revenge tragedy and Restoration comedy.

For such a type to be successful means that its conventions have imposed themselves upon the general consciousness and become the accepted vehicles of a particular set of attitudes and a particular aesthetic effect. One goes to any individual example of the type with very definite expectations, and originality is to be welcomed only in the degree that it intensifies the expected experience without fundamentally altering it. Moreover, the relationship between the conventions which go to make up such a type and the real experience of its audience or the real facts of whatever situation it pretends to describe is of only secondary importance and does not determine its aesthetic force. It is only in an ultimate sense that the type appeals to its audience's expe-

---

* Efforts have been made from time to time to bring the gangster film into line with the prevailing optimism and social constructiveness of our culture; *Kiss of Death* is a recent example. These efforts are usually unsuccessful; the reasons for their lack of success are interesting in themselves, but I shall not be able to discuss them here.

rience of reality; much more immediately, it appeals to previous experience of the type itself: it creates its own field of reference.

Thus the importance of the gangster film, and the nature and intensity of its emotional and aesthetic impact, cannot be measured in terms of the place of the gangster himself or the importance of the problem of crime in American life. Those European moviegoers who think there is a gangster on every corner in New York are certainly deceived, but defenders of the "positive" side of American culture are equally deceived if they think it relevant to point out that most Americans have never seen a gangster. What matters is that the experience of the gangster *as an experience of art* is universal to Americans. There is almost nothing we understand better or react to more readily or with quicker intelligence. The Western film, though it seems never to diminish in popularity, is for most of us no more than the folklore of the past, familiar and understandable only because it has been repeated so often. The gangster film comes much closer. In ways that we do not easily or willingly define, the gangster speaks for us, expressing that part of the American psyche which rejects the qualities and the demands of modern life, which rejects "Americanism" itself.

The gangster is the man of the city, with the city's language and knowledge, with its queer and dishonest skills and its terrible daring, carrying his life in his hands like a placard, like a club. For everyone else, there is at least the theoretical possibility of another world—in that happier American culture which the gangster denies, the city does not really exist; it is only a more crowded and more brightly lit country—but for the gangster there is only the city; he must inhabit it in order to personify it: not the real city, but that dangerous and sad city of the imagination which is so much more important, which is the modern world. And the gangster—though there are real gangsters—is also, and primarily, a creature of the imagination. The real city, one might say, produces only criminals; the imaginary city produces the gangster: he is what we want to be and what we are afraid we may become.

Thrown into the crowd without background or advantages, with only those ambiguous skills which the rest of us—the real people of the real city—can only pretend to have, the gangster is required to make his way, to make his life and impose it on others. Usually, when we come upon him, he has already made his choice or the choice has already been made for him, it doesn't matter which: we are not permitted to ask whether at some point he could have chosen to be something else than what he is.

The gangster's activity is actually a form of rational enterprise, involving fairly definite goals and various techniques for achieving them. But this rationality is usually no more than a vague background; we know, perhaps, that the gangster sells liquor or that he operates a numbers racket; often we are not given even that much information. So his activity becomes a kind of pure criminality: he hurts people. Certainly our response to the gangster film is most consistently and most universally a response to sadism; we gain the double satisfaction of participating vicariously in the gangster's sadism and then seeing it turned against the gangster himself.

But on another level the quality of irrational brutality and the quality of rational enterprise become one. Since we do not see the rational and routine aspects of the gangster's behavior, the practice of brutality—the quality of unmixed criminality—becomes the totality of his career. At the same time, we are always conscious that the whole meaning of this career is a drive for success: the typical gangster film presents a steady upward progress followed by a very precipitate fall. Thus brutality itself becomes at once the means to success and the content of success—a success that is defined in its most general terms, not as accomplishment or specific gain, but simply as the unlimited possibility of aggression. (In the same way, film presentations of businessmen tend to make it appear that they achieve their success by talking on the telephone and holding conferences and that success is talking on the telephone and holding conferences.)

From this point of view, the initial contact between the film and its audience is an agreed conception of human life: that man is a being with the possibilities of success or failure. This principle, too, belongs to the city; one must emerge from the crowd or else one is nothing. On that basis the necessity of the action is established, and it progresses by inalterable paths to the point where the gangster lies dead and the principle has been modified: there is really only one possibility—failure. The final meaning of the city is anonymity and death.

In the opening scene of *Scarface*, we are shown a successful man; we know he is successful because he has just given a party of opulent proportions and because he is called Big Louie. Through some monstrous lack of caution, he permits himself to be alone for a few moments. We understand from this immediately that he is about to be killed. No convention of the gangster film is more strongly established than this: it is dangerous to be alone. And yet the very conditions of success make it impossible not to be alone, for success is always the establishment of an *individual* preeminence that must be imposed on others, in whom it automatically arouses hatred; the successful man is an outlaw. The gangster's whole life is an effort to assert himself as an individual, to draw himself out of the crowd, and he always dies *because* he is an individual; the final bullet thrusts him back, makes him, after all, a failure. "Mother of God," says the dying Little Caesar, "is this the end of Rico?"—speaking of himself thus in the third person because what has been brought low is not the undifferentiated *man*, but the individual with a name, the gangster, the success; even to himself he is a creature of the imagination. (T. S. Eliot has pointed out that a number of Shakespeare's tragic heroes have this trick of looking at themselves dramatically; their true identity, the thing that is destroyed when they die, is something outside themselves—not a man, but a style of life, a kind of meaning.)

At bottom, the gangster is doomed because he is under the obligation to succeed, not because the means he employs are unlawful. In the deeper layers of the modern consciousness, *all* means are unlawful, every attempt to succeed is an act of aggression, leaving one alone and guilty and defenseless among enemies: one is *punished* for success. This is our intolerable dilemma: that failure is a kind of death and success is evil and dangerous, is—ultimately—impossible. The effect of the gangster film is to embody this dilemma in the person of the gangster and resolve it by his death. The dilemma is resolved because it is *his* death, not ours. We are safe; for the moment, we can acquiesce in our failure, we can choose to fail.

Harold Rosenberg (1906–1978) was a major art critic who coined the term "Action Painting" for Abstract Expressionists such as Willem de Kooning, Jackson Pollock, and Franz Kline. He and Clement Greenberg dominated the postwar art scene, often jousting in print, though they tended to like the same artists. An active member of the New York Intellectuals set, Rosenberg in his robust, contentious essay "The Herd of Independent Minds" poked fun at many of his contemporaries for their political posturing and opportunism.

THE HERD OF INDEPENDENT MINDS

The basis of mass culture in all its forms is an experience recognized as common to many people. It is because millions are known to react in the same way to scenes of love or battle, because certain colors or certain combinations of sounds will call up certain moods, because assent or antagonism will inevitably be evoked by certain moral or political opinions, that popular novels, movies, radio programs, magazines, advertisements, ideologies can be contrived. The more exactly he grasps, whether by instinct or through study, the existing element of sameness in people, the more successful is the mass-culture maker. Indeed, so deeply is he committed to the concept that men are alike that he may even fancy that there exists a kind of human dead center in which everyone is identical with everyone else, and that if he can hit that psychic bull's-eye he can make all of mankind twitch at once. In the democracy of mass culture, the proposition "All men are alike" replaces the proposition "All men are equal," thus making it possible for rich or politically powerful mass-culture leaders to enjoy their advantages while still regarding themselves as "men of the people."

On the other hand, the producer of mass culture has no use for experience, his own or another's, which cannot be immediately shared. What is endured by one human being alone seems to him unreal, or even an effect of madness. The "alienation" of the artist, his characteristic neurosis, which we hear so much about today, is an essential axiom of mass-culture thinking: every departure from the common experience appears to be an abnormality requiring some form of explanation—medical, sociological, etc. Actually, the concept that the artist is "alienated from reality" has little to support it either in the psychology of artists or in the history of art. As Thomas Mann said, it depends on who gets sick; the sickness of a Nietzsche may bring him much closer to the truth of the situation, and in that sense be much more "normal," than the health of a thousand editorial writers.

The theory of the "alienated individual" is, in American critical literature, largely derived from Marx. Marx, however, sees alienation as the condition not of the artist but of the common man of industrial society; for him it is the factory worker, the businessman, the professional, who is "alienated in his work" through being hurled into the fetish-world of the market. The artist is the only figure in this society who is able *not to be alienated*, because he works directly with the materials of his own experience and transforms them. Marx therefore conceives the artist as the model of the man of the future. But when critics influenced by Marxist terminology talk of alienation, they mean something directly contrary to Marx's philosophical and revolutionary conception. They mean not the tragic separation of the human individual from himself, but the failure of certain sensitive spirits (themselves) to participate emotionally and intellectually in the fictions and conventions of mass culture. And this removal from popular hallucination and inertia they conceive as a form of pathos.

Nothing could be more vulgar, in the literal meaning of the term, than whining about separation from the mass. That being oneself and not others should be deplored as a condition of misery is the most unambiguous sign of the triumph in the individual of the ideology of mass culture over spiritual independence. It is a renunciation of everything that has been gained during the past centuries through the liberation of mankind from the authoritarian community.

The opposition of mass-culture-making to anything individual goes far beyond mere rejection or even social condemnation. It claims to assert a truth regarding the very nature of human reality: that the real situation of the individual is that in which he is aware of himself in mass terms. The most explicit and aggressive formulation of this metaphysical bias is to be found in the Soviet Union, where the mass-culture principle has been carried to its logical conclusion. There, individual experience is denounced officially as an aberration from real life.

Discussing "plays dealing with the situation arising from the return home of Russian soldiers," Drew Middleton reported* that "the fidelity or infidelity of the soldier's wife, his own amorous affairs at the front, were not considered essential problems of *real life* by the dramatic critics of the Kremlin" (my italics). Middleton then cited the list of situations with which Soviet art is bidden to concern itself: the victory in World War II, socialist reconstruction, and so forth. The list comprises only situations common to Soviet citizens, and the artist is directed to create an emotional and pictorial equivalent of this "real" experience. Needless to add, the recent attack on "formalism" in music means that too much individuality must not be allowed to sneak into even the *manner* in which the artist deals with the mass experience.

It may be argued that what is wrong with Soviet art is not that it restricts itself to the common experience but that its version of that experience is false; were it faithfully to reflect the true experience of the Soviet masses, it might be valid art. But how can one speak of a common Soviet experience without taking into account that it itself is formed by Soviet mass culture? Mass-cultural statements are constantly *in the process of mak-*

---

* *New York Times*, February 11, 1948.

ing themselves true by causing people to experience their common lives in those terms. To illustrate: Several years ago the WPA writers program interviewed old Negroes who had been slaves in the South before Emancipation. A large majority had an image of their own slavery identical with that of the romantic apologists of plantation life. One was left to assume either that the romantic picture is a true description of what slavery was like, or that it became true in regard to the ex-slaves by absorbing their actual experience into itself.

Thus we may take it for granted that the collective experience of the Russians resembles at any given moment the version of it presented by Soviet novels and movies to roughly the same degree that the common experience of Americans corresponds to the Hollywood, TV, or Sunday Supplement presentation of it. Each American knows that these slick and *understandable* portraits are not faithful to *him*. But he does not know that they do not truly picture other Americans. In sum, mass-culture-making operates according to certain laws that cause it to be potentially "true" of the mass but inevitably false to each individual. It is not just Soviet mass culture that is false. What is "experientially" (moral and political values are something else) wrong with Soviet mass culture is simply that it is mass culture—and what is wrong with the Soviet Union is that its mass culture is ordained by a political force that checks the creation of any other kind of culture. But we, too, have less of "the other kind" than we imagine, as I shall show later.

Let me make it clear that the difference between mass culture and authentic art is *not* that the first deals with the community or mass while the second depicts only the single individual. There is a mass culture of "individuals" too, obviously—as in the myriad applications of the Boy Meets Girl formula. On the other hand, there is an authentic art, even in modern times, of masses and of crowds—e.g., the battle panoramas of Tolstoy, Zola, or Malraux, or the street movements of Romains.

What counts is not the number of people involved in the situation but the nature of the experience that goes into the work. The significant distinction is between the formulated *common experiences* which are the substance of mass culture and the *common situations* in which human beings find themselves. The common situation is precisely what the common experience with its mass-culture texture conceals, *and is often intended to conceal.*

The genuine work of art, going past the formulated common experience, may succeed in communicating the common situation—all too clearly from the point of view of the promoters of social myth. I doubt that those in authority would be so systematically opposed to authentic art if, as they claim, it revealed only the private personality of the artist and had no further reference. On the contrary, I am inclined to believe that when modern art is condemned as "lacking broad meaning" or as "unrelated to real life," these accusations often disguise the fear that the exact opposite is true—that this deviation from popular forms has too much meaning and bears too acute a relation to life to be reconciled with the common beliefs.

To penetrate through the common experience to the actual situation from which all suffer requires a creative act—that is to say, an act that directly grasps the life of people during, say, a war, that grasps the war from the inside, so to speak, as a situation with a human being in it. But the moment an artist, ignoring the war as an external fact known to all, approaches it as a possibility that must be endured in the imagination by anyone who would genuinely experience it, he puts the existing mass conception of it into question. Consequently, the result of such a creative act is to arouse not only hostility on the part of officials who have a stake in the perpetuation of some agreed-upon version of the war, but also a general distrust and uneasiness. For the work of art takes away from its audience its sense of knowing where it stands in relation to what has happened to it and suggests to the audience that its situation might be quite different than it has suspected, that the situation is jammed with elements not yet perceived and lies open to the unknown, even though the event has already taken place.

Exactly insofar as he touches the common situation of man in the twentieth century, Kafka goes against the common experience; he undermines the self-confidence of official high culture, which rests on a system of assumptions which are as "false to reality" as the formulas of behavior in a bestseller; and for this

reassuring common experience he substitutes only the tension of
an individual struggling for self-knowledge, a cloudy and painful
seeing and not-seeing. Along this rocky road to the actual it is
only possible to go Indian file, one at a time, so that "art" means
"breaking up the crowd"—not "reflecting" its experience.

If the essential principle of mass-culture-making is that only
experience recognized to be common is real, the operation of this
principle is a means by which to distinguish items of mass culture
from genuine works of art. In the Soviet Union there is no confusion on this score. Non-mass art is outlawed, and any expression
of non-mass experience is dangerous. Here in the United States,
the principle of the common experience operates more or less
in disguise to produce different levels of mass culture, including
a specifically anti-mass-culture mass culture. From "significant"
novels, through "highbrow" radio programs, to "little" magazine
articles and stories, a variety of mass-culture forms pits the mass
culture of small groups against the mass culture of the masses.
The result is not the creation of an artistic culture but of a pyramid of "masses" of different sizes, each with expressions of its
own common experience.

Now the interesting thing about this pyramid is that the farther each level gets above the mass base of the multi-millions *the
closer it is presumed to get to genuine art*. Thus even radio and
Hollywood have their Norman Corwin and Orson Welles, who
by the scale of the mass-culture structure are true artists because
they appeal to "small" audiences. And magazines designed for
college professors and writers are assumed to be more culturally
pertinent than those whose audiences are housewives or prurient
bon vivants.

Yet a single conviction falls like a plumbline through all the
levels of the pyramid, from its apex to its base: the conviction
that the artist ought to communicate the common experience of
his audience level, and that if he fails to do this it is because he
is an egoist and irresponsible. On the basis of this conviction,
each level of mass culture holds the level above it to be filled with
"nuts," that is, with artists and an audience "cut off from the
people," snobs who insist on "expressing themselves" and shirk

the true labors of art and enlightenment. Thus an editor of *Look* once disclosed to me his mingled awe and contempt for the esoteric highbrows who write for the tiny audience of the *Atlantic Monthly*, and the same feeling prevails in the advertising agencies toward Corwin as a writer of "sustainers."

The irresponsible-artist, or artist-nut, formula, based on audience scale, works both ways: on the one hand, anybody who has a "small" audience (from a million in radio to five in poetry) is automatically credited with being a genuine artist; on the other, any artist whose experience seals him off from the mass, big or small, is regarded as a megalomaniac. A literary agent said the other day of a writer appearing in little magazines: "Oh, he writes for posterity. An even worse egotist than the rest."

It is amusing, however, to trace this same artist-egotist formula into an anti-mass-culture organ like *Partisan Review*. In issues closely following one another, *Partisan Review*ers meted out the following judgments: that Dostoevsky and Kafka were neurotics; that there was little in Thomas Mann's *Essays of Three Decades* that had meaning beyond the author's literary exhibitionism— "In the end," said the review (entitled "The Sufferings and Greatness of Self-Love"), "[Mann] continues to love only himself"; that Paul Valéry failed "to convey any substantial doctrine beyond the existence of the particular man and writer" and therefore fell down both as artist and thinker; that "in the *Journal* Gide's self-analysis too often begins and ends with Gide," so that André Gide too had been destroyed by self-interestedness.

Each of these artists, according to *Partisan Review*'s intellectual captains of thousands, is an egotist lost in himself, "alienated" from others, incapable of a valid formulation of the common experience of the modern intellectual and of a "substantial doctrine" for him, and to that extent is a failure as an artist. In the phrase once popular in radical circles, it is "no accident" that these estimates of Dostoevsky, Kafka, Mann, Gide, and Valéry are shared with *Partisan Review* by Soviet criticism. Mass culture, whether of the flat plain of the One Big Mass or of the pyramid of the Many Small Masses, must deny the validity of the single human being's effort to arrive at a consciousness of

himself and of his situation, and must be blind to his practice of
a distinctive method of giving form to his experience. The insight
of the "particular man" must be crushed by the "substantial
doctrine," even when, unhappily, one happens to be, as are the
*Partisan Review*ers, without such a doctrine.

Thus the reduced audience scope of a mass-culture undertaking, be it a radio program or a publisher's book list, does not
alter its mass-culture character; just as the popularity of a Jimmy
Durante or Charlie Chaplin does not prevent him from being a
genuine artist, regardless of the attitude of the little mass. True,
the masses do not read Kafka or Henry James. But a literary
magazine, no matter how "little," does not escape being a mass-
culture organ simply by interesting itself in these writers, when
in discussing them it reduces their work to formulas of common
experience. This reduction is the very method by which Hollywood or the Church or the Communist Party appropriates the
artist and his creation to its own uses—e.g., the capture of Dostoevsky by Hollywood, Rimbaud by the Church, van Gogh by
the CP—under the pretext of "bringing culture to the people."
The peak of the mass-culture pyramid and its base are made of
the same material.

Intellectuals who set themselves against mass culture become
contributors to it by shifting small-mass perspectives to previously neglected fields, as in the "novelization" of the Okies by
Steinbeck or of the Chicago Irish by Farrell. This activity might
be understood as part of the general expansion of mass culture, its imperialist dynamic, so to speak, by which humanity
is increasingly converted into "the common man" through the
discovery and penetration of new areas of experience in order to
derive from them the raw materials of new cultural commodities.

The area which intellectuals have most recently staked out for
themselves as belonging to culture par excellence is the common
historical experience. While down below one still hears about
love, crime, and ambition, the top of the pyramid is reserved
exclusively for the history-conscious small mass. There, the talk
is of "*the* experience of the twenties" or of "the thirties," "*the*
experience of the younger generation" or of "the depression
generation," "*the* epoch of the concentration camp," and so on.

To be accepted by the intellectual mass, experience must come wrapped in a time package.

It is to the credit of a writer like Jean-Paul Sartre that when he makes contemporary historical experience his point of departure for literature, he does so with full consciousness of what this means. Sartre knows that beginning with the common experience implies mass culture. Hence Sartre is in favor of reaching a big audience, of writing for the movies and for radio in order to inform and convert the popular mind. He rejects the individual as an object of literary interest and attacks Valéry and Gide on principled grounds. He insists on the "engagement" or participation of the artist in the social problems of his time and place and in political activity. In this respect his view corresponds to that of the Communists and the Gaullists against whom he is struggling.

American intellectuals are, however, reluctant to face the mass-culture consequences of their historical self-definitions. They retain a nostalgia for the personal and unique, for esoteric art, for small-group attitudes, even while they deplore the inadequacy of these standpoints. As individuals they see themselves in terms of what they have in common with others; in the mass they sense themselves despondently as individuals. Thus they cannot act creatively either for the individual or for the mass.

This spirit of mass-individual evasion is expressed poetically in the verse of Auden and Spender, which has had the widest and to my mind the most stupefying dead-end influence upon the so-called younger generation. Here is an excellent example of the voice of this spirit, picked at random out of a review of Spender's poems in *The New York Times*:

> The shame of what I never was
> That when I lived my life among these dead
> I did not live enough—that when I loved
> Among these dead I did not love enough—
> That when I looked the murderers in their eyes
> I did not die enough—
> I lacked
> That which makes cities not to fall
> The drop of agonizing sweat which changes

Into impenetrable crystal—
And every stone of the stone city
To moments held through time.

According to the *Times*, Spender here "rises to magnificence and *responsibility*" (my italics). To me this poem is pure cant. It brings in "these dead" to bestow significance upon the poet's feelings, which had nothing to do with them and which are *not described*—thus avoiding the individual experience through giving the impression of solidarity with mass experience; and then it claims for this nonexistent individual a fantastic power over the destiny of others, by his passion to "make cities not to fall." Such a combination of avoidance of responsibility for individual experience and avoidance of responsibility for social thinking is now known as "responsible" poetry. And, of course, every truly independent mind must believe in "responsible literature," as well as in "alienation," the "failure" of radicalism, the obsolescence of the individual, and so forth.

Writing of "The Legacy of the 30's,"* Robert Warshow expresses an antagonism to mass culture per se. Unlike the French Existentialists, Warshow feels not only hemmed in but internally invaded by the intellectual commodities of contemporary society. Mass culture for him is the alien within the gate, the slot machine on the altar, the Trojan horse that brings the ready-made into the halls of the original. "Its mere existence—" he says, "this climate in which one had to live—was a standing threat to one's personality, was in a sense a deep personal humiliation." Warshow correctly notes the presence of a "mass culture of the educated classes" and recognizes in its surface seriousness a further obstacle to individual experience.

Yet despite his horror of mass culture, Warshow's entire approach is an "us" approach, that is to say, a mass-culture approach—though his "us" is not the masses but the small mass of the intellectuals. "For most American intellectuals," he begins his article, "the Communist movement of the 1930s was a crucial experience." He is referring, obviously, to the fact that American

---

* *Commentary*, December 1947.

writers, artists, and students, had various relations with Marxist parties and Marxist ideas. I don't know, and neither does Warshow, what this contact has meant to each of these people in terms of the total structure of his consciousness—that is, we cannot say whether for any individual his "Communist experience" was crucial or not. Perhaps it was crucial for certain men who went to Spain and got killed. But even then, in the instances I happen to be familiar with, other experiences played at least as important a part in such decisions as "the experience of Communism."

Warshow is able to state flatly that this was "crucial" only because he is discussing "the" Communist experience as *a mass event*. Yet from this point of view, it seems that Marxism in the United States became a renunciation or negation of experience, a plunging of the individual into mass inertia, precisely because he yielded himself up to the general intellectual "climate." There wasn't any significant group experience of Communism in America except in the negative sense, and this is one of the main reasons why people ran away from it. Then why talk about it as "crucial"? Or, better still, why not talk about some other kind of experience? Because since it happened to a historical "us," it seems to Warshow most significant: "It is for *us* what the First World War and the experience of expatriation were for an earlier generation. If *our* intellectual life is stunted and full of frustration,* this is in large part because *we* have refused to assimilate that experience . . . never trying to understand what it means as part of *our* lives." (My italics.)

Warshow then goes on to measure the success of Edmund Wilson's and Lionel Trilling's "assimilation" and expression of "that experience" as efforts in an essential task that lies before the modern intelligence.

Now I too was alive in the thirties and also underwent the intellectual impact of the Marxist movement, as well as popular-front novels and movies, the New Deal, peculiarities of the erotic in the urban human being, and a good portion of other contem-

---

* In my opinion, if someone's intellectual life is "stunted and full of frustration," it may be because he belongs to a crowd, but it is not because of something that happened to a crowd.

poraneous phenomena. Yet I find that there is very little that is of interest to me in my thoughts and my feelings that is dealt with by either Edmund Wilson or Lionel Trilling.

Yes, what they describe sounds familiar; one had heard about it, even run into it personally. But somehow the experience of these men does not communicate with mine nor seem very pertinent to it—to think it important, I should have to impose upon my reactions some external literary or historical or social "value." Maybe this is because Wilson and Trilling are dealing with "that experience," that is, with something common in the thirties, but not with any significant experience or hypothesis of their own. Perhaps the faintness of my response to this historical souvenir only proves that my experience lacks universality or is even out of date. All right, I confess—the tension of my experience never belongs to the right time or place. Besides my experience of "the thirties," it contains all sorts of anachronisms and cultural fragments: the Old Testament and the Gospels, Plato, eighteenth-century music, the notion of freedom as taught in the New York City school system, the fantastic emotional residues of the Jewish family. If one extended and deepened this compendium, one might get to a kind of tiny *Finnegans Wake*, which, incidentally, in contrast to *Memoirs of Hecate County*, I do find very communicative.

At any rate, the rhythm of my experience is broken and complicated by all sorts of time-lags, symbolic substitutions, decayed absolutes, experimental hypotheses. Because I am so peculiarly (and also not so peculiarly) mixed up, I confess, too, that it doesn't matter to me much whether I belong to Wilson's and Trilling's generation or to Warshow's. There was a journalism of Americans in the First World War and an even wider journalism perhaps of American expatriation. Yet when the "assimilations" of all these literary epochs and generations that take me back to the cradle are added up, for some reason they seem to have communicated less to me about my situation, to have less deeply penetrated my experience, and to have contributed less to my verbal and intellectual resources than, say, Poe, Rimbaud, Dostoevsky, Gide, Miró, Klee, and a lot of other people who didn't participate in this American experience of "ours," or William Carlos

Williams or Wallace Stevens, whose poetry contains scarcely a word about their "generation," or E. E. Cummings, who said some very private things about his.

What I am getting at is that when someone says, as Warshow does, of any one common experience that "that experience is the most important experience of our time," such a statement can have only a mass-culture meaning. And once you've taken this position, to call for a writer to communicate that experience "as it really is, as it really feels," is simply to ask for a "better" mass culture, in the way that Hollywood or some Soviet writers' union periodically calls for a more real and more passionate and even a more original and inspired rendering of the Most Epic Event of Our Times. If Warshow, having properly rejected Trilling's novel for dealing with modern life as if it were entirely a question of which opinions to hold, is really interested in "making it possible for the writer himself to have a meaningful experience in the first place," he should stop trying to decide in advance what is meaningful to everybody and concentrate instead on what is meaningful to him. For individual experience it is necessary to begin with the individual. Maybe there is no individual in the old sense of the term. This cannot be gone into here. But whatever there is, one will not arrive at it by reflecting oneself in a "we."

No one will deny that common situations exist. It may be, too, that the most profound, or even the most ephemeral, individual experiences are, or may prove to be after they have been authentically set down, in essential respects duplicated in many men and sometimes perhaps in all men. In fact, "most profound" may *ultimately* turn out to be the same as "most common." The question is not of uniqueness as a goal, of the artist as a lone wolf programmatically dissociating himself from society and the pathos of human life; it is a question of where to begin and toward what kind of communication to move.

Acceptance of the mass-culture dogma that the artist must become the medium of a common experience will result in the same contrived and unseeing art, whether the assignment is made by a movie producer, a party cultural official, or by the artist himself as a theoretician of social relevance. That genuine art can be created to order *in modern times* has never been demonstrated. Apologists for popular art are fond of referring to Egypt, Greece, medieval or Renaissance Europe, where the artist-as-craftsman was the creator of a high art, officially commissioned, and more or less immediately accessible to its intended audience. But these apologists neglect the fundamental differences between the sources and content of inspiration in the authentic communities of the past, on the one hand, and within the relations that exist in modern industrial society, on the other. Under present conditions, a true work of art may accidentally attract a large audience, but more and more elements in it tend to fall outside the range of the audience's responses. Even works once popular become increasingly esoteric by comparison with, and under the pressure of, the mass consumption of manufactured novels, movies, radio programs, and so on.

The writer seems confronted by the following alternative. He may accept the common experience as a point of beginning, embrace mass culture, start "enlightening" some public about itself, and forget about art and about experience "as it really is, as it really feels." The writer who makes this choice will obtain from outside his work—from politics, from sociology, from religion, from "public opinion," from the policy representative of some corporation or group—a set of "values" which he will endeavor, through such feelings, fancies, and "ideas" as he can muster to his subject, to communicate to a prefabricated audience of experience-comrades. Here communication means a formula, whether in the images of a work of art or in the rhetoric of opinions, by which the member of the audience learns from the author what he already knows, or could have found out—that together with others he is an ex-radical, or a Jew, or feels frustrated, or lives in a postwar world, or prefers freedom to tyranny. Repetition of these mass-cultural themes with all the resources of fancy may prove of practical value to humanity—as when a group of "bad" fictions, like anti-minority caricatures, are replaced with "good" fictions, images of men as equal—and to this service the writer may choose to dedicate himself.

Or the writer may choose to break through mass culture. In that case he will reject the time packages and sociology packages in which experience is delivered fresh every morning, and begin with the tension of what most agitates and conceals itself from him. He will enter into a kind of Socratic ignorance. For he will accept the fact that he cannot know, except through the lengthy unfolding of his work itself, what will prove to be central to his experiencing; it is his way of revealing his existence to his consciousness and of bringing his consciousness into play upon his existence. And this art communicates itself as an experience to others, not because one man's experience is the same as other men's, but because each of those others, like the author, is unique to himself and can therefore recognize in his own experience the matchless experience of another human being and even perhaps the presence of some common situation and the operation of some hidden human principle. The authentic artist arrives at the common situation *at the end* of his effort—e.g., the emergence of decadent French society in *Remembrance of Things Past*—or rather he does not arrive at it, for no one can arrive at the whole, but by way of his own humanity he moves spontaneously towards the humanity of others.

Only the individual can communicate experience, and only another individual can receive such a communication. The individual is *in* society—that goes without saying. He is also isolated and, like Ivan Ilyich, dies alone. I find it no more noble or picturesque to stress the isolation at the expense of participation than to stress the sentiment for the social at the expense of isolation. Poses are a matter of taste, sometimes of achieving spiritual efficiency. I should like only to make sure that nobody is bullied by the abstract concept of social responsibility into becoming useless to himself and to his fellow men, or even becoming a menace. Obviously, the isolation of an artist's work, or his personal loneliness, if that happens to be his fate, does not deprive his accomplishment of social meaning. Nor in rejecting the "responsibility" of the representative of mass-thought for the sake of his concrete experience does he make himself an "irresponsible." (It is humiliating to have to repeat these truisms and to mention such examples of artistic responsibility by way of concrete experiencing as Gide's *Trip to the Congo* or Cummings' *The Enor-*

mous Room—but I here testify to my own social responsibility by acknowledging the power of vulgar antitheses and doing my bit about them.)

The mass-culture maker, who takes his start from the experience of others, is essentially a reflector of myths, and lacks concrete experiences to communicate. To him man is an object seen from the outside. Indeed it could be demonstrated that the modern mass-culture elite, even when it trots around the globe in search of historical hotspots where every six months the destiny of man is decided, actually has less experience than the rest of humanity, less even than the consumers of its products. To the professional of mass culture, knowledge is the knowledge of what is going on in other people; he trades his own experience for an experience of experience. Everyone has met those culture-conscious "responsibles" who think a book or movie or magazine wonderful not because it illuminates or pleases them but because it tells "the people" what they "ought to know."

The makers of mass culture are its first and most complete victims. The anonymous human being to whom they bring their messages has at least the metaphysical advantage of being forced to deal daily with material things and real situations—tools, working conditions, personal passions. The fact that his experience has a body means that mass culture is, as far as he is concerned, like a distorting mirror in an amusement park; whereas the formulators of shared "crucial experiences," whose world is made up of mental constructions, live inside the mirror.

Robert K. Merton (1910–2003) was a giant among American sociologists. He originated such concepts as "the self-fulfilling prophecy," "role models," and "unintended consequences." His middle-range studies of public housing, bureaucracies, and deviance set a standard followed by many sociologists. He was also a leading proponent of the sociology of science. He was a distinguished professor at Columbia University who received every professional award; perhaps most noteworthy for this essay anthology was his possession of a felicitous, lucid prose style, rare among social scientists.

THE SELF-FULFILLING PROPHECY

In a series of works seldom consulted outside the academic fraternity, W. I. Thomas, the dean of American sociologists, set forth a theorem basic to the social sciences: "If men define situations as real, they are real in their consequences." Were the Thomas theorem and its implications more widely known more men would understand more of the workings of our society. Though it lacks the sweep and precision of a Newtonian theorem, it possesses the same gift of relevance, being instructively applicable to many, if indeed not most, social processes.

"If men define situations as real, they are real in their consequences," wrote Professor Thomas. The suspicion that he was driving at a crucial point becomes all the more insistent when we note that essentially the same theorem had been repeatedly set forth by disciplined and observant minds long before Thomas.

When we find such otherwise discrepant minds as the redoubtable Bishop Bossuet in his passionate seventeenth-century defense of Catholic orthodoxy; the ironic Mandeville in his eighteenth-century allegory honeycombed with observations on the paradoxes of human society; the irascible genius Marx in his revision of Hegel's theory of historical change; the seminal Freud in works which have perhaps gone further than any others of his day toward modifying man's outlook on man; and the erudite, dogmatic, and occasionally sound Yale professor William Graham Sumner, who lives on as the Karl Marx of the middle classes—when we find this mixed company (and I select from a longer if less distinguished list) agreeing on the truth and the pertinence of what is substantially the Thomas theorem, we may conclude that perhaps it's worth our attention as well.

To what, then, are Thomas and Bossuet, Mandeville, Marx, Freud and Sumner directing our attention?

The first part of the theorem provides an unceasing reminder that men respond not only to the objective features of a situation, but also, and at times primarily, to the meaning this situation has for them. And once they have assigned some meaning to the situation, their consequent behavior and some of the consequences of that behavior are determined by the ascribed meaning. But this is still rather abstract, and abstractions have a way of becoming unintelligible if they are not occasionally tied to concrete data. What is a case in point?

It is the year 1932. The Last National Bank is a flourishing institution. A large part of its resources is liquid without being watered. Cartwright Millingville has ample reason to be proud of the banking institution over which he presides. Until Black Wednesday. As he enters his bank, he notices that business is unusually brisk. A little odd, that, since the men at the AMOK steel plant and the KOMA mattress factory are not usually paid until Saturday. Yet here are two dozen men, obviously from the factories, queued up in front of the tellers' cages. As he turns into his private office, the president muses rather compassionately: "Hope they haven't been laid off in midweek. They should be in the shop at this hour."

But speculations of this sort have never made for a thriving bank, and Millingville turns to the pile of documents upon his desk. His precise signature is affixed to fewer than a score of papers when he is disturbed by the absence of something familiar and the intrusion of something alien. The low discreet hum of bank business has given way to a strange and annoying stridency of many voices. A situation has been defined as real. And that is the beginning of what ends as Black Wednesday—the last Wednesday, it might be noted, of the Last National Bank.

Cartwright Millingville had never heard of the Thomas theorem. But he had no difficulty in recognizing its workings. He knew that, despite the comparative liquidity of the bank's assets, a rumor of insolvency, once believed by enough depositors, would result in the insolvency of the bank. And by the close of Black Wednesday—and Blacker Thursday—when the long lines of anxious depositors, each frantically seeking to salvage his own, grew to longer lines of even more anxious depositors, it turned out that he was right.

The stable financial structure of the bank had depended upon one set of definitions of the situation: belief in the validity of the interlocking system of economic promises men live by. Once depositors had defined the situation otherwise, once they questioned the possibility of having these promises fulfilled, the consequences of this unreal definition were real enough.

A familiar type-case, this, and one doesn't need the Thomas theorem to understand how it happened—not, at least, if one is old enough to have voted for Franklin Roosevelt in 1932. But with the aid of the theorem the tragic history of Millingville's bank can perhaps be converted into a sociological parable which may help us understand not only what happened to hundreds of banks in the thirties but also what happens to the relations between Negro and white, between Protestant and Catholic and Jew in these days.

The parable tells us that public definitions of a situation (prophecies or predictions) become an integral part of the situation and thus affect subsequent developments. This is peculiar to human affairs. It is not found in the world of nature. Predictions of the return of Halley's Comet do not influence its orbit. But the rumored insolvency of Millingville's bank did affect the actual outcome. The prophecy of collapse led to its own fulfillment.

So common is the pattern of the self-fulfilling prophecy that each of us has his favored specimen. Consider the case of the examination neurosis. Convinced that he is destined to fail, the anxious student devotes more time to worry than to study and then turns in a poor examination. The initially fallacious anxiety is transformed into an entirely justified fear. Or it is believed that war between two nations is "inevitable." Actuated by this conviction, representatives of the two nations become progressively alienated, apprehensively countering each "offensive" move of the other with a "defensive" move of their own. Stockpiles of armaments, raw materials, and armed men grow larger and eventually the anticipation of war helps create the actuality.

The self-fulfilling prophecy is, in the beginning, a *false* definition of the situation evoking a new behavior which makes the originally false conception come *true*. The specious validity of the self-fulfilling prophecy perpetuates a reign of error. For the prophet will cite the actual course of events as proof that he was right from the very beginning. (Yet we know that Millingville's bank was solvent, that it would have survived for many years had not the misleading rumor *created* the very conditions of its own fulfillment.) Such are the perversities of social logic.

It is the self-fulfilling prophecy which goes far toward explaining the dynamics of ethnic and racial conflict in the America of today. That this is the case, at least for relations between Negroes and whites, may be gathered from the fifteen hundred pages which make up Gunnar Myrdal's *An American Dilemma*. That the self-fulfilling prophecy may have even more general bearing upon the relations between ethnic groups than Myrdal has indicated is the thesis of the considerably briefer discussion which follows. *

---

* Counterpart of the self-fulfilling prophecy is the "suicidal prophecy" which so alters human behavior from what would have been its course had the prophecy not been made, that it *fails* to be borne out. The prophecy destroys itself. This important type is not considered here. For examples of both types of social prophecy, see R. M. MacIver, *The More Perfect Union* (Macmillan, 1948); for a general statement, see R. K. Merton, "The Unanticipated Consequences of Purposive Social Action," *American Sociological Review*, 1936, I: 894–904.

II

As a result of their failure to comprehend the operation of the self-fulfilling prophecy, many Americans of goodwill are (sometimes reluctantly) brought to retain enduring ethnic and racial prejudices. They experience these beliefs, not as prejudices, not as prejudgments, but as irresistible products of their own observation. "The facts of the case" permit them no other conclusion.

Thus our fair-minded white citizen strongly supports a policy of excluding Negroes from his labor union. His views are, of course, based not upon prejudice, but upon the cold hard facts. And the facts seem clear enough. Negroes, "lately from the nonindustrial South, are undisciplined in traditions of trade unionism and the art of collective bargaining." The Negro is a strikebreaker. The Negro, with his "low standard of living," rushes in to take jobs at less than prevailing wages. The Negro is, in short, "a traitor to the working class," and should manifestly be excluded from union organizations. So run the facts of the case as seen by our tolerant but hard-headed union member, innocent of any understanding of the self-fulfilling prophecy as a basic process of society.

Our unionist fails to see, of course, that he and his kind have produced the very "facts" which he observes. For by defining the situation as one in which Negroes are held to be incorrigibly at odds with principles of unionism and by excluding Negroes from unions, he invited a series of consequences which indeed made it difficult if not impossible for many Negroes to avoid the role of scab. Out of work after World War I, and kept out of unions, thousands of Negroes could not resist strikebound employers who held a door invitingly open upon a world of jobs from which they were otherwise excluded.

History creates its own test of the theory of self-fulfilling prophecies. That Negroes were strikebreakers because they were excluded from unions (and from a large range of jobs) rather than excluded because they were strikebreakers can be seen from the virtual disappearance of Negroes as scabs in industries where they have gained admission to unions in the last decades.

The application of the Thomas theorem also suggests how the tragic, often vicious, circle of self-fulfilling prophecies can be broken. The initial definition of the situation which has set the circle in motion must be abandoned. Only when the original assumption is questioned and a new definition of the situation introduced, does the consequent flow of events give the lie to the assumption. Only then does the belief no longer father the reality.

But to question these deep-rooted definitions of the situation is no simple act of the will. The will, or, for that matter, goodwill, cannot be turned on and off like a faucet. Social intelligence and goodwill are themselves *products* of distinct social forces. They are not brought into being by mass propaganda and mass education, in the usual sense of these terms so dear to the sociological panaceans. In the social realm, no more than in the psychological realm, do false ideas quietly vanish when confronted with the truth. One does not expect a paranoiac to abandon his hard-won distortions and delusions upon being informed that they are altogether groundless. If psychic ills could be cured merely by the dissemination of truth, the psychiatrists of this country would be suffering from technological unemployment rather than from overwork. Nor will a continuing "educational campaign" itself destroy racial prejudice and discrimination.

This is not a particularly popular position. The appeal to "education" as a cure-all for the most varied social problems is rooted deep in the mores of America. Yet it is nonetheless illusory for all that. For how would this program of racial education proceed? Who is to do the educating? The teachers in our communities? But, in some measure like many other Americans, the teachers share the very prejudices they are being urged to combat. And when they don't, aren't they being asked to serve as conscientious martyrs in the cause of educational utopianism? How long would be the tenure of an elementary school teacher in Alabama or Mississippi or Georgia who attempted meticulously to disabuse his young pupils of the racial beliefs they acquired at home? Education may serve as an operational adjunct but not as the chief basis for any but excruciatingly slow change in the prevailing patterns of race relations.

To understand further why educational campaigns cannot

be counted on to eliminate prevailing ethnic hostilities, we must examine the operation of "in-groups" and "out-groups" in our society. Ethnic out-groups, to adopt Sumner's useful bit of sociological jargon, consist of all those who are believed to differ significantly from "ourselves" in terms of nationality, race, or religion. Counterpart of the ethnic out-group is of course the ethnic in-group, constituted by those who "belong." There is nothing fixed or eternal about the lines separating the in-group from out-groups. As situations change, the lines of separation change. For a large number of white Americans, Joe Louis is a member of an out-group—when the situation is defined in racial terms. On another occasion, when Louis defeated the nazified Schmeling, many of these same white Americans acclaimed him as a member of the (national) in-group. National loyalty took precedence over racial separatism. These abrupt shifts in group boundaries sometimes prove embarrassing. Thus, when Negro-Americans ran away with the honors in the Olympic games held in Berlin, the Nazis, pointing to the second-class citizenship assigned Negroes in various regions of this country, denied that the United States had really won the games, since the Negro athletes were by our own admission "not full-fledged" Americans. And what could Bilbo or Rankin say to that?

Under the benevolent guidance of the dominant in-group, ethnic out-groups are continuously subjected to a lively process of prejudice which, I think, goes far toward vitiating mass education and mass propaganda for ethnic tolerance. This is the process whereby "in-group virtues become out-group vices," to paraphrase a remark by the sociologist Donald Young. Or, more colloquially and perhaps more instructively, it may be called the "damned-if-you-do and damned-if-you-don't" process in ethnic and racial relations.

III

To discover that ethnic out-groups are damned if they do embrace the values of white Protestant society and damned if they don't, we have only to turn to one of the in-group culture heroes, examine the qualities with which he is endowed by biographers and popular belief, and thus distill the qualities of mind and action and character which are generally regarded as altogether admirable.

Periodic public opinion polls are not needed to justify the selection of Abe Lincoln as the culture hero who most fully embodies the cardinal American virtues. As the Lynds point out in *Middletown*, the people of that typical small city allow George Washington alone to join Lincoln as the greatest of Americans. He is claimed as their very own by almost as many well-to-do Republicans as by less well-to-do Democrats.

Even the inevitable schoolboy knows that Lincoln was thrifty, hardworking, eager for knowledge, ambitious, devoted to the rights of the average man, and eminently successful in climbing the ladder of opportunity from the lowermost rung of laborer to the respectable heights of merchant and lawyer. (We need follow his dizzying ascent no further.)

If one did not know that these attributes and achievements are numbered high among the values of middle-class America, one would soon discover it by glancing through the Lynds' account of "the Middletown Spirit." For there we find the image of the Great Emancipator fully reflected in the values in which Middletown believes. And since these are their values, it is not surprising to find the Middletowns of America condemning and disparaging those individuals and groups who fail, presumably, to exhibit these virtues. If it appears to the white in-group that Negroes are *not* educated in the same measure as themselves, that they have an "unduly" high proportion of unskilled workers and an "unduly" low proportion of successful business and professional men, that they are thriftless, and so on through the catalog of middle-class virtue and sin, it is not difficult to understand the charge that the Negro is "inferior" to the white.

Sensitized to the workings of the self-fulfilling prophecy, we should be prepared to find that the anti-Negro charges which are not patently false are only speciously true. The allegations are "true" in the Pickwickian sense that we have found self-fulfilling prophecies in general to be true. Thus, if the dominant in-group believes that Negroes are inferior, and sees to it that funds for education are not "wasted on these incompetents" and then proclaims as final evidence of this inferiority that Negroes have proportionately "only" one-fifth as many college graduates as whites, one can scarcely be amazed by this transparent bit of social legerdemain. Having seen the rabbit carefully though not too adroitly placed in the hat, we can only look askance at the triumphant air with which it is finally produced. (In fact, it is a little embarrassing to note that a larger proportion of Negro than of white high school graduates go on to college; obviously, the Negroes who are hardy enough to scale the high walls of discrimination represent an even more highly selected group than the run-of-the-high-school white population.)

So, too, when the gentleman from Mississippi (a state which spends five times as much on the average white pupil as on the average Negro pupil) proclaims the essential inferiority of the Negro by pointing to the per capita ratio of physicians among Negroes as less than one-fourth that of whites, we are impressed more by his scrambled logic than by his profound prejudices. So plain is the mechanism of the self-fulfilling prophecy in these instances that only those forever devoted to the victory of sentiment over fact can take these specious evidences seriously. Yet the spurious evidence often creates a genuine belief. Self-hypnosis through one's own propaganda is a not infrequent phase of the self-fulfilling prophecy.

So much for out-groups being damned if they don't (apparently) manifest in-group virtues. It is a tasteless bit of ethnocentrism, seasoned with self-interest. But what of the second phase of this process? Can one seriously mean that out-groups are also damned if they do possess these virtues? Precisely.

Through a faultlessly bisymmetrical prejudice, ethnic and racial out-groups get it coming and going. The systematic condemnation of the out-grouper continues largely *irrespective of what he does*. More: through a freakish exercise of capricious judicial logic, the victim is punished for the crime. Superficial appearances notwithstanding, prejudice and discrimination aimed at the out-group are not a result of what the out-group does, but are rooted deep in the structure of our society and the social psychology of its members.

To understand how this happens, we must examine the moral alchemy through which the in-group readily transmutes virtue into vice and vice into virtue, as the occasion may demand. Our studies will proceed by the case-method.

We begin with the engagingly simple formula of moral alchemy: the same behavior must be differently evaluated according to the person who exhibits it. For example, the proficient alchemist will at once know that the word "firm" is properly declined as follows:

I am firm,
Thou art obstinate,
He is pigheaded.

There are some, unversed in the skills of this science, who will tell you that one and the same term should be applied to all three instances of identical behavior. Such unalchemical nonsense should simply be ignored.

With this experiment in mind, we are prepared to observe how the very same behavior undergoes a complete change of evaluation in its transition from the in-group Abe Lincoln to the out-group Abe Cohen or Abe Kurokawa. We proceed systematically. Did Lincoln work far into the night? This testifies that he was industrious, resolute, perseverant, and eager to realize his capacities to the full. Do the out-group Jews or Japanese keep these same hours? This only bears witness to their sweatshop mentality, their ruthless undercutting of American standards, their unfair competitive practices. Is the in-group hero frugal, thrifty, and sparing? Then the out-group villain is stingy, miserly, and penny-pinching. All honor is due the in-group Abe for his having been smart, shrewd, and intelligent, and by the same token, all contempt is owing the out-group Abes for their being sharp, cunning, crafty, and too clever by far. Did the indomitable Lincoln refuse to remain content with a life of work with the hands? Did he prefer to make use of his brain? Then, all praise for his plucky climb up the shaky ladder of opportunity. But, of course, the eschewing of manual work for brain work among the merchants and lawyers of the out-group deserves nothing but censure for a parasitic way of life. Was Abe Lincoln eager to learn the accumulated wisdom of the ages by unending study? The trouble with the Jew is that he's a greasy grind, with his head always in a book, while decent people are going to a show or a ball game. Was the resolute Lincoln unwilling to limit his standards to those of his provincial community? That is what we should expect of a man of vision. And if the out-groupers criticize the vulnerable areas in our society, then send 'em back where they came from. Did Lincoln, rising high above his origins, never forget the rights of the common man and applaud the right of workers to strike? This testifies only that, like all real Americans, this greatest of Americans was deathlessly devoted to the cause of freedom. But, as you examine the recent statistics on strikes, remember that these un-American practices are the result of out-groupers pursuing their evil agitation among otherwise contented workers.

Once stated, the classical formula of moral alchemy is clear enough. Through the adroit use of these rich vocabularies of encomium and opprobrium, the in-group readily transmutes its own virtues into others' vices. But why do so many in-groupers qualify as moral alchemists? Why are so many in the dominant in-group so fully devoted to this continuing experiment in moral transmutation?

An explanation may be found by putting ourselves at some distance from this country and following the anthropologist Malinowski to the Trobriand Islands. For there we find an instructively similar pattern. Among the Trobrianders, to a degree which Americans, despite Hollywood and the confession magazines, have apparently not yet approximated, success with women confers honor and prestige on a man. Sexual prowess is a positive value, a moral virtue. But if a rank-and-file Trobriander has "too much" sexual success, if he achieves "too many" triumphs of the heart, an achievement which should of course be limited to the elite, the chiefs or men of power, then this glorious record becomes a scandal and an abomination. The chiefs are quick *to resent any personal achievement not warranted by social position*. The moral virtues remain virtues only so long as they are jealously confined to the proper in-group. The right activity by the wrong people becomes a thing of contempt, not of honor.

For clearly, only in this way, by holding these virtues exclusively to themselves, can the men of power retain their distinction, their prestige, and their power. No wiser procedure could be devised to hold intact a system of social stratification and social power.

The Trobrianders can teach us more. For it seems clear that the chiefs have not calculatingly devised this program of entrenchment. Their behavior is spontaneous, unthinking, and immediate. Their resentment of "too much" ambition or "too much" success in the ordinary Trobriander is not contrived, it is genuine. It just happens that this prompt emotional response to the "misplaced" manifestation of in-group virtues also serves the useful expedient of reinforcing the chiefs' special claims to the good things of Trobriand life. Nothing could be more remote from the truth and more distorted a reading of the facts than to assume that this conversion of in-group virtues into out-group vices is part of a calculated, deliberate plot of Trobriand chiefs to keep Trobriand commoners in their place. It is merely that the chiefs have been indoctrinated with an appreciation of the proper order of things, and see it as their heavy burden to enforce the mediocrity of others.

Nor, in quick revulsion from the culpabilities of the moral alchemists, need we succumb to the equivalent error of simply upending the moral status of the in-group and the out-groups. It is not that Jews and Negroes are one and all angelic while Gentiles and whites are one and all fiendish. It is not that individual virtue will now be found exclusively on the wrong side of the ethnic-racial tracks and individual viciousness on the right side. It is conceivable even that there are as many corrupt and vicious men and women among Negroes and Jews as among Gentile whites. It is only that the ugly fence which encloses the in-group happens to exclude the people who make up the out-groups from being treated with the decency ordinarily accorded human beings.

IV

We have only to look at the consequences of this peculiar moral alchemy to see that there is no paradox at all in damning out-groupers if they do and if they don't exhibit in-group virtues. Condemnation on these two scores performs one and the same social function. Seeming opposites coalesce. When Negroes are tagged as incorrigibly inferior because they (apparently) don't manifest these virtues, this confirms the natural rightness of their being assigned an inferior status in society. And when Jews or Japanese are tagged as having too many of the in-group values, it becomes plain that they must be securely controlled by the high walls of discrimination. In both cases, the special status assigned the several out-groups can be seen to be eminently reasonable.

Yet this distinctly reasonable arrangement persists in having most unreasonable consequences, both logical and social. Consider only a few of these.

In some contexts, the limitations enforced upon the out-group—say, rationing the number of Jews permitted to enter colleges and professional schools—logically imply a fear of the alleged superiority of the out-group. Were it otherwise, no discrimination need be practiced. The unyielding, impersonal forces of academic competition would soon trim down the number of Jewish (or Japanese or Negro) students to an "appropriate" size.

This implied belief in the superiority of the out-group seems premature. There is simply not enough scientific evidence to demonstrate Jewish or Japanese or Negro superiority. The effort of the in-group discriminator to supplant the myth of Aryan superiority with the myth of non-Aryan superiority is condemned to failure by science. Moreover, such myths are ill-advised. Eventually, life in a world of myth must collide with fact in the world of reality. As a matter of simple self-interest and social therapy, therefore, it might be wise for the in-group to abandon the myth and cling to the reality.

The pattern of being damned-if-you-do and damned-if-you-don't has further consequences—among the out-groups themselves. The response to alleged deficiencies is as clear as it is predictable. If one is repeatedly told that one is inferior, that one lacks any positive accomplishments, it is all too human to seize upon every bit of evidence to the contrary. The in-group definitions force upon the allegedly inferior out-group a defensive tendency to magnify and exalt "race accomplishments." As the

distinguished Negro sociologist Franklin Frazier has noted, the
Negro newspapers are "intensely race conscious and exhibit considerable pride in the achievements of the Negro, most of which
are meagre performances as measured by broader standards."
Self-glorification, found in some measure among all groups,
becomes a frequent counter-response to persistent belittlement
from without.

It is the damnation of out-groups for "excessive achievement,"
however, which gives rise to truly bizarre behavior. For, after
a time and often as a matter of self-defense, these out-groups
become persuaded that their virtues really are vices. And this
provides the final episode in a tragicomedy of inverted values.

Let us try to follow the plot through its intricate maze of self-
contradictions. Respectful admiration for the arduous climb
from office boy to president is rooted deep in American culture.
This long and strenuous ascent carries with it a twofold testimonial: it testifies that careers are abundantly open to genuine talent
in American society and it testifies to the worth of the man who
has distinguished himself by his heroic rise. It would be invidious
to choose among the many stalwart figures who have fought their
way up, against all odds, until they have reached the pinnacle,
there to sit at the head of the long conference table in the longer
conference room of The Board. Taken at random, the saga of
Frederick H. Ecker, chairman of the board of one of the largest
privately managed corporations in the world, the Metropolitan
Life Insurance Company, will suffice as the prototype. From a
menial and poorly paid job, he rose to a position of eminence.
Appropriately enough, an unceasing flow of honors has come
to this man of large power and large achievement. It so happens,
though it is a matter personal to this eminent man of finance,
that Mr. Ecker is a Presbyterian. Yet at last report, no elder of
the Presbyterian church has risen publicly to announce that
Mr. Ecker's successful career should not be taken too seriously,
that, after all, relatively few Presbyterians have risen from rags to
riches and that Presbyterians do not actually "control" the world
of finance—or life insurance, or investment housing. Rather, one
would suppose, Presbyterian elders join with other Americans
imbued with middle-class standards of success to felicitate the

eminently successful Mr. Ecker and to acclaim other sons of the faith who have risen to almost equal heights. Secure with their in-group status, they point the finger of pride rather than the finger of dismay at individual success.

Prompted by the practice of moral alchemy, noteworthy achievements by out-groupers elicit other responses. Patently, if achievement is a vice, the achievement must be disclaimed—or at least, discounted. Under these conditions, what is an occasion for Presbyterian pride must become an occasion for Jewish dismay. If the Jew is condemned for his educational or professional or scientific or economic success, then, understandably enough, many Jews will come to feel that these accomplishments must be minimized in simple self-defense. Thus is the circle of paradox closed by out-groupers busily engaged in assuring the powerful in-group that they have not, in fact, been guilty of inordinate contributions to science, the professions, the arts, the government, and the economy.

In a society which ordinarily looks upon wealth as a warrant of ability, an out-group is compelled by the inverted attitudes of the dominant in-group to deny that many men of wealth are among its members. "Among the 200 largest nonbanking corporations . . . only ten have a Jew as president or chairman of the board." Is this an observation of an anti-Semite, intent on proving the incapacity and inferiority of Jews who have done so little "to build the corporations which have built America"? No; it is a retort of the Anti-Defamation League of B'nai B'rith to anti-Semitic propaganda.

In a society where, as a recent survey by the National Opinion Research Center has shown, the profession of medicine ranks higher in social prestige than any other of ninety occupations (save that of United States Supreme Court justice), we find some Jewish spokesmen maneuvered by the attacking in-group into the fantastic position of announcing their "deep concern" over the number of Jews in medical practice, which is "disproportionate to the number of Jews in other occupations." In a nation suffering from a notorious undersupply of physicians, the Jewish doctor becomes a deplorable occasion for deep concern, rather than receiving applause for his hard-won acquisition of knowledge and skills and for his social utility. Only when the New York Yankees publicly announce deep concern over their eleven World Series titles, so disproportionate to the number of triumphs achieved by other major league teams, will this self-abnegation seem part of the normal order of things.

In a culture which consistently judges the professionals higher in social value than even the most skilled hewers of wood and drawers of water, the out-group finds itself in the anomalous position of pointing with defensive relief to the large number of Jewish painters and paper hangers, plasterers and electricians, plumbers and sheet-metal workers.

But the ultimate reversal of values is yet to be noted. Each succeeding census finds more and more Americans in the city and its suburbs. Americans have traveled the road to urbanization until less than one-fifth of the nation's population live on farms. Plainly, it is high time for the Methodist and the Catholic, the Baptist and the Episcopalian to recognize the iniquity of this trek of their coreligionists to the city. For, as is well-known, one of the central accusations leveled against the Jew is his heinous tendency to live in cities. Jewish leaders, therefore, find themselves in the incredible position of defensively urging their people to move into the very farm areas being hastily vacated by city-bound hordes of Christians. Perhaps this is not altogether necessary. As the Jewish crime of urbanism becomes ever more popular among the in-group, it may be reshaped into transcendent virtue. But, admittedly, one can't be certain. For in this daft confusion of inverted values, it soon becomes impossible to determine when virtue is sin and sin, moral perfection.

Amid this confusion, one fact remains unambiguous. The Jews, like other peoples, have made distinguished contributions to world culture. Consider only an abbreviated catalog. In the field of creative literature (and with acknowledgment of large variations in the caliber of achievement), Jewish authors include Heine, Karl Kraus, Börne, Hofmannsthal, Schnitzler, Kafka. In the realm of musical composition, there are Meyerbeer, Felix Mendelssohn, Offenbach, Mahler, and Schönberg. Among the musical virtuosi, consider only Rosenthal, Schnabel, Godowsky, Pachmann, Kreisler, Hubermann, Milstein, Elman, Heifetz, Joachim, and Menuhin. And among scientists of a stature sufficient to merit the Nobel Prize, examine the familiar list which includes Beranyi, Mayerhof, Ehrlich, Michelson, Lippmann, Haber, Willstätter, and Einstein. Or in the esoteric and imaginative universe of mathematical invention, take note only of Kronecker, the creator of the modern theory of numbers; Hermann Minkowski,* who supplied the mathematical foundations of the special theory of relativity; or Jacobi, with his basic work in the theory of elliptical functions. And so through each special province of cultural achievement, we are supplied with a list of preeminent men and women who happened to be Jews.

And who is thus busily engaged in singing the praises of the Jews? Who has so assiduously compiled the list of many hundreds of distinguished Jews who contributed so notably to science, literature and the arts—a list from which these few cases were excerpted? A philo-Semite, eager to demonstrate that his people have contributed their due share to world culture? No, by now we should know better than that. The complete list will be found in the thirty-sixth edition of an anti-Semitic handbook by the racist Fritsch. In accord with the alchemical formula for transmuting in-group virtues into out-group vices, he presents this as a roll call of sinister spirits who have usurped the accomplishments properly owing the Aryan in-group.

Once we comprehend the predominant role of the in-group in defining the situation, the further paradox of the seemingly opposed behavior of the Negro out-group and the Jewish out-group falls away. The behavior of both minority groups is in response to the majority-group allegations.

If the Negroes are accused of inferiority, and their alleged failure to contribute to world culture is cited in support of this accusation, the human urge for self-respect and a concern for security leads them *defensively* often to magnify each and every achievement by members of the race. If Jews are accused of "excessive"

---

* Obviously, the forename must be explicitly mentioned here, else Hermann Minkowski, the mathematician, may be confused with Eugen Minkowski, who contributed so notably to our knowledge of schizophrenia, or with Mieczyslaw Minkowski, high in the ranks of brain anatomists, or even with Oskar Minkowski, discoverer of pancreatic diabetes.

achievements and "excessive" ambitions, and lists of preeminent Jews are compiled in support of this counter-accusation, then the urge for security leads them *defensively* to minimize the actual achievements of members of the group. Apparently opposed types of behavior have the same psychological and social functions. Self-assertion and self-effacement become the devices for seeking to cope with condemnation for alleged group deficiency and condemnation for alleged group excesses, respectively. And with a fine sense of moral superiority, the secure in-group looks on these curious performances by the out-groups with mingled derision and contempt.

V

Will this desolate tragicomedy run on and on, marked only by minor changes in the cast? Not necessarily.

Were moral scruples and a sense of decency the only bases for bringing the play to an end, one would indeed expect it to continue an indefinitely long run. In and of themselves, moral sentiments are not much more effective in curing social ills than in curing physical ills. Moral sentiments no doubt help to motivate efforts for change, but they are no substitute for hardheaded instrumentalities for achieving the objective, as the thickly populated graveyard of softheaded utopias bears witness.

There are ample indications that a deliberate and planned halt can be put to the workings of the self-fulfilling prophecy and the vicious circle in society. The sequel to our sociological parable of the Last National Bank provides one clue to the way in which this can be achieved. During the fabulous twenties, when Coolidge undoubtedly caused a Republican era of lush prosperity, an average of 635 banks a year quietly suspended operations. And during the four years immediately before and after the Crash, when Hoover undoubtedly did not cause a Republican era of sluggish depression, this zoomed to the more spectacular average of 2,276 bank suspensions annually. But, interestingly enough, in the twelve years following the establishment of the Federal Deposit Insurance Corporation and the enactment of other banking legislation while Roosevelt presided over Democratic depression and revival, recession and boom, bank suspensions dropped to a niggardly average of twenty-eight a year. Perhaps money panics have not been institutionally exorcized by legislation. Nevertheless, millions of depositors no longer have occasion to give way to panic-motivated runs on banks simply because deliberate institutional change has removed the grounds for panic. Occasions for racial hostility are no more inborn psychological constants than are occasions for panic. Despite the teachings of amateur psychologists, blind panic and racial aggression are not rooted in "human nature." These patterns of human behavior are largely a product of the modifiable structure of society.

For a further clue, return to our instance of widespread hostility of white unionists toward the Negro strikebreakers brought into industry by employers after the close of the very first World War. Once the initial definition of Negroes as not deserving of union membership had largely broken down, the Negro, with a wider range of work opportunities, no longer found it necessary to enter industry through the doors held open by strikebound employers. Again, appropriate institutional change broke through the tragic circle of the self-fulfilling prophecy. Deliberate social change gave the lie to the firm conviction that "it just ain't in the nature of the nigra" to join cooperatively with his white fellows in trade unions.

A final instance is drawn from a study of a biracial housing project which I have been conducting with Patricia J. Salter, under a grant from the Lavanburg Foundation. Located in Pittsburgh, this community of Hilltown is made up of 50 percent Negro families and 50 percent white. It is not a twentieth-century utopia. There is some interpersonal friction here, as elsewhere. But in a community made up of equal numbers of the two races, fewer than a fifth of the whites and less than a third of the Negroes report that this friction occurs between members of *different* races. By their own testimony, it is very largely confined to disagreements *within* each racial group. Yet only one in every twenty-five whites initially *expected* relations between the races in this community to run smoothly, whereas five times as many expected serious trouble, the remainder anticipating a tolerable, if not altogether pleasant, situation. So much for expectations. Upon reviewing their actual experience, three of every four of the most apprehensive whites subsequently found that the "races get along fairly well," after all. This is not the place to report the findings of the Lavanburg study in detail, but substantially these demonstrate anew that under *appropriate institutional and administrative conditions*, the experience of interracial amity can supplant the fear of interracial conflict.

These changes, and others of the same kind, do not occur automatically. *The self-fulfilling prophecy, whereby fears are translated into reality, operates only in the absence of deliberate institutional controls.* And it is only with the rejection of social fatalism implied in the notion of unchangeable human nature that the tragic circle of fear, social disaster, reinforced fear can be broken.

Ethnic prejudices do die—but slowly. They can be helped over the threshold of oblivion, not by insisting that it is unreasonable and unworthy of them to survive, but by cutting off their sustenance now provided by certain institutions of our society.

If we find ourselves doubting man's capacity to control man and his society, if we persist in our tendency to find in the patterns of the past the chart of the future, it is perhaps time to take up anew the wisdom of Tocqueville's 112-year-old apothegm: "What we call necessary institutions are often no more than institutions to which we have grown accustomed."

Nor can widespread, even typical, failures in planning human relations between ethnic groups be cited as evidence for pessimism. In the world laboratory of the sociologist, as in the more secluded laboratories of the physicist and chemist, it is the successful experiment which is decisive and not the thousand-and-one failures which preceded it. More is learned from the single success than from the multiple failures. A single success proves it can be done. Thereafter, it is necessary only to learn what made it work. This, at least, is what I take to be the sociological sense of those revealing words of Thomas Love Peacock: "Whatever is, is possible."

Leslie Fiedler (1917–2003) was an American literary critic whose daring essay "Come Back to the Raft Ag'in, Huck Honey!" was the opening salvo in an attempt to apply Freudian psychological premises to the canon. He teased out mythological strands in the plots of classical American novels, emphasizing their homoerotic tendencies and evasions of domesticity and women. A professor at SUNY Buffalo, Fiedler's essays, collected in books such as No! In Thunder *and* Love and Death in the American Novel, *achieved a crossover popularity unusual among literary scholars.*

COME BACK TO THE RAFT AG'IN, HUCK HONEY!

It is perhaps to be expected that the Negro and the homosexual should become stock literary themes in a period when the exploration of responsibility and failure has become again a primary concern of our literature. It is the discrepancy they represent that haunts us, that moral discrepancy before which we are helpless, having no resources (no tradition of courtesy, no honored mode of cynicism) for dealing with a conflict of principle and practice. It used once to be fashionable to think of puritanism as a force in our lives encouraging hypocrisy; quite the contrary, its emphasis upon the singleness of belief and action, its turning of the most prosaic areas of life into arenas where one's state of grace is tested, confuse the outer and the inner and make hypocrisy among us, perhaps more strikingly than ever elsewhere, *visible*, visibly detestable, the cardinal sin. It is not without significance that the shrug of the shoulders (the acceptance of circumstance as a sufficient excuse, the sign of self-pardon before the inevitable lapse) seems in America an unfamiliar, an alien gesture.

And yet before the continued existence of physical homosexual love (our crudest epithets notoriously evoke the mechanics of such affairs), before the blatant ghettos in which the Negro conspicuously creates the gaudiness and stench that offend him, the white American must make a choice between coming to terms with institutionalized discrepancy or formulating radically new ideologies. There are, to be sure, stopgap devices, evasions of that final choice; not the least interesting is the special night-club: the "queer" café, the black-and-tan joint, in which fairy or Negro exhibits their fairy-ness, their Negro-ness as if they were mere divertissements, gags thought up for the laughs and having no reality once the lights go out and the chairs are piled on the tables by the cleaning women. In the earlier minstrel show, a Negro performer was required to put on with greasepaint and burnt cork the formalized mask of blackness; while the queer must exaggerate flounce and flutter into the convention of his condition.

The situations of the Negro and the homosexual in our society pose quite opposite problems, or at least problems suggesting quite opposite solutions. Our laws on homosexuality and the context of prejudice they objectify must apparently be changed to accord with a stubborn social fact; whereas it is the social fact, our overt behavior toward the Negro, that must be modified to accord with our laws and the, at least official, morality they objectify. It is not, of course, quite so simple. There is another sense in which the fact of homosexual passion contradicts a national myth of masculine love, just as our real relationship with the Negro contradicts a myth of that relationship; and those two myths with their betrayals are, as we shall see, one.

The existence of overt homosexuality threatens to compromise an essential aspect of American sentimental life: the camaraderie of the locker room and ball park, the good fellowship of the poker game and fishing trip, a kind of passionless passion, at once gross and delicate, homoerotic in the boy's sense, possessing an innocence above suspicion. To doubt for a moment this innocence, which can survive only as *assumed*, would destroy our stubborn belief in a relationship simple, utterly satisfying, yet immune to lust; physical as the handshake is physical, this side of copulation. The nineteenth-century myth of the Immaculate Young Girl has failed to survive in any *felt* way into our time. Rather, in the dirty jokes shared among men in the smoking car, the barracks, or the dormitory, there is a common male revenge against women for having flagrantly betrayed that myth; and under the revenge, the rather smug assumption of the chastity of the revenging group, in so far as it is a purely male society. From what other source could arise that unexpected air of good clean fun which overhangs such sessions? It is this self-congratulatory buddy-buddiness, its astonishing naïveté that breed at once endless opportunities for inversion and the terrible reluctance to admit its existence, to surrender the last believed-in stronghold of love without passion.

It is, after all, what we know from a hundred other sources that is here verified: the regressiveness, in a technical sense, of American life, its implacable nostalgia for the infantile, at once wrongheaded and somehow admirable. The mythic America is boyhood—and who would dare be startled to realize that the two most popular, most *absorbed*, I am sure, of the handful of great books in our native heritage are customarily to be found, illustrated, on the shelves of the children's library. I am referring, of course, to *Moby-Dick* and *Huckleberry Finn*, so different in technique and language, but alike children's books or, more precisely, *boys'* books.

There are the Leatherstocking Tales of Cooper, too, as well as Dana's *Two Years Before the Mast* and a good deal of Stephen Crane, books whose continuing favor depends more and more on the taste of boys; and one begins to foresee a similar improbable fate for Ernest Hemingway. Among the most distinguished novelists of the American past, only Henry James completely escapes classification as a writer of juvenile classics; even Hawthorne, who did write sometimes for children, must in his most adult novels endure, though not as Mark Twain and Melville submit to, the child's perusal. A child's version of *The Scarlet Letter* would seem a rather farfetched joke if it were not a part of our common experience. Finding in the children's department of the local library what Hawthorne liked to call his "hell-fired book," and remembering that *Moby-Dick* itself has as its secret motto "*Ego te baptizo in nomine diaboli*," one can only bow in awed silence before the mysteries of public morality, the American idea of "innocence." Everything goes except the frank description of adult heterosexual love. After all, boys will be boys!

What, then, do all these books have in common? As boys' books we should expect them shyly, guiltlessly as it were, to proffer a chaste male love as the ultimate emotional experience—and this is spectacularly the case. In Dana, it is the narrator's melancholy love for the *kanaka*, Hope; in Cooper, the lifelong affection of Natty Bumppo and Chingachgook; in Melville, Ishmael's love for Queequeg; in Twain, Huck's feeling for Nigger Jim. At the focus of emotion, where we are accustomed to find in the world's great novels some heterosexual passion, be it "platonic" love or adultery, seduction, rape, or long-drawn-out flirtation, we come instead on the fugitive slave and the no-account boy lying side by side on a raft borne by the endless river toward an impossible escape, or the pariah sailor waking in the tattooed arms of the brown harpooner on the verge of their impossible quest. "*Aloha, aikane, aloha nui,*" Hope cries to the lover who prefers him to all his fellow-whites; and Ishmael in utter frankness tells us: "I found Queequeg's arm thrown over me in the most loving and affectionate manner. You had almost thought I had been his wife . . . he still hugged me tightly, as though naught but death should part us twain . . . Thus, then, in our heart's honeymoon, lay I and Queequeg—a cosy, loving pair . . . he pressed his forehead against mine, clasped me around the waist, and said that henceforth we were married."

In Melville, the ambiguous relationship is most explicitly rendered; almost, indeed, openly explained. Not by a chance phrase or camouflaged symbol (the dressing of Jim in a woman's gown in *Huck Finn*, for instance, which can mean anything or nothing at all), but in a step-by-step exposition, the Pure Marriage of Ishmael and Queequeg is set before us: the initial going to bed together and the first shyness overcome, that great hot tomahawk-pipe accepted in a familiarity that dispels fear; next, the wedding ceremony itself (for in this marriage like so many others the ceremonial follows the deflowering), with the ritual touching of foreheads; then, the queasiness and guilt the morning after the *official* First Night, the suspicion that one has joined himself irrevocably to his own worst nightmare; finally, a symbolic portrayal of the continuing state of marriage through the image of the "monkey rope" which binds the lovers fast waist to waist (for the sake of this symbolism, Melville changes a *fact* of whaling practice—the only time in the book), a permanent alliance that provides mutual protection but also threatens mutual death.

Physical it all is, certainly, yet somehow ultimately innocent. There lies between the lovers no naked sword but a childlike ignorance, as if the possibility of a fall to the carnal had not yet been discovered. Even in the *Vita Nuova* of Dante, there is no vision of love less offensively, more unremittingly chaste; that it is not adult seems beside the point. Ishmael's sensations as he wakes under the pressure of Queequeg's arm, the tenderness of Huck's repeated loss and refinding of Jim, the role of almost Edenic helpmate played for Bumppo by the Indian—these shape us from childhood: we have no sense of first discovering them or of having been once without them.

Of the infantile, the homoerotic aspects of these stories we are, though vaguely, aware; but it is only with an effort that we can wake to a consciousness of how, among us who at the level of adulthood find a difference in color sufficient provocation for distrust and hatred, they celebrate, all of them, the mutual love of *a white man and a colored*. So buried at a level of acceptance which does not touch reason, so desperately repressed from overt recognition, so contrary to what is usually thought of as our ultimate level of taboo—the sense of that love can survive only in the obliquity of a symbol, persistent, obsessive, in short, an archetype: the boy's homoerotic crush, the love of the black fused at this level into a single thing.

I hope I have been using here a hopelessly abused word with some precision; by "archetype" I mean a coherent pattern of beliefs and feelings so widely shared at a level beneath consciousness that there exists no abstract vocabulary for representing it, and so "sacred" that unexamined, irrational restraints inhibit any explicit analysis. Such a complex finds a formula or pattern story, which serves both to embody it, and, at first at least, to conceal its full implications. Later, the secret may be revealed, the archetype "analyzed" or "allegorically" interpreted according to the language of the day.

I find the complex we have been examining genuinely mythic; certainly it has the invisible character of the true archetype, eluding the wary pounce of Howells or Mrs. Twain, who excised from *Huckleberry Finn* the cussing as unfit for children, but who left, unperceived, a conventionally abhorrent doctrine of ideal love. Even the writers in whom we find it attained it, in a sense, dreaming. The felt difference between *Huckleberry Finn* and Twain's other books must lie in part in the release from conscious restraint inherent in the author's assumption of the character of Huck; the passage in and out of darkness and river mist, the constant confusion of identities (Huck's ten or twelve names; the question of who is the real uncle, who the true Tom), the sudden intrusions into alien violences without past or future, give the whole work, for all its carefully observed detail, the texture of a dream. For *Moby-Dick* such a point need scarcely be made. Even Cooper, despite his insufferable gentlemanliness, his tedium, cannot conceal from the kids who continue to read him the secret behind his overconscious prose: the childish, impossible dream. D. H. Lawrence saw in him clearly the boy's Utopia: the absolute wilderness in which the stuffiness of home yields to the wigwam, and "My Wife" to Chingachgook.

I do not recall ever having seen in the commentaries of the social anthropologist or psychologist an awareness of the role of this profound child's dream of love in our relation to the Negro. (I say Negro, though the beloved in the books I have mentioned is variously Indian and Polynesian, because the Negro has become more and more exclusively for us *the* colored man, the colored man par excellence.) Trapped in what have by now become shackling clichés—the concept of the white man's sexual envy of the Negro male, the ambivalent horror of miscegenation— they do not sufficiently note the complementary factor of physical attraction, the archetypal love of white male and black. But either the horror or the attraction is meaningless alone; only together do they make sense. Just as the pure love of man and man is in general set off against the ignoble passion of man for woman, so more specifically (and more vividly) the dark desire which leads to miscegenation is contrasted with the ennobling love of a white man and a colored one. James Fenimore Cooper is our first poet of this ambivalence; indeed, miscegenation is the secret theme of the Leatherstocking novels, especially of *The Last of the Mohicans*. Natty Bumppo, the man who boasts always of having "no cross" in *his* blood, flees by nature from the defilement of all women, but never with so absolute a revulsion as he displays toward the *squaw* with whom at one point he seems at the point of being forced to cohabit; and the threat of the dark-skinned rapist sends pale woman after pale woman skittering through Cooper's imagined wilderness. Even poor Cora, who already has a fatal drop of alien blood that cuts her off from any marriage with a white man, in so far as she is white cannot be mated with Uncas, the noblest of redmen. Only in death can they be joined in an embrace as chaste as that of males. There's no good woman but a dead woman! Yet Chingachgook and the Deerslayer are permitted to sit night after night over their campfire in the purest domestic bliss. So long as there is no mingling of blood, soul may couple with soul in God's undefiled forest.

Nature undefiled—this is the inevitable setting of the Sacred Marriage of males. Ishmael and Queequeg, arm in arm, about to ship out, Huck and Jim swimming beside the raft in the peaceful flux of the Mississippi—here it is the motion of water which completes the syndrome, the American dream of isolation afloat. The notion of the Negro as the unblemished bride blends with the myth of running away to sea, of running the great river down to the sea. The immensity of water defines a loneliness that demands love; its strangeness symbolizes the disavowal of the conventional that makes possible all versions of love. In *Two Years Before the Mast*, in *Moby-Dick*, in *Huckleberry Finn* the water is there, is the very texture of the novel; the Leatherstocking Tales propose another symbol for the same meaning: the virgin forest. Notice the adjectives—the virgin forest and the forever inviolable sea. It is well to remember, too, what surely must be more than a coincidence, that Cooper, who could dream this myth, also invented for us the novel of the sea, wrote for the first time in history the sea story proper.

The rude pederasty of the forecastle and the captain's cabin, celebrated in a thousand jokes, is the profanation of a dream; yet Melville, who must have known such blasphemies, refers to them only once and indirectly, for it was *his* dream that they threatened. And still the dream survives; in a recent book by Gore Vidal, an incipient homosexual, not yet aware of the implications of his feelings, indulges in the reverie of running off to sea with his dearest friend. The buggery of sailors is taken for granted everywhere, yet is thought of usually as an inversion forced on men by their isolation from women; though the opposite case may well be true: the isolation sought more or less consciously as an occasion for male encounters. At any rate, there is a context in which the legend of the sea as escape and solace, the fixated sexuality of boys, the myth of the dark beloved, are one. In Melville and Twain at the center of our tradition, in the lesser writers at the periphery, the archetype is at once formalized and perpetuated. Nigger Jim and Queequeg make concrete for us what was without them a vague pressure on the threshold of our consciousness; the proper existence of the archetype is in the realized character, who waits, as it were, only to be asked his secret. Think of Oedipus biding in silence from Sophocles to Freud!

Unwittingly, we are possessed in childhood by these characters and their undiscriminated meaning, and it is difficult for us to dissociate them without a sense of disbelief. What—these household figures clues to our subtlest passions! The foreigner finds it easier to perceive the significances too deep within us to be brought into focus. D. H. Lawrence discovered in our classics a linked mythos of escape and immaculate male love; Lorca in *Poet in New York* grasped instinctively (he could not even read English) the kinship of Harlem and Walt Whitman, the fairy as bard. But of course we do not have to be conscious of what possesses us; in every generation of our own writers the archetype reappears, refracted, half-understood, but *there*. In the gothic reverie of Capote's *Other Voices, Other Rooms*, both elements of the syndrome are presented, though disjunctively: the boy moving between the love of a Negro maidservant and his inverted cousin. In Carson McCullers' *The Member of the Wedding*, another variant is invented: a *female* homosexual romance between the boy-girl Frankie and a Negro cook. This time the Father-Slave-Beloved is converted into the figure of a Mother-Sweetheart-Servant, but remains still, of course, satisfactorily black. It is not strange, after all, to find this archetypal complex in latter-day writers of a frankly homosexual sensibility; but it recurs, too, in such resolutely masculine writers as Faulkner, who evokes the myth in the persons of the Negro and the boy of *Intruder in the Dust*.

In the myth, one notes finally, it is typically in the role of outcast, ragged woodsman, or despised sailor ("Call me Ishmael!"), or unregenerate boy (Huck before the prospect of being "sivilized" cries out, "I been there before!"), that we turn to the love of a colored man. But how, we cannot help asking, does the vision of the white American as a pariah correspond with our long-held public status: the world's beloved, the success? It is perhaps only the artist's portrayal of *himself*, the notoriously alienated writer in America, at home with such images, child of the town drunk, the hapless survivor. But no, Ishmael is in all of us, our unconfessed universal fear objectified in the writer's status as in the outcast sailor's: that compelling anxiety, which every foreigner notes, that we may not be loved, that we are loved for our possessions and not our selves, that we are really—*alone*. It is that underlying terror which explains our incredulity in the face of adulation or favor, what is called (once more the happy adjective) our "boyish modesty."

Our dark-skinned beloved will take us in, we assure ourselves, when we have been cut off, or have cut ourselves off, from all others, without rancor or the insult of forgiveness. He will fold us in his arms saying, "Honey" or "Aikane"; he will comfort us, as if our offense against him were long ago remitted, were never truly *real*. And yet we cannot ever really forget our guilt; the stories that embody the myth dramatize as if compulsively the role of the colored man as the victim. Dana's Hope is shown dying of the white man's syphilis; Queequeg is portrayed as racked by fever, a pointless episode except in the light of this necessity; Crane's Negro is disfigured to the point of monstrosity; Cooper's Indian smolders to a hopeless old age conscious of the imminent disappearance of his race; Jim is shown loaded down with chains, weakened by the hundred torments dreamed up by Tom in the name of bulliness. The immense gulf of guilt must not be mitigated any more than the disparity of color (Queequeg is not merely brown but monstrously tattooed; Chingachgook is horrid with paint; Jim is portrayed as the sick A-rab dyed blue), so that the final reconciliation may seem more unbelievable and tender. The archetype makes no attempt to deny our outrage as fact; it portrays it as meaningless in the face of love.

There would be something insufferable, I think, in that final vision of remission if it were not for the presence of a motivating anxiety, the sense always of a last chance. Behind the white American's nightmare that someday, no longer tourist, inheritor, or liberator, he will be rejected, refused, he dreams of his acceptance at the breast he has most utterly offended. It is a dream so sentimental, so outrageous, so desperate, that it redeems our concept of boyhood from nostalgia to tragedy.

In each generation we *play out* the impossible mythos, and we live to see our children play it: the white boy and the black we can discover wrestling affectionately on any American sidewalk, along which they will walk in adulthood, eyes averted from each other, unwilling to touch even by accident. The dream recedes; the immaculate passion and the astonishing reconciliation become a memory, and less, a regret, at last the unrecognized motifs of a child's book. "It's too good to be true, Honey," Jim says to Huck. "It's too good to be true."

James Baldwin (1924–1987) was the most prominent American essayist in the second half of the twentieth century. His essays matter: they have an urgency, breadth of concern, and vocal eloquence like no other. His main subject was the wounds of racism, which he dissected not only sociologically but personally, drawing a riveting self-portrait in his nonfiction books (Notes of a Native Son, Nobody Knows My Name, The Fire Next Time). *In 1948, seeking a respite from American racism, he moved to Europe, where he encountered a different kind of alienation, as described in "Stranger in the Village." Baldwin was energized by the African countries then throwing off colonialism and acquiring independence, but he was aware that, as a black American, he himself would always be caught in a no-man's-land between white Western culture and the global future, with its promise of a rising majority of people of color.*

STRANGER IN THE VILLAGE

From all available evidence no black man had ever set foot in this tiny Swiss village before I came. I was told before arriving that I would probably be a "sight" for the village; I took this to mean that people of my complexion were rarely seen in Switzerland, and also that city people are always something of a "sight" outside of the city. It did not occur to me—possibly because I am an American—that there could be people anywhere who had never seen a Negro.

It is a fact that cannot be explained on the basis of the inaccessibility of the village. The village is very high, but it is only four hours from Milan and three hours from Lausanne. It is true that it is virtually unknown. Few people making plans for a holiday would elect to come here. On the other hand, the villagers are able, presumably, to come and go as they please—which they do: to another town at the foot of the mountain, with a population of approximately five thousand, the nearest place to see a movie or go to the bank. In the village there is no movie house, no bank, no library, no theater; very few radios, one jeep, one station wagon; and at the moment, one typewriter, mine, an invention which the woman next door to me here had never seen. There are about six hundred people living here, all Catholic— I conclude this from the fact that the Catholic church is open all year round, whereas the Protestant chapel, set off on a hill a little removed from the village, is open only in the summertime when the tourists arrive. There are four or five hotels, all closed now, and four or five *bistros*, of which, however, only two do any business during the winter. These two do not do a great deal, for life in the village seems to end around nine or ten o'clock. There are a few stores, butcher, baker, *épicerie*, a hardware store, and a money-changer—who cannot change travelers' checks, but must send them down to the bank, an operation which takes two or three days. There is something called the *Ballet Haus*, closed in the winter and used for God knows what, certainly not ballet, during the summer. There seems to be only one schoolhouse in the village, and this for the quite young children; I suppose this to mean that their older brothers and sisters at some point descend from these mountains in order to complete their education— possibly, again, to the town just below. The landscape is absolutely forbidding, mountains towering on all four sides, ice and snow as far as the eye can reach. In this white wilderness, men and women and children move all day, carrying washing, wood, buckets of milk or water, sometimes skiing on Sunday afternoons. All week long boys and young men are to be seen shoveling snow off the rooftops, or dragging wood down from the forest in sleds. The village's only real attraction, which explains the tourist season, is the hot spring water. A disquietingly high proportion of these tourists are cripples, or semi-cripples, who come year after year—from other parts of Switzerland, usually—to take the waters. This lends the village, at the height of the season, a rather terrifying air of sanctity, as though it were a lesser Lourdes. There is often something beautiful, there is always something awful, in the spectacle of a person who has lost one of his faculties, a faculty he never questioned until it was gone, and who struggles to recover it. Yet people remain people, on crutches or indeed on deathbeds; and wherever I passed, the first summer I was here, among the native villagers or among the lame, a wind passed with me—of astonishment, curiosity, amusement and outrage. That first summer I stayed two weeks and never intended to return. But I did return in the winter, to work; the village offers, obviously, no distractions whatever and has the further advantage of being extremely cheap. Now it is winter again, a year later, and I am here again. Everyone in the village knows my name, though they scarcely ever use it, knows that I come from America—though, this, apparently, they will never really believe: black men come from Africa—and everyone knows that I am the friend of the son of a woman who was born here, and that I am staying in their chalet. But I remain as much a stranger today as I was the first day I arrived, and the children shout *Neger! Neger!* as I walk along the streets.

It must be admitted that in the beginning I was far too shocked to have any real reaction. In so far as I reacted at all, I reacted by trying to be pleasant—it being a great part of the American Negro's education (long before he goes to school) that he must make people "like" him. This smile-and-the-world-smiles-with-you routine worked about as well in this situation as it had in the situation for which it was designed, which is to say that it did not work at all. No one, after all, can be liked whose human weight and complexity cannot be, or has not been, admitted. My smile was simply another unheard-of phenomenon which allowed them to see my teeth—they did not, really, see my smile and I began to think that, should I take to snarling, no one would notice any difference. All of the physical characteristics of the Negro which had caused me, in America, a very different and almost forgotten pain were nothing less than miraculous—or infernal—in the eyes of the village people. Some thought my hair was the color of tar, that it had the texture of wire, or the texture of cotton. It was jocularly suggested that I might let it all grow long and make myself a winter coat. If I sat in the sun for more than five minutes some daring creature was certain to come along and gingerly put his fingers on my hair, as though he were afraid of an electric shock, or put his hand on my hand, astonished that the color did not rub off. In all of this, in which it must be conceded there was the charm of genuine wonder and in which there was certainly no element of intentional unkindness, there was yet no suggestion that I was human: I was simply a living wonder.

I knew that they did not mean to be unkind, and I know it now; it is necessary, nevertheless, for me to repeat this to myself each time that I walk out of the chalet. The children who shout *Neger!* have no way of knowing the echoes this sound raises in me. They are brimming with good humor and the more daring swell with pride when I stop to speak with them. Just the same, there are days when I cannot pause and smile, when I have no heart to play with them; when, indeed, I mutter sourly to myself, exactly as I muttered on the streets of a city these children have never seen, when I was no bigger than these children are now: *Your* mother *was a nigger*. Joyce is right about history being a nightmare—but it may be the nightmare from which no one *can* awaken. People are trapped in history and history is trapped in them.

There is a custom in the village—I am told it is repeated in many villages—of "buying" African natives for the purpose of converting them to Christianity. There stands in the church all year round a small box with a slot for money, decorated with a black figurine, and into this box the villagers drop their francs. During the *carnaval* which precedes Lent, two village children have their faces blackened—out of which bloodless darkness their blue eyes shine like ice—and fantastic horsehair wigs are placed on their blond heads; thus disguised, they solicit among the villagers for money for the missionaries in Africa. Between the box in the church and the blackened children, the village "bought" last year six or eight African natives. This was reported to me with pride by the wife of one of the *bistro* owners and I was careful to express astonishment and pleasure at the solicitude shown by the village for the souls of black folk. The *bistro* owner's wife beamed with a pleasure far more genuine than my own and seemed to feel that I might now breathe more easily concerning the souls of at least six of my kinsmen.

I tried not to think of these so lately baptized kinsmen, of the price paid for them, or the peculiar price they themselves would pay, and said nothing about my father, who having taken his own conversion too literally never, at bottom, forgave the white world (which he described as heathen) for having saddled him with a Christ in whom, to judge at least from their treatment of him, they themselves no longer believed. I thought of white men arriving for the first time in an African village, strangers there, as I am a stranger here, and tried to imagine the astounded populace touching their hair and marveling at the color of their skin. But there is a great difference between being the first white man to be seen by Africans and being the first black man to be seen by whites. The white man takes the astonishment as tribute, for he arrives to conquer and to convert the natives, whose inferiority in relation to himself is not even to be questioned; whereas I, without a thought of conquest, find myself among a people whose culture controls me, has even, in a sense, created me, people who have cost me more in anguish and rage than they will ever know, who yet do not even know of my existence. The astonishment with which I might have greeted them, should they have stumbled into my African village a few hundred years ago, might have rejoiced their hearts. But the astonishment with which they greet me today can only poison mine.

And this is so despite everything I may do to feel differently, despite my friendly conversations with the *bistro* owner's wife, despite their three-year-old son who has at last become my friend, despite the *salut*s and *bonsoir*s which I exchange with people as I walk, despite the fact that I know that no individual can be taken to task for what history is doing, or has done. I say that the culture of these people controls me—but they can scarcely be held responsible for European culture. America comes out of Europe, but these people have never seen America, nor have most of them seen more of Europe than the hamlet at the foot of their mountain. Yet they move with an authority which I shall never have; and they regard me, quite rightly, not only as a stranger in the village but as a suspect latecomer, bearing no credentials, to everything they have—however unconsciously—inherited.

For this village, even were it incomparably more remote and incredibly more primitive, is the West, the West onto which I have been so strangely grafted. These people cannot be, from the point of view of power, strangers anywhere in the world; they have made the modern world, in effect, even if they do not know it. The most illiterate among them is related, in a way that I am not, to Dante, Shakespeare, Michelangelo, Aeschylus, Da Vinci, Rembrandt, and Racine; the cathedral at Chartres says something to them which it cannot say to me, as indeed would New York's Empire State Building, should anyone here ever see it. Out of their hymns and dances come Beethoven and Bach. Go back a few centuries and they are in their full glory—but I am in Africa, watching the conquerors arrive.

The rage of the disesteemed is personally fruitless, but it is also absolutely inevitable; this rage, so generally discounted, so little understood even among the people whose daily bread it is, is one of the things that makes history. Rage can only with difficulty, and never entirely, be brought under the domination of the intelligence and is therefore not susceptible to any arguments whatever. This is a fact which ordinary representatives of the *Herrenvolk*, having never felt this rage and being unable to imagine it, quite fail to understand. Also, rage cannot be hidden, it can only be dissembled. This dissembling deludes the thoughtless, and strengthens rage and adds, to rage, contempt. There are, no doubt, as many ways of coping with the resulting complex of tensions as there are black men in the world, but no black man can hope ever to be entirely liberated from this internal warfare— rage, dissembling, and contempt having inevitably accompanied his first realization of the power of white men. What is crucial here is that since white men represent in the black man's world so heavy a weight, white men have for black men a reality which is far from being reciprocal; and hence all black men have toward all white men an attitude which is designed, really, either to rob the white man of the jewel of his naïveté, or else to make it cost him dear.

The black man insists, by whatever means he finds at his disposal, that the white man cease to regard him as an exotic rarity and recognize him as a human being. This is a very charged and difficult moment, for there is a great deal of willpower involved in the white man's naïveté. Most people are not naturally reflective any more than they are naturally malicious, and the white man prefers to keep the black man at a certain human remove because it is easier for him thus to preserve his simplicity and avoid being called to account for crimes committed by his forefathers, or his neighbors. He is inescapably aware, nevertheless, that he is in a better position in the world than black men are, nor can he quite put to death the suspicion that he is hated by black men therefore. He does not wish to be hated, neither does he wish to change places, and at this point in his uneasiness he can scarcely avoid having recourse to those legends which white men have created about black men, the most usual effect of which is that the white man finds himself enmeshed, so to speak, in his own language which describes hell, as well as the attributes which lead one to hell, as being as black as night.

Every legend, moreover, contains its residuum of truth, and the root function of language is to control the universe by describing it. It is of quite considerable significance that black men remain, in the imagination, and in overwhelming numbers in fact, beyond the disciplines of salvation; and this despite the fact that the West has been "buying" African natives for centuries. There is, I should hazard, an instantaneous necessity to be divorced from this so visibly unsaved stranger, in whose heart, moreover, one cannot guess what dreams of vengeance are being nourished; and, at the same time, there are few things on earth more attractive than the idea of the unspeakable liberty which is allowed the unredeemed. When, beneath the black mask, a human being begins to make himself felt one cannot escape a certain awful wonder as to what kind of human being it is. What one's imagination makes of other people is dictated, of course, by the laws of one's own personality and it is one of the ironies of black-white relations that, by means of what the white man imagines the black man to be, the black man is enabled to know who the white man is.

I have said, for example, that I am as much a stranger in this village today as I was the first summer I arrived, but this is not quite true. The villagers wonder less about the texture of my hair than they did then, and wonder rather more about me. And the fact that their wonder now exists on another level is reflected in their attitudes and in their eyes. There are the children who make those delightful, hilarious, sometimes astonishingly grave overtures of friendship in the unpredictable fashion of children; other children, having been taught that the devil is a black man, scream in genuine anguish as I approach. Some of the older women never pass without a friendly greeting, never pass, indeed, if it seems that they will be able to engage me in conversation; other women look down or look away or rather contemptuously smirk. Some of the men drink with me and suggest that I learn how to ski—partly, I gather, because they cannot imagine what I would look like on skis—and want to know if I am married, and ask questions about my *métier*. But some of the men have accused *le sale nègre*—behind my back—of stealing wood and there is already in the eyes of some of them that peculiar, intent, paranoiac malevolence which one sometimes surprises in the eyes of American white men when, out walking with their Sunday girl, they see a Negro male approach.

There is a dreadful abyss between the streets of this village and the streets of the city in which I was born, between the children who shout *Neger!* today and those who shouted *Nigger!* yesterday—the abyss is experience, the American experience. The syllable hurled behind me today expresses, above all, wonder: I am a stranger here. But I am not a stranger in America and the same syllable riding on the American air expresses the war my presence has occasioned in the American soul.

For this village brings home to me this fact: that there was a day, and not really a very distant day, when Americans were scarcely Americans at all but discontented Europeans, facing a great unconquered continent and strolling, say, into a market-place and seeing black men for the first time. The shock this spectacle afforded is suggested, surely, by the promptness with which they decided that these black men were not really men but cattle. It is true that the necessity on the part of the settlers of the New

World of reconciling their moral assumptions with the fact—and the necessity—of slavery enhanced immensely the charm of this idea, and it is also true that this idea expresses, with a truly American bluntness, the attitude which to varying extents all masters have had toward all slaves.

But between all former slaves and slave-owners and the drama which begins for Americans over three hundred years ago at Jamestown, there are at least two differences to be observed. The American Negro slave could not suppose, for one thing, as slaves in past epochs had supposed and often done, that he would ever be able to wrest the power from his master's hands. This was a supposition which the modern era, which was to bring about such vast changes in the aims and dimensions of power, put to death; it only begins in unprecedented fashion, and with dreadful implications, to be resurrected, today. But even had this supposition persisted with undiminished force, the American Negro slave could not have used it to lend his condition dignity, for the reason that this supposition rests on another: that the slave in exile yet remains related to his past, has some means—if only in memory—of revering and sustaining the forms of his former life, is able, in short, to maintain his identity.

This was not the case with the American Negro slave. He is unique among the black men of the world in that his past was taken from him, almost literally, at one blow. One wonders what on earth the first slave found to say to the first dark child he bore. I am told that there are Haitians able to trace their ancestry back to African kings, but any American Negro wishing to go back so far will find his journey through time abruptly arrested by the signature on the bill of sale which served as the entrance paper for his ancestor. At the time—to say nothing of the circumstances—of the enslavement of the captive black man who was to become the American Negro, there was not the remotest possibility that he would ever take power from his master's hands. There was no reason to suppose that his situation would ever change, nor was there, shortly, anything to indicate that his situation had ever been different. It was his necessity, in the words of E. Franklin Frazier, to find a "motive for living under American culture or die." The identity of the American Negro comes out of this extreme situation, and the evolution of this identity was a source of the most intolerable anxiety in the minds and the lives of his masters.

For the history of the American Negro is unique also in this: that the question of his humanity, and of his rights therefore as a human being, became a burning one for several generations of Americans, so burning a question that it ultimately became one of those used to divide the nation. It is out of this argument that the venom of the epithet *Nigger!* is derived. It is an argument which Europe has never had, and hence Europe quite sincerely fails to understand how or why the argument arose in the first place, why its effects are frequently disastrous and always so unpredictable, why it refuses until today to be entirely settled. Europe's black possessions remained—and do remain—in Europe's colonies, at which remove they represented no threat whatever to European identity. If they posed any problem at all for the European conscience, it was a problem which remained comfortingly abstract: in effect, the black man, *as a man*, did not exist for Europe. But in America, even as a slave, he was an inescapable part of the general social fabric and no American could escape having an attitude toward him. Americans attempt until today to make an abstraction of the Negro, but the very nature of these abstractions reveals the tremendous effects the presence of the Negro has had on the American character.

When one considers the history of the Negro in America it is of the greatest importance to recognize that the moral beliefs of a person, or a people, are never really as tenuous as life— which is not moral—very often causes them to appear; these create for them a frame of reference and a necessary hope, the hope being that when life has done its worst they will be enabled to rise above themselves and to triumph over life. Life would scarcely be bearable if this hope did not exist. Again, even when the worst has been said, to betray a belief is not by any means to have put oneself beyond its power; the betrayal of a belief is not the same thing as ceasing to believe. If this were not so there would be no moral standards in the world at all. Yet one must also recognize that morality is based on ideas and that all ideas are dangerous— dangerous because ideas can only lead to action and where the action leads no man can say. And dangerous in this respect: that confronted with the impossibility of remaining faithful to one's beliefs, and the equal impossibility of becoming free of them, one can be driven to the most inhuman excesses. The ideas on which American beliefs are based are not, though Americans often seem to think so, ideas which originated in America. They came out of Europe. And the establishment of democracy on the American continent was scarcely as radical a break with the past as was the necessity, which Americans faced, of broadening this concept to include black men.

This was, literally, a hard necessity. It was impossible, for one thing, for Americans to abandon their beliefs, not only because these beliefs alone seemed able to justify the sacrifices they had endured and the blood that they had spilled, but also because these beliefs afforded them their only bulwark against a moral chaos as absolute as the physical chaos of the continent it was their destiny to conquer. But in the situation in which Americans found themselves, these beliefs threatened an idea which, whether or not one likes to think so, is the very warp and woof of the heritage of the West, the idea of white supremacy.

Americans have made themselves notorious by the shrillness and the brutality with which they have insisted on this idea, but they did not invent it; and it has escaped the world's notice that those very excesses of which Americans have been guilty imply a certain, unprecedented uneasiness over the idea's life and power, if not, indeed, the idea's validity. The idea of white supremacy rests simply on the fact that white men are the creators of civilization (the present civilization, which is the only one that matters; all previous civilizations are simply "contributions" to our own) and are therefore civilization's guardians and defenders. Thus it was impossible for Americans to accept the black man as one of themselves, for to do so was to jeopardize their status as white men. But not so to accept him was to deny his human reality, his human weight and complexity, and the strain of denying the overwhelmingly undeniable forced Americans into rationalizations so fantastic that they approached the pathological.

At the root of the American Negro problem is the necessity of the American white man to find a way of living with the Negro in order to be able to live with himself. And the history of this problem can be reduced to the means used by Americans—lynch law and law, segregation and legal acceptance, terrorization and concession—either to come to terms with this necessity, or to find a way around it, or (most usually) to find a way of doing both these things at once. The resulting spectacle, at once foolish and dreadful, led someone to make the quite accurate observation that "the Negro-in-America is a form of insanity which overtakes white men."

In this long battle, a battle by no means finished, the unforeseeable effects of which will be felt by many future generations, the white man's motive was the protection of his identity; the black man was motivated by the need to establish an identity. And despite the terrorization which the Negro in America endured and endures sporadically until today, despite the cruel and totally inescapable ambivalence of his status in his country, the battle for his identity has long ago been won. He is not a visitor to the West, but a citizen there, an American; as American as the Americans who despise him, the Americans who fear him, the Americans who love him—the Americans who became less than themselves, or rose to be greater than themselves by virtue of the fact that the challenge he represented was inescapable. He is perhaps the only black man in the world whose relationship to white men is more terrible, more subtle, and more meaningful than the relationship of bitter possessed to uncertain possessor. His survival depended, and his development depends, on his ability to turn his peculiar status in the Western world to his own advantage and, it may be, to the very great advantage of that world. It remains for him to fashion out of his experience that which will give him sustenance, and a voice.

The cathedral at Chartres, I have said, says something to the people of this village which it cannot say to me; but it is important to understand that this cathedral says something to me which it cannot say to them. Perhaps they are struck by the power of the spires, the glory of the windows; but they have known God, after all, longer than I have known him, and in a different way, and I am terrified by the slippery bottomless well to be found in the crypt, down which heretics were hurled to death, and by the obscene, inescapable gargoyles jutting out of the stone and seeming to say that God and the devil can never be divorced. I doubt that the villagers think of the devil when they face a cathedral because they have never been identified with the devil. But I must accept the status which myth, if nothing else, gives me in the West before I can hope to change the myth.

Yet, if the American Negro has arrived at his identity by virtue of the absoluteness of his estrangement from his past, American white men still nourish the illusion that there is some means of recovering the European innocence, of returning to a state in which black men do not exist. This is one of the greatest errors Americans can make. The identity they fought so hard to protect has, by virtue of that battle, undergone a change: Americans are as unlike any other white people in the world as it is possible to be. I do not think, for example, that it is too much to suggest that the American vision of the world—which allows so little reality, generally speaking, for any of the darker forces in human life, which tends until today to paint moral issues in glaring black and white—owes a great deal to the battle waged by Americans to maintain between themselves and black men a human separation which could not be bridged. It is only now beginning to be borne in on us—very faintly, it must be admitted, very slowly, and very much against our will—that this vision of the world is dangerously inaccurate, and perfectly useless. For it protects our moral high-mindedness at the terrible expense of weakening our grasp of reality. People who shut their eyes to reality simply invite their own destruction, and anyone who insists on remaining in a state of innocence long after that innocence is dead turns himself into a monster.

The time has come to realize that the interracial drama acted out on the American continent has not only created a new black man, it has created a new white man, too. No road whatever will lead Americans back to the simplicity of this European village where white men still have the luxury of looking on me as a stranger. I am not, really, a stranger any longer for any American alive. One of the things that distinguishes Americans from other people is that no other people has ever been so deeply involved in the lives of black men, and vice versa. This fact faced, with all its implications, it can be seen that the history of the American Negro problem is not merely shameful, it is also something of an achievement. For even when the worst has been said, it must also be added that the perpetual challenge posed by this problem was always, somehow, perpetually met. It is precisely this black-white experience which may prove of indispensable value to us in the world we face today. This world is white no longer, and it will never be white again.

Mary McCarthy (1912–1989) began her writing career as a critic, with a sharp, take-no-prisoners approach. The title of her first essay collection, On the Contrary, *indicated her willingness to engage in argument, both with received opinion and with herself. Given to frank self-analysis, she had no compunction about presenting her I-character in a less-than-attractive light, as can be seen in her indispensable* Memories of a Catholic Girlhood. *In her narrative essay "Artists in Uniform," McCarthy displayed the scene-making brio and subtle character analysis that her novels (*The Company She Keeps, The Group*) would also feature.*

ARTISTS IN UNIFORM

The Colonel went out sailing.
He spoke with Turk and Jew . . .

"Pour it on, Colonel," cried the young man in the Dacron suit excitedly, making his first sortie into the club-car conversation. His face was white as Roquefort and of a glistening, cheese-like texture; he had a shock of tow-colored hair, badly cut and greasy, and a snub nose with large gray pores. Under his darting eyes were two black craters. He appeared to be under some intense nervous strain and had sat the night before in the club car drinking bourbon with beer chasers and leafing magazines which he frowningly tossed aside, like cards into a discard heap. This morning he had come in late, with a hangdog, hangover look, and had been sitting tensely forward on a settee, smoking cigarettes and following the conversation with little twitches of the nose and quivers of the body, as a dog follows a human conversa-

tion, veering its mistrustful eyeballs from one speaker to another
and raising its head eagerly at its master's voice. The colonel's
voice, rich and light and plausible, had in fact abruptly risen and
swollen, as he pronounced his last sentence. "I can tell you one
thing," he said harshly. "They weren't named Ryan or Murphy!"

A sort of sigh, as of consummation, ran through the club car.
"Pour it on, Colonel, give it to them, Colonel, that's right, Colonel," urged the young man in a transport of admiration. The
colonel fingered his collar and modestly smiled. He was a thin,
hawklike, black-haired handsome man with a bright blue blood-
shot eye and a well-pressed, well-tailored uniform that did not
show the effects of the heat—the train, westbound for St. Louis,
was passing through Indiana, and, as usual in a heat wave, the
air-conditioning had not met the test. He wore the Air Force
insignia, and there was something in his light-boned, spruce figure and keen, knifelike profile that suggested a classic image of
the aviator, ready to cut, piercing, into space. In base fact, however, the colonel was in procurement, as we heard him tell the
mining engineer who had just bought him a drink. From several
silken hints that parachuted into the talk, it was patent to us that
the colonel was a man who knew how to enjoy this earth and its
pleasures: he led, he gave us to think, a bachelor's life of abste-
mious dissipation and well-rounded sensuality. He had accepted
the engineer's drink with a mere nod of the glass in acknowledgment, like a genial Mars quaffing a libation; there was clearly no
prospect of his buying a second in return, not if the train were
to travel from here to the Mojave Desert. In the same way, an
understanding had arisen that I, the only woman in the club car,
had become the colonel's perquisite; it was taken for granted,
without an invitation's being issued, that I was to lunch with him
in St. Louis, where we each had a wait between trains—my plans
for seeing the city in a taxicab were dished.

From the beginning, as we eyed each other over my volume of
Dickens ("*The Christmas Carol?*" suggested the colonel, opening relations), I had guessed that the colonel was of Irish stock,
and this, I felt, gave me an advantage, for he did not suspect the
same of me; strangely so, for I am supposed to have the map
of Ireland written on my features. In fact, he had just wagered,

with a jaunty, sidelong grin at the mining engineer, that my people "came from Boston from way back," and that I—narrowed
glance, running, like steel measuring-tape, up and down my
form—was a professional sculptress. I might have laughed this
off, as a crudely bad guess like his *Christmas Carol*, if I had not
seen the engineer nodding gravely, like an idol, and the peculiar
young man bobbing his head up and down in mute applause and
agreement. I was wearing a bright apple-green raw silk blouse
and a dark-green rather full raw silk skirt, plus a pair of pink
glass earrings; my hair was done up in a bun. It came to me, for
the first time, with a sort of dawning horror, that I had begun,
in the course of years, without ever guessing it, to look irrevocably Bohemian. Refracted from the three men's eyes was a strange
vision of myself as an artist, through and through, stained with
my occupation like the dyer's hand. All I lacked, apparently, was
a pair of sandals. My sick heart sank to my Ferragamo shoes;
I had always particularly preened myself on being an artist in
disguise. And it was not only a question of personal vanity—it
seemed to me that the writer or intellectual had a certain mis-
sionary usefulness in just such accidental gatherings as this, if he
spoke not as an intellectual but as a normal member of the public. Now, thanks to the colonel, I slowly became aware that my
contributions to the club-car conversation were being watched
and assessed as coming from *a certain quarter*. My costume, it
seemed, carefully assembled as it had been at an expensive shop,
was to these observers simply a uniform that blazoned a caste
and allegiance just as plainly as the colonel's khaki and eagles.
"*Gardez*," I said to myself. But, as the conversation grew tenser
and I endeavored to keep cool, I began to writhe within myself,
and every time I looked down, my contrasting greens seemed to
be growing more and more lurid and taking on an almost menacing light, like leaves just before a storm that lift their bright
undersides as the air becomes darker. We had been speaking, of
course, of Russia, and I had mentioned a study that had been
made at Harvard of political attitudes among Iron Curtain refu-
gees. Suddenly, the colonel had smiled. "They're pretty Red at
Harvard, I'm given to understand," he observed in a comfortable tone, while the young man twitched and quivered urgently.

The eyes of all the men settled on me and waited. I flushed as I saw myself reflected. The woodland greens of my dress were turning to their complementary red, like a color-experiment in psychology or a traffic light changing. Down at the other end of the club car, a man looked up from his paper. I pulled myself together. "Set your mind at rest, Colonel," I remarked dryly. "I know Harvard very well and they're conservative to the point of dullness. The only thing crimson is the football team." This disparagement had its effect. "So . . . ?" queried the colonel. "I thought there was some professor. . . ." I shook my head. "Absolutely not. There used to be a few fellow-travelers, but they're very quiet these days, when they haven't absolutely recanted. The general atmosphere is more anti-Communist than the Vatican." The colonel and the mining engineer exchanged a thoughtful stare and seemed to agree that the Delphic oracle that had just pronounced knew whereof it spoke. "Glad to hear it," said the colonel. The engineer frowned and shook his fat wattles; he was a stately, gray-haired, plump man with small hands and feet and the pampered, finical tidiness of a small-town widow. "There's so much hearsay these days," he exclaimed vexedly. "You don't know *what* to believe."

I reopened my book with an air of having closed the subject and read a paragraph three times over. I exulted to think that I had made a modest contribution to sanity in our times, and I imagined my words pyramiding like a chain letter—the colonel telling a fellow-officer on the veranda of a club in Texas, the engineer halting a works-superintendent in a Colorado mine shaft: "I met a woman on the train who claims . . . Yes, absolutely. . . ." Of course, I did not know Harvard as thoroughly as I pretended, but I forgave myself by thinking it was the convention of such club-car symposia in our positivistic country to speak from the horse's mouth.

Meanwhile, across the aisle, the engineer and the colonel continued their talk in slightly lowered voices. From time to time, the colonel's polished index-fingernail scratched his burnished black head and his knowing blue eye forayed occasionally toward

me. I saw that still I was a doubtful quantity to them, a movement in the bushes, a noise, a flicker, that was figuring in their
crenelated thought as "she." The subject of Reds in our colleges
had not, alas, been finished; they were speaking now of another
university and a woman faculty-member who had been issuing
Communist statements. This story somehow, I thought angrily,
had managed to appear in the newspapers without my knowledge, while these men were conversant with it; I recognized a big
chink in the armor of my authority. Looking up from my book,
I began to question them sharply, as though they were reporting
some unheard-of natural phenomenon. "When?" I demanded.
"Where did you see it? What was her name?" This request for the
professor's name was a headlong attempt on my part to buttress
my position, the implication being that the identities of all university professors were known to me and that if I were but given
the name I could promptly clarify the matter. To admit that there
was a single Communist in our academic system whose activities were hidden from me imperiled, I instinctively felt, all the
small good I had done here. Moreover, in the back of my mind, I
had a supreme confidence that these men were wrong: the story,
I supposed, was some tattered piece of misinformation they had
picked up from a gossip column. Pride, as usual, preceded my
fall. To the colonel, the demand for the name was not specific
but generic: what *kind* of name was the question he presumed
me to be asking. "Oh," he said slowly with a luxurious yawn,
"Finkelstein or Fishbein or Feinstein." He lolled back in his seat
with a side glance at the engineer, who deeply nodded. There
was a voluptuary pause, as the implication sank in. I bit my
lip, regarding this as a mere diversionary tactic. "Please!" I said
impatiently. "Can't you remember exactly?" The colonel shook
his head and then his spare cheekbones suddenly reddened and
he looked directly at me. "I can tell you one thing," he exclaimed
irefully. "They weren't named Ryan or Murphy."

The colonel went no further; it was quite unnecessary. In an
instant, the young man was at his side, yapping excitedly and
actually picking at the military sleeve. The poor thing was
transformed, like some creature in a fairy tale whom a magic
word releases from silence. "That's right, Colonel," he happily

repeated. "I know them. I was at Harvard in the business school, studying accountancy. I left. I couldn't take it." He threw a poisonous glance at me, and the colonel, who had been regarding him somewhat doubtfully, now put on an alert expression and inclined an ear for his confidences. The man at the other end of the car folded his newspaper solemnly and took a seat by the young man's side. "They're all Reds, Colonel," said the young man. "They teach it in the classroom. I came back here to Missouri. It made me sick to listen to the stuff they handed out. If you didn't hand it back, they flunked you. Don't let anybody tell you different." "You are wrong," I said coldly, and closed my book and rose. The young man was still talking eagerly, and the three men were leaning forward to catch his every gasping word, like three astute detectives over a dying informer, when I reached the door and cast a last look over my shoulder at them. For an instant, the colonel's eye met mine, and I felt his scrutiny processing my green back as I tugged open the door and met a blast of hot air, blowing my full skirt wide. Behind me, in my fancy, I saw four sets of shrugging brows.

In my own car, I sat down, opposite two fat nuns, and tried to assemble my thoughts. I ought to have spoken, I felt, and yet what could I have said? It occurred to me that the four men had perhaps not realized why I had left the club car with such abruptness: was it possible that they thought I was a Communist, who feared to be unmasked? I spurned this possibility, and yet it made me uneasy. For some reason, it troubled my *amour-propre* to think of my anti-Communist self living on, so to speak, green in their collective memory as a Communist or fellow-traveler. In fact, though I did not give a fig for the men, I hated the idea, while a few years ago I should have counted it a great joke. This, it seemed to me, was a measure of the change in the social climate. I had always scoffed at the notion of liberals "living in fear" of political demagoguery in America, but now I had to admit that if I was not fearful, I was at least uncomfortable in the supposition that anybody, anybody whatever, could think of me, precious me, as a Communist. A remoter possibility was, of course, that back there my departure was being ascribed to Jewishness, and this too annoyed me. I am in fact a quarter Jewish, and though I did not "hate" the idea of being taken for a Jew, I did not precisely like it, particularly under these circumstances. I wished it to be clear that I had left the club car for intellectual and principled reasons; I wanted those men to know that it was not I, but my principles, that had been offended. To let them conjecture that I had left because I was Jewish would imply that only a Jew could be affronted by an anti-Semitic outburst: a terrible idea. Aside from anything else, it voided the whole concept of transcendence, which was very close to my heart, the concept that man is more than his circumstances, more even than himself.

However you looked at the episode, I said to myself nervously, I had not acquitted myself well. I ought to have done or said something concrete and unmistakable. From this, I slid glassily to the thought that those men ought to be punished, the colonel, in particular, who occupied a responsible position. In a minute, I was framing a businesslike letter to the chief of staff, deploring the colonel's conduct as unbecoming to an officer and identifying him by rank and post, since unfortunately I did not know his name. Earlier in the conversation, he had passed some comments on "Harry" that bordered positively on treason, I said to myself triumphantly. A vivid image of the proceedings against him presented itself to my imagination: the long military tribunal with a row of stern soldierly faces glaring down at the colonel. I myself occupied only an inconspicuous corner of this tableau, for, to tell the truth, I did not relish the role of the witness. Perhaps it would be wiser to let the matter drop . . . ? We were nearing St. Louis now; the colonel had come back into my car, and the young accountant had followed him, still talking feverishly. I pretended not to see them and turned to the two nuns, as if for sanctuary from this world and its hatreds and revenges. Out of the corner of my eye, I watched the colonel, who now looked wry and restless; he shrank against the window as the young man made a place for himself amid the colonel's smart luggage and continued to express his views in a pale breathless voice. I smiled to think that the colonel was paying the piper. For the colonel, anti-Semitism was simply an aspect of urbanity, like a knowledge of hotels or women. This frantic psychopath of an accountant was serving him as a nemesis, just as the German people had been served by their psychopath, Hitler. Colonel, I adjured him, you have chosen, between him and me; measure the depth of your error and make the best of it! No intervention on my part was now necessary; justice had been meted out. Nevertheless, my heart was still throbbing violently, as if I were on the verge of some dangerous action. What was I to do, I kept asking myself, as I chatted with the nuns, if the colonel were to hold me to that lunch? And I slowly and apprehensively revolved this question, just as though it were a matter of the most serious import. It seemed to me that if I did not lunch with him—and I had no intention of doing so—I had the dreadful obligation of telling him why.

He was waiting for me as I descended the car steps. "Aren't you coming to lunch with me?" he called out, and moved up to take my elbow. I began to tremble with audacity. "No," I said firmly, picking up my suitcase and draping an olive-green linen duster over my arm. "I can't lunch with you." He quirked a wiry black eyebrow. "Why not?" he said. "I understood it was all arranged." He reached for my suitcase. "No," I said, holding on to the suitcase. "I can't." I took a deep breath. "I have to tell you. I think you should be *ashamed* of yourself, Colonel, for what you said in the club car." The colonel stared; I mechanically waved for a red-cap, who took my bag and coat and went off. The colonel and I stood facing each other on the emptying platform. "What do you mean?" he inquired in a low, almost clandestine tone. "Those anti-Semitic remarks," I muttered, resolutely. "You ought to be *ashamed*." The colonel gave a quick, relieved laugh. "Oh, come now," he protested. "I'm sorry," I said. "I can't have lunch with anybody who feels that way about the Jews." The colonel put down his attaché case and scratched the back of his lean neck. "Oh, come now," he repeated, with a look of amusement. "You're not Jewish, are you?" "No," I said quickly. "Well, then . . . ," said the colonel, spreading his hands in a gesture of bafflement. I saw that he was truly surprised and slightly hurt by my criticism, and this made me feel wretchedly embarrassed and even apologetic, on my side, as though I had called attention to some physical defect in him, of which he himself was unconscious. "But I might have been," I stammered. "You had no way of knowing. You oughtn't to talk like that." I recognized, too late, that I was strangely reducing the whole matter to a question of etiquette: "Don't start anti-Semitic talk before making sure there are no Jews present." "Oh, hell," said the colonel, easily. "I can tell a Jew." "No, you can't," I retorted, thinking of my Jewish grandmother, for by Nazi criteria I was Jewish. "Of course I can," he insisted. "So can you." We had begun to walk down the platform side by side, disputing with a restrained passion that isolated us like a pair of lovers. All at once, the colonel halted, as though struck with a thought. "What *are* you, anyway?" he said meditatively, regarding my dark hair, green blouse, and pink earrings. Inside myself, I began to laugh. "Oh," I said gaily, playing out the trump I had been saving, "I'm Irish, like you, Colonel." "How did you know?" he said amazedly. I laughed aloud. "I can tell an Irishman," I taunted. The colonel frowned. "What's your family name?" he said brusquely. "McCarthy." He lifted an eyebrow, in defeat, and then quickly took note of my wedding ring. "That your maiden name?" I nodded. Under this peremptory questioning, I had the peculiar sensation that I get when I am lying; I began to feel that "McCarthy" was a nom de plume, a coinage of my artistic personality. But the colonel appeared to be satisfied. "Hell," he said, "come on to lunch, then. With a fine name like that, you and I should be friends." I still shook my head, though by this time we were pacing outside the station restaurant; my baggage had been checked in a locker; sweat was running down my face and I felt exhausted and hungry. I knew that I was weakening and I wanted only an excuse to yield and go inside with him. The colonel seemed to sense this. "Hell," he conceded. "You've got me wrong. I've nothing against the Jews. Back there in the club car, I was just stating a simple fact: you won't find an Irishman sounding off for the Commies. You can't deny that, can you?"

His voice rose persuasively; he took my arm. In the heat, I wilted and we went into the air-conditioned cocktail lounge. The colonel ordered two old-fashioneds. The room was dark as a cave and produced, in the midst of the hot midday, a hallucinated feeling, as though time had ceased, with the weather, and we were in eternity together. As the colonel prepared to relax, I made a tremendous effort to guide the conversation along rational, purposive lines; my only justification for being here would be to convert the colonel. "There *have* been Irishmen associated with the Communist Party," I said suddenly, when the drinks came. "I can think of two." "Oh, hell," said the colonel, "every race and nation has its traitors. What I mean is, you won't find them in numbers. You've got to admit that the Communists in this country are ninety percent Jewish." "But the Jews in this country aren't ninety percent Communist," I retorted.

As he stirred his drink, restively, I began to try to show him the reasons why the Communist movement in America had attracted such a large number, relatively, of Jews: how the Communists had been anti-Nazi when nobody else seemed to care what happened to the Jews in Germany; how the Communists still capitalized on a Jewish fear of fascism; how many Jews had become, after Buchenwald, traumatized by this fear. . . .

But the colonel was scarcely listening. An impatient frown rested on his jaunty features. "I don't get it," he said slowly. "Why should you be for them, with a name like yours?" "I'm *not* for the Communists," I cried. "I'm just trying to explain to you—" "For the Jews," the colonel interrupted, irritable now himself. "I've heard of such people but I never met one before." "I'm not 'for' them," I protested. "You don't understand. I'm not for *any* race or nation. I'm against those who are against them." This word, *them*, with a sort of slurring circle drawn round it, was beginning to sound ugly to me. Automatically, in arguing with him, I seemed to have slipped into the colonel's style of thought. It occurred to me that defense of the Jews could be a subtle and safe form of anti-Semitism, an exercise of patronage: as a rational Gentile, one could feel superior both to the Jews and the anti-Semites. There could be no doubt that the Jewish question evoked a curious stealthy lust or concupiscence. I could feel it now vibrating between us over the dark table. If I had been a good person, I should unquestionably have got up and left.

"I don't get it," repeated the colonel. "How were you brought up? Were your people this way too?" It was manifest that an odd reversal had taken place; each of us regarded the other as "abnormal" and was attempting to understand the etiology of the disease. "Many of my people think just as you do," I said, smiling coldly. "It seems to be a sickness to which the Irish are prone. Perhaps it's due to the potato diet," I said sweetly, having divined that the colonel came from a social stratum somewhat lower than my own.

But the colonel's hide was tough. "You've got me wrong," he reiterated, with an almost plaintive laugh. "I don't dislike the Jews. I've got a lot of Jewish friends. Among themselves, they think just as I do, mark my words. I tell you what it is," he added ruminatively, with a thoughtful prod of his muddler, "I draw a distinction between a kike and a Jew." I groaned. "Colonel, I've never heard an anti-Semite who didn't draw that distinction. You know what Otto Kahn said? 'A kike is a Jewish gentleman who has just left the room.' " The colonel did not laugh. "I don't hold it against some of them," he persisted, in a tone of pensive justice. "It's not their fault if they were born that way. That's what I tell them, and they respect me for my honesty. I've had a lot of discussions; in procurement, you have to do business with them, and the Jews are the first to admit that you'll find more chiselers among their race than among the rest of mankind." "It's not a race," I interjected wearily, but the colonel pressed on. "If I deal with a Jewish manufacturer, I can't bank on his word. I've seen it again and again, every damned time. When I deal with a Gentile, I can trust him to make delivery as promised. That's the difference between the two races. They're just a different breed. They don't have standards of honesty, even among each other." I sighed, feeling unequal to arguing the colonel's personal experience.

"Look," I said, "you may be dealing with an industry where the Jewish manufacturers are the most recent comers and feel they have to cut corners to compete with the established firms. I've heard that said about Jewish cattle-dealers, who are supposed to be extra sharp. But what I think, really, is that you notice it when a Jewish firm fails to meet an agreement and don't notice it when it's a Yankee." "Hah," said the colonel. "They'll tell you what I'm telling you themselves, if you get to know them and go into their homes. You won't believe it, but some of my best friends are Jews," he said, simply and thoughtfully, with an air of originality. "They may be *your* best friends, Colonel," I retorted, "but you are not theirs. I defy you to tell me that you talk to them as you're talking now." "Sure," said the colonel, easily. "More or less." "They must be very queer Jews you know," I observed tartly, and I began to wonder whether there indeed existed a peculiar class of Jews whose function in life was to be "friends" with such people as the colonel. It was difficult to think that all the anti-Semites who made the colonel's assertion were the victims of a cruel self-deception.

A dispirited silence followed. I was not one of those liberals who believed that the Jews, alone among peoples, possessed no characteristics whatever of a distinguishing nature—this would mean they had no history and no culture, a charge which should be leveled against them only by an anti-Semite. Certainly, types of Jews could be noted and patterns of Jewish thought and feeling: Jewish humor, Jewish rationality, and so on, not that every Jew reflected every attribute of Jewish life or history. But somehow, with the colonel, I dared not concede that there was such a thing as a Jew: I saw the sad meaning of the assertion that a Jew was a person whom other people thought was Jewish.

Hopeless, however, to convey this to the colonel. The desolate truth was that the colonel was extremely stupid, and it came to me, as we sat there, glumly ordering lunch, that for extremely stupid people anti-Semitism was a form of intellectuality, the sole form of intellectuality of which they were capable. It represented, in a rudimentary way, the ability to make categories, to generalize. Hence a thing I had noted before but never understood: the fact that anti-Semitic statements were generally delivered in an atmosphere of profundity. Furrowed brows attended these speculative distinctions between a kike and a Jew, these little empirical laws that you can't know one without knowing them all. To arrive, indeed, at the idea of a Jew was, for these grouping minds, an exercise in Platonic thought, a discovery of essence, and to be able to add the great corollary, "Some of my best friends are Jews," was to find the philosopher's cleft between essence and existence. From this, it would seem, followed the querulous obstinacy with which the anti-Semite clung to his concept; to be deprived of this intellectual tool by missionaries of tolerance would be, for persons like the colonel, the equivalent of Western man's losing the syllogism: a lapse into animal darkness. In the club car, we had just witnessed an example: the colonel with his anti-Semitic observation had come to the mute young man like the paraclete, bearing the gift of tongues.

In the bar, it grew plainer and plainer that the colonel did not regard himself as an anti-Semite but merely as a heavy thinker. The idea that I considered him anti-Semitic sincerely outraged his feelings. "Prejudice" was the last trait he could have imputed to himself. He looked on me, almost respectfully, as a "Jew lover," a kind of being he had heard of but never actually encountered, like a centaur or a Siamese twin, and the interest of relating this prodigy to the natural state of mankind overrode any personal distaste. There I sat, the exception which was "proving" or testing the rule, and he kept pressing me for details of my history that might explain my deviation in terms of the norm. On my side, of course, I had become fiercely resolved that he would learn nothing from me that would make it possible for him to dismiss my anti-anti-Semitism as the product of special circumstances: I was stubbornly sitting on the fact of my Jewish grandmother like a hen on a golden egg. I was bent on making *him* see himself as a monster, a deviation, a heretic from Church and State. Unfortunately, the colonel, owing perhaps to his military training, had not the glimmering of an idea of what democracy meant; to him, it was simply a slogan that was sometimes useful in war. The notion of an ordained inequality was to him "scientific."

"Honestly," he was saying in lowered tones, as our drinks were taken away and the waitress set down my sandwich and his corned-beef hash, "don't you, brought up the way you were, feel about them the way I do? Just between ourselves, isn't there a sort of inborn feeling of horror that the very word, Jew, suggests?" I shook my head, roundly. The idea of an *innate* anti-Semitism was in keeping with the rest of the colonel's thought, yet it shocked me more than anything he had yet said. "No," I sharply replied. "It doesn't evoke any feeling one way or the other." "Honest Injun?" said the colonel. "Think back; when you were a kid, didn't the word, Jew, make you feel sick?" There was a dreadful sincerity about this that made me answer in an almost kindly tone. "No, truthfully, I assure you. When we were children, we learned to call the old-clothes man a sheeny, but that was just a dirty word to us, like 'Hun' that we used to call after workmen we thought were Germans."

"I don't get it," pondered the colonel, eating a pickle. "There must be something wrong with you. Everybody is born with that feeling. It's natural; it's part of nature." "On the contrary," I said. "It's something very unnatural that you must have been taught as a child." "It's not something you're *taught*," he protested. "You must have been," I said. "You simply don't remember it. In any case, you're a man now; you must rid yourself of that feeling. It's psychopathic, like that horrible young man on the train." "You thought he was crazy?" mused the colonel, in an idle, dreamy tone. I shrugged my shoulders. "Of course. Think of his color. He was probably just out of a mental institution. People don't get that tattletale gray except in prison or mental hospitals." The colonel suddenly grinned. "You might be right," he said. "He was quite a case." He chuckled.

I leaned forward. "You know, Colonel," I said quickly, "anti-Semitism is contrary to the Church's teaching. God will make you do penance for hating the Jews. Ask your priest; he'll tell you I'm right. You'll have a long spell in Purgatory, if you don't rid yourself of this sin. It's a deliberate violation of Christ's commandment, 'Love thy neighbor.' The Church holds that the Jews have a sacred place in God's design. Mary was a Jew and Christ was a Jew. The Jews are under God's special protection. The Church teaches that the millennium can't come until the conversion of the Jews; therefore, the Jews must be preserved that the Divine Will may be accomplished. Woe to them that harm them, for they controvert God's Will!" In the course of speaking, I had swept myself away with the solemnity of the doctrine. The Great Reconciliation between God and His chosen people, as envisioned by the Evangelist, had for me at that moment a piercing, majestic beauty, like some awesome Tintoretto. I saw a noble spectacle of blue sky, thronged with gray clouds, and a vast white desert, across which God and Israel advanced to meet each other, while below in hell the demons of disunion shrieked and gnashed their teeth.

"Hell," said the colonel, jovially. "I don't believe in all that. I lost my faith when I was a kid. I saw that all this God stuff was a lot of bushwa." I gazed at him in stupefaction. His confidence had completely returned. The blue eyes glittered debonairly; the eagles glittered; the narrow polished head cocked and listened to itself like a trilling bird. I was up against an air man with a bird's-eye view, a man who believed in nothing but the law of kind: the epitome of godless materialism. "You still don't hold with that bunk?" the colonel inquired in an undertone, with an expression of stealthy curiosity. "No," I confessed, sad to admit to a meeting of minds. "You know what got me?" exclaimed the colonel. "That birth-control stuff. Didn't it kill you?" I made a neutral sound. "I was beginning to play around," said the colonel, with a significant beam of the eye, "and I just couldn't take that guff. When I saw through the birth-control talk, I saw through the whole thing. They claimed it was against nature, but I claim, if that's so, an operation's against nature. I told my old man that when he was having his kidney stones out. You ought to have heard him yell!" A rich, reminiscent satisfaction dwelt in the colonel's face.

This period of his life, in which he had thrown off the claims of the spiritual and adopted a practical approach, was evidently one of those "turning points" to which a man looks back with pride. He lingered over the story of his break with church and parents with a curious sort of heat, as though the flames of old sexual conquests stirred within his body at the memory of those old quarrels. The looks he rested on me, as a sharer of that experience, grew more and more lickerish and assaying. "What got *you* down?" he finally inquired, settling back in his chair and pushing his coffee cup aside. "Oh," I said wearily, "it's a long story. You can read it when it's published." "You're an author?" cried the colonel, who was really very slow-witted. I nodded, and the colonel regarded me afresh. "What do you write? Love stories?" He gave a half-wink. "No," I said. "Various things. Articles. Books. Highbrowish stories." A suspicion darkened in the colonel's sharp face. "That McCarthy," he said. "Is that your pen name?" "Yes," I said, "but it's my real name too. It's the name I write under *and* my maiden name." The colonel digested this thought. "Oh," he concluded.

A new idea seemed to visit him. Quite cruelly, I watched it take possession. He was thinking of the power of the press and the indiscretions of other military figures, who had been rewarded with demotion. The consciousness of the uniform he wore appeared to seep uneasily into his body. He straightened his shoulders and called thoughtfully for the check. We paid in silence, the colonel making no effort to forestall my dive into my pocketbook. I should not have let him pay in any case, but it startled me that he did not try to do so, if only for reasons of vanity. The whole business of paying, apparently, was painful to him; I watched his facial muscles contract as he pocketed the change and slipped two dimes for the waitress onto the table, not daring quite to hide them under the coffee cup—he had shortchanged me on the bill and the tip, and we both knew it. We walked out into the steaming station and I took my baggage out of the checking locker. The colonel carried my suitcase and we strolled along without speaking. Again, I felt horribly embarrassed for him. He was meditative, and I supposed that he too was mortified by his meanness about the tip.

"Don't get me wrong," he said suddenly, setting the suitcase down and turning squarely to face me, as though he had taken a big decision. "I may have said a few things back there about the Jews getting what they deserved in Germany." I looked at him in surprise; actually, he had not said that to me. Perhaps he had let it drop in the club car. "But that doesn't mean I approve of Hitler." "I should hope not," I said. "What I mean is," said the colonel, "that they probably gave the Germans a lot of provocation, but that doesn't excuse what Hitler did." "No," I said, somewhat ironically, but the colonel was unaware of anything satiric in the air. His face was grave and determined; he was sorting out his philosophy for the record. "I mean, I don't approve of his methods," he finally stated. "No," I agreed. "You mean, you don't approve of the gas chamber." The colonel shook his head very severely. "Absolutely not! That was terrible." He shuddered and drew out a handkerchief and slowly wiped his brow. "For God's sake," he said, "don't get me wrong. I think they're human beings." "Yes," I assented, and we walked along to my track. The colonel's spirits lifted, as though, having stated his credo, he had both got himself in line with public policy and achieved an autonomous thought. "I mean," he resumed, "you may not care for them, but that's not the same as killing them, in cold blood, like that." "No, Colonel," I said.

He swung my bag onto the car's platform and I climbed up behind it. He stood below, smiling, with upturned face. "I'll look for your article," he cried, as the train whistle blew. I nodded, and the colonel waved, and I could not stop myself from waving back at him and even giving him the corner of a smile. After all, I said to myself, looking down at him, the colonel was "a human being." There followed one of those inane intervals in which one prays for the train to leave. We both glanced at our watches. "See you some time," he called. "What's your married name?" "Broadwater," I called back. The whistle blew again. "Brodwa- ter?" shouted the colonel, with a dazed look of unbelief and growing enlightenment; he was not the first person to hear it as a Jewish name, on the model of Goldwater. "B-r-o-a-d," I began, automatically, but then I stopped. I disdained to spell it out for him; the victory was his. "One of the chosen, eh?" his brief gri- mace seemed to commiserate. For the last time, and in the final fullness of understanding, the hawk eye patrolled the green dress, the duster, and the earrings; the narrow flue of his nostril con- tracted as he curtly turned away. The train commenced to move.

Irving Howe (1920–1993), a prominent social and literary critic, was perhaps the country's foremost spokesman for democratic socialism, at a time when the Left seemed much weakened. His shrewd analyses of literature in Politics and the Novel *intertwined moral and political concerns with formal aesthetics. As founder/editor of the magazine* Dissent, *he continued to advocate for a more just, equitable society, dissenting from both the complacencies of corporate America and the rigidities of Stalinist ideologues. Disappointed as he often was with the nation's policies, he still managed to project a worldly, ironic tone on the page that eschewed outrage and retained a certain optimism that humanity, for all its follies, might ultimately right itself.*

THIS AGE
OF CONFORMITY

Intellectuals have always been partial to grandiose ideas about themselves, whether of a heroic or a masochistic kind, but surely no one has ever had a more grandiose idea about the destiny of modern intellectuals than the brilliant economist Joseph Schumpeter. Though he desired nothing so much as to be realistic and hard-boiled, Schumpeter had somehow absorbed all those romantic notions about the revolutionary potential and critical independence of the intellectuals which have now and again swept through the radical and bohemian worlds. Marx, said Schumpeter, was wrong in supposing that capitalism would break down from inherent economic contradictions; it would break down, instead, from an inability to claim people through ties of loyalty and value. "Unlike any other type of society, capitalism inevitably . . . creates, educates and subsidizes a vested interest in social unrest." The intellectuals, bristling with neurotic aspirations and deranged by fantasies of utopia made possible by the very society they would destroy, become agents of discontent who infect rich and poor, high and low. In drawing this picture Schumpeter hardly meant to praise the intellectuals, yet until a few years ago many of them would have accepted it as both truth and tribute, though a few of the more realistic ones might have smiled a doubt as to their capacity to do *all that*.

Schumpeter's picture of the intellectuals is not, of course, without historical validity, but at the moment it seems spectacularly, even comically wrong. And wrong for a reason that Schumpeter, with his elaborate sense of irony, would have appreciated: he who had insisted that capitalism is "a form or method of economic change and not only never is but never can be stationary" had failed sufficiently to consider those new developments in our society which have changed the whole position and status of the intellectuals. Far from creating and subsidizing unrest, capitalism in its most recent stage has found an honored place for the intellectuals; and the intellectuals, far from thinking of themselves as a desperate "opposition," have been enjoying a return to the bosom of the nation. Were Archibald MacLeish again tempted to play Cato and chastise the Irresponsibles, he could hardly find a victim. We have all, even the handful who still try to retain a glower of criticism, become responsible and moderate.

II

In 1932 not many American intellectuals saw any hope for the revival of capitalism. Few of them could support this feeling with any well-grounded theory of society; many held to a highly simplified idea of what capitalism was; and almost all were committed to a vision of the *crisis* of capitalism which was merely a vulgarized model of the class struggle in Europe. Suddenly, with the appearance of the New Deal, the intellectuals saw fresh hope: capitalism was not to be exhausted by the naïve specifications they had assigned it, and consequently the "European" policies of the Roosevelt administration might help dissolve their "Europeanized" sense of crisis. So that the more American society became Europeanized, adopting measures that had been common practice on the Continent for decades, the more the American intellectuals began to believe in . . . American uniqueness. Somehow, the major capitalist power in the world would evade the troubles afflicting capitalism as a world economy.

The two central policies of the New Deal, social legislation and state intervention in economic life, were not unrelated, but they were separable as to time; in Europe they had not always appeared together. Here, in America, it was the simultaneous introduction of these two policies that aroused the enthusiasm, as it dulled the criticism, of the intellectuals. Had the drive toward bureaucratic state regulation of a capitalist economy appeared by itself, so that one could see the state becoming a major buyer and hence indirect controller of industry, and industries on the verge of collapse being systematically subsidized by the state, and the whole of economic life being rationalized according to the long-run needs, if not the immediate tastes, of corporate economy—had all this appeared in isolation, the intellectuals would have reacted critically, they would have recognized the trend toward "state capitalism" as the danger it was. But their desire for the genuine social reforms that came with this trend made them blind or indifferent to the danger. Still, one may suppose that their enthusiasm would have mellowed had not the New Deal been gradually transformed into a permanent war economy; for whatever the theoretical attractions of the Keynesian formula for salvaging capitalism, it has thus far "worked" only in times of war or preparation for war. And it was in the war economy, itself closely related to the trend toward statification, that the intellectuals came into their own.

Statification, war economy, the growth of a mass society and mass culture—all these are aspects of the same historical process. The kind of society that has been emerging in the West, a society in which bureaucratic controls are imposed upon (but not fundamentally against) an interplay of private interests, has need for intellectuals in a way the earlier, "traditional" capitalism never did. It is a society in which ideology plays an unprecedented part: as social relations become more abstract and elusive, the human object is bound to the state with ideological slogans and abstractions—and for this chore intellectuals are indispensable; no one else can do the job as well. Because industrialism grants large quantities of leisure time without any creative sense of how to employ it, there springs up a vast new industry that must be staffed by intellectuals and quasi-intellectuals: the industry of mass culture. And because the state subsidizes mass education and our uneasy prosperity allows additional millions to gain a "higher" education, many new jobs suddenly become available in the academy: some fall to intellectuals. Bohemia gradually disappears as a setting for our intellectual life, and what remains of it seems willed or fake. Looking upon the prosperous ruins of Greenwich Village, one sometimes feels that a full-time bohemian career has become as arduous, if not as expensive, as acquiring a Ph.D.

Bohemia, said Flaubert, was "the fatherland of my breed." If so, his breed, at least in America, is becoming extinct. The most exciting periods of American intellectual life tend to coincide with the rise of bohemia, with the tragic yet liberating rhythm of the break from the small town into the literary roominess of the city, or from the provincial immigrant family into the centers of intellectual experiment. Given the nature of contemporary life, bohemia flourishes in the city—but that has not always been so. Concord too was a kind of bohemia, sedate, subversive, and transcendental all at once. Today, however, the idea of bohemia, which was a strategy for bringing artists and writers together in their struggle with and for the world—this idea has become disreputable, being rather nastily associated with the kinds of exhibitionism that have only an incidental relationship to bohemia. Nonetheless, it is the disintegration of bohemia that is a major cause for the way intellectuals feel, as distinct from and far more important than what they say or think. Those feelings of loneliness one finds among so many American intellectuals, feelings of damp dispirited isolation which undercut the ideology of liberal optimism, are partly due to the breakup of bohemia. Where young writers would once face the world together, they now sink into suburbs, country homes, and college towns. And the price they pay for this rise in social status is to be measured in more than an increase in rent.

It is not my purpose to berate anyone, for the pressures of conformism are at work upon all of us, to say nothing of the need to earn one's bread; and all of us bend under the terrible weight of our time—though some take pleasure in learning to enjoy it. Nor do I wish to indulge in the sort of good-natured condescension with which Malcolm Cowley recently described the younger writers as lugubrious and timid longhairs huddling in chill academies and poring over the gnostic texts of Henry James—by contrast, no doubt, to Cowley's own career of risk-taking. Some intellectuals, to be sure, have "sold out" and we can all point to examples, probably the same examples. But far more prevalent and far more insidious is that slow attrition which destroys one's ability to stand firm and alone: the temptations of an improved standard of living combined with guilt over the historical tragedy that has made possible our prosperity; one's sense of being swamped by the rubbish of a reactionary period together with the loss of those earlier certainties that had the advantage, at least, of making resistance easy. Nor, in saying these things, do I look forward to any sort of material or intellectual asceticism. Our world is to be neither flatly accepted nor rejected: it must be engaged, resisted, and—who knows, perhaps still—transformed.

All of life, my older friends often tell me, is a conspiracy against that ideal of independence with which a young intellectual begins; but if so, wisdom consists not in premature surrender but in learning when to evade, when to stave off, and when to oppose head-on. Conformity, as Arthur Koestler said some years ago, "is often a form of betrayal which can be carried out with a clear conscience." Gradually we make our peace with the world, and not by anything as exciting as a secret pact; nowadays Lucifer is a very patient and reasonable fellow with a gift for indulging one's most legitimate desires; and we learn, if we learn anything at all, that betrayal may consist in a chain of small compromises, even while we also learn that in this age one cannot survive without compromise. What is most alarming is not that a number of intellectuals have abandoned the posture of iconoclasm: let the zeitgeist give them a jog and they will again be radical, all too radical. What is most alarming is that the whole idea of the intellectual vocation—the idea of a life dedicated to values that cannot possibly be realized by a commercial civilization—has gradually lost its allure. And it is this, rather than the abandonment of a particular program, which constitutes our rout.

In a recent number of *Perspectives* Lionel Trilling addressed himself to some of these problems; his perspective is sharply different from mine. Trilling believes that "there is an unmistakable improvement in the American cultural situation of today over that of, say, thirty years ago," while to me it seems that any comparison between the buoyant free-spirited cultural life of 1923 with the dreariness of 1953, or between their literary achievements, must lead to the conclusion that Trilling is indulging in a pleasant fantasy. More important, however, is his analysis of how this "improvement" has occurred:

> In many civilizations there comes a point at which wealth shows a tendency to submit itself, in some degree, to the rule of mind and imagination, to apologize for its existence by a show of taste and sensitivity. In America the signs of this submission have for some time been visible. . . . Intellect has associated itself with power, perhaps as never before in history, and is now conceded to be in itself a kind of power.

Such stately terms as "wealth" and "intellect" hardly make for sharp distinctions, yet the drift of Trilling's remarks is clear enough—and, I think, disastrous.

It is perfectly true that in the government bureaucracy and institutional staff, in the mass-culture industries and the academy, intellectuals have been welcomed and absorbed as never before. It is true, again, that "wealth" has become far more indulgent in its treatment of intellectuals, and for good reasons: it needs them more than ever, they are tamer than ever, and its own position is more comfortable and expansive than it has been for a long time. But if "wealth" has made a mild bow toward "intellect" (sometimes while picking its pocket), then "intellect" has engaged in some undignified prostrations before "wealth." Thirty years ago "wealth" was on the defensive, and twenty years ago it was frightened, hesitant, apologetic. "Intellect" was self-confident, aggressive, secure in its belief or, if you wish, delusions. Today the ideology of American capitalism, with its claim to a unique and immaculate destiny, is trumpeted through every medium of communication: official propaganda, institutional advertising, and the scholarly writings of people who, until a few years ago, were its major opponents. Marx baiting, that least risky of occupations, has become a favorite sport in the academic journals; a whining genteel chauvinism is widespread among intellectuals; and the bemoaning of their own fears and timidities a constant theme among professors. Is this to be taken as evidence that "wealth" has subordinated itself to "intellect"? Or is the evidence to be found in the careers of such writers as Max Eastman and James Burnham? To be sure, culture has acquired a more honorific status, as restrained ostentation has replaced conspicuous consumption: wealthy people collect more pictures or at least more modern ones, they endow foundations with large sums—but all this is possible because "intellect" no longer pretends to challenge "wealth."

What has actually been taking place is the absorption of large numbers of intellectuals, previously independent, into the world of government bureaucracy and public committees; into the constantly growing industries of pseudo culture; into the adult-education business, which subsists on regulated culture-anxiety. This process of bureaucratic absorption does not proceed without check: the Eisenhower administration has recently dismissed a good many intellectuals from government posts. Yet it seems likely that such stupidity will prove temporary and that one way or another, in one administration or another, the intellectuals will drift back into the government: they must, they are indispensable.

Some years ago C. Wright Mills wrote an article in which he labeled the intellectuals as "powerless people." He meant, of course, that they felt incapable of translating their ideas into action and that their consequent frustration had become a major motif in their behavior. His description was accurate enough; yet we might remember that the truly powerless people are those intellectuals—the new realists—who attach themselves to the seats of power, where they surrender their freedom of expression without gaining any significance as political figures. For it is crucial to the history of the American intellectuals in the past few decades—as well as to the relationship between "wealth" and "intellect"—that whenever they become absorbed into the accredited institutions of society they not only lose their traditional rebelliousness but to one extent or another *they cease to function as intellectuals*. The institutional world needs intellectuals *because* they are intellectuals but it does not want them *as* intellectuals. It beckons to them because of what they are but it will not allow them, at least within its sphere of articulation, to either remain or entirely cease being what they are. It needs them for their knowledge, their talent, their inclinations and passions; it insists that they retain a measure of these endowments, which it means to employ for its own ends, and without which the intellectuals would be of no use to it whatever. A simplified but useful equation suggests itself: the relation of the institutional world to the intellectuals is like the relation of middlebrow culture to serious culture. The one battens on the other, absorbs and raids it with increasing frequency and skill, subsidizes and encourages it enough to make further raids possible—at times the parasite will support its victim. Surely this relationship must be one reason for the high incidence of neurosis that is supposed to prevail among intellectuals. A total estrangement from the sources of power and prestige, even a blind unreasoning rejection of every aspect of our culture, would be far healthier, if only because it would permit a free discharge of aggression.

I do not mean to suggest that for intellectuals all institutions are equally dangerous or disadvantageous. Even during the New Deal, the life of those intellectuals who journeyed to Washington was far from happy. The independence possible to a professor of sociology is usually greater than that possible to a writer of television scripts, and a professor of English, since the world will not take his subject seriously, can generally enjoy more intellectual leeway than a professor of sociology. Philip Rieff, a sociologist, has caustically described a major tendency among his colleagues as a drift from "science" to "policy" in which "loyalty, not truth, provides the social condition by which the intellectual discovers his new environment." It is a drift "from the New School to the Rand Corporation."

There is, to be sure, a qualitative difference between the academy and the government bureau or the editorial staff. The university is still committed to the ideology of freedom, and many professors try hard and honestly to live by it. If the intellectual cannot subsist independently, off his work or his relatives, the academy is usually his best bet. But no one who has a live sense of what the literary life has been and might still be, in either Europe or this country, can accept the notion that the academy is the natural home of intellect. What seems so unfortunate is that the whole *idea* of independence is losing its traditional power. Scientists are bound with chains of official secrecy; sociologists compete for government research chores; foundations become indifferent to solitary writers and delight in "teams"; the possibility of living in decent poverty from moderately serious literary journalism becomes more and more remote. Compromises are no doubt necessary, but they had better be recognized for what they are.

Perhaps something should be said here about "alienation." Involved, primarily, is a matter of historical fact. During most of the bourgeois epoch, the European intellectuals grew increasingly alienated from the social community because the very ideals that had animated the bourgeois revolution were now being violated by bourgeois society; their "alienation" was prompted not by bohemian willfulness or socialist dogmatism but by a loyalty to Liberty, Fraternity, Equality, or to a vision of a preindustrial society that, by a trick of history, came pretty much to resemble Liberty, Fraternity, Equality. Just as it was the triumph of capitalism which largely caused this sense of estrangement, so it was the expansion of capitalism that allowed the intellectuals enough freedom to express it. As Philip Rahv has put it: "During the greater part of the bourgeois epoch . . . [writers] preferred alienation from the community to alienation from themselves." Precisely this choice made possible their strength and boldness, precisely this "lack of roots" gave them their speculative power. Almost always, the talk one hears these days about "the need for roots" veils a desire to compromise the tradition of intellectual independence, to seek in a nation or religion or party a substitute for the tenacity one should find in oneself. Isaac Rosenfeld's remark that "the ideal society . . . cannot afford to include many deeply rooted individuals" is not merely a clever mot but an important observation.

It may be that the issue is no longer relevant; that, with the partial submission of "wealth" to "intellect," the clash between a business civilization and the values of art is no longer as urgent as we once thought; but if so, we must discard a great deal, and mostly the best, of the literature, the criticism, and the speculative thought of the twentieth century. For to deny the historical fact of "alienation" (as if that would make it any the less real!) is to deny our heritage, both as burden and advantage, and also, I think, to deny our possible future as a community.

Much of what I have been describing here must be due to a feeling among intellectuals that the danger of Stalinism allows them little or no freedom in their relations with bourgeois society. This feeling seems to me only partly justified, and I do not suffer from any inclination to minimize the Stalinist threat. To be sure, it does limit our possibilities for action—if, that is, we still want to engage in any dissident politics—and sometimes it may force us into political alignments that are distasteful. But here a crucial distinction should be made: the danger of Stalinism may require temporary expedients in the area of *power* such as would have seemed compromising some years ago, but there is no reason, at least no good reason, why it should require compromise or conformity in the area of *ideas*, no reason why it should lead us to become partisans of bourgeois society, which is itself, we might remember, heavily responsible for the Stalinist victories.

III

"In the United States at this time liberalism is not only the dominant but even the sole intellectual tradition." This sentence of
Lionel Trilling's contains a sharp insight into the political life of
contemporary America. If I understand him correctly, he is saying that our society is at present so free from those pressures of
conflicting classes and interests which make for sharply defined
ideologies, that liberalism colors, or perhaps the word should
be, bleaches all political tendencies. It becomes a loose shelter,
a poncho rather than a program; to call oneself a liberal one
doesn't really have to believe in anything. In such a moment of
social slackness, the more extreme intellectual tendencies have
a way, as soon as an effort is made to put them into practice, of
sliding into and becoming barely distinguishable from the dominant liberalism. Both conservatism and radicalism can retain, at
most, an intellectual recalcitrance, but neither is presently able to
engage in a sustained practical politics of its own; which does not
mean they will never be able to.

The point is enforced by looking at the recent effort to affirm
a conservative ideology. Russell Kirk, who makes this effort with
some earnestness, can hardly avoid the eccentricity of appealing
to Providence as a putative force in American politics: an appeal
that suggests both the intensity of his conservative desire and
the desperation behind the intensity. Peter Viereck, a friskier sort
of writer, calls himself a conservative, but surely this is nothing more than a mystifying pleasantry, for aside from the usual
distinctions of temperament and talent it is hard to see how his
conservatism differs from the liberalism of Arthur Schlesinger,
Jr. For Viereck conservatism is a shuffling together of attractive formulas, without any effort to discover their relationship
to deep *actual* clashes of interest: he fails, for example, even to
consider that in America there is today neither opportunity nor
need for conservatism (since the liberals do the necessary themselves) and that if an opportunity were to arise, conservatism
could seize upon it only by acquiring a mass, perhaps reaction-

ary dynamic, that is, by "going into the streets." And that, surely, Viereck doesn't want.

If conservatism is taken to mean, as in some "classical" sense it should be, a principled rejection of industrial economy and a yearning for an ordered, hierarchical society that is not centered on the city, then conservatism in America is best defended by a group of literary men whose seriousness is proportionate to their recognition that such a politics is now utterly hopeless and, in any but a utopian sense, meaningless. Such a conservatism, in America, goes back to Fenimore Cooper, who anticipates those implicit criticisms of our society which we honor in Faulkner; and in the hands of serious imaginative writers, but hardly in the hands of political writers obliged to deal with immediate relations of power, it can become a myth which, through abrasion, profoundly challenges modern experience. As for the "conservatism" of the late Senator Robert Taft, which consists of nothing but liberal economics and wounded nostalgia, it lacks intellectual content and, more important, when in power it merely continues those "statist" policies it had previously attacked.

This prevalence of liberalism yields, to be sure, some obvious and substantial benefits. It makes us properly skeptical of the excessive claims and fanaticisms that accompany ideologies. It makes implausible those "aristocratic" rantings against democracy which were fashionable in some literary circles a few years ago. And it allows for the hope that any revival of American radicalism will acknowledge not only its break from, but also its roots in, the liberal tradition.

At the same time, however, the dominance of liberalism contributes heavily to our intellectual conformity. Liberalism dominates, but without confidence or security; it knows that its victories at home are tied to disasters abroad; and for the élan it cannot summon, it substitutes a blend of complacence and anxiety. It makes for an atmosphere of blur in the realm of ideas, since it has a stake in seeing momentary concurrences as deep harmonies. In an age that suffers from incredible catastrophes it scoffs at theories of social apocalypse—as if any *more* evidence were needed; in an era convulsed by war, revolution and counterrevolution it discovers the virtues of "moderation." And when the dominant school of liberalism, the school of realpolitik, scores points in attacking "the ritualistic liberals," it also betrays a subterranean desire to retreat into the caves of bureaucratic caution. Liberalism as an ideology, as "the haunted air," has never been stronger in this country; but can as much be said of the appetite for freedom?

Sidney Hook discovers merit in the Smith Act: he was not for its passage but doubts the wisdom of its repeal.* Mary McCarthy, zooming to earth from never-never land, discovers in the American war economy no less than paradise: "Class barriers disappear or tend to become porous; the factory worker is an economic aristocrat in comparison to the middle-class clerk. . . . The America . . . of vast inequalities and dramatic contrasts is rapidly ceasing to exist." Daniel Boorstin—he cannot be charged with the self-deceptions peculiar to idealism—discovers that "the genius of American politics" consists not in the universal possibilities of democracy but in a uniquely fortunate geography which, obviously, cannot be exported. David Riesman is so disturbed by Veblen's rebelliousness toward American society that he explains it as a projection of father-hatred; and what complex is it, one wonders, which explains a writer's assumption that Veblen's view of America is so inconceivable as to require a home-brewed psychoanalysis? Irving Kristol writes an article minimizing the threat to civil liberties and shortly thereafter is chosen to be public spokesman for the American Committee for Cultural Freedom. And in the committee itself, it is possible for serious intellectuals to debate—none is *for* Senator McCarthy— whether the public activities of the Wisconsin hooligan constitute a serious menace to freedom.

One likes to speculate: suppose Simone de Beauvoir and Bertrand Russell didn't exist; would not many of the political writers for *Commentary* and the *New Leader* have to invent them? It is all very well, and even necessary, to demonstrate that Russell's description of America as subject to "a reign of terror" is mali-

---

* The Smith Act, passed in 1940, was a loosely worded piece of legislation that made it unlawful to "conspire to advocate the overthrow of the government by force and violence."

cious and ignorant, or that Beauvoir's picture of America is a blend of Stalinist clichés and second-rate literary fantasies; but this hardly disposes of the problem of civil liberties or of the justified alarm many sober European intellectuals feel with regard to America. Between the willfulness of those who see only terror and the indifference of those who see only health, there is need for simple truth: that intellectual freedom in the United States is under severe attack and that the intellectuals have, by and large, shown a painful lack of militancy in defending the rights which are a precondition of their existence.*

It is in the pages of the influential magazine *Commentary* that liberalism is most skillfully and systematically advanced as a strategy for adapting to the American status quo. Until the last few months, when a shift in editorial temper seems to have occurred, the magazine was more deeply preoccupied, or preoccupied at deeper levels, with the dangers to freedom stemming from people like Freda Kirchwey and Arthur Miller than the dangers from people like Senator McCarthy. In March 1952 Irving Kristol, then an editor of *Commentary*, could write that "there is one thing the American people know about Senator McCarthy: he, like them, is unequivocally anti-Communist. About the spokesmen for American liberalism, they feel they know no such thing. And with some justification." In September 1952, at the very moment when McCarthy had become a central issue in the presidential campaign, Elliot Cohen, the senior editor of *Commentary*, could write that McCarthy "remains in the popular mind an unreliable, second-string blowhard; his *only* support as a great national figure is from the fascinated fears of the intelligentsia" (emphasis mine). As if to blot out the memory of these performances, Nathan Glazer, still another editor, wrote an

---

* It must in honesty be noted that many of the intellectuals least alive to the problem of civil liberties are former Stalinists or radicals; and this, more than the vast anti-Marxist literature of recent years, constitutes a serious criticism of American radicalism. For the truth is that the "old-fashioned liberals" like John Dewey and Alexander Meiklejohn, at whom it was once so fashionable to sneer, have displayed a finer sensitivity to the need for defending domestic freedoms than the more "sophisticated" intellectuals who leapt from Marx to Machiavelli.

excellent analysis of McCarthy in the March 1953 issue; but at the end of his article, almost as if from another hand, there again appeared the magazine's earlier line: "All that Senator McCarthy can do on his own authority that someone equally unpleasant and not a Senator can't, is to haul people down to Washington for a grilling by his committee. It is a shame and an outrage that Senator McCarthy should remain in the Senate; yet I cannot see that it is an imminent danger to personal liberty in the United States." It is, I suppose, this sort of thing that is meant when people speak about the need for replacing the outworn formulas and clichés of liberalism and radicalism with *new ideas*.

IV

To what does one conform? To institutions, obviously. To the dead images that rot in one's mind, unavoidably. And almost always, to the small grating necessities of day-to-day survival. In these senses it may be said that we are all conformists to one or another degree. When Sidney Hook writes, "I see no specific virtue in the attitude of conformity or non-conformity," he is right if he means that no human being can, or should, entirely accept or reject the moral and social modes of his time. And he is right in adding that there are occasions, such as the crisis of the Weimar republic, when the nonconformism of a Stefan George or an Oswald Spengler can have unhappy consequences.

But Professor Hook seems to me quite wrong in supposing that his remark applies significantly to present-day America. It would apply if we lived in a world where ideas could be weighed in free and delicate balance, without social pressures or contaminations, so that our choices would be made solely from a passion for truth. As it happens, however, there are tremendous pressures in America that make for intellectual conformism and consequently, in this tense and difficult age, there are very real virtues in preserving the attitude of critical skepticism and distance. Even some of the more extreme antics of the professional "bohemians" or literary anarchists take on a certain value which in cooler moments they might not have.*

What one conforms to most of all—despite and against one's intentions—is the zeitgeist, that vast insidious sum of pressures and fashions; one drifts along, anxious and compliant, upon the favored assumptions of the moment; and not a soul in the intellectual world can escape this. Only, some resist and some don't. Today the zeitgeist presses down upon us with a greater insistence than at any other moment of the century. In the 1930s many of those who hovered about the *New Masses* were mere camp followers of success; but the conformism of the party-line intellectual, at least before 1936, did sometimes bring him into conflict with established power: he had to risk something. Now, by contrast, established power and the dominant intellectual tendencies have come together in a harmony such as this country has not seen since the Gilded Age; and this, of course, makes the temptations of conformism all the more acute. The carrots, for once, are real.

Real even for literary men, who these days prefer to meditate upon symbolic vegetables. I would certainly not wish to suggest any direct correlation between our literary assumptions and the nature of our politics; but surely some of the recent literary trends and fashions owe something to the more general intellectual drift toward conformism. Not, of course, that liberalism dominates literary life, as it dominates the rest of the intellectual world. Whatever practical interest most literary men have in politics comes to little else than the usual liberalism, but their efforts at constructing literary ideologies—frequently as forced marches to discover values our society will not yield them—result in something quite different from liberalism. Through much of our writing, both creative and critical, there run a number of ideological motifs, the importance of which is hardly diminished by

---

* It may be asked whether a Stalinist's "nonconformism" is valuable. No, it isn't; the Stalinist is anything but a nonconformist; he has merely shifted the object of his worship, as later, when he abandons Stalinism, he usually shifts it again.

the failure of the men who employ them to be fully aware of their implications. Thus, a major charge that might be brought against some New Critics is not that they practice formal criticism but that they don't; not that they see the work of art as an object to be judged according to laws of its own realm but that, often unconsciously, they weave ideological assumptions into their writings.* Listening last summer to Cleanth Brooks lecture on Faulkner, I was struck by the deep hold that the term "orthodox" has acquired on his critical imagination, and not, by the way, on his alone. But "orthodox" is not, properly speaking, a critical term at all; it pertains to matters of religious or other belief rather than to literary judgment; and a habitual use of such terms can only result in the kind of "slanted" criticism Mr. Brooks has been so quick, and right, to condemn.

Together with "orthodox" there goes a cluster of terms which, in their sum, reveal an implicit ideological bias. The word "traditional" is especially tricky here, since it has legitimate uses in both literary and moral-ideological contexts. What happens, however, in much contemporary criticism is that these two contexts are taken to either be one or to be organically related, so that it becomes possible to assume that a sense of literary tradition necessarily involves and sanctions a "traditional" view of morality. There is a powerful inclination here—it is the doing of the impish zeitgeist—to forget that literary tradition can be fruitfully seen as a series of revolts, literary but sometimes more than literary, of generation against generation, age against age.

---

* This may be true of all critics, but is most perilous to those who suppose themselves free of ideological coloring. In a review of my Faulkner book—rather favorable, so that no ego wounds prompt what follows—Robert Daniel writes that "because of Mr. Howe's connections with . . . the *Partisan Review*, one might expect his literary judgments to be shaped by political and social preconceptions, but that does not happen often." Daniel is surprised that a critic whose politics happen to be radical should try to keep his literary views distinct from his nonliterary ones. To be sure, this is sometimes very difficult, and perhaps no one entirely succeeds. But the one sure way of not succeeding is to write, as Daniel does, from no very pressing awareness that it is a problem for critics who appear in the *Sewanee Review* quite as much as for those who appear in *Partisan Review*.

The emphasis on "tradition" has other contemporary implications: it is used as a not very courageous means of countering the experimental and the modern; it can enclose the academic assumption—and this is the curse of the Ph.D. system—that the whole of the literary past is at every point equally relevant to a modern intelligence; and it frequently includes the provincial American need to be more genteel than the gentry, more English than the English. Basically, it has served as a means of asserting conservative or reactionary moral-ideological views not, as they should be asserted, in their own terms, but through the refining medium of literary talk.

In general, there has been a tendency among critics to subsume literature under their own moral musings, which makes for a conspicuously humorless kind of criticism.* Morality is assumed to be a sufficient container for the floods of experience, and poems or novels that gain their richness from the complexity with which they dramatize the incommensurability between man's existence and his conceptualizing, are thinned, pruned, and allegorized into moral fables. Writers who spent—in both senses of the word—their lives wrestling with terrible private demons are elevated into literary dons and deacons. It is as if Stendhal had never come forth, with his subversive wit, to testify how often life and literature find the whole moral apparatus irrelevant or tedious, as if Lawrence had never written *The Man Who Died*, as if Nietzsche had never launched his great attack on the Christian impoverishment of the human psyche. One can only be relieved, therefore, at knowing a few critics personally: how pleasant the discrepancy between their writings and their lives!

But it is Original Sin that today commands the highest prestige in the literary world. Like nothing else, it allows literary men to enjoy a sense of profundity and depth—to relish a disenchant-

---

* Writing about *Wuthering Heights* Mark Schorer solemnly declares that "the theme of the moral magnificence of unmoral passion is an impossible theme to sustain, and the needs of her temperament to the contrary, all personal longing and reverie to the contrary, Emily Brontë teaches herself that this was indeed not at all what her material must mean as art." What is more, if Emily Brontë had lived a little longer she would have been offered a Chair in Moral Philosophy.

ment which allows no further risk of becoming enchanted—as against the superficiality of *mere* rationalism. It allows them to appropriate to the "tradition" the greatest modern writers, precisely those whose values and allegiances are most ambiguous, complex, and enigmatic, while at the same time generously leaving, as Leslie Fiedler once suggested, Dreiser and Farrell as the proper idols for that remnant benighted enough to maintain a naturalist philosophy. To hold, as Dickens remarks in *Bleak House*, "a loose belief that if the world go wrong, it was, in some offhand manner, never meant to go right," this becomes the essence of wisdom. (Liberals too have learned to cast a warm eye on "man's fallen nature," so that one gets the high comedy of Arthur Schlesinger, Jr., interrupting his quite worldly political articles with uneasy bows in the direction of Kierkegaard.) And with this latest dispensation come, of course, many facile references to the ideas supposedly held by Rousseau* and Marx, that man is "perfectible" and that progress moves in a steady upward curve.

I say, facile references, because no one who has troubled to read Rousseau or Marx could write such things. Exactly what the "perfectibility of man" is supposed to mean, if anything at all, I cannot say; but it is not a phrase intrinsic to the *kind* of thought one finds in the mature Marx or, most of the time, in Rousseau. Marx did not base his argument for socialism on any view that one could isolate a constant called "human nature"; he would certainly have agreed with Ortega that man has not a nature, but a history. Nor did he have a very rosy view of the human beings who were his contemporaries or recent predecessors: see in *Capital* the chapter on the Working Day, a grisly catalog of human bestiality. Nor did he hold to a naïve theory of progress: he wrote that the victories of progress "seem bought by the loss of character. At the same pace that mankind masters nature, man seems to become enslaved to other men or to his own infamy."

As for Rousseau, the use of even a finger's worth of histori-

---

* Randall Jarrell, who usually avoids fashionable cant: "Most of us know, now, that Rousseau was wrong; that man, when you knock his chains off, sets up the death camps." Which chains were knocked off in Germany to permit the setting up of death camps? And which chains must be put up again to prevent a repetition of the death camps?

cal imagination should suggest that the notion of "a state of nature," which modern literary people so enjoy attacking, was a political metaphor employed in a prerevolutionary situation, and not, therefore, to be understood outside its context. Rousseau explicitly declared that he did not suppose the "state of nature" to have existed in historical time; it was, he said, "a pure idea of reason" reached by abstraction from the observable state of society. As G. D. H. Cole remarks, "in political matters at any rate, the 'state of nature' is for [Rousseau] only a term of controversy . . . he means by 'nature' not the original state of a thing, nor even its reduction to the simplest terms; he is passing over to the conception of 'nature' as identical with the full development of [human] capacity. . . ." There are, to be sure, elements in Rousseau's thought which one may well find distasteful, but these are not the elements commonly referred to when he is used in literary talk as a straw man to be beaten with the cudgels of "orthodoxy."

What then is the significance of the turn to Original Sin among so many intellectuals? Surely not to inform us, at this late moment, that man is capable of evil. Or is it, as Cleanth Brooks writes, to suggest that man is a "limited" creature, limited in possibilities and capacities, and hence unable to achieve his salvation through social means? Yes, to be sure; but the problem of history is to determine, by action, how far those limits may go. Conservative critics like to say that "man's fallen nature" makes unrealistic the liberal-radical vision of the good society—apparently, when Eve bit the apple she predetermined, with one fatal crunch, that her progeny could work its way up to capitalism, and not a step further. But the liberal-radical vision of the good society does not depend upon a belief in the "unqualified goodness of man"; nor does it locate salvation in society: anyone in need of being saved had better engage in a private scrutiny. The liberal-radical claim is merely that the development of technology has now made possible—possible, not inevitable—a solution of those material problems that have burdened mankind for centuries. These problems solved, man is then on his own, to make of his self and his world what he can.

The literary prestige of Original Sin cannot be understood

without reference to the current cultural situation; it cannot be understood except as a historical phenomenon reflecting, like the whole turn to religion and religiosity, the weariness of intellectuals in an age of defeat and their yearning to remove themselves from the bloodied arena of historical action and choice, which necessarily means, of secular action and choice. Much sarcasm and anger has been expended on the "failure of nerve" theory, usually by people who take it as a personal affront to be told that there is a connection between what happens in their minds and what happens in the world; but if one looks at the large-scale shifts among intellectuals during the past twenty-five years, it becomes impossible to put *all* of them down to a simultaneous, and thereby miraculous, discovery of Truth; some at least must be seen as a consequence of those historical pressures which make this an age of conformism. Like other efforts to explain major changes in belief, the "failure of nerve" theory does not tell us why certain people believed in the thirties what was only to become popular in the fifties and why others still believe in the fifties what was popular in the thirties; but it does tell us something more important: why a complex of beliefs is dominant at one time and subordinate at another.

V

I have tried to trace a rough pattern from social history through politics and finally into literary ideology, as a means of explaining the power of the conformist impulse in our time. But it is obvious that in each intellectual "world" there are impulses of this kind that cannot easily be shown to have their sources in social or historical pressures. Each intellectual world gives rise to its own patterns of obligation and preference. The literary world, being relatively free from the coarser kinds of social pressure, enjoys a considerable degree of detachment and autonomy. (Not as much as it likes to suppose, but a considerable degree.) That the general intellectual tendency is to acquiesce in what one no longer feels able to change or modify strongly encourages the internal patterns of conformism in the literary world and intensifies the yearning, common to all groups but especially to small and insecure groups, to draw together in a phalanx of solidarity. Then too, those groups that live by hostility to the dominant values of society—in this case, cultural values—find it extremely difficult to avoid an inner conservatism as a way of balancing their public role of opposition; anyone familiar with radical politics knows this phenomenon only too well. Finally, the literary world, while quite powerless in relation to, say, the worlds of business and politics, disposes of a measurable amount of power and patronage within its own domain; which makes, again, for predictable kinds of influence.

Whoever would examine the inner life of the literary world should turn first not to the magazines or the dignitaries or famous writers but to the graduate students, for like it or not the graduate school has become the main recruiting grounds for critics and sometimes even for writers. Here, in conversation with the depressed classes of the academy, one sees how the Ph.D. system—more powerful today than it has been for decades, since so few other choices are open to young literary men—grinds and batters personality into a mold of cautious routine. And what one finds among these young people, for all their intelligence and devotion and eagerness, is often appalling: a remarkable desire to be "critics," not as an accompaniment to the writing of poetry or the changing of the world or the study of man and God, but just critics—as if criticism were a *subject*, as if one could be a critic without having at least four nonliterary opinions, or as if criticism "in itself" could adequately engage an adult mind for more than a small part of its waking time. An equally astonishing indifference to the ideas that occupy the serious modern mind—Freud, Marx, Nietzsche, Frazer, Dewey are not great thinkers in their own right, but reservoirs from which one dredges up "approaches to criticism"—together with a fabulous knowledge of what Ransom said about Winters with regard to what Winters had said about Eliot. And a curiously humble discipleship—but also arrogant to those beyond the circle—so that one meets not fresh minds in growth but apostles of Burke or Trilling or Winters or Leavis or Brooks or neo-Aristotle.

Very little of this is the fault of the graduate students themselves, for they, like the distinguished figures I have just listed, are the victims of an unhappy cultural moment. What we have today in the literary world is a gradual bureaucratization of opinion and taste; not a dictatorship, not a conspiracy, not a coup, not a Machiavellian plot to impose a mandatory "syllabus"; but the inevitable result of outer success and inner hardening. Fourth-rate exercises in exegesis are puffed in the magazines while so remarkable and provocative a work as Arnold Hauser's *Social History of Art* is hardly reviewed, its very title indicating the reason. Learned young critics who have never troubled to open a novel by Turgenev can rattle off reams of Kenneth Burke, which gives them, understandably, a sensation of having enlarged upon literature. Literature itself becomes a raw material which critics work up into schemes of structure and symbol; to suppose that it is concerned with anything so gauche as human experience or obsolete as human beings—"You mean," a student said to me, "that you're interested in the *characters* of novels!" Symbols clutter the literary landscape like the pots and pans a two-year-old strews over the kitchen floor; and what is wrong here is not merely the transparent absence of literary tact—the gift for saying when a pan is a pan and when a pan is a symbol—but far more important, a transparent lack of interest in represented experience. For Robert Wooster Stallman the fact that Stephen Crane looking at the sun felt moved to compare it to a wafer is not enough, the existence of suns and wafers and their possible conjunction is not sufficiently marvelous: both objects must be absorbed into Christian symbolism (an ancient theory of literature developed by the church fathers to prove that suns, moons, vulva, chairs, money, hair, pots, pans, and words are really crucifixes). Techniques for reading a novel that have at best a limited relevance are frozen into dogmas: one might suppose from glancing at the more imposing literary manuals that "point of view" is the crucial means of judging a novel. (Willa Cather, according to Caroline Gordon, was "astonishingly ignorant of her craft," for she refrained from "using a single consciousness as a prism of moral reflection." The very mistake Tolstoy made, too!) Criticism itself, far from being the reflection of a solitary mind upon a work of art and therefore, like the solitary mind, incomplete and subjective, comes increasingly to be regarded as a problem in mechanics, the tools, methods, and trade secrets of which can be picked up, usually during the summer, from the more experienced operatives. In the mind of Stanley Hyman, who serves the indispensable function of reducing fashionable literary notions, criticism seems to resemble Macy's on bargain day: *First floor, symbols; second floor, myths (rituals to the rear on your right); third floor, ambiguities and paradoxes; fourth floor, word counting; fifth floor, Miss Harrison's antiquities; attic, Marxist remnants; basement, Freud; sub-basement, Jung. Watch your step, please.*

What is most disturbing, however, is that writing about literature and writers has become an industry. The preposterous academic requirement that professors write books they don't want to write and no one wants to read, together with the obtuse assumption that piling up more and more irrelevant information about an author's life helps us understand his work—this makes for a vast flood of books that have little to do with literature, criticism, or even scholarship. Would you care to know the contents of the cargo (including one elephant) carried by the vessel of which Hawthorne's father was captain in 1795? Robert Cantwell has an itemized list, no doubt as an aid to reading *The Scarlet Letter*. Jay Leyda knows what happened to Melville day by day and it is hardly his fault that most days nothing very much happened. Edgar Johnson does as much for Dickens and adds plot summaries too, no doubt because he is dealing with a little-read author. Another American scholar has published a full book on *Mardi*, which is astonishing not because he wrote the book but because he managed to finish reading *Mardi* at all.

I have obviously chosen extreme examples and it would be silly to contend that they adequately describe the American literary scene; but like the distorting mirrors in Coney Island they help bring into sharper contour the major features. Or as Donald Davie writes in the English journal *Twentieth Century*:

The professional poet has already disappeared from the literary scene, and the professional man of letters is following him into the grave. . . . It becomes more and more difficult, and will soon be impossible, for a man to make his living as a literary dilettante. . . . And instead of the professional man of letters we have the professional critic, the young don writing in the first place for other dons, and only incidentally for that supremely necessary fiction, the common reader. In other words, an even greater proportion of what is written about literature, and even of what literature is written, is "academic." . . . Literary standards are now in academic hands; for the freelance man of letters, who once supplemented and corrected the don, is fast disappearing from the literary scene. . . .

The pedant is as common as he ever was. And now that willy-nilly so much writing about literature is in academic hands, his activities are more dangerous than ever. But he has changed his habits. Twenty years ago he was to be heard asserting that his business was with hard facts, that questions of value and technique were not his affair, and that criticism could therefore be left to the impressionistic journalist. Now the pedant is proud to call himself a critic; he prides himself on evaluation and analysis; he aims to be penetrating, not informative. . . .

The pedant is a very adaptable creature, and can be as comfortable with Mr. Eliot's "objective correlative," Mr. Empson's "ambiguities" and Dr. Leavis's "complexities" as in the older suit of critical clothes that he has now, for the most part, abandoned.

Davie has in mind the literary situation in England, but all one needs for applying his remarks to America is an ability to multiply.

VI

All of the tendencies toward cultural conformism come to a head in the assumption that the avant-garde, as both concept and intellectual grouping, has become obsolete or irrelevant. Yet the future quality of American culture, I would maintain, largely depends on the survival, and the terms of survival, of precisely the kind of dedicated group that the avant-garde has been.

The avant-garde first appeared on the American scene some twenty-five or thirty years ago, as a response to the need for absorbing the meanings of the cultural revolution that had taken place in Europe during the first two decades of the century. The achievements of Joyce, Proust, Schoenberg, Bartók, Picasso, Matisse, to mention only the obvious figures, signified one of the major turnings in the cultural history of the West, a turning made all the more crucial by the fact that it came not during the vigor of a society but during its crisis. To counter the hostility which the work of such artists met among all the official spokesmen of culture, to discover formal terms and modes through which to secure these achievements, to insist upon the continuity between their work and the accepted, because dead, artists of the past—this became the task of the avant-garde. Somewhat later a section of the avant-garde also became politically active, and not by accident; for precisely those aroused sensibilities that had responded to the innovations of the modern masters now responded to the crisis of modern society. Thus, in the early years of a magazine like *Partisan Review*—roughly between 1936 and 1941—these two radical impulses came together in an uneasy but fruitful union; and it was in those years that the magazine seemed most exciting and vital as a link between art and experience, between the critical consciousness and the political conscience, between the avant-garde of letters and the independent left of politics.

That union has since been dissolved, and there is no likelihood that it will soon be reestablished. American radicalism exists only as an idea, and that barely; the literary avant-garde—it has become a stock comment for reviewers to make—is rapidly disintegrating, without function or spirit, and held together only by an inert nostalgia.

Had the purpose of the avant-garde been to establish the currency of certain names, to make the reading of *The Waste Land* and *Ulysses* respectable in the universities, there would be no further need for its continuance. But clearly this was not the central purpose of the avant-garde; it was only an unavoidable fringe of snobbery and fashion. The struggle for Joyce mattered only as it was a struggle for literary standards; the defense of Joyce was a defense not merely of modern innovation but of that traditional culture which was the source of modern innovation. And at its best it was a defense against those spokesmen for the genteel, the respectable, and the academic who had established a stranglehold over traditional culture. At the most serious level, the avant-garde was trying to face the problem of the quality of our culture, and when all is said and done, it faced that problem with a courage and honesty that no other group in society could match.

If the history of the avant-garde is seen in this way, there is every reason for believing that its survival is as necessary today as it was twenty-five years ago. To be sure, our immediate prospect is not nearly so exciting as it must then have seemed: we face no battle on behalf of great and difficult artists who are scorned by the official voices of culture. Today, in a sense, the danger is that the serious artists are not scorned enough. Philistinism has become very shrewd: it does not attack its enemies as much as it disarms them through reasonable cautions and moderate amendments. But this hardly makes the defense of those standards that animated the avant-garde during its best days any the less a critical obligation.

It has been urged in some circles that only the pressure of habit keeps serious writers from making "raids" upon the middlebrow world, that it is now possible to win substantial outposts in that world if we are ready to take risks. Perhaps. But surely no one desires a policy of highbrow isolation, and no one could oppose raids, provided that is what they really are. The precondition for successful raids, however, is that the serious writers themselves have a sense—not of belonging to an exclusive club—but of representing those cultural values which alone can sustain them while making their raids. Thus far the incursions of serious writers into the middlebrow world have not been remarkably successful: for every short story writer who has survived *The New Yorker* one could point to a dozen whose work became trivial and frozen after they had begun to write for it. Nor do I advocate, in saying this, a policy of evading temptations. I advocate overcoming them. Writers today have no choice, often enough, but to write for magazines like *The New Yorker*—and worse, far worse. But what matters is the terms upon which the writer enters into such relationships, his willingness to understand with whom he is dealing, his readiness not to deceive himself that an unpleasant necessity is a desirable virtue.

It seems to me beyond dispute that, thus far at least, in the encounter between high and middle culture, the latter has come off by far the better. Every current of the zeitgeist, every imprint of social power, every assumption of contemporary American life favors the safe and comforting patterns of middlebrow feeling. And then too the gloomier Christian writers may have a point when they tell us that it is easier for a soul to fall than to rise.*

Precisely at the time that the highbrows seem inclined to abandon what is sometimes called their "proud isolation," the middlebrows have become more intransigent in their opposition to everything that is serious and creative in our culture (which does not, of course, prevent them from exploiting and contaminating, for purposes of mass gossip, everything that is serious and creative in our culture). What else is the meaning of the coarse attack launched by the *Saturday Review* against the highbrows, under the guise of discussing the Pound case? What, for that matter, is the meaning of the hostility with which the *Partisan Review* symposium on "Our Country and Our Culture" was received? It would take no straining of texts to see this symposium as a disconcerting sign of how far intellectuals have drifted in the direction of cultural adaptation, yet the middlebrows wrote of

---

* Thus Professor Gilbert Highet, the distinguished classicist, writing in *Harper's* finds André Gide "an abominably wicked man. His work seems to me to be either shallowly based symbolism, or else cheap cynicism made by inverting commonplaces or by grinning through them. . . . Gide had the curse of perpetual immaturity. But then I am always aware of the central fact about Gide—that he was a sexual pervert who kept proclaiming and justifying his perversion; and perhaps this blinds me to his merits . . . the garrulous, Pangloss-like, pimple-scratching, self-exposure of Gide." I don't mean to suggest that many fall so low, but then not many philistines are so well educated as Highet.

it with blunt enmity. And perhaps because they too sensed this drift in the symposium, the middlebrows, highly confident at the moment, became more aggressive, for they do not desire compromise, they know that none is possible. So genial a middlebrow as Elmer Davis, in a long review of the symposium, entitled with a characteristic smirk "The Care and Feeding of Intellectuals," ends up on a revealing note: "The highbrows seem to be getting around to recognizing what the middlebrows have known for the past thirty years. This is progress." It is also the best possible argument for the maintenance of the avant-garde, even if only as a kind of limited defense.

Much has been written about the improvement of cultural standards in America, though a major piece of evidence—the wide circulation of paperbound books—is still an unweighed and unanalyzed quantity. The basic relations of cultural power remain unchanged, however: the middlebrows continue to dominate. The most distinguished newspaper in this country retains as its music critic a mediocrity named Olin Downes; the literary critic for that newspaper is a philistine named Orville Prescott; the most widely read book reviewer in this country is a buffoon named Sterling North; the most powerful literary journal, read with admiration by many librarians and professors, remains the *Saturday Review*. Nothing here gives us cause for reassurance or relaxation; nothing gives us reason to dissolve that compact in behalf of critical intransigence known as the avant-garde.

No formal ideology or program is entirely adequate for coping with the problems that intellectuals face in the twentieth century. No easy certainties and no easy acceptance of uncertainty. All the forms of authority, the states and institutions and monster bureaucracies, that press in upon modern life—what have these shown us to warrant the surrender of independence?

The most glorious vision of the intellectual life is still that which is loosely called humanist: the idea of a mind committed yet dispassionate, ready to stand alone, curious, eager, skeptical. The banner of critical independence, ragged and torn though it may be, is still the best we have.

E. B. White (1899–1985) was and remains one of the United States' most important, beloved essayists. Writing regularly for publications such as The New Yorker *and* Harper's, *he created a self-mocking, humorous persona of an amiable average citizen entangled in the absurdities and chagrins of daily life. Less recognized is how often he took civic-minded stances on the major political problems of the day, such as the essay below, which addresses the dangers of nuclear proliferation and environmental pollution with urgency and prescient awareness.*

SOOTFALL AND FALLOUT

Turtle Bay, October 18, 1956

This is a dark morning in the apartment, but the block is gay with yellow moving vans disgorging Mary Martin's belongings in front of a house a couple of doors east of here, into which (I should say from the looks of things) she is moving. People's lives are so exposed at moments like this, their possessions lying naked in the street, the light of day searching out every bruise and mark of indoor living. It is an unfair exposé—end tables with nothing to be at the end of, standing lamps with their cords tied up in curlers, bottles of vermouth craning their long necks from cartons of personal papers, and every wastebasket carrying its small cargo of miscellany. The vans cause a stir in the block. Heads appear in the windows of No. 230, across the way.

Passersby stop on the sidewalk and stare brazenly into the new home through the open door. I have a mezzanine seat for the performance; like a Peeping Tom, I lounge here in my bathrobe and look down, held in the embrace of a common cold, before which scientists stand in awe although they have managed to split the atom, infect the topsoil with strontium 90, break the barrier of sound, and build the Lincoln Tunnel.

What a tremendous lot of stuff makes up the cumulus called "the home"! The trivet, the tiny washboard, the fire tools, the big copper caldron large enough to scald a hog in, the metal filing cabinets, the cardboard filing cabinets, the record player, the glass and the china invisible in their barrels, the carpet sweeper. (I wonder whether Miss Martin knows that she owns an old-fashioned carpet sweeper in a modern shade of green.) And here comes a bright little hacksaw, probably the apple of Mr. Halliday's eye. When a writing desk appears, the movers take the drawers out, to lighten the load, and I am free to observe what a tangle Mary Martin's stationery and supplies are in—like my wife's, everything at sixes and sevens. And now the bed, under the open sky above Forty-Eighth Street. And now the mattress. A wave of decency overtakes me. I avert my gaze.

The movers experience the worst trouble with two large houseplants, six-footers, in their great jars. The jars, on being sounded, prove to be a third full of water and have to be emptied into the gutter. Living things are always harder to lift, somehow, than inanimate objects, and I think any mover would rather walk up three flights with a heavy bureau than go into a waltz with a rubber plant. There is really no way for a man to put his arms around a big houseplant and still remain a gentleman.

Out in back, away from the street, the prospect is more pleasing. The yellow cat mounts the wisteria vine and tries to enter my bedroom, stirred by dreams of a bullfinch in a cage. The air is hazy, smoke and fumes being pressed downward in what the smog reporter of the *Times* calls "a wigwam effect." I don't know what new gadget the factories of Long Island are making today to produce such a foul vapor—probably a new jet applicator for the relief of nasal congestion. But whatever it is, I would swap it for a breath of fresh air. On every slight stirring of the breeze, the willow behind Mary Martin's wigwam lets drop two or three stylish yellow leaves, and they swim lazily down like golden fish to where Paul, the handyman, waits with his broom. In the ivy border along the wall, watchful of the cat, three thrushes hunt about among the dry leaves. I can't pronounce "three thrushes," but I can see three thrushes from this window, and this is the first autumn I have ever seen three at once. An October miracle. I think they are hermits, but the visibility is so poor I can't be sure.

This section of Manhattan boasts the heaviest sootfall in town, and the United States of America boasts the heaviest fall-out in the world, and when you take the sootfall and the fallout and bring smog in on top of them, I feel I am in a perfect position to discuss the problem of universal pollution. The papers, of course, are full of the subject these days, as they follow the presidential campaigners around the nation from one contaminated area to another.

I have no recent figures on sootfall in the vicinity of Third Avenue, but the *Times* last Saturday published some figures on fallout from Dr. Willard F. Libby, who said the reservoir of radioactive materials now floating in the stratosphere from the tests of all nations was roughly twenty-four billion tons. That was Saturday. Sunday's *Times* quoted Dr. Laurence H. Snyder as saying, "In assessing the potential harm [of weapons-testing], statements are always qualified by a phrase such as 'if the testing of weapons continues at the present rate . . .' This qualification is usually obsolete by the time the statement is printed." I have an idea the figure twenty-four billion tons may have been obsolete when it appeared in the paper. It may not have included, for instance, the radioactive stuff from the bomb the British set off in Australia a week or two ago. Maybe it did, maybe it didn't. The point of Dr. Snyder's remark is clear; a thermonuclear arms race is, as he puts it, self-accelerating. Bomb begets bomb. A begets H. Anything you can build, I can build bigger.

"Unhappily," said Governor Harriman the other night, "we are still thinking in small, conventional terms, and with unwarranted complacency."

The habit of thinking in small, conventional terms is, of course, not limited to us Americans. You could drop a leaflet or a

Hubbard squash on the head of any person in any land and you would almost certainly hit a brain that was whirling in small, conventional circles. There is something about the human mind that keeps it well within the confines of the parish, and only one outlook in a million is nonparochial. The impression one gets from campaign oratory is that the sun revolves around the earth, the earth revolves around the United States, and the United States revolves around whichever city the speaker happens to be in at the moment. This is what a friend of mine used to call the Un-Copernican system. During a presidential race, candidates sometimes manage to create the impression that their thoughts are ranging widely and that they have abandoned conventional thinking. I love to listen to them when they are in the throes of these quadrennial seizures. But I haven't heard much from either candidate that sounded unconventional—although I have heard some things that sounded sensible and sincere. A candidate could easily commit political suicide if he were to come up with an unconventional thought during a presidential tour.

I think man's gradual, creeping contamination of the planet, his sending up of dust into the air, his strontium additive in our bones, his discharge of industrial poisons into rivers that once flowed clear, his mixing of chemicals with fog on the east wind add up to a fantasy of such grotesque proportions as to make everything said on the subject seem pale and anemic by contrast. I hold one share in the corporate earth and am uneasy about the management. Dr. Libby said there is new evidence that the amount of strontium reaching the body from topsoil impregnated by fallout is "considerably less than the 70 percent of the topsoil concentration originally estimated." Perhaps we should all feel elated at this, but I don't. The correct amount of strontium with which to impregnate the topsoil is *no* strontium. To rely on "tolerances" when you get into the matter of strontium 90, with three sovereign bomb testers already testing, independently of one another, and about fifty potential bomb testers ready to enter the stratosphere with their contraptions, is to talk with unwarranted complacency. I belong to a small, unconventional school that believes that *no* rat poison is the correct amount to spread in the kitchen where children and puppies can get at it. I believe that *no* chemical waste is the correct amount to discharge into the fresh rivers of the world, and I believe that if there is a way to trap the fumes from factory chimneys, it should be against the law to set these deadly fumes adrift where they can mingle with fog and, given the right conditions, suddenly turn an area into another Donora, Pennsylvania.

"I have seen the smoky fury of our factories—rising to the skies," said President Eisenhower pridefully as he addressed the people of Seattle last night. Well, I can see the smoky fury of our factories drifting right into this room this very minute; the fury sits in my throat like a bundle of needles, it explores my nose, chokes off my breath, and makes my eyes burn. The room smells like a slaughterhouse. And the phenomenon gets a brief mention in the morning press.

One simple, unrefuted fact about radioactive substances is that scientists do not agree about the "safe" amount. All radiation is harmful, all of it shortens life, all is cumulative, nobody keeps track of how much he gets in the form of X-rays and radio therapy, and all of it affects not only the recipient but his heirs. Both President Eisenhower and Governor Stevenson have discussed H-bomb testing and the thermonuclear scene, and their views differ. Neither of them, it seems to me, has quite told the changing facts of life on earth. Both tend to speak of national security as though it were still capable of being dissociated from universal well-being; in fact, sometimes in these political addresses it sounds as though this nation, or any nation, through force of character or force of arms, could damn well rise *above* planetary considerations, as though we were greater than our environment, as though the national verve somehow transcended the natural world.

"Strong we shall stay free," said President Eisenhower in Pittsburgh. And Governor Stevenson echoed the statement in Chicago: ". . . only the strong can be free."

This doctrine of freedom through strength deserves a second look. It would have served nicely in 1936, but nobody thought of it then. Today, with the H-bomb deterring war, we are free and we are militarily strong, but the doctrine is subject to a queer, embarrassing amendment. Today it reads, "Strong we shall stay free, *provided we do not have to use our strength.*" That's not quite the same thing. What was true in 1936, if not actually false today, is at best a mere partial, or half truth. A nation wearing atomic armor is like a knight whose armor has grown so heavy he is immobilized; he can hardly walk, hardly sit his horse, hardly think, hardly breathe. The H-bomb is an extremely effective deterrent to war, but it has little virtue as a *weapon* of war, because it would leave the world uninhabitable.

For a short while following the release of atomic energy, a strong nation was a secure nation. Today, no nation, whatever its thermonuclear power, is a strong nation in the sense that it is a fully independent nation. All are weak, and all are weak from the same cause: each depends on the others for salvation, yet none likes to admit this dependence, and there is no machinery for interdependence. The big nations are weak because the strength has gone out of their arms—which are too terrifying to use, too poisonous to explode. The little nations are weak because they have always been relatively weak and now they have to breathe the same bad air as the big ones. Ours is a balance, as Mr. Stevenson put it, not of power but of terror. If anything, the H-bomb rather favors small nations that don't as yet possess it; they feel slightly more free to jostle other nations, having discovered that a country can stick its tongue out quite far these days without provoking war, so horrible are war's consequences.

The atom, then, is a proper oddity. It has qualified the meaning of national security, it has very likely saved us from a third world war, it has given a new twist to the meaning of power, and it has already entered our bones with a cancer-producing isotope. Furthermore, it has altered the concept of personal sacrifice for moral principle. Human beings have always been willing to shed their blood for what they believed in. Yesterday this was clear and simple; we would pay in blood because, after the price was exacted, there was still a chance to make good the gain. But the modern price tag is not blood. Today our leaders and the leaders of other nations are, in effect, saying, "We will defend our beliefs not alone with our blood—by God, we'll defend them, if we have to, with our genes." This is bold, resolute talk, and one can't help admiring the spirit of it. I admire the spirit of it, but the logic of it eludes me. I doubt whether any noble principle—or any ignoble principle, either, for that matter—can be preserved at the price of genetic disintegration.

The thing I watch for in the speeches of the candidates is some hint that the thermonuclear arms race may be bringing people nearer together, rather than forcing them farther apart. I suspect that because of fallout we may achieve a sort of universality sooner than we bargained for. Fallout may compel us to fall in. The magic-carpet ride on the mushroom cloud has left us dazed—we have come so far so fast. There is a passage in Anne Lindbergh's book *North to the Orient* that captures the curious lag between the mind and the body during a plane journey, between the slow unfolding of remembered images and the swift blur of modern flight. Mrs. Lindbergh started her flight to the Orient by way of North Haven, her childhood summer home. "The trip to Maine," she wrote, "used to be a long and slow one. There was plenty of time in the night, spattered away in the sleeper, in the morning spent ferrying across the river at Bath, in the afternoon syncopated into a series of calls on one coast town after another—there was plenty of time to make the mental change coinciding with our physical change. . . . But on this swift flight to North Haven in the *Sirius* my mind was so far behind my body that when we flew over Rockland Harbor the familiar landmarks below me had no reality."

Like the girl in the plane, we have arrived, but the familiar scene lacks reality. We cling to old remembered forms, old definitions, old comfortable conceptions of national coziness, national self-sufficiency. The Security Council meets solemnly and takes up Suez, eleven sovereign fellows kicking a sovereign ditch around while England threatens war to defend her "lifelines," when modern war itself means universal contamination, universal deathlines, and the end of ditches. I would feel more hopeful, more *secure*, if the councilmen suddenly changed their tune and began arguing the case for mud turtles and other ancient denizens of ponds and ditches. That is the thing at stake now, and it is what will finally open the canal to the world's ships in perfect concord.

Candidates for political office steer clear of what Mrs. Luce used to call "globaloney," for fear they may lose the entire American Legion vote and pick up only Norman Cousins. Yet there are indications that supranational ideas are alive in the back of a few men's minds. Through the tangle of verbiage, the idea of "common cause" skitters like a shy bird. Mr. Dulles uses the word "interdependent" in one sentence, then returns promptly to the more customary, safer word "independent." We give aid to Yugoslavia to assure her "independence," and the very fact of the gift is proof that neither donor nor recipient enjoys absolute independence anymore; the two are locked in mortal *inter*dependence. Mr. Tito says he is for "new forms and new laws." I haven't the vaguest notion of what he means by that, and I doubt whether he has, either. Certainly there are no *old* laws, if by "laws" he means enforceable rules of conduct by which the world community is governed. But I'm for new forms, all right. Governor Stevenson, in one of his talks, said, "Nations have become so accustomed to living in the dark that they find it hard to learn to live in the light." What light? The light of government? If so, why not say so? President Eisenhower ended a speech the other day with the phrase "a peace of justice in a world of law." Everything else in his speech dealt with a peace of justice in a world of anarchy.

The riddle of disarmament, the riddle of peace, seems to me to hang on the interpretation of these conflicting and contradictory phrases—and on whether or not the men who use them really mean business. Are we independent or interdependent? We can't possibly be both. Do we indeed seek a peace of justice in a world of law, as the president intimates? If so, when do we start, and how? Are we for "new forms," or will the old ones do? In 1945, after the worst bloodbath in history, the nations settled immediately back into old forms. In its structure, the United Nations reaffirms everything that caused the Second World War. At the end of a war fought to defeat dictators, the UN welcomed Stalin and Perón to full membership, and the Iron Curtain quickly descended to put the seal of authority on this inconsistent act. The drafters of the charter assembled in San Francisco and defended their mild, inadequate format with the catchy phrase "Diplomacy is the art of the possible." Meanwhile, a little band of physicists met in a squash court and said, "The hell with the art of the possible. Watch this!"

The world organization debates disarmament in one room and, in the next room, moves the knights and pawns that make national arms imperative. This is not justice and law, and this is not light. It is not new forms. The UN is modern in intent, old-fashioned in shape. In San Francisco in 1945, the victor nations failed to create a constitution that placed a higher value on principle than on sovereignty, on common cause than on special cause. The world of 1945 was still 100 percent parochial. The world of 1956 is still almost 100 percent parochial. But at last we have a problem that is clearly a community problem, devoid of nationality—the problem of the total pollution of the planet.

We have, in fact, a situation in which the deadliest of all weapons, the H-bomb, together with its little brother, the A-bomb, is the latent source of great agreement among peoples. The bomb is universally hated, and it is universally feared. We cannot escape it with collective security; we shall have to face it with united action. It has given us a few years of grace without war, and now it offers us a few millenniums of oblivion. In a paradox of unbelievable jocundity, the shield of national sovereignty suddenly becomes the challenge of national sovereignty. And, largely because of events beyond our control, we are able to sniff the faint stirring of a community ferment—something every man can enjoy.

The president speaks often of "the peaceful uses of atomic energy," and they are greatly on his mind. I believe the peaceful use of atomic energy that should take precedence over all other uses is this: stop it from contaminating the soil and the sea, the rain and the sky, and the bones of man. This is elementary. It comes ahead of "goodwill" ships and it comes ahead of cheap power. What good is cheap power if your child already has an incurable cancer?

The hydrogen-garbage-disposal program unites the people of the earth in a common antilitterbug drive for salvation. Radio-active dust has no nationality, is not deflected by boundaries; it falls on Turk and Texan impartially. The radio-strontium isotope finds its way into the milk of Soviet cow and English cow with equal ease. This simple fact profoundly alters the political scene and calls for political leaders to echo the physicists and say, "Never mind the art of the possible. Watch this!"

To me, living in the light means an honest attempt to discover the germ of common cause in a world of special cause, even against the almost insuperable odds of parochialism and national fervor, even in the face of the dangers that always attend political growth. Actually, nations are already enjoying little pockets of unity. The European coal-steel authority is apparently a success. The UN, which is usually impotent in political disputes, has nevertheless managed to elevate the world's children and the world's health to a community level. The trick is to encourage and hasten this magical growth, this benign condition—encourage it and get it on paper, while children still have healthy bones and before we have all reached the point of no return. It will not mean the end of nations; it will mean the true beginning of nations.

Paul-Henri Spaak, addressing himself to the Egyptian government the other day, said, "We are no longer at the time of the absolute sovereignty of states." We are not, and we ought by this time to know we are not. I just hope we learn it in time. In the beautiful phrase of Mrs. Lindbergh's, there used to be "plenty of time in the night." Now there is hardly any time at all.

Well, this started out as a letter and has turned into a discourse. But I don't mind. If a candidate were to appear on the scene and come out for the dignity of mud turtles, I suppose people would hesitate to support him, for fear he had lost his reason. But he would have my vote, on the theory that in losing his reason he had kept his head. It is time men allowed their imagination to infect their intellect, time we all rushed headlong into the wilder regions of thought where the earth again revolves around the sun instead of around the Suez, regions where no individual and no group can blithely assume the right to sow the sky with seeds of mischief, and where the sovereign nation at last begins to function as the true friend and guardian of sovereign man.

PS (May 1962). The dirty state of affairs on earth is getting worse, not better. Our soil, our rivers, our seas, our air carry an ever-increasing load of industrial wastes, agricultural poisons, and military debris. The seeds of mischief are in the wind—in the warm sweet airs of spring. Contamination continues in greater force and new ways, and with new excuses: the Soviet tests last autumn had a double-barreled purpose—to experiment and to intimidate. This was the first appearance of the diplomacy of dust; the breaking of the moratorium by Russia was a high crime, murder in the first degree. President Kennedy countered with the announcement that he would reply in kind unless a test-ban agreement could be reached by the end of April. None was reached, and our tests are being conducted. One more nation, France, has joined the company of testers. If Red China learns the trick, we will probably see the greatest pyrotechnic display yet, for the Chinese love fireworks of all kinds.

I asked myself what I would have done, had I been in the president's shoes, and was forced to admit I would have taken the same course—test. The shattering of the moratorium was for the time being the shattering of our hopes of good nuclear conduct. In a darkening and dirt-ridden world the course of freedom must be maintained even by desperate means, while there is a time of grace, and the only thing worse than being in an arms race is to be in one and not compete. The president's decision to resume testing in the atmosphere was, I believe, a correct decision, and I think the people who protest by lying down in the street have not come up with an alternative course that is sensible and workable. But the time of grace will run out, sooner or later, for all nations. We are in a vast riddle, all of us—dependence on a strength that is inimical to life—and what we are really doing is fighting a war that uses the lives of future individuals, rather than the lives of existing young men. The president did his best to lighten the blow by pointing out that fallout isn't as bad as it used to be, that our tests would raise the background radiation by only 1 percent. But this is like saying that it isn't dangerous to go in the cage with the tiger because the tiger is taking a nap. I am not calmed by the news of fallout's mildness, or deceived by drowsy tigers. The percentages will increase, the damage will mount steadily unless a turn is made somehow. Because our adversary tests, we test; because we test, they test. Where is the end of this dirty habit? I think there is no military solution, no economic solution, only a political solution, and this is the area to which we should give the closest attention and in which we should show the greatest imaginative powers.

These nuclear springtimes have a pervasive sadness about them, the virgin earth having been the victim of rape attacks. This is a smiling morning; I am writing where I can look out at our garden piece, which has been newly harrowed, ready for planting. The rich brown patch of ground used to bring delight to eye and mind at this fresh season of promise. For me the scene has been spoiled by the maggots that work in the mind. Tomorrow we will have rain, and the rain falling on the garden will carry its cargo of debris from old explosions in distant places. Whether the amount of this freight is great or small, whether it is measurable by the farmer or can only be guessed at, one thing is certain: the character of rain has changed, the joy of watching it soak the waiting earth has been diminished, and the whole meaning and worth of gardens has been brought into question.

Vladimir Nabokov (1899–1977) was born in Russia and raised in an aristocratic, cultivated environment, which he lovingly describes in his outstanding memoir, Speak, Memory. *Fleeing his native country when the Bolsheviks took over, he moved to England and Paris before settling down in the United States, where he taught for many years at Cornell University. There he composed some of his most celebrated novels (Pnin, Lolita, Pale Fire, Ada). A passionate hunter of butterflies, Nabokov was cherished by the happy few as a supremely refined master of prose, but it was the sensation around* Lolita *that brought him notoriety and popular success. Though he kept insisting he regarded Humbert Humbert, the book's pedophile narrator, as a monster, some readers continued to associate the author with his character, or else excoriated him for allowing any sympathy to cling to the villain. Nabokov's defensive position that he was just doing the fiction writer's job may be gleaned from the essay below.*

ON A BOOK ENTITLED *LOLITA*

After doing my impersonation of suave John Ray, the character in *Lolita* who pens the foreword, any comments coming straight from me may strike one—may strike me, in fact—as an impersonation of Vladimir Nabokov talking about his own book. A few points, however, have to be discussed; and the autobiographic device may induce mimic and model to blend.

Teachers of Literature are apt to think up such problems as

"What is the author's purpose?" or still worse "What is the guy trying to say?" Now, I happen to be the kind of author who in starting to work on a book has no other purpose than to get rid of that book and who, when asked to explain its origin and growth, has to rely on such ancient terms as Interreaction of Inspiration and Combination—which, I admit, sounds like a conjurer explaining one trick by performing another.

The first little throb of *Lolita* went through me late in 1939 or early in 1940, in Paris, at a time when I was laid up with a severe attack of intercostal neuralgia. As far as I can recall, the initial shiver of inspiration was somehow prompted by a newspaper story about an ape in the Jardin des Plantes, who, after months of coaxing by a scientist, produced the first drawing ever charcoaled by an animal: this sketch showed the bars of the poor creature's cage. The impulse I record had no textual connection with the ensuing train of thought, which resulted, however, in a prototype of my present novel, a short story some thirty pages long. I wrote it in Russian, the language in which I had been writing novels since 1924 (the best of these are not translated into English, and all are prohibited for political reasons in Russia). The man was a Central European, the anonymous nymphet was French, and the loci were Paris and Provence. I had him marry the little girl's sick mother who soon died, and after a thwarted attempt to take advantage of the orphan in a hotel room, Arthur (for that was his name) threw himself under the wheels of a truck. I read the story one blue-papered wartime night to a group of friends— Mark Aldanov, two social revolutionaries, and a woman doctor; but I was not pleased with the thing and destroyed it sometime after moving to America in 1940.

Around 1949, in Ithaca, upstate New York, the throbbing, which had never quite ceased, began to plague me again. Combination joined inspiration with fresh zest and involved me in a new treatment of the theme, this time in English—the language of my first governess in St. Petersburg, circa 1903, a Miss Rachel Home. The nymphet, now with a dash of Irish blood, was really much the same lass, and the basic marrying-her-mother idea also subsisted; but otherwise the thing was new and had grown in secret the claws and wings of a novel.

The book developed slowly, with many interruptions and asides. It had taken me some forty years to invent Russia and Western Europe, and now I was faced by the task of inventing America. The obtaining of such local ingredients as would allow me to inject a modicum of average "reality" (one of the few words which mean nothing without quotes) into the brew of individual fancy, proved at fifty a much more difficult process than it had been in the Europe of my youth when receptiveness and retention were at their automatic best. Other books intervened. Once or twice I was on the point of burning the unfinished draft and had carried my Juanita Dark as far as the shadow of the leaning incinerator on the innocent lawn, when I was stopped by the thought that the ghost of the destroyed book would haunt my files for the rest of my life.

Every summer my wife and I go butterfly hunting. The specimens are deposited at scientific institutions, such as the Museum of Comparative Zoology at Harvard or the Cornell University collection. The locality labels pinned under these butterflies will be a boon to some twenty-first-century scholar with a taste for recondite biography. It was at such of our headquarters as Telluride, Colorado; Afton, Wyoming; Portal, Arizona; and Ashland, Oregon, that *Lolita* was energetically resumed in the evenings or on cloudy days. I finished copying the thing out in longhand in the spring of 1954, and at once began casting around for a publisher.

At first, on the advice of a wary old friend, I was meek enough to stipulate that the book be brought out anonymously. I doubt that I shall ever regret that soon afterwards, realizing how likely a mask was to betray my own cause, I decided to sign *Lolita*. The four American publishers, W, X, Y, Z, who in turn were offered the typescript and had their readers glance at it, were shocked by *Lolita* to a degree that even my wary old friend FP had not expected.

While it is true that in ancient Europe, and well into the eighteenth century (obvious examples come from France), deliberate lewdness was not inconsistent with flashes of comedy, or vigorous satire, or even the verve of a fine poet in a wanton mood, it is also true that in modern times the term "pornography" connotes mediocrity, commercialism, and certain strict rules of narration. Obscenity must be mated with banality because every kind of aesthetic enjoyment has to be entirely replaced by simple sexual stimulation which demands the traditional word for direct action upon the patient. Old rigid rules must be followed by the pornographer in order to have his patient feel the same security of satisfaction as, for example, fans of detective stories feel— stories where, if you do not watch out, the real murderer may turn out to be, to the fan's disgust, artistic originality (who for instance would want a detective story without a single dialogue in it?). Thus, in pornographic novels, action has to be limited to the copulation of clichés. Style, structure, imagery should never distract the reader from his tepid lust. The novel must consist of an alternation of sexual scenes. The passages in between must be reduced to sutures of sense, logical bridges of the simplest design, brief expositions and explanations, which the reader will probably skip but must know they exist in order not to feel cheated (a mentality stemming from the routine of "true" fairy tales in childhood). Moreover, the sexual scenes in the book must follow a crescendo line, with new variations, new combinations, new sexes, and a steady increase in the number of participants (in a Sade play they call the gardener in), and therefore the end of the book must be more replete with lewd lore than the first chapters.

Certain techniques in the beginning of *Lolita* (Humbert's journal, for example) misled some of my first readers into assuming that this was going to be a lewd book. They expected the rising succession of erotic scenes; when these stopped, the readers stopped, too, and felt bored and let down. This, I suspect, is one of the reasons why not all the four firms read the typescript to the end. Whether they found it pornographic or not did not interest me. Their refusal to buy the book was based not on my treatment of the theme but on the theme itself, for there are at least three themes which are utterly taboo as far as most American publishers are concerned. The two others are: a Negro-white marriage which is a complete and glorious success resulting in lots of children and grandchildren; and the total atheist who lives a happy and useful life, and dies in his sleep at the age of 106.

Some of the reactions were very amusing: one reader suggested that his firm might consider publication if I turned my Lolita into a twelve-year-old lad and had him seduced by Humbert, a farmer, in a barn, amidst gaunt and arid surroundings, all this set forth in short, strong, "realistic" sentences ("He acts crazy. We all act crazy, I guess. I guess God acts crazy." Etc.). Although everybody should know that I detest symbols and allegories (which is due partly to my old feud with Freudian voodooism and partly to my loathing of generalizations devised by literary mythists and sociologists), an otherwise intelligent reader who flipped through the first part described *Lolita* as "old Europe debauching young America," while another flipper saw in it "young America debauching old Europe." Publisher X, whose advisers got so bored with Humbert that they never got beyond page 188, had the naïveté to write me that Part Two was too long. Publisher Y, on the other hand, regretted there were no good people in the book. Publisher Z said if he printed *Lolita*, he and I would go to jail.

No writer in a free country should be expected to bother about the exact demarcation between the sensuous and the sensual; this is preposterous; I can only admire but cannot emulate the accuracy of judgment of those who pose the fair young mammals photographed in magazines where the general neckline is just low enough to provoke a past master's chuckle and just high enough not to make a postmaster frown. I presume there exist readers who find titillating the display of mural words in those hopelessly banal and enormous novels which are typed out by the thumbs of tense mediocrities and called "powerful" and "stark" by the reviewing hack. There are gentle souls who would pronounce *Lolita* meaningless because it does not teach them anything. I am neither a reader nor a writer of didactic fiction, and, despite John Ray's assertion, *Lolita* has no moral in tow. For me a work of fiction exists only insofar as it affords me what I shall bluntly call aesthetic bliss, that is a sense of being somehow, somewhere, connected with other states of being where art (curiosity, tenderness, kindness, ecstasy) is the norm. There are not many such books. All the rest is either topical trash or what some call the Literature of Ideas, which very often is topical trash

corning in huge blocks of plaster that are carefully transmitted
from age to age until somebody comes along with a hammer and
takes a good crack at Balzac, at Gorki, at Mann.

Another charge which some readers have made is that *Lolita*
is anti-American. This is something that pains me considerably
more than the idiotic accusation of immorality. Considerations
of depth and perspective (a suburban lawn, a mountain meadow)
led me to build a number of North American sets. I needed a
certain exhilarating milieu. Nothing is more exhilarating than
philistine vulgarity. But in regard to philistine vulgarity there is
no intrinsic difference between Palearctic manners and Nearctic
manners. Any proletarian from Chicago can be as bourgeois (in
the Flaubertian sense) as a duke. I chose American motels instead
of Swiss hotels or English inns only because I am trying to be an
American writer and claim only the same rights that other American writers enjoy. On the other hand, my creature Humbert is
a foreigner and an anarchist, and there are many things, besides
nymphets, in which I disagree with him. And all my Russian
readers know that my old worlds—Russian, British, German,
French—are just as fantastic and personal as my new one is.

Lest the little statement I am making here seem an airing of
grudges, I must hasten to add that besides the lambs who read
the typescript of *Lolita* or its Olympia Press edition in a spirit
of "Why did he have to write it?" or "Why should I read about
maniacs?" there have been a number of wise, sensitive, and
staunch people who understood my book much better than I can
explain its mechanism here.

Every serious writer, I dare say, is aware of this or that published book of his as of a constant comforting presence. Its pilot
light is steadily burning somewhere in the basement and a mere
touch applied to one's private thermostat instantly results in a
quiet little explosion of familiar warmth. This presence, this
glow of the book in an ever accessible remoteness is a most com-
panionable feeling, and the better the book has conformed to its
prefigured contour and color the ampler and smoother it glows.
But even so, there are certain points, byroads, favorite hollows
that one evokes more eagerly and enjoys more tenderly than the
rest of one's book. I have not reread *Lolita* since I went through

the proofs in the spring of 1955 but I find it to be a delightful presence now that it quietly hangs about the house like a summer day which one knows to be bright behind the haze. And when I thus think of *Lolita*, I seem always to pick out for special delectation such images as Mr. Taxovich, or that class list of Ramsdale School, or Charlotte saying "waterproof," or Lolita in slow motion advancing toward Humbert's gifts, or the pictures decorating the stylized garret of Gaston Godin, or the Kasbeam barber (who cost me a month of work), or Lolita playing tennis, or the hospital at Elphinstone, or pale, pregnant, beloved, irretrievable Dolly Schiller dying in Gray Star (the capital town of the book), or the tinkling sounds of the valley town coming up the mountain trail (on which I caught the first known female of *Lycaeides sublivens* Nabokov). These are the nerves of the novel. These are the secret points, the subliminal coordinates by means of which the book is plotted—although I realize very clearly that these and other scenes will be skimmed over or not noticed, or never even reached, by those who begin reading the book under the impression that it is something on the lines of *Memoirs of a Woman of Pleasure* or *Les Amours de Milord Grosvit*. That my novel does contain various allusions to the physiological urges of a pervert is quite true. But after all we are not children, not illiterate juvenile delinquents, not English public school boys who after a night of homosexual romps have to endure the paradox of reading the Ancients in expurgated versions.

It is childish to study a work of fiction in order to gain information about a country or about a social class or about the author. And yet one of my very few intimate friends, after reading *Lolita*, was sincerely worried that I (I!) should be living "among such depressing people"—when the only discomfort I really experienced was to live in my workshop among discarded limbs and unfinished torsos.

After Olympia Press, in Paris, published the book, an American critic suggested that *Lolita* was the record of my love affair with the romantic novel. The substitution "English language" for "romantic novel" would make this elegant formula more correct. But here I feel my voice rising to a much too strident pitch. None of my American friends have read my Russian books and thus every appraisal on the strength of my English ones is bound to be out of focus. My private tragedy, which cannot, and indeed should not, be anybody's concern, is that I had to abandon my natural idiom, my untrammeled, rich, and infinitely docile Russian tongue for a second-rate brand of English, devoid of any of those apparatuses—the baffling mirror, the black velvet backdrop, the implied associations and traditions—which the native illusionist, frac-tails flying, can magically use to transcend the heritage in his own way.

Saul Bellow (1915–2005) was a Nobel Prize in Literature win-ner and one of America's greatest fiction writers in our time. His masterly novels (such as The Adventures of Augie March, Seize the Day, Henderson the Rain King, Herzog, *and* Humboldt's Gift*) display not only a magnificently fluent prose style but a capturing of the dance of thought on the page that might well be described as essayistic. If he poured his best reflective energies into his fiction, he also wrote many full-voiced, humorous, astute essays, which were collected posthumously in the aptly named* There Is Simply Too Much to Think About.

THE UNIVERSITY AS VILLAIN

Are writers greatly harmed by teaching in universities? The first reply that comes to me is that a man may make a damn fool of himself anywhere.

But the question probably deserves more serious considera-tion. Any number of serious people have given it their best thought. Some believe it is harmful beyond measure, others that nothing can be nicer for both the writers and the universities. I was once told by Nelson Algren, "Some teach school; some would rather run a poker game." Poker is probably better but not everyone can be so lucky. I am too stupid a poker player to make a living at cards.

Exactly twenty years ago I graduated from Northwestern University. Of those twenty years five or six have been given to teaching, the rest to writing, and I think I am able to weigh the arguments of either side with an equal hand.

In 1952, when I was teaching at Princeton, I met in New York a man I had known in Chicago in less happy times (for me) when he was connected with the University of Chicago and I was connected with nothing. He had been one of Chancellor Robert Maynard Hutchins's assistants; now he was near the summit of a huge advertising corporation in New York. We had always been fond of each other and we met with pleasure. He was dressed in such high style that I could hardly keep from touching his tweed. He had a fine red, conservative straight face and was smoking the biggest and shiningest pipe that Madison Avenue had to sell, so there was no need for me to ask how *he* was doing.

"But what are *you* up to these days?" he said.

"Well," I told him, "you'll find it hard to believe, but this year I am teaching at Princeton."

It had never occurred to him that I might be connected with anything so classy and because of his respect for higher learning, probably absorbed from the chancellor, he was upset. So I was very sorry and I said, "It's only temporary."

"What do your academic colleagues think about this?" he said.

"Oh, it's probably a joke to them, but they still have most of the joint to themselves. What's the matter, Mack? Why does this bother you?"

"Well," he said, "writers have always come out of the gutter. The gutter is their proper place."

I can't think just now which of the one hundred Great Books of the Western World contains this historic idea. But perhaps the books were not to blame at all. And in justice to my friend I must make it clear that he was not upset because of the academic colleagues alone; he viewed the matter also from my side—a little. He seemed to feel that society was right to build universities to shelter men of learning and to pay them and protect them and keep them. It could not, however, do this for writers. It could not be friendly to them without softening and taming them and making them fat, checking their necessary vices, damaging their freedom and harmfully curbing their madness.

But I have seen full-blown lunatics in universities, too, and as for the vices, they may be found on the campus not less than on the Bowery. It seemed crazy to explain to the executive of a large corporation how powerfully pervasive life could be; and I didn't think it would be suitable to tell the chancellor's former assistant that his implied view of professors was not flattering. Were they fat, tame and lazy, or did they take no harm from the special protection of society? Were they too good for the gutter, or not good enough for it? How was it that a philosopher might live in the *tour d'ivoire* whereas a writer belonged out in the *marais de merde* by which Flaubert thought the tower to be surrounded?

Sharp questions. Too bad they didn't come to me then. But I like to continue old debates in my mind and today I can tell Mack that the old tower ain't what it used to be. From its remoteness there now come things like rocket-launched satellites that loop over us, the writers, as we sit in our gutters playing poker.

I will certainly hear it argued that professors of physics and professors of literature are altogether different, and it must be conceded right away that the differences are great. For the professor of physics is reinforced, as animal psychologists might put it, by a sense of being needed (by the Air Force and the Navy and Oak Ridge), whereas the professor of literature is likely to feel that the dull canal, all that remains of the once sweet Thames, is his only portion, and that he is foolishly watching the rats in the vegetation while he ponders the problem of Hamlet's uncle, unrelated to the gas tanks behind him and Sputnik overhead. Professors of humanities often have a keen sense of their inferiority to the great mass of Americans. Is the real realer where the mass is thicker? So they seem to believe. Perhaps, too, it is their feeling that there is something shameful for grown men in sitting with a parcel of kids in a corner. Callicles in the *Gorgias* accuses Socrates of doing just that. To which Socrates replies that if you follow Philosophy you must give it what it calls for. It is true that in the English departments to which writers find their way, there are sometimes to be found discouraged people who stand dully upon a brilliant plane, in charge of masterpieces but not themselves inspired, people who are to literature what Samuel Butler's clergymen were to religion. But belief does not end with the Reverend Pontifex nor literature with Professor This-or-That. If the professor will not give it what it calls for, somebody else will. And the writer, if he is a lively soul, does not need to feel so depressed. If he knows his own mind and if the university thinks it can get along with him—well, why not?

He will very often find good conversation in university communities, and he may find a Whitehead or an Einstein as well worth writing about as saloonkeepers or big-game hunters. Everything depends on the amount of energy he has the boldness to release, regardless of the restraints of his environment. Is he more likely to achieve this boldness in Greenwich Village; in the air; on the water; in the "literary life"; in the mines; on an assembly line?

If you, the writer, love rough company and need to knock around, why then, do as Walt Whitman did, go into the streets, ride up and down Broadway or go and dig clams. But under no circumstances should you select any of these things deliberately and do them for the sake of writing. *What* an idea! You must give the thing what it calls for. But there is no prescription to follow.

A man's life from the standpoint of Experience—and it is a notion about Experience which is at the heart of the gutter position—is made up from varied and balanced experiences of a specified sort. There are people who are intensely proud of having met the specifications and who have made very special efforts in the fields of sex, drunkenness, violence and even poverty. Not to have met these specifications can be, for them, a source of shame. The shame of never having been down and out! I have heard young fellows boast that they had been on the bum and that they have been run in for panhandling (not that there were no checks from home). I have even been envied my good luck in having grown up during the Depression.

Now I don't want to make jokes on serious matters, and it is serious when people feel that they must be able to demonstrate that reality has happened to them, certified and approved reality in the form of Experience. Have they met life, not fled it? That's fine. Very good. But Experience in this aspect is something resembling a merit badge; something like a commodity. Let us admit it, Experience with the capital E *is* something of a writer's commodity and the reason for this, I think, is that modern fiction has taken it upon itself to show experience as ever new and ever valuable. The very form of fiction is that of experience itself. Everything is to be viewed as though for the first time. The representation of things is imperative, for the things of a modern man's life are important. They are important because man's career on this earth is held to be important. Literature has been committed to the assertion of this importance for a long time. Unquestioned value. But what is the source of the value?

For some time now the whole fictional enterprise has been running backward. It is not importance that illuminates the facts. The facts as facts are assumed to be important. We bring forward characters, enumerate the facts and try to put it over on everyone that such numbering or naming is all that is necessary.

"He opened the door." Did he, now?

"She lit his cigarette." So what?

It is assumed that these declarations are important or will seem so. But why? Documentation, observation, details of action cannot by themselves give life, no matter how authentic or faithful to experience they may be. You can't construct a tree with twigs. You cannot give importance to events by the authority of Experience, merely.

The life of a civilized man is, increasingly, an internalized one, and toward this internalized life writers have been encouraged to take a gross and foolish attitude. They are the playboys of Experience. More Lord Byron? More Kipling? More *Noa Noa*? More Zola? These are very old-fashioned postures. It is ridiculous for writers to continue them.

Well now, does it harm writers to teach in universities? I am not sure the question is a real one. It is to some extent a *postural* question. It assumes that by doing the right things we get the desired results. Those right things are conventional. Leave your hometown; don't leave your hometown; don't write for the movies; travel; don't be a sissy; don't tie yourself down—and you will turn out fine. But the wind of the spirit is capricious. I have known men of foresight who avoided every trap of bourgeois life, some after the manner of Rimbaud, and some after the manner of Baudelaire; I have known faithful followers of Fitzgerald and Hemingway, and D. H. Lawrence–men, *semper fidelis*, grown old and wrinkled and red-nosed and cat-whiskered and bad-tempered. But that wind! It bloweth where it listeth. And in the end a correct posture can give you nothing more than the satisfaction that comes of fidelity to good form.

It is not easy to find the right way. You must learn to govern yourself, you must learn autonomy, you must manage your freedom or drown in it. You may strain the will after Experience because you need it for your books. Or you may perish under the heavy weight of Culture. You may make a fool of yourself anywhere. You may find illumination anywhere—in the gutter, in the college, in the corporation, in a submarine, in the library. No one man holds a patent on it. No man knows what it is likely to tell him to do. For this reason universities and corporations may find the illuminable type unreliable from a *personnel* point of view. A writer may do better in the anxiety of the gutter; he may do better in the heavy security of the college. Despite the purity of your posture he may do well. It's up to the spirit, altogether, and the spirit prints no timetable.

*Lionel Trilling (1905–1975) was a distinguished critic and professor, and a living embodiment of the liberal humanist tradition (*The Liberal Imagination, Beyond Culture, Sincerity and Authenticity*). Writing essays in journals such as* Partisan Review *and* Commentary, *he mastered a style of measured inquiry, often questioning received opinion with an internal argument. Circling some paradox, he would consider the contentious relationships between art and life, social thought and literature, manners and history. In analyzing the controversial* Lolita, *he knew he was on dangerous ground and took a characteristic approach of disentangling patiently, strand by strand, the categories and concerns that the novel evoked.*

THE LAST LOVER

I

Vladimir Nabokov's novel *Lolita* was first published in Paris in 1955. Its reputation was not slow to reach the country in which it had been written and in which, presumably, it could not be published. Reviews of the book appeared in some of the more advanced literary journals, and in 1956 the *Anchor Review* published a sizable portion of the novel, together with a thoughtful comment on the whole work by F. W. Dupee. Copies of the book in the Olympia Press edition were brought back to the United States by returning travelers and were passed from hand to hand in a manner somewhat reminiscent of the early circulation of *Ulysses* in the 1920s and *Lady Chatterley's Lover* in the 1930s.

I use the qualifying "somewhat" because the borrowing and lending of *Lolita* did not proceed in the aura of righteous indignation which had attended the private circulation of the two earlier books. The bland acceptance of what would once have been called censorship and denounced as such—actually there never was an American legal ruling on *Lolita*, only a caginess on the part of the American publishers—was perhaps the result of a general cultural change from the 1920s and 1930s, an aspect of the diminished capacity for indignation that has often been noted of the 1950s. Or it may imply the recognition that Mr. Nabokov's book, in tune with the temper of the times, is very much less weighty and solemn than Joyce's or Lawrence's, that it does not proclaim itself to be, and is not, a work of genius. Or, again, it may suggest that readers have discovered that *Lolita* really is, as the conditions of its first publication would lead us to suppose, a shocking and scandalous book.

Certainly its scandalous reputation was affirmed by the action of the French government in suppressing it. When I was in Paris not long after its publication I tried to buy a copy, and as I stood at that foremost counter in Galignani's on which are piled the standard dirty books for English and American tourists, I was told by the clerk that the sale of *Lolita* had been made illegal just the day before. This was at a time when the French were going in for suppressing books on a rather large scale. I heard it said that they were doing so in response to representations made by the English government, which was concerned to stop the flow of indecent or questionable literature across the Channel. Perhaps this was true, although it is really not necessary to account in any special and elaborate way for the displays of literary squeamishness that the French make every now and then. But this time their heart was not in it, and shortly after my visit *Lolita* became again available.

So much for the pre-history of *Lolita*. Now the book has been brought out by an American publishing firm of entire respectability and everyone may buy it and read it and judge it for himself.

The legitimizing of *Lolita* must not mislead us about its nature. It must not tempt us into taking the correct enlightened attitude—"Well, now, what was all the fuss about? Here is the book brought into the full light of day, and of course we can very plainly see that there is nothing shocking about it." The fact is that *Lolita* is indeed a shocking book. It means to be shocking and it succeeds in its intention.

But it is not shocking in the way that books which circulate in secret are usually said to be shocking. I shall presently try to say in what ways—there are several—the book does, or should, shock us. Now I shall simply report that *Lolita* is not pornographic as that word would be used in any legal complaint that might conceivably be made against it.

I specify the legal use of the word in order to distinguish that from my own use of it. As I use the word, its meaning is neutrally descriptive, not pejorative.* I take it to mean the explicit representation in literature (or the graphic arts—or music, for that matter) of the actual sexual conduct of human beings. (I suppose I should include anthropomorphic gods, demons, etc.) It seems to me that this representation is a perfectly acceptable artistic enterprise. I expect that, if it is carried out with some skill, it will raise lustful thoughts in the reader, and I believe that this in itself provides no ground for objection.

I should like to be entirely clear on this point. I am not taking the position of liberal and progressive lawyers and judges. I am not saying that literature should be permitted its moments of pornography because such moments are essential to the moral truth which a particular work of literature is aiming at; or because they are essential to its objective truth; or because, when taken in context, they cannot really arouse the normal mature reader to thoughts of lust. I am saying that I see no reason in morality (or in aesthetic theory) why literature should not have as one of its intentions the arousing of thoughts of lust. It is one of the effects, perhaps one of the functions, of literature to

---

* I am aware that a pejorative meaning is, as it were, built into the word, that it derives from *porne*, the Greek word for prostitute. But we have no other word to express the idea; and the attempt to invent a prettier one is bound to compromise the position I wish to maintain.

arouse desire, and I can discover no ground for saying that sexual pleasure should not be among the objects of desire which literature presents to us, along with heroism, virtue, peace, death, food, wisdom, God, etc.

This, as I say, is not the position taken by the liberal lawyers and judges. And having read a good many of the American legal opinions in matters of literary censorship, I have come to think that the liberal line of argument, although it comes out on the right side in some ways, is shallow and evasive. I have been told by lawyers that there is no other way for them to go about things, that they must defend indicted books by taking a hypocritical view of their sexual passages, owlishly arguing that these passages when "read in context" have no special significance or effect, that they are "essential" to the "total artistic effect of the work." No doubt the forensic necessity is what the lawyers say it is, but their submission to it does not advance the cause of honesty.

My position in this matter does not lead me to argue that censorship is always indefensible. My use of the word "pornographic" follows, of course, that of D. H. Lawrence in his famous essay "Pornography and Obscenity," and I go along with Lawrence in distinguishing the pornographic from the obscene. It seems to me that if we are going to be frank in our demand that sexuality be accepted as an element of human life which should be available to literature like any other, we must be no less frank in recognizing its unique nature as a literary subject. For most people it is the very most interesting subject, the subject that is most sought for, even though with shame and embarrassment. It is, if we look at it truthfully, a uniquely influential subject— no part of the individual life is so susceptible to literature as the sexual expectations and emotions. As Lawrence said in effect, there are discriminations to be made among kinds of lust, of which some tend to humanize, others to dehumanize us. This gives society an unusually high stake in sexuality as a literary subject, and although I have no great confidence in the ability of society, through the agency of the courts of law, to make the discrimination accurately, it seems to me natural that the effort at discrimination should be made, and appropriate that it should be made through the courts.

The purpose of my digression on censorship is simply to make plain the grounds for my saying that in the sense in which the courts use the word, it is not possible to call *Lolita* a pornographic book. It is, to be sure, the story of an erotic episode, and the story is told in such a way that erotic emotions and sensations are always before the reader. By my own definition of pornography, there is one scene to which the word can be applied—other readers may perhaps find more—but it is unlikely that any court, working under the standards of acceptation that have been established over the last few years, would apply the word in the legal sense even to that scene. And, indeed, *Lolita* takes very little of the wide latitude in the representation of sexual behavior that is nowadays permitted to fiction, in point either of language or of explicitness of description.

That is what I mean when I say that if *Lolita* is, as I have called it, a shocking book, it is not for the reason that books are commonly thought to be shocking.

II

Lolita is the story of the love of a man in his forties for a girl of twelve. The narrative is in the first person, the memoir or confession of the lover, written by him while awaiting trial for murder. Upon his sudden death before the trial begins, his manuscript is edited by John Ray, Jr., Ph.D., presumably a professor of psychology.

Humbert Humbert is the fictitious name under which the narrator presents himself. It is, as the "editor" remarks in his solemn preface, a bizarre name, and Humbert himself says that of the possible pseudonyms that had occurred to him, this one "expresses the nastiness best." It is in some way indicative of his nature that he takes a kind of pleasure in its being misheard and misremembered; he adopts the distortions and represents himself variously as Humbug, Humbird, Humburger, Hamburg,

Homberg. He is, as the editor says, "a mixture of ferocity and jocularity that betrays supreme misery perhaps, but is not conducive to attractiveness." He is indeed anything but attractive. The jocularity can sometimes rise to wit, sometimes to wildness, but it can also sink to facetiousness and reach the brink of silliness. Humbert is a man without friends, and he desires none. His characteristic mode of thought is contemptuous and satirical, but we do not know what makes his standard of judgment, for it is never clear what, besides female beauty of a certain kind, has ever won his admiration. His ferocity takes the form of open brutality to women. He is the less attractive by reason of the style in which he chiefly writes about himself—whoever has tried to keep a journal and has been abashed at reading it by the apologetic, self-referring, self-exculpating whine of the prose, and by the very irony which is used to modify this deplorable tone, will recognize the manner of most of *Lolita*. Humbert himself recognizes it and asks forgiveness for it—he is nothing if not self-conscious and he is as self-contemptuous as he is self-defensive.

By no means attractive, then. Yet he does not fail to effect an intimacy with us. His unrelenting self-reference, his impious greediness, seduce us into kinship with him. He is in every way a nonhero, an anti-hero; but his lack of all admirable qualities leaves perfectly clear—was no doubt devised to leave perfectly clear—the force of the obsessive passion of which he is capable.

Humbert is the son of a generally European (Swiss, French, Austrian, Danubian) father, who owned a luxury hotel on the Riviera, and of an English mother. His European birth and rearing are of considerable importance, for if the narrative is primarily the history of his love affair with an American girl-child, it is incidentally the history of his love affair with America. It is a relationship sufficiently ambivalent, charged with as much scorn and dislike as tenderness and affection, but perhaps for that reason the more interesting, and yielding a first-rate account of the life of the American road, of hotels and motels, of dead towns and flashy resorts, of skating rinks and tourist caves, of Coke machines and jukeboxes, of all that pertains to mobility and transience, to youth and uninvolvement.

By the time he has reached maturity HH (as he sometimes

calls himself) has come to the realization of the most important fact about his nature. Grown women repel him, not in the degree that he cannot have sexual relations with them, but in the degree that they can give him no pleasure. His sexual desire can be aroused and truly gratified only by girls between the ages of nine and fourteen.

The social sanctions against the indulgence of this taste being of the most extreme sort, HH lives a deprived life. On several occasions he has had to take refuge in mental hospitals. He makes no great claims for his sanity, all he insists on is the madness of psychiatrists, and it is a chief dogma of his view of his erotic idiosyncrasy that no explanation of it can possibly be made. He tells us that his "very photogenic mother died in a freak accident (picnic, lightning)" when he was three, and nothing seems to him more absurd than the idea that his passional life might have been influenced by this event. It is probable that the author does not intend an irony here, that he quite agrees with Humbert in thinking the idea comical.

But Humbert does trace the strict condition imposed upon his love to a childhood episode, to his first passionate attachment, experienced as a boy one summer on the Riviera. The object of his passion, who reciprocated it, was a little girl named Annabel, who soon after died of typhus. Her name and her fate are significant, intended to recall the Annabel Lee of Poe's poem. The marriage of Poe to the fourteen-year-old Virginia Clemm is touched upon several times in the course of the story, and can, I think, be made to throw light on what the novel is up to.

The image of the lost Annabel fixes itself upon HH's mind. To girls of her kind, having her beauty, charm, and sexual responsiveness, he gives the name "nymphets." "Between the age limits of nine and fourteen there occur maidens who, to certain bewitched travellers, twice or many times older than they, reveal their true nature which is not human, but nymphic (that is, demoniac); and those chosen creatures I propose to designate as 'nymphets.'" [The accent should probably come on the first syllable, otherwise we get, as someone pointed out to me when I put it on the second, the heavy sound and eventually the ugly appearance of "nymphette," which must inevitably suggest the very opposite

of a nymphet, a drum-majorette.] The further description of the
nymphet emphasizes the demoniac quality—"the fey grace, the
elusive, shifty, soul-shattering, insidious charm"—upon which
the Greeks based their idea of the disease of nympholepsy and
later peoples their conceptions of Undines, Belles Dames Sans
Merci, and White Goddesses.

In middle age, in a New England town, Humbert discovers
Dolores Haze, called Lolita, a middle-class schoolgirl of twelve,
and conceives for her an irresistible desire. In order to be near
Lolita and to make opportunity to possess her, Humbert marries
her mother. It cannot be said that he exactly murders his new
wife—it is only that, having read his diary in which he had set
forth his reasons for marrying her and the details of his dislike of
her, she runs distractedly out of the house and is providentially
hit by a passing car. The way is now quite clear for the stepfather.
Believing that Lolita's innocence must not be offended, he has for
some time made elaborate plans to drug the child, but in the end
it is Lolita who ravishes Humbert; a month at a summer camp
had served to induct her into the mysteries of sex, which to her
are no mysteries at all, and she considers that HH is rather lacking in address.

The relation that is now established between Humbert and
Lolita is of a double kind. His sexual obsession, so far from abat-
ing, grows by what it feeds on. Lolita accepts his sensuality with
cool acquiescence, and even responds to it physically, but she
is not moved by desire, and she is frequently bored and has to
be bribed into compliance. Sensuality, however, does not com-
prise the whole of Humbert's feeling. He is *in loco parentis*—
I have forgotten whether or not he makes a joke on this—and his
emotions are in some part paternal. Lolita passes for his daughter, and his brooding concern for her, his jealousy of her interest in other males, his nervous desire to please or to placate her,
constitute a mode of behavior not very different from that of
any American father to his adolescent daughter. Nor is Lolita's
response to Humbert very different from that which American
girls of her age make to their fathers. She maintains toward him
the common alternation of remote indifference and easy accep-

tance, and finds his restriction of her freedom a burden which is not much lightened by his indulgence.

Inevitably, of course, she undertakes to "get away," and inevitably she makes another man the instrument of an escape from a tyranny which for her is less that of a lover than of a father. All Humbert's jealous fantasies come true; Lolita takes up with a perverse middle-aged playwright—who is as much concerned to torture Humbert as to win Lolita—and after a period of very skillful deception, runs off with her lover. Her desertion of Humbert brings his life to an end and he exists only to dream of regaining her love and of destroying her seducer. After the passage of some years, he does at last find Lolita; she is married, not to the perverse lover but to a deaf and worthy young technician, by whom she is pregnant. At seventeen, her status as a nymphet has quite gone, yet for Humbert her charm is unabated, still absolute. It is so even though he observes "how womanish and somehow never seen that way before was the shadowy division between her pale breasts." He begs her to return to him. She refuses—it is to her a surprising idea that he loves her or had ever loved her: she is as unrecognizing of his feeling for her as if she were indeed his daughter—and Humbert goes off to murder the playwright. We learn from the editor's preface that Lolita dies in childbed. Humbert dies of heart disease.

III

This, then, is the story of *Lolita* and it is indeed shocking. In a tone which is calculatedly not serious, it makes a prolonged assault on one of our unquestioned and unquestionable sexual prohibitions, the sexual inviolability of girls of a certain age (and compounds the impiousness with what amounts to incest).

It is all very well for us to remember that Juliet was fourteen when she was betrothed to Paris and gave herself, with our full approval, to Romeo. It is all very well for us to find a wry idyllic charm in the story of the aged David and the little maid Abishag. And gravely to receive Dante's account of being struck to the heart by an eight-year-old Beatrice. And to say that distant cultures—HH gives a list of them to put his idiosyncrasy in some moral perspective—and hot climates make a difference in ideas of the right age for female sexuality to begin. All very well for us to have long ago got over our first horror at what Freud told us about the sexuality of children, and to receive blandly what he has told us about the "family romance" and its part in the dynamics of the psyche. All very well for the family and society to take approving note of the little girl's developing sexual charms, to find a sweet comedy in her growing awareness of them and her learning to use them, and for her mother to be open and frank and delighted and ironic over the teacups about the clear signs of the explosive force of her sexual impulse. We have all become so nicely clear-eyed, so sensibly Coming-of-Age-in-Samoa. But let an adult male seriously think about the girl as a sexual object and all our sensibility is revolted.

The response is not reasoned but visceral. Within the range of possible heterosexual conduct, this is one of the few prohibitions which still seem to us to be confirmed by nature itself. Virginity once seemed so confirmed, as did the marital fidelity of women, but they do so no longer. No novelist would expect us to respond with any moral intensity to his representing an unmarried girl having a sexual experience, whether in love or curiosity; the infidelity of a wife may perhaps be a little more interesting, but not much. The most serious response the novelist would expect from us is that we should "understand," which he would count on us to do automatically.

But our response to the situation that Mr. Nabokov presents to us is that of shock. And we find ourselves the more shocked when we realize that, in the course of reading the novel, we have come virtually to condone the violation it presents. Charles Dickens, by no means a naïve man, was once required to meet a young woman who had lived for some years with a man out of wedlock; he was dreadfully agitated at the prospect, and when he met the girl he was appalled to discover that he was not confronting a piece of depravity but a principled, attractive young person, virtually a lady. It was a terrible blow to the certitude of his moral feelings. That we may experience the same loss of certitude about the sexual behavior that *Lolita* describes is perhaps suggested by the tone of my summary of the story—I was plainly not able to muster up the note of moral outrage. And it is likely that any reader of *Lolita* will discover that he comes to see the situation as less and less abstract and moral and horrible, and more and more as human and "understandable." Less and less, indeed, do we see a *situation*; what we become aware of is people. Humbert is perfectly willing to say that he is a monster; no doubt he is, but we find ourselves less and less eager to say so. Perhaps his depravity is the easier to accept when we learn that he deals with a Lolita who is not innocent, and who seems to have very few emotions to be violated; and I suppose we naturally incline to be lenient toward a rapist—legally and by intention HH is that—who eventually feels a deathless devotion to his victim!

But we have only to let the immediate influence of the book diminish a little with time, we have only to free ourselves from the rationalizing effect of HH's obsessive passion, we have only to move back into the real world where twelve-year-olds are being bored by Social Studies and plagued by orthodonture, to feel again the outrage at the violation of the sexual prohibition. And to feel this the more because we have been seduced into conniving in the violation, because we have permitted our fantasies to accept what we know to be revolting.

What, we must ask, is Mr. Nabokov's purpose in making this occasion for outrage?

I have indicated that his purpose cannot be explained by any interest in the "psychological" aspects of the story; he has none whatever. His novel is as far as possible from being a "study of" the emotions it presents. The malice which HH bears to psychiatry is quite Mr. Nabokov's own; for author as for character, psychiatric concepts are merely occasions for naughty irreverence. Psychiatry and the world may join in giving scientific or ugly names to Humbert's sexual idiosyncrasy; the novel treats of it as a condition of love like another.

And we can be sure that Mr. Nabokov has not committed himself to moral subversion. He is not concerned to bring about a sexual revolution which will make pedophilia a rational and respectable form of heterosexuality. Humbert's "ferocity and jocularity," what we might call his moral facetiousness reaching the point of anarchic silliness, make the pervasive tone of the narrative, and that tone does have its curious influence upon us, as does the absoluteness of Humbert's passional obsession. Yet any anarchic power to which we may respond in the novel is quite negated when, near the end of the history, HH reflects, in a tone never used before, on the havoc he has made of Lolita's life.

It is of course possible that Mr. Nabokov wanted to shock us merely for shocking's sake, that he had in mind the intention of what might be called general satire, the purpose of which is to make us uneasy with ourselves, less sure of our moral simplicity than we have been: this he brings about by contriving the effect I have described, of leading us to become quite at ease with a sexual situation that should outrage us and then facing us with our facilely given acquiescence.

And then of course Mr. Nabokov may be intending a more particular satire, upon the peculiar sexual hypocrisy of American life. I have in mind the perpetual publicity we give to sexuality, the unending invitation made by our popular art and advertising to sexual awareness, competence, and competition. To what end is a girl-child taught from her earliest years to consider the brightness and fragrance of her hair, and the shape of her body, and her look of readiness for adventure? Why, what other end than that she shall someday be a really capable airline hostess? Or that she shall have the shining self-respect which, as we know, underlies all true virtue and efficiency? Or that her husband and her children shall not be ashamed of her but, on the contrary, proud to claim her as their own? So say the headmistresses, the principals, the deans of women, the parents. But in every other culture that Mr. Nabokov is aware of, which is a good many, the arts of the boudoir were understood to point to the bed, and if they were taught early, they were understood to point to the bed early.

But I think that the real reason why Mr. Nabokov chose his outrageous subject matter is that he wanted to write a story about love.

IV

Lolita is about love. Perhaps I shall be better understood if I put the statement in this form: *Lolita* is not about sex, but about love. Almost every page sets forth some explicit erotic emotion or some overt erotic action and still it is not about sex. It is about love.

This makes it unique in my experience of contemporary novels. If our fiction gives accurate testimony, love has disappeared from the Western world, just as Denis de Rougemont said it should. The contemporary novel can tell us about sex, and about sexual communion, and about mutuality, and about the strong fine relationships that grow up between men and women; and it can tell us about marriage. But about love, which was once one of its chief preoccupations, it can tell us nothing at all.

My having mentioned Denis de Rougemont and his curious, belated, supererogatory onslaught on love will indicate that I have in mind what I seem to remember he calls passion-love, a kind of love with which European literature has dealt since time immemorial but with especial intensity since the Arthurian romances and the code of courtly love. Passion-love was a mode of feeling not available to everyone—the authorities on the subject restricted it to the aristocracy—but it was always of the greatest interest to almost everyone who was at all interested in the feelings, and it had a continuing influence on other kinds of love and on the literary conventions through which love was represented.

The essential condition of this kind of love was that it had nothing to do with marriage and could not possibly exist in marriage. Alanus Capellanus in his manual on courtly love set it down as perfectly obvious doctrine that a husband and wife cannot be lovers. The reason was that theirs was a practical and contractual relationship, having reference to estates and progeny. It was not a relation of the heart, and the inclination and the situation of the lady made it impossible for her to give herself in free will because it was expected that she give herself in obedience. That the possibility of love could exist only apart from and more or less in opposition to marriage has been, by and large, the traditional supposition of the European upper classes, which have placed most of their expectations of erotic pleasure outside of marriage.

It was surely one of the most interesting and important of cultural revisions when the middle classes, which had been quite specifically excluded from the pleasure and dignity of love (one cannot be both busy and a lover), began to appropriate the prestige of this mode of feeling and to change it in the process of adopting it. For they assimilated it to marriage itself, and required of married love that it have the high brilliance and significance of passion-love. Something of that expectation still persists—it is still the love-poetry and the love-music and the love-dramas of passion-love in its later forms that shape our notions of what the erotic experience can be in intensity, in variety, in grace.

But inevitably the sexual revolution of our time brought the relationship between marriage and passion-love to a virtual end. Perhaps all that the two now have in common is the belief that the lovers must freely choose each other and that their choice has the highest sanctions and must not be interfered with. Apart from this, every aspect of the new relationship is a denial of the old ideal of love. If one can rely on the evidence of fiction to discover the modern idea of the right relation between a man and a woman, it would probably begin with a sexual meeting, more or less tentative or experimental, and go on to sexual communion, after which marriage would take place. There would follow a period in which husband and wife would each make an effort to get rid of their *merely symbolic* feelings for the other *partner* in the marriage and to learn to see each other *without illusion* and as they are *in reality*. To do this is the sign of *maturity*. It enables husband and wife to *build a life together*. In the *mutuality* and *warmth* of their *togetherness* their children are included. Toward each other, as toward their children, they show *tolerance* and *understanding*, which they find it easier to do if they have a *good sexual relationship*.

The condition toward which such a marriage aspires is *health*—a marriage is praised by being called a *healthy* marriage. This will suggest how far the modern ideal of love is from passion-love. The literal meaning of the word "passion" will indicate the distance. Nowadays we use the word chiefly to mean an intense feeling, forgetting the old distinction between a passion and an emotion, the former being an emotion before which we are helpless, which we have to *suffer*, in whose grip we are *passive*. The passion-lover was a sick man, a *patient*. It was the convention for him to say that he was sick and to make a show of his physical and mental derangement. And indeed by any modern standard of emotional health what he was expected to display in the way of obsessional conduct and masochism would make his condition deserve some sort of pretty grave name. His passion filled his whole mind to the exclusion of everything else; he submitted himself to his *mistress* as her *servant*, even her *slave*, he gloried in her *power* over him and expected that she would make him suffer, that she would be *cruel*.

Obviously I am dealing with a convention of literature, not describing the actual relationship between men and women. But it was a convention of a peculiar explicitness and force and it exerted an influence upon the management of the emotions down through the nineteenth century. At that time, it may be observed, the creative genius took over some of the characteristics of the lover: his obsessiveness, his masochism, his noble subservience to an ideal, and his antagonism to the social conventions, his propensity for making a scandal.

For scandal was of the essence of passion-love, which not only inverted the marital relationship of men and women but subverted marriage itself. It could also subvert a man's social responsibility, his honor. In either case, a scandal resulted, the extent of which measured the force of the love. Typically it led to disaster for the lovers, to death. For one aspect of the pathology of love was that it made of no account certain established judgments, denying the reality and the good of much in the world that is indeed real and good. In this respect lovers were conceived of much as we conceived of the artist—that is, as captivated by a reality and a good that are not of the ordinary world.

Now it may well be that all this is absurd, and really and truly a kind of pathology, and that we are much the better for being quite done with it, and that our contemporary love-ideal of a firm, tolerant, humorous, wry, happy marriage is a great advance from it. The world seems to be agreed that this is so—the evidence is to be found in a wide range of testimony from the most elementary fiction and the simplest handbook of marriage up to psychoanalysis and the works of D. H. Lawrence, for whom "love" was anathema. But the old ideal, as I have said, still has its charm for us—we still understand it in some degree; it still speaks to us of an intensity and grace of erotic emotion and behavior that we do not want to admit is entirely beyond our reach.

If a novelist wanted, for whatever strange reason, to write a novel about the old kind of love, how would he go about it? How would he find or contrive the elements that make love possible?

For example, if love requires scandal, what could the novelist count on to constitute a scandal? Surely not—as I have already suggested—adultery. The very word is archaic; we recognize the possibility of its use only in law or in the past. Marital infidelity is not thought of as necessarily destructive of marriage, and, indeed, the word "unfaithful," which once had so terrible a charge of meaning, begins to sound quaint, seeming to be inappropriate to our modern code. A few years ago William Barrett asked, *à propos* the effect of *Othello* on a modern audience, whether anyone nowadays could really comprehend and be interested in the spectacle of Othello's jealousy. I think that both comprehension and interest are possible. There are more than enough of the old feelings still left—nothing is ever thrown out of the attic of the mind—to permit us to understand perfectly well what Othello feels. Here we must be aware of the difference between life and literature. It is of course not true that people do not feel sexual jealousy; it is still one of the most intense of emotions. But they find it ever harder to believe that they are justified in feeling it, that they do right to give this emotion any authority. A contemporary writer would not be able to interest us in a situation like Othello's because, even if he had proof in his own experience of the actuality of jealousy, he could not give intellectual credence, or expect his readers to give it, to an emotion which in Shakespeare was visceral, unquestionable, of absolute authority.

But the breaking of the taboo about the sexual unavailability of very young girls has for us something of the force that a wife's infidelity had for Shakespeare. HH's relation with Lolita defies society as scandalously as did Tristan's relation with Iseult, or Vronsky's with Anna. It puts the lovers, as lovers in literature must be put, beyond the pale of society.

Then the novelist, if he is to maintain the right conditions for a story of passion-love, must see to it that his lovers do not approach the condition of marriage. That is, their behavior to each other must not be touched by practicality, their virtues must not be of a kind that acknowledges the claims of the world. As soon as mutuality comes in, and common interests, and cooperation, and tolerance, and a concern for each other's welfare or prestige in the world, the ethos of the family, of marriage, has asserted itself and they lose their status of lovers. Their behavior to each other must be precisely not what we call "mature"—they must see each other and the world with the imperious absolutism of children. So that a man in the grip of an obsessional lust and a girl of twelve make the ideal couple for a story about love written in our time. At least at the beginning of his love for Lolita there are no practical moral considerations, no practical personal considerations, that qualify HH's behavior. As for Lolita, there is no possibility of her bringing the relation close to the condition of marriage because she cannot even imagine the female role in marriage. She remains perpetually the cruel mistress; even after her lover has won physical possession of her, she withholds the favor of her feeling, for she has none to give, by reason of her age, possibly by reason of her temperament.

Then the novelist must pay due attention to making the lover's obsession believable and not ridiculous. Nowadays we find it difficult to give credence to the idea that a man might feel that his reason and his very life depended on the response to him of a particular woman. Recently I read *Liber Amoris* with some graduate students and found that they had no understanding whatever of Hazlitt's obsessive commitment to Sarah Walker. They could see no reason why a man could not break the chains of a passion so unrewarding, so humiliating. I later regretted having been cross at their stupidity when I found myself doubting the verisimilitude of Proust's account of the relation of Swann to Odette. But our doubts are allayed if the obsession can be accounted for by the known fact of a sexual peculiarity, an avowed aberration. Pathology naturalizes the strange particularity of the lover's preference.

I may seem to have been talking about *Lolita* as if in writing it Mr. Nabokov had undertaken a job of emotional archaeology. This may not be quite fair to Mr. Nabokov's whole intention, but it does suggest how regressive a book *Lolita* is, how, although it strikes all the most approved modern postures and attitudes, it is concerned to restore a foregone mode of feeling. And in nothing is *Lolita* so archaic as in its way of imaging the beloved. We with our modern latitude in these matters are likely to be amused by the minor details of his mistress's person that caught the lover's fancy in the novels of the nineteenth century—the expressiveness of the eyes, a certain kind of glance, a foot, an ankle, a wrist, an ear, a ringlet; with our modern reader's knowledge of the size and shape of the heroine's breasts, thighs, belly, and buttocks, these seem trifling and beside the point. Yet the interest in the not immediately erotic details of the female person was not forced on the lover or the novelist by narrow conventions; rather, it was an aspect of the fetishism which seems to attend passion-love, a sort of synecdoche of desire, in which the part stands for the whole, and even the glove or the scarf of the beloved has an erotic value. This is the mode of HH's adoration of Lolita, and against the background of his sexual greed, which he calls "ape-like," it comes over us as another reason for being shocked, that in recent fiction no lover has thought of his beloved with so much tenderness, that no woman has been so charmingly evoked, in such grace and delicacy, as Lolita; the description of her tennis game, in which even her racket has an erotic charm, is one of the few examples of rapture in modern writing.

It seems to me that it is impossible to miss the *parti pris* in Mr. Nabokov's archaeological undertaking, the impulse to mock and discredit all forms of progressive rationalism not only because they are stupid in themselves but because they have brought the madness of love to an end. But Mr. Nabokov is not partisan to the point of being dishonest about the true nature of love. It is HH, that mixture of ferocity and jocularity, who reminds us that "love seeketh only self to please. . . . And builds a Hell in

Heaven's despite." The passages in which Humbert gives voice to this judgment are not as well done as one might wish; they stand in an awkward relation to the tone and device of the book. Yet perhaps for that very reason they are the more startling and impressive (if we do not read them in a mood which makes them seem to verge upon the maudlin).

And in the end HH succumbs, and happily, to the dialectic of the history of love. I have represented passion-love as being the antithesis of marriage and as coming to an end when the conditions characteristic of marriage impose themselves, by whatever means, upon the lovers. Yet it is always to marriage that passion-love aspires, unique marriage, ideal marriage, marriage available to no other pair, but marriage nonetheless, with all the cramping vows and habitualness of marriage. And it is just this that HH eventually desires. Mr. Nabokov is, among his other accomplishments, an eminent entomologist and I shall leave it to some really rigorous close-reader of fiction to tell us what an entomological novelist wants us to do with the fact that "nymph" is the name for the young of an insect without complete metamorphosis. Probably nothing. But he is also a scholar of languages and he knows that "nymph" is the Greek word for "bride." He does not impart this information to us, yet he is at pains, as I have remarked, to put us in mind of the rapturous, tortured marriage of Poe and Virginia, and one of his last meditations on Lolita is of the constancy she evokes from him despite the ravages of time having destroyed the old incitements to lust:

> . . . There she was with her ruined looks and her adult, rope-veined narrow hands and her goose-flesh white arms, and her shallow ears, and her unkempt armpits, there she was (my Lolita), hopelessly worn at seventeen, with that baby, dreaming already in her of becoming a big shot and retiring around 2020 A.D.—and I looked and looked at her, and knew as clearly as I know I am to die, that I loved her more than anything I had ever seen or imagined on earth, or hoped for anywhere else. She was only the faint violet whiff and dead leaf echo of the nymphet I had rolled myself upon with such cries in the past; an echo on the brink of a

russet ravine, with a far wood under a white sky, and brown leaves choking the brook and one last cricket in the crisp weeds . . . but thank God it was not that echo alone that I worshipped. What I used to pamper among the tangled vines of my heart, *mon grand péché radieux*, had dwindled in its essence: sterile and selfish vice, all that I cancelled and cursed. You may jeer at me, and threaten to clear the court, but until I am gagged and half-throttled, I will shout my poor truth. I insist the world know how much I loved my Lolita, *this* Lolita, pale and polluted, and big with another's child, but still grey-eyed, still sooty-lashed, still auburn and almond. . . .

I am not sure just how I respond to the moral implication of this passage—I am not sure that with it, as with other passages in which HH speaks of the depth and wild solemnity of his love and remorse, Mr. Nabokov has not laid an emotional trap for the reader, that perhaps HH's last intensities ought not to be received with considerably more irony than at first they call for. I don't say this with the least certitude. It may be that Mr. Nabokov really wants us to believe with entire seriousness that we are witnessing the culmination of HH's moral evolution. Perhaps he even wants us to believe that his ascent from "ape-like" lust to a love which challenges the devils below and the angels up over the sea to ever dissever his soul from the soul of the lovely Annabel Lee constitutes the life cycle of the erotic instinct. I can, I think, manage to take seriously a tragic Humbert, but I find myself easier with Humbert the anti-hero, with Humbert as cousin-german to Rameau's nephew.

I don't want to put my uneasiness with the tragic Humbert as an objection. Indeed, for me one of the attractions of *Lolita* is its ambiguity of tone—which is pretty well exemplified in the passage I have quoted—and its ambiguity of intention, its ability to arouse uneasiness, to throw the reader off balance, to require him to change his stance and shift his position and move on. *Lolita* gives us no chance to settle and sink roots. Perhaps it is the curious moral mobility it urges on us that accounts for its remarkable ability to represent certain aspects of American life.

A. J. Liebling (1904–1963) mastered the art of the lively essay: fluently written, focused on pleasurable activities, and attuned to his readers' enjoyment. A foreign correspondent during World War II, he was a valuable member of The New Yorker *stable of reportorial belletrists that included E. B. White, John McNulty, and Joseph Mitchell. Liebling's specialties were boxing, the press, knavish politicians, New York City, Paris, food, and wine. His collection* Between Meals *starts with the piece below, "A Good Appetite," which the portly Liebling certainly had: he was both gourmet and gourmand. Because of the way he incorporated aspects of his own irrepressible personality into his pieces, he is considered a forerunner of the New Journalism.*

A GOOD APPETITE

The Proust madeleine phenomenon is now as firmly established in folklore as Newton's apple or Watt's steam kettle. The man ate a tea biscuit, the taste evoked memories, he wrote a book. This is capable of expression by the formula TMB, for Taste > Memory > Book. Some time ago, when I began to read a book called *The Food of France*, by Waverley Root, I had an inverse experience: BMT, for Book > Memory > Taste. Happily, the tastes that *The Food of France* re-created for me—small birds, stewed rabbit, stuffed tripe, Côte Rôtie, and Tavel—were more robust than that of the madeleine, which Larousse defines as "a light cake made with sugar, flour, lemon juice, brandy, and eggs." (The quantity of brandy in a madeleine would not furnish a gnat with an alcohol rub.) In the light of what Proust wrote with so mild a stimulus, it is the world's loss that he did not have a heartier appetite.

On a dozen Gardiners Island oysters, a bowl of clam chowder, a peck of steamers, some bay scallops, three sautéed soft-shelled crabs, a few ears of fresh-picked corn, a thin swordfish steak of generous area, a pair of lobsters, and a Long Island duck, he might have written a masterpiece.

The primary requisite for writing well about food is a good appetite. Without this, it is impossible to accumulate, within the allotted span, enough experience of eating to have anything worth setting down. Each day brings only two opportunities for field work, and they are not to be wasted minimizing the intake of cholesterol. They are indispensable, like a prizefighter's hours on the road. (I have read that the late French professional gourmand Maurice Curnonsky ate but one meal a day—dinner. But that was late in his life, and I have always suspected his attainments anyway; so many mediocre witticisms are attributed to him that he could not have had much time for eating.) A good appetite gives an eater room to turn around in. For example, a nonprofessional eater I know went to the Restaurant Pierre, in the Place Gaillon, a couple of years ago, his mind set on a sensibly light meal: a dozen, or possibly eighteen, oysters, and a thick chunk of steak topped with beef marrow, which M. Pierre calls a *Délice de la Villette*—the equivalent of a "Stockyards' Delight." But as he arrived, he heard M. Pierre say to his headwaiter, "Here comes Monsieur L. Those two portions of cassoulet that are left—put them aside for him." A cassoulet is a substantial dish, of a complexity precluding its discussion here. (Mr. Root devotes three pages to the great controversy over what it should contain.) M. Pierre is the most amiable of restaurateurs, who prides himself on knowing in advance what his friends will like. A client of limited appetite would be obliged either to forgo his steak or to hurt M. Pierre's feelings. Monsieur L., however, was in no difficulty. He ate the two cassoulets, as was his normal practice; if he had consumed only one, his host would have feared that it wasn't up to standard. He then enjoyed his steak. The oysters offered no problem, since they present no bulk.

In the heroic age before the First World War, there were men and women who ate, in addition to a whacking lunch and a glorious dinner, a voluminous *souper* after the theater or the other amusements of the evening. I have known some of the survivors, octogenarians of unblemished appetite and unfailing good humor—spry, wry, and free of the ulcers that come from worrying about a balanced diet—but they have had no emulators in France since the doctors there discovered the existence of the human liver. From that time on, French life has been built to an increasing extent around that organ, and a niggling caution has replaced the old recklessness; the liver was the seat of the Maginot mentality. One of the last of the great around-the-clock gastronomes of France was Yves Mirande, a small, merry author of farces and musical-comedy books. In 1955, Mirande celebrated his eightieth birthday with a speech before the curtain of the Théâtre Antoine, in the management of which he was associated with Mme B., a protégée of his, forty years younger than himself. But the theater was only half of his life. In addition, M. Mirande was an unofficial director of a restaurant on the Rue Saint-Augustin, which he had founded for another protégée, also forty years younger than himself; this was Mme G., a Gasconne and a magnificent cook. In the restaurant on the Rue Saint-Augustin, M. Mirande would dazzle his juniors, French and American, by dispatching a lunch of raw Bayonne ham and fresh figs, a hot sausage in crust, spindles of filleted pike in a rich rose *sauce Nantua*, a leg of lamb larded with anchovies, artichokes on a pedestal of foie gras, and four or five kinds of cheese, with a good bottle of Bordeaux and one of champagne, after which he would call for the Armagnac and remind Madame to have ready for dinner the larks and ortolans she had promised him, with a few langoustes and a turbot—and, of course, a fine civet made from the *marcassin*, or young wild boar, that the lover of the leading lady in his current production had sent up from his estate in the Sologne. "And while I think of it," I once heard him say, "we haven't had any woodcock for days, or truffles baked in the ashes, and the cellar is becoming a disgrace—no more 'thirty-fours and hardly any 'thirty-sevens. Last week, I had to offer my publisher a bottle that was far too good for him, simply because there was nothing between the insulting and the superlative."

M. Mirande had to his credit a hundred produced plays, including a number of great Paris hits, but he had just written his first book for print, so he said "my publisher" in a special mock-impressive tone. "An informal sketch for my definitive autobiography," he would say of this production. The informal sketch, which I cherish, begins with the most important decision in Mirande's life. He was almost seventeen and living in the small Breton port of Lannion—his offstage family name was Le Querrec—when his father, a retired naval officer, said to him, "It is time to decide your future career. Which will it be, the Navy or the Church?" No other choice was conceivable in Lannion. At dawn, Yves ran away to Paris.

There, he had read a thousand times, all the famous wits and cocottes frequented the tables in front of the Café Napolitain, on the Boulevard des Capucines. He presented himself at the café at nine the next morning—late in the day for Lannion—and found that the place had not yet opened. Soon he became a newspaperman. It was a newspaper era as cynically animated as the corresponding period of the Bennett-Pulitzer-Hearst competition in New York, and in his second or third job he worked for a press lord who was as notional and niggardly as most press lords are; the publisher insisted that his reporters be well turned out, but did not pay them salaries that permitted cab fares when it rained. Mirande lived near the fashionable Montmartre cemetery and solved his rainy-day pants-crease problem by crashing funeral parties as they broke up and riding, gratis, in the carriages returning to the center of town. Early in his career, he became personal secretary to Clemenceau and then to Briand, but the gay theater attracted him more than politics, and he made the second great decision of his life after one of his political patrons had caused him to be appointed *sous-préfet* in a provincial city. A *sous-préfet* is the administrator of one of the districts into which each of the ninety *départements* of France is divided, and a young *sous-préfet* is often headed for a precocious rise to high positions of state. Mirande, attired in the magnificent uniform that was then de rigueur, went to his "capital," spent one night there, and then ran off to Paris again to direct a one-act farce. Nevertheless, his connections with the serious world remained cordial. In the restaurant on the Rue Saint-Augustin, he introduced me to Colette, by that time a national glory of letters.

The regimen fabricated by Mirande's culinary protégée, Mme. G., maintained him *en pleine forme*. When I first met him, in the restaurant, during the summer of the Liberation, he was a sprightly sixty-nine. In the spring of 1955, when we renewed a friendship that had begun in admiration of each other's appetite, he was as good as ever. On the occasion of our reunion, we began with a *truite au bleu*—a fine trout simply done to death in hot water, like a Roman emperor in his bath. It was served up doused with enough melted butter to thrombose a regiment of Paul Dudley Whites, and accompanied, as was right, by an Alsatian wine—a Lacrimae Sanctae Odiliae, which once contributed slightly to my education. Long ago, when I was very young, I took out a woman in Strasbourg and, wishing to impress her with my knowledge of local customs, ordered a bottle of Ste. Odile. I was making the same mistake as if I had taken out a girl in Boston and offered her baked beans. "How quaint!" the woman in Strasbourg said. "I haven't drunk that for years." She excused herself to go to the telephone, and never came back.

After the trout, Mirande and I had two meat courses, since we could not decide in advance which we preferred. We had a magnificent *daube provençale*, because we were faithful to *la cuisine bourgeoise*, and then *pintadous*—young guinea hens, simply and tenderly roasted—with the first asparagus of the year, to show our fidelity to *la cuisine classique*. We had clarets with both courses—a Pétrus with the *daube*, a Cheval Blanc with the guineas. Mirande said that his doctor had discounseled Burgundies. It was the first time in our acquaintance that I had heard him admit he had a doctor, but I was reassured when he drank a bottle and a half of Krug after luncheon. We had three bottles between us—one to our loves, one to our countries, and one for symmetry, the last being on the house.

Mirande was a small, alert man with the face of a Celtic terrier—salient eyebrows and an upturned nose. He looked like an intelligent Lloyd George. That summer, in association with

Mme B., his theatrical protégée, he planned to produce a new play of Sartre's. His mind kept young by the theater of Mme B., his metabolism protected by the restaurant of Mme G., Mirande seemed fortified against all eventualities for at least another twenty years. Then, perhaps, he would have to recruit new protégées. The Sunday following our reunion, I encountered him at Longchamp, a racecourse where the restaurant does not face the horses, and diners can keep first things first. There he sat, radiant, surrounded by celebrities and champagne buckets, sending out a relay team of commissionaires to bet for him on the successive tips that the proprietors of stables were ravished to furnish him between races. He was the embodiment of a happy man. (I myself had a nice thing at 27–1.)

The first alteration in Mirande's fortunes affected me so directly that I did not at once sense its gravity for him. Six weeks later, I was again in Paris. (That year, I was shuttling frequently between there and London.) I was alone on the evening I arrived, and looked forward to a pleasant dinner at Mme G.'s, which was within two hundred meters of the hotel, in the Square Louvois, where I always stop. Madame's was more than a place to eat, although one ate superbly there. Arriving, I would have a bit of talk with the proprietress, then with the waitresses—Germaine and Lucienne—who had composed the original staff. Waiters had been added as the house prospered, but they were of less marked personality. Madame was a bosomy woman—voluble, tawny, with a big nose and lank black hair—who made one think of a Saracen. (The Saracens reached Gascony in the eighth century.) Her conversation was a chronicle of letters and the theater—as good as a subscription to *Figaro Littéraire*, but more advanced. It was somewhere between the avant-garde and the main body, but within hailing distance of both and enriched with the names of the great people who had been in recently—M. Cocteau, Gene Kelly, la Comtesse de Vogüé. It was always well to give an appearance of listening, lest she someday fail to save for you the last order of larks *en brochette* and bestow them on a more attentive customer. With Germaine and Lucienne, whom I had known when we were all younger, in 1939, the year of the *drôle de guerre*, flirtation was now perfunctory, but the *carte du jour* was still the serious topic—for example, how the fat Belgian industrialist from Tournai had reacted to the *caille vendangeuse*, or quail potted with fresh grapes. "You know the man," Germaine would say. "If it isn't dazzling, he takes only two portions. But when he has three, then you can say to yourself . . ." She and Lucienne looked alike—compact little women, with high foreheads and cheekbones and solid, muscular legs, who walked like *chasseurs à pied*, 130 steps to the minute. In 1939, and again in 1944, Germaine had been a brunette and Lucienne a blonde, but in 1955 Germaine had become a blonde, too, and I found it hard to tell them apart.

Among my fellow customers at Mme G.'s I was always likely to see some friend out of the past. It is a risk to make an engagement for an entire evening with somebody you haven't seen for years. This is particularly true in France now. The almost embarrassingly pro-American acquaintance of the Liberation may be by now a Communist Party–line hack; the idealistic young Resistance journalist may have become an editorial writer for the reactionary newspaper of a textile magnate. The Vichy apologist you met in Washington in 1941, who called de Gaulle a traitor and the creation of the British Intelligence Service, may now tell you that the general is the best thing ever, while the fellow you knew as a de Gaulle aide in London may now compare him to Sulla destroying the Roman Republic. As for the women, who is to say which of them has resisted the years? But in a good restaurant that all have frequented, you are likely to meet any of them again, for good restaurants are not so many nowadays that a Frenchman will permanently desert one—unless, of course, he is broke, and in that case it would depress you to learn of his misfortunes. If you happen to encounter your old friends when they are already established at their tables, you have the opportunity to greet them cordially and to size them up. If you still like them, you can make a further engagement.

On the ghastly evening I speak of—a beautiful one in June—I perceived no change in the undistinguished exterior of Mme G.'s restaurant. The name—something like Prospéria—was the same, and since the plate-glass windows were backed with scrim, it was impossible to see inside. Nor, indeed, did I notice any difference when I first entered. The bar, the tables, the banquettes covered with leatherette, the simple décor of mirrors and pink marble slabs were the same. The premises had been a business employees' bar-and-café before Mme G., succeeding a long string of obscure proprietors, made it illustrious. She had changed the fare and the clientele but not the cadre. There are hundreds of identical fronts and interiors in Paris, turned out by some mass producer in the late twenties. I might have been warned by the fact that the room was empty, but it was only eight o'clock and still light outdoors. I had come unusually early because I was so hungry. A man whom I did not recognize came to meet me, rubbing his hands and hailing me as an old acquaintance. I thought he might be a waiter who had served me. (The waiters, as I have said, were not the marked personalities of the place.) He had me at a table before I sensed the trap.

"Madame goes well?" I asked politely.

"No, Madame is lightly ill," he said, with what I now realize was a guilty air.

He presented me with a *carte du jour* written in the familiar purple ink on the familiar wide sheet of paper with the name and telephone number of the restaurant at the top. The content of the menu, however, had become Italianized, the spelling had deteriorated, and the prices had diminished to a point where it would be a miracle if the food continued distinguished.

"Madame still conducts the restaurant?" I asked sharply.

I could now see that he was a Piedmontese of the most evasive description. From rubbing his hands he had switched to twisting them.

"Not exactly," he said, "but we make the same cuisine."

I could not descry anything in the smudged ink but misspelled noodles and unorthographical "*escaloppinis*"; Italians writing French by ear produce a regression to an unknown ancestor of both languages.

"Try us," my man pleaded, and, like a fool, I did. I was hungry. Forty minutes later, I stamped out into the street as purple as an aubergine with rage. The minestrone had been cabbage scraps in greasy water. I had chosen *côtes d'agneau* as the safest item in the mediocre catalog that the Prospéria's prospectus of bliss had turned into overnight. They had been cut from a tired Alpine billy goat and seared in machine oil, and the haricots verts with which they were served resembled decomposed whiskers from a theatrical-costume beard.

"The same cuisine?" I thundered as I flung my money on the falsified *addition* that I was too angry to verify. "You take me for a jackass!"

I am sure that as soon as I turned my back the scoundrel nodded. The restaurant has changed hands at least once since then.

In the morning, I telephoned Mirande. He confirmed the disaster. Mme G., ill, had closed the restaurant. Worse, she had sold the lease and the goodwill, and had definitely retired.

"What is the matter with her?" I asked in a tone appropriate to fatal disease.

"I think it was trying to read Simone de Beauvoir," he said. "A syncope."

Mme G. still lives, but Mirande is dead. When I met him in Paris the following November, his appearance gave no hint of decline. It was the season for his sable-lined overcoat *à l'impresario*, and a hat that was a furry cross between a porkpie and a homburg. Since the restaurant on the Rue Saint-Augustin no longer existed, I had invited him to lunch with me at a very small place called the Gratin Dauphinois, on the Rue Chabanais, directly across from the building that once housed the most celebrated sporting house in Paris. The Rue Chabanais is a short street that runs from the Square Louvois to the Rue des Petits Champs—perhaps a hundred yards—but before the reform wave stimulated by a municipal councilor named Marthe Richard at the end of the Second World War, the name Chabanais had a cachet all its own. Mme Richard will go down in history as the Carry Nation of sex. Now the house is closed, and the premises are devoted to some low commercial purpose. The walls of the midget Gratin Dauphinois are hung with cartoons that have a nostalgic reference to the past glories of the street.

Mirande, when he arrived, crackled with jokes about the locale. He taunted me with being a criminal who haunts the scene of his misdeeds. The fare at the Gratin is robust, as it is in Dauphine, but it did not daunt Mirande. The wine card, similarly, is limited to the strong, rough wines of Arbois and the like, with a couple of Burgundies for clients who want to show off. There are no clarets; the proprietor hasn't heard of them. There are, of course, a few champagnes, for wedding parties or anniversaries, so Mirande, with Burgundies discounseled by his doctor, decided on champagne throughout the meal. This was a *drôle* combination with the mountain food, but I had forgotten about the lack of claret when I invited him.

We ordered a couple of dozen *escargots en pots de chambre* to begin with. These are snails baked and served, for the client's convenience, in individual earthenware crocks, instead of being forced back into shells. The snail, of course, has to be taken out of his shell to be prepared for cooking. The shell he is forced back into may not be his own. There is thus not even a sentimental justification for his reincarceration. The frankness of the service *en pot* does not improve the preparation of the snail, nor does it detract from it, but it does facilitate and accelerate his consumption. (The notion that the shell proves the snail's authenticity, like the head left on a woodcock, is invalid, as even a suburban housewife knows nowadays; you can buy a tin of snail shells in a supermarket and fill them with a mixture of nutted cream cheese and chopped olives.)

Mirande finished his dozen first, meticulously swabbing out the garlicky butter in each *pot* with a bit of bread that was fitted to the bore of the crock, as precisely as a bullet to a rifle barrel. Tearing bread like that takes practice. We had emptied the first bottle of champagne when he placed his right hand delicately on the point of his waistcoat farthest removed from his spinal column.

"Liebling," he said, "I am not well."

It was like the moment when I first saw Joe Louis draped on the ropes. A great pity filled my heart. "*Maître*," I said, "I will take you home."

The dismayed *patronne* waved to her husband in the kitchen (he could see her through the opening he pushed the dishes through) to suspend the preparation of the *gendarme de Morteau*—the great smoked sausage in its tough skin—that we had proposed to follow the snails with. ("Short and broad in shape, it is made of pure pork and . . . is likely to be accompanied . . . by hot potato salad." —Root, page 217.) We had decided to substitute for the *pommes à l'huile* the *gratin dauphinois* itself. ("Thinly sliced potatoes are moistened with boiled milk and beaten egg, seasoned with salt, pepper, and nutmeg, and mixed with grated cheese, of the Gruyère type. The potatoes are then put into an earthenware dish which has been rubbed with garlic and then buttered, spotted with little dabs of butter, and sprinkled with more grated cheese. It is then cooked slowly in not too hot an oven." —Root, page 228.) After that, we were going to have a fowl in cream with *morilles*—wild black mushrooms of the mountains. We abandoned all.

I led Mirande into the street and hailed a taxi.

"I am not well, Liebling," he said. "I grow old."

He lived far from the restaurant, beyond the Place de l'Etoile, in the Paris of the successful. From time to time on our way, he would say, "It is nothing. You must excuse me. I am not well."

The apartment house in which he and Mme B. lived resembled one of the chic modern museums of the quarter, with entrance gained through a maze of garden patches sheathed in glass. Successive metal grilles swung open before us as I pushed buttons that Mirande indicated—in these modern palaces there are no visible flunkies—until we reached an elevator that smoothly shot us upward to his apartment, which was rather larger in area than the Square Louvois. The décor, with basalt columns and floors covered with the skin of jumbo Siberian tigers—a special strain force-fed to supply old-style movie stars—reminded me of the sets for *Belphégor*, a French serial of silent days that I enjoyed when I was a student at the Sorbonne in 1926. (It was, I think, about an ancient Egyptian high priest who came to life and set up bachelor quarters in Paris in the style of the Temple of Karnak.) Three or four maids rushed to relieve Mirande of his sable-lined coat, his hat, and his cane topped with the horn of an albino chamois. I helped him to a divan on which two Theda Baras could have defended their honor simultaneously against two villains of the silents without either couple's getting in the other's way. Most of the horizontal surfaces in the room were covered with sculpture and most of the vertical ones with large paintings. In pain though he was, Mirande called my attention to these works of art.

"All the sculptures are by Renoir," he said. "It was his hobby. And all the paintings are by Maillol. It was *his* hobby. If it were the other way around, I would be one of the richest chaps in France. Both men were my friends. But then, one doesn't give one's friends one's bread and butter. And, after all, it's less banal as it is."

After a minute, he asked me to help him to his bedroom, which was in a wing of the apartment all his own. When we got there, one of the maids came in and took his shoes off.

"I am in good hands now, Liebling," he said. "Farewell until next time. It is nothing."

I telephoned the next noon, and he said that his doctor, who was a fool, insisted that he was ill.

Again I left Paris, and when I returned, late the following January, I neglected Mirande. A Father William is a comforting companion for the middle-aged—he reminds you that the best is yet to be and that there's a dance in the old dame yet—but a sick old man is discouraging. My conscience stirred when I read in a gossip column in *France-Dimanche* that Toto Mirande was convalescing nicely and was devouring caviar at a great rate— with champagne, of course. (I had never thought of Mirande as Toto, which is baby slang for "little kid," but from then on I never referred to him in any other way; I didn't want anybody to think I wasn't in the know.) So the next day I sent him a pound of fresh caviar from Kaspia, in the Place de la Madeleine. It was the kind of medication I approved of.

I received a note from Mirande by tube next morning, reproaching me for spoiling him. He was going better, he wrote, and would telephone in a day or two to make an appointment for a return bout. When he called, he said that the idiotic doctor would not yet permit him to go out to a restaurant, and he invited me, instead, to a family dinner at Mme B.'s. "Only a few old friends, and not the cuisine I hope to give you at Maxim's next time," he said. "But one makes out."

On the appointed evening, I arrived early—or on time, which amounts to the same thing—chez Mme B.; you take taxis when you can get them in Paris at the rush hours. The handsome quarter overlooking the Seine above the Trocadéro is so dull that when my taxi deposited me before my host's door, I had no inclination to stroll to kill time. It is like Park Avenue or the near North Side of Chicago. So I was the first or second guest to arrive, and Mme B.'s fourteen-year-old daughter, by a past marriage, received me in the Belphégor room, apologizing because her mother was still with Toto—she called him that. She need not have told me, for at that moment I heard Madame, who is famous for her determined voice, storming at an unmistakable someone: "You go too far, Toto. It's disgusting. People all over Paris are kind enough to send you caviar, and because you call it monotonous, you throw it at the maid! If you think servants are easy to come by . . ."

When they entered the room a few minutes later, my old friend was all smiles. "How did you know I adore caviar to such a point?" he asked me. But I was worried because of what I had heard; the Mirande I remembered would never have been irritated by the obligation to eat a few extra kilos of fresh caviar. The little girl, who hoped I had not heard, embraced Toto. "Don't be angry with Maman!" she implored him.

My fellow guests included the youngish new wife of an old former premier, who was unavoidably detained in Lille at a congress of the party he now headed; it mustered four deputies, of whom two formed a Left Wing and two a Right Wing. ("If they had elected a fifth at the last election, or if, by good luck, one had been defeated, they could afford the luxury of a Center," Mirande told me in identifying the lady. "*C'est malheureux*, a party without a Center. It limits the possibilities of maneuver.") There was also an amiable couple in their advanced sixties or beginning seventies, of whom the husband was the grand manitou of Veuve Clicquot champagne. Mirande introduced them by their right name, which I forget, and during the rest of the evening addressed them as M. and Mme Clicquot. There was a forceful, black-haired man from the Midi, in the youth of middle age—square-shouldered, stocky, decisive, blatantly virile—who, I was told, managed Mme B.'s vinicultural enterprises in Provence. There were two guests of less decided individuality, whom I barely remember, and filling out the party were the young girl—shy, carefully unsophisticated and unadorned—Mme B., Mirande, and me. Mme B. had a strong triangular face on a strong triangular base—a strong chin, high cheekbones, and a wide, strong jaw, but full of stormy good nature. She was a woman who, if she had been a man, would have wanted to be called Honest John. She had a high color and an iron hand-grip, and repeatedly affirmed that there was no affectation about her, that she was *sans façon*, that she called her shots as she saw them. "I won't apologize," she said to me. "I know you're a great feeder, like Toto here, but I won't offer you the sort of menu he used to get in that restaurant you know of, where he ruined his plumbing. Oh, that woman! I used to be so jealous. I can offer only a simple home dinner." And she waved us toward a marble table about twenty-two feet long. Unfortunately for me, she meant it. The dinner began with a kidney-and-mushroom mince served in a giant popover—the kind of thing you might get at a literary hotel in New York. The inner side of the pastry had the feeling of a baby's palm, in the true tearoom tradition.

"It is savory but healthy," Madame said firmly, setting an example by taking a large second helping before starting the dish on its second round. Mirande regarded the untouched doughy fabric on his plate with diaphanously veiled horror, but he had an excuse in the state of his health. "It's still a little rich for me, darling," he murmured. The others, including me, delivered salvos of compliments. I do not squander my moral courage on minor crises. M. Clicquot said, "Impossible to obtain anything like this chez Lapérouse!" Mme Clicquot said, "Not even at the Tour d'Argent!"

"And what do you think of my little wine?" Mme B. asked M. Clicquot. "I'm so anxious for your professional opinion—as a rival producer, you know."

The wine was a thin *rosé* in an Art Nouveau bottle with a label that was a triumph of lithography; it had spires and monks and troubadours and blondes in wimples on it, and the name of the *cru* was spelled out in letters with Gothic curlicues and pennons. The name was something like Château Guillaume d'Aquitaine, *grand vin*.

"What a madly gay little wine, my dear!" M. Clicquot said, repressing, but not soon enough, a grimace of pain.

"One would say a Tavel of a good year," I cried, "if one were a complete bloody fool." I did not say the second clause aloud.

My old friend looked at me with new respect. He was discovering in me a capacity for hypocrisy that he had never credited me with before.

The main course was a shoulder of mutton with white beans—the poor relation of a gigot, and an excellent dish in its way, when not too dry. This was.

For the second wine, the man from the Midi proudly produced a red, in a bottle without a label, which he offered to M. Clicquot with the air of a tomcat bringing a field mouse to its master's feet. "Tell me what you think of this," he said as he filled the champagne man's glass.

M. Clicquot—a veteran of such challenges, I could well imagine—held the glass against the light, dramatically inhaled the bouquet, and then drank, after a slight stiffening of the features that indicated to me that he knew what he was in for. Having emptied half the glass, he deliberated.

"It has a lovely color," he said.

"But what is it? What is it?" the man from the Midi insisted.

"There are things about it that remind me of a Beaujolais," M. Clicquot said (he must have meant that it was wet), "but on the whole I should compare it to a Bordeaux" (without doubt unfavorably).

Mme B.'s agent was beside himself with triumph. "Not one or the other!" he crowed. "It's from the domaine—the Château Guillaume d'Aquitaine!"

The admirable M. Clicquot professed astonishment, and I, when I had emptied a glass, said that there would be a vast market for the wine in America if it could be properly presented. "Unfortunately," I said, "the cost of advertising . . . ," and I rolled my eyes skyward.

"Ah, yes," Mme B. cried sadly. "The cost of advertising!"

I caught Mirande looking at me again, and thought of the Pétrus and the Cheval Blanc of our last meal together chez Mme G. He drank a glass of the red. After all, he wasn't going to die of thirst.

For dessert, we had a simple fruit tart with milk—just the thing for an invalid's stomach, although Mirande didn't eat it.

M. Clicquot retrieved the evening, oenologically, by producing two bottles of a wine "impossible to find in the cellars of any restaurant in France"—Veuve Clicquot '19. There is at present a great to-do among wine merchants in France and the United States about young wines, and an accompanying tendency to cry down the "legend" of the old. For that matter, hardware clerks, when you ask for a can opener with a wooden handle that is thick enough to give a grip and long enough for leverage, try to sell you complicated mechanical folderols. The motivation in both cases is the same—simple greed. To deal in wines of varied ages requires judgment, the sum of experience and flair. It involves the risk of money, because every lot of wine, like every human being, has a life span, and it is this that the good vintner must estimate. His object should be to sell his wine at its moment of maximum value—to the drinker as well as the merchant. The vintner who handles only young wines is like an insurance company that will write policies only on children; the unqualified dealer wants to risk nothing and at the same time to avoid tying up his money. The client misled by brochures warning him off clarets and champagnes that are over ten years old and assuring him that Beaujolais should be drunk green will miss the major pleasures of wine drinking. To deal wisely in wines and merely to sell them are things as different as being an expert in ancient coins and selling Indian-head pennies over a souvenir counter.

Despite these convictions of mine about wine, I should never have tried a thirty-seven-year-old champagne on the recommendation of a lesser authority than the blessed M. Clicquot. It is the oldest by far that I have ever drunk. (H. Warner Allen, in *The Wines of France*, published circa 1924, which is my personal wine bible, says, "In the matter of age, champagne is a capricious wine. As a general rule, it has passed its best between fifteen and twenty, yet a bottle thirty years old may prove excellent, though all its fellows may be quite undrinkable." He cites Saintsbury's note that "a Perrier Jouet of 1857 was still majestical in 1884," adding, "And all wine-drinkers know of such amazing discoveries." Mr. Root, whose book is not a foolish panegyric of everything French, is hard on champagne, in my opinion. He falls into a critical error more common among writers less intelligent: he attacks it for not being something else. Because its excellences are not those of Burgundy or Bordeaux, he underrates the peculiar qualities it does not share with them, as one who would chide Dickens for not being Stendhal, or Marciano for not being Benny Leonard.)

The Veuve Clicquot '19 was tart without brashness—a refined but effective understatement of younger champagnes, which run too much to rhetoric, at best. Even so, the force was all there, to judge from the two glasses that were a shade more than my share. The wine still had a discreet *cordon*—the ring of bubbles that forms inside the glass—and it had developed the color known as "partridge eye." I have never seen a partridge's eye, because the bird, unlike woodcock, is served without the head, but the color the term indicates is that of serous blood or a maple leaf on the turn.

"How nice it was, life in 1919, eh, M. Clicquot?" Mirande said as he sipped his second glass.

After we had finished M. Clicquot's offering, we played a game called lying poker for table stakes, each player being allowed a capital of five hundred francs, not to be replenished under any circumstances. When Mme B. had won everybody's five hundred francs, the party broke up. Mirande promised me that he would be up and about soon, and would show me how men reveled in the heroic days of *la belle époque*, but I had a feeling that the bell was cracked.

I left Paris and came back to it seven times during the next year, but never saw him. Once, being in his quarter in the company of a remarkably pretty woman, I called him up, simply because I knew he would like to look at her, but he was too tired.

I forget when I last talked to him on the telephone. During the next winter, while I was away in Egypt or Jordan or someplace where French papers don't circulate, he died, and I did not learn of it until I returned to Europe.

When Mirande first faltered, in the Rue Chabanais, I had failed to correlate cause and effect. I had even felt a certain selfish alarm. If eating well was beginning to affect Mirande at eighty, I thought, I had better begin taking in sail. After all, I was only thirty years his junior. But after the dinner at Mme B.'s, and in the light of subsequent reflection, I saw that what had undermined his constitution was Mme G.'s defection from the restaurant business. For years, he had been able to escape Mme B.'s solicitude for his health by lunching and dining in the restaurant of Mme G., the sight of whom Mme B. could not support. Entranced by Mme G.'s magnificent food, he had continued to live "like a cock in a pie"—eating as well, and very nearly as much, as when he was thirty. The organs of the interior—never very intelligent, in spite of what the psychosomatic quacks say—received each day the amount of pleasure to which they were accustomed, and never marked the passage of time; it was the indispensable roadwork of the prizefighter. When Mme G., good soul, retired, moderation began its fatal inroads on his resistance. My old friend's appetite, insufficiently stimulated, started to loaf—the insidious result, no doubt, of the advice of the doctor whose existence he had revealed to me by that slip of the tongue about why he no longer drank Burgundy. Mirande commenced, perhaps, by omitting the fish course after the oysters, or the oysters before the fish, then began neglecting his cheeses and skipping the second bottle of wine on odd Wednesdays. What he called his pipes ("*ma tuyauterie*"), being insufficiently exercised, lost their tone, like the leg muscles of a retired champion. When, in his kindly effort to please me, he challenged the *escargots en pots de chambre*, he was like an old fighter who tries a comeback without training for it. That, however, was only the revelation of the rot that had already taken place. What always happens happened. The damage was done, but it could so easily have been averted had he been warned against the fatal trap of abstinence.

Seymour Krim (1922–1989) has come to seem a uniquely American essayist with the passage of time. He evolved a nonfiction style of manic melancholy exuberance that was inspired by the Beats, the comic Lenny Bruce, and bebop jazz, with driving riffs building rhythmically, paragraph by paragraph. His great subject was failure, and the chagrin, humiliation, and envy of being a "loser" outsider in a success-driven culture. He is the American grandchild of Dostoevsky's Underground Man. Though "Making It!" purports to be a prescription for selling out, it is of course ironically shot through with a romantic's bruised idealism.

MAKING IT!

When has an inside phrase like "making it" or so-and-so's "got it made" shot with such reality through the museum of official English? In this terse verbal shorthand lies a philosophy of life that puts a gun in the back of Chase Manhattan rhetoric and opens up, like a money bag, the true values that make the Sammys and Susies of modern city life run today. *You've got it made.* How the words sing a swift jazz poem of success, hi-fi, the best chicks (or guys), your name in lights, pot to burn, jets to LA and London, bread in the bank, baby, and a fortress built around your ego like a magic suit of armor! You've got it made. Royalties pouring in, terraces stretching out, hip movie starlets strutting in butt-parade, nothing but Jack Daniel's with your water, your name in Skolsky's column, Tennessee for lunch, dinner with—somebody who swings, sweetheart! And tomorrow the world (as a starter).

Middle-class ideals of success once curled the lip of the intellectual; today he grins not, neither does he snide. Columbia pro-

fessor, poet, painter, ex-Trotskyite, *Partisan Review* editor, GE
engineer, Schenley salesman—they all live in the same world for
a change and that world says, go! The Marxist, neo-Christian,
romantic, humanitarian values of twenty years ago are great for
the mind's library and its nighttime prayer mat; but will they fill
the cancerous hunger in the soul for getting what *you* want today?
Softies become tough, toughies get harder, men dig that they'd
rather be women, women say to hell with lilacs and become men,
the road gets rougher (as Frankie lays his smart-money message
on us) and you've got to move, hustle, go for the ultimate broke
or you'll be left with a handful of nothing, Jack and Jill! What
happened to the world out *there*, the one you always thought you
loved and honestly-couldn't-get-enough-of-without-wanting-a-
sou-in-return for your pure and holy feelings? *Baby, that world
went up in the cornball illusions of yesterday! Forget it just like
it never knew you were alive. This bit about being a fine writer, a
dedicated actor, a movie-maker with Modern Museum notions
of heaven, a musician because you truly love it, a painter because
you die when you smell the color? Don't make me laugh—it's
not good for the stitches, dad. This world (nuts, this rutting universe!) is a Mt. Everest, kiddo, and you've got to start climbing
now or the dumbwaiter of this age will slam you down into the
black basement. Use whatever you've got and use what you* ain't
got, too!

Throughout the jumping metropolis of New York one sees
vertical fanaticism, the Thor-type upward thrust of the entire
being, replacing pale, horizontal, mock-Christian love of fellow-
creature; the man or woman who is High Inside, hummingly self-
aware, the gunner and gunnerette in the turret of the aircraft that
is Self, is watching out for number one with a hundred new-born
eyes. He or she has been slicked down by the competition to a
lean, lone-eagle, universe-supporting role. Hey Atlas, did you
ever think that common man and woman would be imprisoned
under the burden of your heroic weight and find it the ultimate
drag rather than the godlike stance, without value, nobility or
purpose? The ancient symphonies of Man have lost their meaning. It is hopelessness that drives the modern whirlwind striver to
put such emphasis on personal achievement.

In every brain-cell of intellectual and artistic life the heat is on in America today no differently than it is in business. Values? Purpose? Selectivity? Principles? *For the birds, Charley! I want to make it and nothing's going to stand in my way because everything is crap, except making it! I want* my *ego to ride high,* my *heart to bank the loot of life,* my *apartment to swing,* my *MG to snarl down the highway,* my *pennant to wave above the scattered turds of broken dreams for a better world! Why don't you level and say you want the same, you hypocrite? Be honest for Chrissakes!*

With the blessings of psychiatry, enlightened (so-called) self-ishness has become the motto of hip city life; the once-Philistine is admired for his thick skin and wallet, the poor slob who translates Artaud but can't make his rent, a girl, or hold his own at a party is used as a dartboard for the wit of others—not by the "enemy," either, but by his very Village brothers who have forsaken a square idealism for a bite-marked realism. The only enemy today is failure, failure, failure, and the only true friend is—success? How? In what line? Whoring yourself a little? Buttering up, sucking up, self-salesmanship, the sweet oh-let-me-kiss-your-ass-please smile? *Don't be naïve, friend. You think this hallucinated world is the moonlight sonata or something? You think anyone cares about your principles or (don't make me puke!) integrity or that they make the slightest ripple in the tempest of contemporary confusion? Go sit at home, then, you model saint and keep pure like the monks with your hands on your own genitalia! Because if you want to make it out in the world, baby, you have to swing, move, love what you hate and love yourself for doing it, too!*

The one unforgivable sin in city life today is not to *make it.* Even though the cush of success may seem hollow to the victor as his true self sifts the spoils, alone and apart from the madding cats who envy him, he knows that his vulnerable heart could not bear the pain of being a loser. Wasn't success drummed at him every day in every way in relation to women, status, loot—Christ, the image of himself in his own eyes? Didn't he see those he admired in his tender years flicked off like so many flies because they'd never made a public victory of their talents? My God, man, what else could he do except be a success (or kill himself)—the world being what it is?

For *making it* today has become the only tangible value in an environment quaking with insecurity and life's mockery of once-holy goals, which the bored witch of modern history has popped over the rim of the world for sport, like an idle boy with paper pellets. *How can you buy grand abstractions of human brother-hood for that daily fix needed by your ego when Dostoevsky and Freud have taught us we hate our parents, brothers, sisters, and wives, as well as friends? Oh, no, you can't snow us, you peddlers of fake hope! We know you for what you are: Vaseline-tongued frustrates who wanted to make it and lost. Man, how the wound shows behind your pathetic rationalizations!*

The padded values and euphemisms of a more leisurely time have been ruthlessly stripped away under the hospital light of today's world; honesty, integrity, truthfulness, seem sentimental hangovers from a pastoral age, boy-scout ideals trying to cope with an armored tank of actuality that is crumpling the music-box values of the past like matchsticks. It is not Truth that is pertinent today, in the quaint dream of some old philosopher; it is the specific truths of survival, getting, taking, besting, as the old order collapses like a grounded parachute around the stoney vision of the embittered modern adult. *What is left but me?* mutters the voice of reality, *and how else can I save myself except by exhausting every pore in the race with time?* We see in America today a personal ambition unparalleled in fierce egocentricity, getting ahead, achieving the prize, making a score—for the redemption of the self. Are the ends good? Does it matter to the world? Will it pass muster at the gates of judgment? *Such questions are ridiculous: they presume a God above man rather than the god of life who thumps within my chest for more, faster, bigger, conquests for me, me, ME!*

As the individual stands his lonely vigil in the polar night of the desolation of all once agreed-upon values—as they have receded like the tide, rolling back into the past—where else, he cries, can he turn but to his own future? Who else will help him? What can he or she do but mount the top of personal fulfillment in a world that has crumbled beneath the foot? Upon the neon-lit plains of the modern city comes the tortured cry of a million selves for a place in the sun of personal godhood. As one by one the lights of the old-fashioned planets Peace, Love, Happiness, have flickered and gone out, plunging all into the spook jazzglow of a new surrealist dawn, the only believable light comes from the soul-jet of need that burns in the private heart. *Let the lousy world crash like a demented P-38! What can I do about it? I'm merely a pawn of this age like you. Man, my only escape-hatch is making it at the highest pitch I can dream of!*

An individualism just short of murder has replaced the phantom of socialism as the idols of the recent past shrink into mere trophies on the mocking walls of history. In an existence so dreamlike, uncertain, swift, the only nailed-down values that remain are those that can be seen in the bankbook of life. *Can honors be taken away from me? Fame? Money? The beauty I can possess (by name or dollar) in both flesh and leather? No! Don't croon to me of art or soul in a world that has flipped loose from its moorings, seen the futility of truth, the platitude of spiritual hope, the self-deception in innocence, the lack of discrimination in goodness, the pettiness of tears! You only live once, Jack, and if you don't swing with the fractured rhythms of this time—if you hide behind the curtains of a former, simpler, child's world of right and wrong—you condemn yourself to the just sneers of those who dig the real world as it is! Baby, there is no significance today but* you *and the sooner you wake up to the full horror of this fact, the better!*

By time-honored esthetic and moral standards the knowing modern man, and woman, is a barely polite gangster; his machine gun is his mind, ideas his bullets, power and possession his goals. The reduction of the real to the usable has been whittled into a necessity by the impossible number of potential choices within himself: he knows, after juggling more thoughts than he can reach conclusions about, that he must snap down the lid on fruitless speculation and use the precious energy for making warheads on the spears of practicality. Victims of their own subjective desperation, pygmies under the heavens of thought that dot the roof of their minds with a million perverse stars, converge upon the external prizes of life like hordes released from prison: eager to bury the intolerable freedom of the mind's insanity in the beautiful sanity of—making it! *Yes, yes, I will convert the self that bugs me into an objective victory in the steel and weighable world! I will take the scalding steam of my spirit and hiss it outward like an acetylene torch upon the hard shale of life, and cut diamonds for myself! You say this therapy of mine adds brutality to the gutter of modernity, that I care only for my private need at the expense of the world? That my fuel is desperation and that I'm marvelously indifferent about adding my shot of cruel self-interest to an already amoral environment? I don't deny it. Survival at its highest conception means making it! To live you must conquer if you're normal enough to hate being stuck with your futile being and smart enough to know you must trade it for success!*

For what else is there? Dying at parties, as I used to, when I saw some headliner bring the fawn out of even the best people, who swooned around this living symbol of magic? Eating my heart out because I didn't have the admiration, the quiff, the loot, the attention I and all human beings demand out of life? Suppose I do know how cheap and unlike my original ideal it all is? You want it too, you envious bastard, you know you do! Spit it out that the ego is the world today for all of us and that without its gratification living is a hell, roasting on the skewer of frustration as you watch others grab the nooky! Jack, life is too far gone—too man-eat-man—for your wistful moralizing and pansy references to the cathedrals of the past. It's only the present that counts in a world that has no foreseeable future and I'm human enough to want to swing my way to the grave—sweetheart, you can have immortality!

In an age that has seen the abandonment, because they are too costly, of cherished political and personal hopes, hypodermic realism inside and businesslike efficiency outside becomes the new style. The address book replaces the soul, doing is the relief of being, talking of thinking, getting of feeling. *I've got to numb myself in action, exhaust this inner fiend, or else all the hopelessness of this so-called life of mine will come bursting through its trapdoor and overwhelm me! I've got to swing, plan, plot, connive, go and get and get some more, because what else is there, Buster?* The frenzied tempo of achievement is matched only by the endless desert within; the futility-powered desperado drives himself ever forward, trying to find in action some publicly applauded significance that is freezingly absent in solitude. Does it matter that he finds his buddies who have made it as rocket-desperate and unsatisfied as himself?

Hell, no. Doesn't the world admire us and isn't it obvious that it's better to be miserable as a storm-trooper than as a Jew? Wasn't my picture in Look, *wasn't I on Mike Wallace's show and didn't I turn down an invitation from Long John? Doesn't my answering service hum with invitations, haven't I made it with that crazy-looking blonde who sings at the Persian Room as well as that distinguished lady novelist who lives near Dash Hammett's old apartment on West Tenth? Don't I jive with Condon as well as Wystan Auden, Jim Jones (when he's in town) as well as Maureen Stapleton, Bill Zeckendorf, Bill Rose, Bill Styron, Bill Faulkner, Bill Basie, Bill Williams, Bill de Kooning, Bill Holden—just on the Bill front? Don't I get tips on the market, complimentary copies of* Big Table *as well as* Holiday, *didn't I put down Dalí at that party for being square and get a big grin from Adlai Stevenson for doing so?*

Man, I know what I'm doing! I'm swinging instead of standing still, I'm racing with a racing age, I'm handling seventeen things at once and I'm scoring with them all! Life's too wild today, sonny, to worry about the fate of the race or private morality or nunlike delicacies of should-I or should-I-not; anyone with brains or even imagination is a self-aware marauder with the wisdom to know that if he hustles hard enough he can have a moat full of gravy and a penthouse-castle high over life's East River! I'm bartering my neuroses for AT&T (not crying over them to Beethoven's Ninth like you, you fake holy man!) and bemoaning my futile existence with Mumm's Extra Dry and the finest hemp from Laredo and my new Jackson Pollock and my new off-Broadway boff and my new book and my new play and my new pad and this TV show they're gonna build around me and— Jesus, I've got it made!

. . . while down below the lusting average man and woman sweats in jealousy at the sight of these Dexedrine angels, the very inspiration of what he and she can become if only they too can put that last shred of shame behind them and swing, extrovert yourself, get with it, make that buck, make that chick, make that poem, make this crazy modern scene *pay off*. O my heart, so I too can sink my teeth in the sirloin and wear the pearls of hell!

*Elizabeth Hardwick (1916–2007) was a literary critic and fiction writer whose stature has continued to grow since her death, and she now stands at the pinnacle of recent American essayists— a respect we can attribute to her formidable intelligence, exigent standards, and elegant prose. Susan Sontag said: "I think she writes more beautiful sentences than any living American writer." In her essay collections (*A View of My Own, Bartleby in Manhattan, *and* Seduction and Betrayal), *which dealt mostly with nineteenth- and twentieth-century writers, she displayed her large grasp of history and literary tradition. Her wry essay on Boston, where she spent a number of years with her poet-professor husband, Robert Lowell, may strike citizens of that great city as unfair, but they would be hard-pressed to deny its merits as sparkling, well-wrought prose.*

BOSTON

With Boston and its mysteriously enduring reputation, "the reverberation is longer than the thunderclap," as Emerson observed about the tenacious fame of certain artists. Boston—wrinkled, spindly-legged, depleted of nearly all her spiritual and cutaneous oils, provincial, self-esteeming—has gone on spending and spending her inflated bills of pure reputation, decade after decade. Now, one supposes it is all over at last. The old jokes embarrass, the anecdotes are so many thrice-squeezed lemons, and no new fruit hangs on the boughs. All the American regions are breaking up, ground down to a standard American corn meal. And why not Boston, which would have been the most difficult to maintain? There has never been anything quite like Boston as a creation of the American imagination, or perhaps one should say as a creation of the American scene. Some of the legend was once real, surely. Our utilitarian, fluid landscape has produced a handful of regional conceptions, popular images, brief and naked: the conservative Vermonter, the boastful Texan, the honeyed Southerner. "Graciousness is ours," brays a coarsened South; and the sheiks of Texas cruise around their desert.

The Boston image is more complex. The city is felt to have, in the end, a pure and special nature, absurd no doubt but somehow valuable. Empiricism will not carry one far; faith and *being*, sheer being above all, are needed. To be it, old Boston, real Boston, very Boston, and—one shrinks before the claim—proper Boston; there lies knowledge. An author can hardly fail to turn a penny or two on this magical subject. Everyone will consent to be informed on it, to be slyly entertained by it. *Actual* Boston is governed largely by people of Irish descent and more and more, recently, by men of Italian descent. Not long ago, the old Yankee Senator Saltonstall remarked wistfully that there were still a good many Anglo-Saxons in Massachusetts, his own family among them. Extinction is foreshadowed in the defense.

Plainness and pretension restlessly feuding and combining; wealth and respectability and firmness of character ending in the production of a number of diverting individual tics or, at the best, instances of high culture—something of that sort is the legendary Boston soul, or so one supposes without full confidence because the old citizens of Boston vehemently hold to the notion that the city and their character are ineffable, unknowable. When asked for an opinion on the admirable novel *Boston Adventure*, or even the light social history *The Proper Bostonians*, the answer invariably comes, "Not Boston." The descriptive intelligence, the speculative mind, the fresh or even the merely open eye are felt to discover nothing but errors here, be they errors of praise or censure. Still, wrongheadedness flourishes, the subject fascinates, and the Athenaeum's list of written productions on this topic is nearly endless.

The best book on Boston is Henry James's novel *The Bostonians*. By the bald and bold use of the place name, the unity of situation and person is dramatized. But poor James, of course, was roundly and importantly informed by everyone, including his brother William, that this too was "not Boston." Stricken, he pushed aside a superb creation, and left the impregnable, unfathomable Boston to its mysteries. James's attitude toward the city's intellectual consequence and social charm is one of absolute impiety. A view of the Charles River reveals, ". . . an horizon indented at empty intervals with wooden spires, the masts of lonely boats, the chimneys of dirty 'works,' over a brackish expanse of anomalous character, which is too big for a river and too small for a bay." A certain house has "a peculiar look of being both new and faded—a kind of modern fatigue— like certain articles of commerce which are sold at a reduction as shopworn." However, there is little natural landscape in James's novel. The picture is, rather, of the psychological Boston of the 1870s, a confused scene, slightly mad with neurotic repressions, provincialism, and earnestness without intellectual seriousness.

James's view of Boston is not the usual one, although his irony and dissatisfaction are shared by Henry Adams, who says that "a simpler manner of life and thought could hardly exist, short of cave-dwelling," and by Santayana, who spoke of Boston as a "moral and intellectual nursery, always busy applying first principles to trifles." The great majority of the writings on Boston are in another spirit altogether—they are frankly unctuous, for the town has always attracted men of quiet and timid and tasteful opinion, men interested in old families and things, in the charms of times recently past, collectors of anecdotes about those Boston worthies hardly anyone can still clearly identify, men who spoke and preached and whose fame deteriorated quickly. Rufus Choate, Dr. Channing, Edward Everett Hale, Phillips Brooks, and Theodore Parker: names that remain in one's mind, without producing an image or a fact, as the marks are left on the wall after the picture has been removed. William Dean Howells held a more usual view than Henry James or Adams or Santayana. Indeed Howells's original enthusiasm for garden and edifice, person and setting, is more than a little *exalté*. The first sight of the chapel at Mount Auburn Cemetery moved him more than the

"Acropolis, Westminster Abbey, and Santa Croce in one." The massive gray stones of "the Public Library and the Athenaeum are hardly eclipsed by the Vatican and the Pitti." And so on.

The importance of Boston was intellectual and as its intellectual donations to the country have diminished, so it has declined from its lofty symbolic meaning, to become a more lowly image, a sort of farce of conservative exclusiveness and snobbish humor. Marquand's George Apley is a figure of the decline—fussy, sentimental, farcically mannered, archaic. He cannot be imagined as an Abolitionist, an author, a speaker; he is merely a "character." The old Boston had something of the spirit of Bloomsbury: it was clannish, worldly, and intellectually alive. About the historian Prescott, Van Wyck Brooks could say, ". . . for at least ten years, Prescott had been hard at work, harder, perhaps, than any Boston merchant."

History, indeed, with its long, leisurely, gentlemanly labors, the books arriving by post, the cards to be kept and filed, the sections to be copied, the documents to be checked, is the ideal pursuit for the New England mind. All the Adamses spent a good deal of their lives on one kind of history or another. The eccentricity, studiousness, and study-window slow pace of life of the historical gentleman lay everywhere about the Boston scene. For money, society, fashion, extravagance, one went to New York. But now, the descendants of the old, intellectual aristocracy live in the respectable suburbs and lead the healthy, restless, outdoor life that atrophies the sedentary nerves of culture. The bluestocking, the eccentric, the intransigent bring a blush of uncertainty and embarrassment to the healthy young couple's cheek.

Boston today can still provide a fairly stimulating atmosphere for the banker, the broker, for doctors and lawyers. "Open end" investments prosper, the fish come in at the dock, the wool market continues, and workers are employed in the shoe factories in the nearby towns. For the engineer, the physicist, the industrial designer, for all the highly trained specialists of the electronic age, Boston and its area are of seemingly unlimited promise. Sleek, well-designed factories and research centers pop up everywhere; the companies plead, in the Sunday papers, for more chemists, more engineers, and humbly relate the executive benefits of salary and pension and advancement they are prepared to offer.

But otherwise, for the artist, the architect, the composer, the writer, the philosopher, the historian, for those humane pursuits for which the town was once noted and even for the delights of entertainment, for dancing, acting, cooking, Boston is a bewildering place. There is, first of all, the question of Boston or New York. (The question is not new; indeed it was answered in the last decades of the last century in favor of New York as the cultural center of America.) It is, in our day, only a private and personal question: where or which of the two Eastern cities should one try to live and work in? It is a one-sided problem. For the New Yorker, San Francisco or Florida, perhaps—Boston, never. In Boston, New York tantalizes; one of the advantages of Boston is said, wistfully, to be its nearness to New York. It is a bad sign when a man, who has come to Boston or Cambridge, Massachusetts, from another place begins to show an undivided acceptance of his new town. Smugness is the great vice of the two places. Between puffy self-satisfaction and the fatiguing wonder if one wouldn't be happier, more productive, more appreciated in New York, a thoughtful man makes his choice.

Boston is not a small New York, as they say a child is not a small adult but is, rather, a specially organized small creature with its small-creature's temperature, balance, and distribution of fat. In Boston there is an utter absence of that wild electric beauty of New York, of the marvelous excited rush of people in taxicabs at twilight, of the great Avenues and Streets, the restaurants, theaters, bars, hotels, delicatessens, shops. In Boston the night comes down with an incredibly heavy, small-town finality. The cows come home; the chickens go to roost; the meadow is dark. Nearly every Bostonian is in his own house or in someone else's house, dining at the home board, enjoying domestic and social privacy. The "nice little dinner party"—for this the Bostonian would sell his soul. In the evenings, the old "accommodators" dart about the city, carrying their black uniforms and white aprons in a paper bag. They are on call to go anywhere, to cook and serve dinners. Many of these women are former cooks and

maids, now living on Social Security retirement pensions, supplemented by the fees for these evening "accommodations" to the
community. Their style and the bland respectability of their cuisine keep up the social tone of the town. They are like those old
slaves who stuck to their places and, even in the greatest deprivation, graciously went on toting things to the Massa'.

There is a curious flimsiness and indifference in the commercial life of Boston. The restaurants are, charitably, to be called
mediocre; the famous seafood is only palatable when raw. Otherwise it usually has to endure the deep-fry method that makes
everything taste like the breaded pork chops of the Middle West,
which in turn taste like the fried sole of Boston. Here, French
restaurants quickly become tearoomy, as if some sort of rapid
naturalization had taken place. There is not a single attractive
eating place on the waterfront. An old downtown restaurant of
considerable celebrity, Locke-Ober, has been expanded, let out,
and "costumed" by one of the American restaurant decorators
whose productions have a ready-make look, as if the designs
had been chosen from a catalog. But for the purest eccentricity,
there is the "famous" restaurant Durgin-Park, which is run like a
boardinghouse in a mining town. And so it goes. Downtown Boston at night is a dreary jungle of honky-tonks for sailors, dreary
department store windows, Loew's movie houses, hillbilly bands,
strippers, parking lots, undistinguished new buildings. Mid-
town Boston—small, expensive shops, the inevitable Elizabeth
Arden and Helena Rubinstein "salons," Brooks Brothers—is
deserted at night, except for people going in and out of the Ritz-
Carlton Hotel, the only public place in Boston that could be
called "smart." The merchandise in the Newbury Street shops is
designed in a high fashion, elaborate, furred, and sequined, but
it is never seen anywhere. Perhaps it is for out-of-town use, like a
traveling man's mistress.

Just as there is no smart life, so there is no Soho, no Greenwich Village. Recently a man was murdered in a parking lot in
the Chinatown area. His address was given as the South End, a
lower-class section, and he was said to be a "free-spender," making enough money as a summer bartender on Cape Cod to lead
a freewheeling life the rest of the year. One paper referred to the

unfortunate man as a "member of the Beacon Hill Bohemia set." This designation is of considerable interest because there is no "Bohemia" in Boston, neither upper nor lower; the detergent of bourgeois Boston cleans everything, effortlessly, completely. If there were a Bohemia, its members *would* live on Beacon Hill, the most beautiful part of Boston and, like the older parts of most cities, fundamentally classless, providing space for the rich in the noble mansions and for the people with little money in the run-down alleys. For both of these groups the walled gardens of Beacon Hill, the mews, the coach houses, the river views, the cobblestone streets are a necessity and the yellow brick structures of the Fenway are poison. *Espresso* bars have sprung up, or rather dug down in basements, but no summer of bohemianism is ushered into town. This reluctance is due to the Boston legend and its endurance as a lost ideal, a romantic quest.

Something transcendental is always expected in Boston. There is, one imagines, behind the drapery on Mount Vernon Street a person of democratic curiosity and originality of expression, someone alas—and this is the tiresome Boston note—*wellborn*. It is likely to be, even in imagination, a *she*, since women now and not the men provide the links with the old traditions. Of her, then, one expects a certain unprofessionalism, but it is not expected that she will be superficial; she is profoundly conventional in manner of life but capable of radical insights. To live in Boston means to seek some connection with this famous local excellence, the regional type and special creation of the city.

An angry disappointment attends the romantic soul bent upon this quest. When the archaeological diggings do turn up an authentic specimen it will be someone old, nearly gone, "whom you should have known when she was young"—and could hear. The younger Bostonians seem in revolt against the old excellence, with its indulgent, unfettered development of the self. Revolt, however, is too active a word for a passive failure to perpetuate the ideal high-mindedness and intellectual effort. With the fashionable young women of Boston, one might just as well be on Long Island. In the nervous, shy, earnest women there is a lingering hint of the peculiar local development. Terrible faux pas are constantly being made by this reasonable, honorable person, followed by blushes and more false steps and explanations and the final blinking, retreating blush.

Among the men, the equivalent of the blushing, blurting, sensitive, and often "fine" woman, is a person who exists everywhere perhaps but nowhere else with such elaboration of type, such purity of example. This is the wellborn failure, the amateur not by choice but from some fatal reticence of temperament. They are often descendants of intellectual Boston, oddball grandsons, charming and sensitive, puzzlingly complicated, living on a "small income." These unhappy men carry on their conscience the weight of unpublished novels, half-finished paintings, impossible historical projects, old-fashioned poems, unproduced plays. Their inevitable "small income" is a sort of dynastic flaw, like hemophilia. Much money seems often to impose obligations of energetic management; from great fortunes the living cells receive the hints of the possibilities of genuine power, enough even to make some enormously rich Americans endure the humiliations and fatigues of political office. Only the most decadent and spoiled think of living in idleness on millions; but this notion does occur to the man afflicted with ten thousand a year. He will commit himself with a dreamy courage to whatever traces of talent he may have and live to see himself punished by the New England conscience which demands accomplishments, duties performed, responsibilities noted, and energies sensibly used. The dying will accuses and the result is a queer kind of Boston incoherence. It is literally impossible much of the time to tell what some of the most attractive men in Boston are talking about. Half-uttered witticisms, grave and fascinating obfuscations, points incredibly qualified, hesitations infinitely refined—one staggers about, charmed and confused by the twilight.

But this person, with his longings, connects with the old possibilities and, in spite of his practical failure, keeps alive the memory of the best days. He may have a brother who has retained the mercantile robustness of nature and easy capacity for action and yet has lost all belief in anything except money and class, who may practice private charities, but entertains profoundly trivial national and world views. A Roosevelt, Harriman, or Stevenson is impossible to imagine as a member of the Boston aristocracy; here the vein of self-satisfaction and public indifference cuts too deeply.

Harvard (across the river in Cambridge) and Boston are two ends of one mustache. Harvard is now so large and international it has altogether avoided the whimsical stagnation of Boston. But the two places need each other, as we knowingly say of a mismatched couple. Without the faculty, the visitors, the events that Harvard brings to the life here, Boston would be intolerable to anyone except genealogists, antique dealers, and those who find repletion in a closed local society.

Unfortunately, Harvard, like Boston, has "tradition," and in America this always carries with it the risk of a special staleness of attitude, and of pride, incredibly and comically swollen like the traits of hypocrisy, selfishness, or lust in the old dramas. At Harvard some of the vices of "society" exist, of Boston society that is—arrogance and the blinding dazzle of being, *being at Harvard.* The moral and social temptations of Harvard's unique position in American academic life are great and the pathos is seen in those young faculty members who are presently at Harvard but whose appointments are not permanent and so they may be thrown down, banished from the beatific condition. The young teachers in this position live in a dazed state of love and hatred, pride and fear; their faces have a look of desperate yearning, for they would rather serve in heaven than reign in hell. For those who are not banished, for the American at least, since the many distinguished foreigners at Harvard need not endure these piercing and fascinating complications, something of Boston seems to seep into their characters. They may come from anywhere in America and yet to be at Harvard unites them with the transcendental, legendary Boston, with New England in flower. They begin to revere the old worthies, the houses, the paths trod by so many before, and they feel a throb of romantic sympathy for the directly-gazing portraits on the walls, for the old graves and old names in the Mount Auburn Cemetery. All of this has charm and may even have a degree of social and intellectual value—and then again it may not. Devious parochialisms, irrelevant snobberies, a bemused exaggeration of one's own productions, pimple the soul of a man upholding tradition in a forest of relaxation, such as most of America is thought to be. Henry James's observation in his book on Hawthorne bears on this:

> . . . it is only in a country where newness and change and brevity of tenure are the common substance of life, that the fact of one's ancestors having lived for a hundred and seventy years in a single spot would become an element of one's morality. It is only an imaginative American that would feel urged to keep reverting to this circumstance, to keep analysing and cunningly considering it.

If the old things of Boston are too heavy and plushy, the new either hasn't been born or is appallingly shabby and poor. As early as Thanksgiving, Christmas decorations unequaled for cheap ugliness go up in the Public Garden and on the Boston Common. Year after year, the city fathers bring out crèches and camels and Mother and Child so badly made and of such caste-less colors they verge on blasphemy, or would seem to do so if it were not for the further degradation of secular little men blowing horns and the canes of peppermint hanging on the lamps. The shock of the first sight is the most interesting; later the critical senses are stilled as year after year the same bits are brought forth and gradually one realizes that the whole thing is a sort of permanent exhibition.

Recently the dying downtown shopping section of Boston was to be graced with flowers, an idea perhaps in imitation of the charming potted geraniums and tulips along Fifth Avenue in New York. Commercial Boston produced a really amazing display: old, gray square bins, in which were stuck a few bits of yellowing, dying evergreen. It had the look of exhausted greenery thrown out in the garbage and soon the dustbins were full of other bits of junk and discard—people had not realized or recognized the decorative hope and saw only the rubbishy result.

The municipal, civic backwardness of Boston does not seem to bother its more fortunate residents. For them and for the observer, Boston's beauty is serene and private, an enclosed, intense personal life, rich with domestic variation, interesting stuffs and things, showing the hearthside vitality of a Dutch genre painting. Of an evening the spirits quicken, not to public entertainment, but instead to the sights behind the draperies, the glimpses of drawing rooms on Louisburg Square, paneled walls and French chandeliers on Commonwealth Avenue, bookshelves and flower-filled bays on Beacon Street. Boston is a winter city. Every apartment has a fireplace. In the town houses, old persons climb steps without complaint, four or five floors of them, cope with the maintenance of roof and gutter and survive the impractical kitchen and resign themselves to the useless parlors. This is life; the house, the dinner party, the charming gardens, one's high ceilings, fine windows, lacy grillings, magnolia trees, inside shutters, glassed-in studios on the top of what were once stables, outlook on the "river side." Setting is serious. When it is not serious, when a splendid old private house passes into less dedicated hands, an almost exuberant swiftness of deterioration can be noticed. A rooming house, although privately owned, is no longer in the purest sense a private house and soon it partakes of some of the feckless, ugly, municipal neglect. The contrasts are startling. One of two houses of almost identical exterior design will have shining windows, a bright brass door knocker, and its twin will show a *"Rooms"* sign peering out of dingy glass, curtained by those lengths of flowered plastic used in the shower bath. Garbage lies about in the alleys behind the rooming houses, discarded furniture blocks old garden gateways. The vulnerability of Boston's way of life, the meanness of most things that fall outside the needs of the upper classes, are shown with a bleak and terrible fullness in the rooming houses on Beacon Street. And even some of the best houses show a spirit of mere "maintenance," which, while useful for the individual with money, leads to civic dullness, architectural torpor, and stagnation. In the Back Bay area, a voluntary, casual association of property owners exists for the purpose of trying to keep the alleys clean, the streets lighted beyond their present medieval darkness, and to pursue other worthy items of neighborhood value. And yet this same group will "protest" against the attractive Café Florian on Newbury Street (smell of coffee too strong!) and against the brilliantly exciting Boston Arts Festival held in the beautiful Public Garden for two weeks in June. The idea that Boston might be a vivacious, convenient place to live in is not uppermost in these residents' thoughts. Trying to buy groceries in the best section of the Back Bay region is an interesting study in commercial apathy.

A great many of the young Bostonians leave town, often taking off with a sullen demand for a freer, more energetic air. And yet many of them return later, if not to the city itself, to the beautiful sea towns and old villages around it. For the city itself, who will live in it after the present human landmarks are gone? No doubt, some of the young people there at the moment will persevere, and as a reward for their fidelity and endurance will themselves later become monuments, old types interesting to students of what our colleges call American Civilization. Boston is defective, out-of-date, vain, and lazy, but if you're not in a hurry it has a deep, secret appeal. Or, more accurately, those who like it may make of its appeal a secret. The weight of the Boston legend, the tedium of its largely fraudulent posture of traditionalism, the disillusionment of the Boston present as a cultural force make quick minds hesitate to embrace a region too deeply compromised. They are on their guard against falling for it, but meanwhile they can enjoy its very defects, its backwardness, its slowness, its position as one of the large, possible cities on the Eastern seacoast, its private, residential charm. They speak of going to New York and yet another season finds them holding back, positively enjoying the Boston life. . . .

. . . Outside it is winter, dark. The curtains are drawn, the wood is on the fire, the table has been checked, and in the stillness one waits for the guests who come stamping in out of the snow. There are lectures in Cambridge, excellent concerts in Symphony Hall, bad plays being tried out for the hungry sheep of Boston before going to the hungry sheep of New York. Arnold Toynbee or T. S. Eliot or Robert Frost or Robert Oppenheimer or Barbara Ward is in town again. The cars are double-parked so thickly along the narrow streets that a moving vehicle can scarcely maneuver; the pedestrians stumble over the cobbles; in the back alleys a cat cries and the rats, enormously fat, run in front of the car lights creeping into the parking spots. Inside it is cozy, Victorian, and gossipy. Someone else has *not* been kept on at Harvard. The old Irish "accommodator" puffs up stairs she had never seen before a few hours previously and announces that dinner is ready. A Swedish journalist is just getting off the train at the Back Bay Station. He has been exhausted by cocktails, reality, life, taxis, telephones, bad connections in New York and Chicago, pulverized by a "good time." Sighing, he alights, seeking old Boston, a culture that hasn't been alive for a long time . . . and rest.

*Flannery O'Connor (1925–1964) was one of the greatest American fiction writers of the twentieth century. In her extraordinary short story collections (*A Good Man Is Hard to Find, Everything That Rises Must Converge*) and novels (*Wise Blood*), she perfected her inimitable style of narrative shocks and grotesque characters driven by violent turns toward sin and redemption. O'Connor was a practicing Catholic, and her writing dramatizes, with a zest for absurdity, the fallen state of man and the uncanny presence of grace. She also wrote lively essays, like the one below, which good-humoredly addresses being pigeonholed both regionally and aesthetically.*

SOME ASPECTS OF THE GROTESQUE IN SOUTHERN FICTION

I think that if there is any value in hearing writers talk, it will be in hearing what they can witness to and not what they can theorize about. My own approach to literary problems is very like the one Dr. Johnson's blind housekeeper used when she poured tea—she put her finger inside the cup.

These are not times when writers in this country can very well speak for one another. In the twenties there were those at Vanderbilt University who felt enough kinship with each other's ideas to issue a pamphlet called *I'll Take My Stand*, and in the thirties there were writers whose social consciousness set them all going in more or less the same direction; but today there are no good writers, bound even loosely together, who would be so bold as to say that they speak for a generation or for each other. Today each writer speaks for himself, even though he may not be sure that his work is important enough to justify his doing so.

I think that every writer, when he speaks of his own approach to fiction, hopes to show that, in some crucial and deep sense, he is a realist; and for some of us, for whom the ordinary aspects of daily life prove to be of no great fictional interest, this is very difficult. I have found that if one's young hero can't be identified with the average American boy, or even with the average American delinquent, then his perpetrator will have a good deal of explaining to do.

The first necessity confronting him will be to say what he is not doing; for even if there are no genuine schools in American letters today, there is always some critic who has just invented one and who is ready to put you into it. If you are a Southern writer, that label, and all the misconceptions that go with it, is pasted on you at once, and you are left to get it off as best you can. I have found that no matter for what purpose peculiar to your special dramatic needs you use the Southern scene, you are still thought by the general reader to be writing about the South and are judged by the fidelity your fiction has to typical Southern life.

I am always having it pointed out to me that life in Georgia is not at all the way I picture it, that escaped criminals do not roam the roads exterminating families, nor Bible salesmen prowl about looking for girls with wooden legs.

The social sciences have cast a dreary blight on the public approach to fiction. When I first began to write, my own particular bête noire was that mythical entity, The School of Southern Degeneracy. Every time I heard about The School of Southern Degeneracy, I felt like Br'er Rabbit stuck on the Tarbaby. There was a time when the average reader read a novel simply for the moral he could get out of it, and however naïve that may have been, it was a good deal less naïve than some of the more limited objectives he now has. Today novels are considered to be entirely concerned with the social or economic or psychological forces that they will by necessity exhibit, or with those details of daily life that are for the good novelist only means to some deeper end.

Hawthorne knew his own problems and perhaps anticipated ours when he said he did not write novels, he wrote romances. Today many readers and critics have set up for the novel a kind of orthodoxy. They demand a realism of fact which may, in the end, limit rather than broaden the novel's scope. They associate the only legitimate material for long fiction with the movement of social forces, with the typical, with fidelity to the way things look and happen in normal life. Along with this usually goes a wholesale treatment of those aspects of existence that the Victorian novelist could not directly deal with. It has only been within the last five or six decades that writers have won this supposed emancipation. This was a license that opened up many possibilities for fiction, but it is always a bad day for culture when any liberty of this kind is assumed to be general. The writer has no rights at all except those he forges for himself inside his own work. We have become so flooded with sorry fiction based on unearned liberties, or on the notion that fiction must represent the typical, that in the public mind the deeper kinds of realism are less and less understandable.

The writer who writes within what might be called the modern romance tradition may not be writing novels which in all respects partake of a novelistic orthodoxy; but as long as these works have vitality, as long as they present something that is alive, however eccentric its life may seem to the general reader, then they have to be dealt with; and they have to be dealt with on their own terms.

When we look at a good deal of serious modern fiction, and particularly Southern fiction, we find this quality about it that is generally described, in a pejorative sense, as grotesque. Of course, I have found that anything that comes out of the South is going to be called grotesque by the Northern reader, unless it is grotesque, in which case it is going to be called realistic. But for this occasion, we may leave such misapplications aside and consider the kind of fiction that may be called grotesque with good reason, because of a directed intention that way on the part of the author.

In these grotesque works, we find that the writer has made alive some experience which we are not accustomed to observe every day, or which the ordinary man may never experience in his ordinary life. We find that connections which we would expect in the customary kind of realism have been ignored, that there are strange skips and gaps which anyone trying to describe manners and customs would certainly not have left. Yet the characters have an inner coherence, if not always a coherence to their social framework. Their fictional qualities lean away from typical social patterns, toward mystery and the unexpected. It is this kind of realism that I want to consider.

All novelists are fundamentally seekers and describers of the real, but the realism of each novelist will depend on his view of the ultimate reaches of reality. Since the eighteenth century, the popular spirit of each succeeding age has tended more and more to the view that the ills and mysteries of life will eventually fall before the scientific advances of man, a belief that is still going strong even though this is the first generation to face total extinction because of these advances. If the novelist is in tune with this spirit, if he believes that actions are predetermined by psychic makeup or the economic situation or some other determinable factor, then he will be concerned above all with an accurate reproduction of the things that most immediately concern man, with the natural forces that he feels control his destiny. Such a writer may produce a great tragic naturalism, for by his responsibility to the things he sees, he may transcend the limitations of his narrow vision.

On the other hand, if the writer believes that our life is and will remain essentially mysterious, if he looks upon us as beings existing in a created order to whose laws we freely respond, then what he sees on the surface will be of interest to him only as he can go through it into an experience of mystery itself. His kind of fiction will always be pushing its own limits outward toward the limits of mystery, because for this kind of writer, the meaning of a story does not begin except at a depth where adequate motivation and adequate psychology and the various determinations have been exhausted. Such a writer will be interested in what we don't understand rather than in what we do. He will be interested in possibility rather than in probability. He will be interested in characters who are forced out to meet evil and grace and who act on a trust beyond themselves—whether they know very clearly what it is they act upon or not. To the modern mind, this kind of character, and his creator, are typical Don Quixotes, tilting at what is not there.

I would not like to suggest that this kind of writer, because his interest is predominantly in mystery, is able in any sense to slight the concrete. Fiction begins where human knowledge begins—with the senses—and every fiction writer is bound by this fundamental aspect of his medium. I do believe, however, that the kind of writer I am describing will use the concrete in a more drastic way. His way will much more obviously be the way of distortion.

Henry James said that Conrad in his fiction did things in the way that took the most doing. I think the writer of grotesque fiction does them in the way that takes the least, because in his work distances are so great. He's looking for one image that will connect or combine or embody two points; one is a point in the concrete, and the other is a point not visible to the naked eye, but believed in by him firmly, just as real to him, really, as the one that everybody sees.

It's not necessary to point out that the look of this fiction is going to be wild, that it is almost of necessity going to be violent and comic, because of the discrepancies that it seeks to combine.

Even though the writer who produces grotesque fiction may not consider his characters any more freakish than ordinary fallen man usually is, his audience is going to; and it is going to ask him—or more often, tell him—why he has chosen to bring such maimed souls alive. Thomas Mann has said that the grotesque is the true anti-bourgeois style, but I believe that in this country, the general reader has managed to connect the grotesque with the sentimental, for whenever he speaks of it favorably, he seems to associate it with the writer's compassion.

It's considered an absolute necessity these days for writers to have compassion. Compassion is a word that sounds good in anybody's mouth and which no book jacket can do without. It is a quality which no one can put his finger on in any exact critical sense, so it is always safe for anybody to use. Usually I think what is meant by it is that the writer excuses all human weakness because human weakness is human. The kind of hazy compassion demanded of the writer now makes it difficult for him to be anti-anything. Certainly when the grotesque is used in a legitimate way, the intellectual and moral judgments implicit in it will have the ascendency over feeling.

In nineteenth-century American writing, there was a good deal of grotesque literature which came from the frontier and was supposed to be funny; but our present grotesque characters, comic though they may be, are at least not primarily so. They seem to carry an invisible burden; their fanaticism is a reproach, not merely an eccentricity. I believe that they come about from the prophetic vision peculiar to any novelist whose concerns I have been describing. In the novelist's case, prophecy is a matter of seeing near things with their extensions of meaning and thus of seeing far things close up. The prophet is a realist of distances, and it is this kind of realism that you find in the best modern instances of the grotesque.

Whenever I'm asked why Southern writers particularly have a penchant for writing about freaks, I say it is because we are still able to recognize one. To be able to recognize a freak, you have to have some conception of the whole man, and in the South the general conception of man is still, in the main, theological. That is a large statement, and it is dangerous to make it, for almost anything you say about Southern belief can be denied in the next breath with equal propriety. But approaching the subject from the standpoint of the writer, I think it is safe to say that while the South is hardly Christ-centered, it is most certainly Christ-haunted. The Southerner, who isn't convinced of it, is very much afraid that he may have been formed in the image and likeness of God. Ghosts can be very fierce and instructive. They cast strange shadows, particularly in our literature. In any case, it is when the freak can be sensed as a figure for our essential displacement that he attains some depth in literature.

There is another reason in the Southern situation that makes for a tendency toward the grotesque and this is the prevalence of good Southern writers. I think the writer is initially set going by literature more than by life. When there are many writers all employing the same idiom, all looking out on more or less the same social scene, the individual writer will have to be more than

ever careful that he isn't just doing badly what has already been
done to completion. The presence alone of Faulkner in our midst
makes a great difference in what the writer can and cannot permit himself to do. Nobody wants his mule and wagon stalled on
the same track the Dixie Limited is roaring down.

The Southern writer is forced from all sides to make his
gaze extend beyond the surface, beyond mere problems, until it
touches that realm which is the concern of prophets and poets.
When Hawthorne said that he wrote romances, he was attempting, in effect, to keep for fiction some of its freedom from social
determinisms, and to steer it in the direction of poetry. I think
this tradition of the dark and divisive romance-novel has combined with the comic-grotesque tradition, and with the lessons all
writers have learned from the naturalists, to preserve our Southern literature for at least a little while from becoming the kind
of thing Mr. Van Wyck Brooks desired when he said he hoped
that our next literary phase would restore that central literature
which combines the great subject matter of the middlebrow writers with the technical expertness bequeathed by the new critics
and which would thereby restore literature as a mirror and guide
for society.

For the kind of writer I have been describing, a literature
which mirrors society would be no fit guide for it, and one which
did manage, by sheer art, to do both these things would have to
have recourse to more violent means than middlebrow subject
matter and mere technical expertness.

We are not living in times when the realist of distances is
understood or well thought of, even though he may be in the
dominant tradition of American letters. Whenever the public is
heard from, it is heard demanding a literature which is balanced
and which will somehow heal the ravages of our times. In the
name of social order, liberal thought, and sometimes even Christianity, the novelist is asked to be the handmaid of his age.

I have come to think of this handmaid as being very like the
Negro porter who set Henry James's dressing case down in a
puddle when James was leaving the hotel in Charleston. James
was then obliged to sit in the crowded carriage with the satchel
on his knees. All through the South the poor man was ignobly

served, and he afterwards wrote that our domestic servants were the last people in the world who should be employed in the way they were, for they were by nature unfitted for it. The case is the same with the novelist. When he is given the function of domestic, he is going to set the public's luggage down in puddle after puddle.

The novelist must be characterized not by his function but by his vision, and we must remember that his vision has to be transmitted and that the limitations and blind spots of his audience will very definitely affect the way he is able to show what he sees. This is another thing which in these times increases the tendency toward the grotesque in fiction.

Those writers who speak for and with their age are able to do so with a great deal more ease and grace than those who speak counter to prevailing attitudes. I once received a letter from an old lady in California who informed me that when the tired reader comes home at night, he wishes to read something that will lift up his heart. And it seems her heart had not been lifted up by anything of mine she had read. I think that if her heart had been in the right place, it would have been lifted up.

You may say that the serious writer doesn't have to bother about the tired reader, but he does, because they are all tired. One old lady who wants her heart lifted up wouldn't be so bad, but you multiply her two hundred and fifty thousand times and what you get is a book club. I used to think it should be possible to write for some supposed elite, for the people who attend universities and sometimes know how to read, but I have since found that though you may publish your stories in *Botteghe Oscure*, if they are any good at all, you are eventually going to get a letter from some old lady in California, or some inmate of the Federal Penitentiary or the state insane asylum or the local poorhouse, telling you where you have failed to meet his needs.

And his need, of course, is to be lifted up. There is something in us, as storytellers and as listeners to stories, that demands the redemptive act, that demands that what falls at least be offered the chance to be restored. The reader of today looks for this motion, and rightly so, but what he has forgotten is the cost of it. His sense of evil is diluted or lacking altogether, and so he has forgotten the price of restoration. When he reads a novel, he wants either his senses tormented or his spirits raised. He wants to be transported, instantly, either to mock damnation or a mock innocence.

I am often told that the model of balance for the novelist should be Dante, who divided his territory up pretty evenly between hell, purgatory, and paradise. There can be no objection to this, but also there can be no reason to assume that the result of doing it in these times will give us the balanced picture that it gave in Dante's. Dante lived in the thirteenth century, when that balance was achieved in the faith of his age. We live now in an age which doubts both fact and value, which is swept this way and that by momentary convictions. Instead of reflecting a balance from the world around him, the novelist now has to achieve one from a felt balance inside himself.

There is no literary orthodoxy that can be prescribed as settled for the fiction writer, not even that of Henry James, who balanced the elements of traditional realism and romance so admirably within each of his novels. But this much can be said. The great novels we get in the future are not going to be those that the public thinks it wants, or those that critics demand. They are going to be the kind of novels that interest the novelist. And the novels that interest the novelist are those that have not already been written. They are those that put the greatest demands on him, that require him to operate at the maximum of his intelligence and his talents, and to be true to the particularities of his own vocation. The direction of many of us will be more toward poetry than toward the traditional novel.

The problem for such a novelist will be to know how far he can distort without destroying, and in order not to destroy, he will have to descend far enough into himself to reach those underground springs that give life to big work. This descent into himself will, at the same time, be a descent into his region. It will be a descent through the darkness of the familiar into a world where, like the blind man cured in the gospels, he sees men as if they were trees, but walking. This is the beginning of vision, and I feel it is a vision which we in the South must at least try to understand if we want to participate in the continuance of a vital Southern literature. I hate to think that in twenty years Southern writers too may be writing about men in gray-flannel suits and may have lost their ability to see that these gentlemen are even greater freaks than what we are writing about now. I hate to think of the day when the Southern writer will satisfy the tired reader.

John Updike (1932–2009) is considered one of America's fore-
most fiction writers (the Rabbit novels, the Maples stories,
Couples), exploring the disordered lives of the suburban, white
middle class with unfailing verbal felicity. He also wrote vol-
*umes of polished essays and memoirs (*Hugging the Shore, Self-
Consciousness*). His tribute to the Boston Red Sox slugger Ted*
Williams is immersed in the lingo of baseball; it captures with
knowledgeable dispassion the exaltations of sports fans obses-
sively involved with their idols, experiencing triumph, disap-
pointment, betrayal, and, ultimately, resignation vicariously
through them.

HUB FANS
BID KID ADIEU

Fenway Park, in Boston, is a lyric little bandbox of a ballpark.
Everything is painted green and seems in curiously sharp focus,
like the inside of an old-fashioned peeping-type Easter egg. It
was built in 1912 and rebuilt in 1934, and offers, as do most Boston artifacts, a compromise between Man's Euclidean determinations and Nature's beguiling irregularities. Its right field is one
of the deepest in the American League, while its left field is the
shortest; the high left-field wall, three hundred and fifteen feet
from home plate along the foul line, virtually thrusts its surface
at right-handed hitters. On the afternoon of Wednesday, September 28th, as I took a seat behind third base, a uniformed ground-
keeper was treading the top of this wall, picking batting-practice
home runs out of the screen, like a mushroom gatherer seen in

Wordsworthian perspective on the verge of a cliff. The day was overcast, chill, and uninspirational. The Boston team was the worst in twenty-seven seasons. A jangling medley of incompetent youth and aging competence, the Red Sox were finishing in seventh place only because the Kansas City Athletics had locked them out of the cellar. They were scheduled to play the Baltimore Orioles, a much nimbler blend of May and December, who had been dumped from pennant contention a week before by the insatiable Yankees. I, and 10,453 others, had shown up primarily because this was the Red Sox's last home game of the season, and therefore the last time in all eternity that their regular left fielder, known to the headlines as TED, KID, SPLINTER, THUMPER, TW, and, most cloyingly, MISTER WONDERFUL, would play in Boston. "WHAT WILL WE DO WITHOUT TED? HUB FANS ASK" ran the headline on a newspaper being read by a bulb-nosed cigar smoker a few rows away. Williams' retirement had been announced, doubted (he had been threatening retirement for years), confirmed by Tom Yawkey, the Red Sox owner, and at last widely accepted as the sad but probable truth. He was forty-two and had redeemed his abysmal season of 1959 with a—considering his advanced age—fine one. He had been giving away his gloves and bats and had grudgingly consented to a sentimental ceremony today. This was not necessarily his last game; the Red Sox were scheduled to travel to New York and wind up the season with three games there.

I arrived early. The Orioles were hitting fungos on the field. The day before, they had spitefully smothered the Red Sox, 17–4, and neither their faces nor their drab gray visiting-team uniforms seemed very gracious. I wondered who had invited them to the party. Between our heads and the lowering clouds a frenzied organ was thundering through, with an appositeness perhaps accidental, "You *maaaade* me love you, I didn't wanna do it, I didn't wanna do it . . ."

The affair between Boston and Ted Williams has been no mere summer romance; it has been a marriage, composed of spats, mutual disappointments, and, toward the end, a mellowing hoard of shared memories. It falls into three stages, which may be termed Youth, Maturity, and Age; or Thesis, Antithesis, and Synthesis; or Jason, Achilles, and Nestor.

First, there was the by now legendary epoch when the young bridegroom came out of the West, announced "All I want out of life is that when I walk down the street folks will say 'There goes the greatest hitter who ever lived.'" The dowagers of local journalism attempted to give elementary deportment lessons to this child who spake as a god, and to their horror were themselves rebuked. Thus began the long exchange of backbiting, hat-flipping, booing, and spitting that has distinguished Williams' public relations. The spitting incidents of 1957 and 1958 and the similar dockside courtesies that Williams has now and then extended to the grandstand should be judged against this background: the left-field stands at Fenway for twenty years have held a large number of customers who have bought their way in primarily for the privilege of showering abuse on Williams. Greatness necessarily attracts debunkers, but in Williams' case the hostility has been systematic and unappeasable. His basic offense against the fans has been to wish that they weren't there. Seeking a perfectionist's vacuum, he has quixotically desired to sever the game from the ground of paid spectatorship and publicity that supports it. Hence his refusal to tip his cap to the crowd or turn the other cheek to newsmen. It has been a costly theory—it has probably cost him, among other evidences of goodwill, two Most Valuable Player awards, which are voted by reporters—but he has held to it from his rookie year on. While his critics, oral and literary, remained beyond the reach of his discipline, the opposing pitchers were accessible, and he spanked them to the tune of .406 in 1941. He slumped to .356 in 1942 and went off to war.

In 1946, Williams returned from three years as a Marine pilot to the second of his baseball avatars, that of Achilles, the hero of incomparable prowess and beauty who nevertheless was to be found sulking in his tent while the Trojans (mostly Yankees) fought through to the ships. Yawkey, a timber and mining maharajah, had surrounded his central jewel with many gems of slightly lesser water, such as Bobby Doerr, Dom DiMaggio, Rudy York, Birdie Tebbetts, and Johnny Pesky. Throughout the late forties, the Red Sox were the best paper team in baseball, yet they had little three-dimensional to show for it, and if this was a tragedy, Williams was Hamlet. A succinct review of the indictment—and a fair sample of appreciative sports-page prose—appeared the very day of Williams' valedictory, in a column by Huck Finnegan in the Boston *American* (no sentimentalist, Huck):

> Williams' career, in contrast [to Babe Ruth's], has been a series of failures except for his averages. He flopped in the only World Series he ever played in (1946) when he batted only .200. He flopped in the playoff game with Cleveland in 1948. He flopped in the final game of the 1949 season with the pennant hinging on the outcome (Yanks 5, Sox 3). He flopped in 1950 when he returned to the lineup after a two-month absence and ruined the morale of a club that seemed pennant-bound under Steve O'Neill. It has always been Williams' records first, the team second, and the Sox non-winning record is proof enough of that.

There are answers to all this, of course. The fatal weakness of the great Sox slugging teams was not-quite-good-enough pitching rather than Williams' failure to hit a home run every time he came to bat. Again, Williams' depressing effect on his teammates has never been proved. Despite ample coaching to the contrary, most insisted that they *liked* him. He has been generous with advice to any player who asked for it. In an increasingly combative baseball atmosphere, he continued to duck beanballs docilely. With umpires he was gracious to a fault. This courtesy itself annoyed his critics, whom there was no pleasing. And against the ten crucial games (the seven World Series games with the St. Louis Cardinals, the 1948 playoff with the Cleveland Indians, and the two-game series with the Yankees at the end of the 1949 season, winning either one of which would have given the Red Sox the pennant) that make up the Achilles' heel of Williams' record, a mass of statistics can be set showing that day in and day out he was no slouch in the clutch. The correspondence columns of the Boston papers now and then suffer a sharp flurry of arithmetic on this score; indeed, for Williams to have distributed all his hits so they did nobody else any good would constitute a feat of placement unparalleled in the annals of selfishness.

Whatever residue of truth remains of the Finnegan charge those of us who love Williams must transmute as best we can, in our own personal crucibles. My personal memories of Williams begin when I was a boy in Pennsylvania, with two last-place teams in Philadelphia to keep me company. For me, "W'ms, lf" was a figment of the box scores who always seemed to be going 3-for-5. He radiated, from afar, the hard blue glow of high purpose. I remember listening over the radio to the All-Star Game of 1946, in which Williams hit two singles and two home runs, the second one off a Rip Sewell "blooper" pitch; it was like hitting a balloon out of the park. I remember watching one of his home runs from the bleachers of Shibe Park; it went over the first baseman's head and rose meticulously along a straight line and was still rising when it cleared the fence. The trajectory seemed qualitatively different from anything anyone else might hit. For me, Williams is the classic ballplayer of the game on a hot August weekday, before a small crowd, when the only thing at stake is the tissue-thin difference between a thing done well and a thing done ill. Baseball is a game of the long season, of relentless and gradual averaging-out. Irrelevance—since the reference point of most individual games is remote and statistical—always threatens its interest, which can be maintained not by the occasional heroics that sportswriters feed upon but by players who always *care*; who care, that is to say, about themselves and their art. Insofar as the clutch hitter is not a sportswriter's myth, he is a vulgarity, like a writer who writes only for money. It may be that, compared to managers' dreams such as Joe DiMaggio and the always helpful Stan Musial, Williams is an icy star. But of all team sports, baseball, with its graceful intermittences of action, its immense and tranquil field sparsely settled with poised men in white, its dispassionate mathematics, seems to me best suited to accommodate, and be ornamented by, a loner. It is an essentially lonely game. No other player visible to my generation has concentrated within himself so much of the sport's poignance, has so assiduously refined his natural skills, has so constantly brought to the plate that intensity of competence that crowds the throat with joy.

By the time I went to college, near Boston, the lesser stars Yawkey had assembled around Williams had faded, and his craftsmanship, his rigorous pride, had become itself a kind of heroism. This brittle and temperamental player developed an unexpected quality of persistence. He was always coming back— back from Korea, back from a broken collarbone, a shattered elbow, a bruised heel, back from drastic bouts of flu and pto- maine poisoning. Hardly a season went by without some enfee- bling mishap, yet he always came back, and always looked like himself. The delicate mechanism of timing and power seemed locked, shockproof, in some case outside his body. In addition to injuries, there were a heavily publicized divorce, and the usual storms with the press, and the Williams Shift—the maneu- ver, custom-built by Lou Boudreau, of the Cleveland Indians, whereby three infielders were concentrated on the right side of the infield, where a left-handed pull hitter like Williams generally hits the ball. Williams could easily have learned to punch singles through the vacancy on his left and fattened his average hugely. This was what Ty Cobb, the Einstein of average, told him to do. But the game had changed since Cobb; Williams believed that his value to the club and to the game was as a slugger, so he went on pulling the ball, trying to blast it through three men, and paid the price of perhaps fifteen points of lifetime average. Like Ruth before him, he bought the occasional home run at the cost of many directed singles—a calculated sacrifice certainly not, in the case of a hitter as average-minded as Williams, entirely selfish.

After a prime so harassed and hobbled, William was granted by the relenting fates a golden twilight. He became at the end of his career perhaps the best *old* hitter of the century. The dividing line came between the 1956 and the 1957 seasons. In September of the first year, he and Mickey Mantle were contending for the batting championship. Both were hitting around .350, and there was no one else near them. The season ended with a three-game series between the Yankees and the Sox, and, living in New York then, I went up to the Stadium. Williams was slightly shy of the four hundred at-bats needed to qualify; the fear was expressed that the Yankee pitchers would walk him to protect Mantle. Instead, they pitched to him—a wise decision. He looked terrible at the plate, tired and discouraged and unconvincing. He never looked very good to me in the Stadium. (Last week, in *Life*, Williams, a sportswriter himself now, wrote gloomily of the Stadium, "There's the bigness of it. There are those high stands and all those people smoking—and, of course, the shadows. . . . It takes at least one series to get accustomed to the Stadium and even then you're not sure.") The final outcome in 1956 was Mantle .353, Williams .345.

The next year, I moved from New York to New England, and it made all the difference. For in September of 1957, in the same situation, the story was reversed. Mantle finally hit .365; it was the best season of his career. But Williams, though sick and old, had run away from him. A bout of flu had laid him low in September. He emerged from his cave in the Hotel Somerset haggard but irresistible; he hit four successive pinch-hit home runs. "I feel terrible," he confessed, "but every time I take a swing at the ball it goes out of the park." He ended the season with thirty-eight home runs and an average of .388, the highest in either league since his own .406, and, coming from a decrepit man of thirty-nine, an even more supernal figure. With eight or so of the "leg hits" that a younger man would have beaten out, it would have been .400. And the next year, Williams, who in 1949 and 1953 had lost batting championships by decimal whiskers to George Kell and Mickey Vernon, sneaked in behind his teammate Pete Runnels and filched his sixth title, a bargain at .328.

In 1959, it seemed all over. The dinosaur thrashed around in the .200 swamp for the first half of the season, and was even benched ("rested," manager Mike Higgins tactfully said). Old foes like the late Bill Cunningham began to offer batting tips. Cunningham thought Williams was jiggling his elbows; in truth, Williams' neck was so stiff he could hardly turn his head to look at the pitcher. When he swung, it looked like a Calder mobile with one thread cut; it reminded you that since 1953 Williams' shoulders had been wired together. A solicitous pall settled over the sports pages. In the two decades since Williams had come to Boston, his status had imperceptibly shifted from that of a naughty prodigy to that of a municipal monument. As his shadow in the record books lengthened, the Red Sox teams around him declined, and the entire American League seemed to be losing life and color to the National. The inconsistency of the new superstars—Mantle, Colavito, and Kaline—served to make Williams appear all the more singular. And off the field, his private philanthropy—in particular, his zealous chairmanship of the Jimmy Fund, a charity for children with cancer—gave him a civic presence somewhat like that of Richard Cardinal Cushing. In religion, Williams appears to be a humanist, and a selective one at that, but he and the cardinal, when their good works intersect and they appear in the public eye together, make a handsome and heartening pair.

Humiliated by his '59 season, Williams determined, once more, to come back. I, as a specimen Williams partisan, was both glad and fearful. All baseball fans believe in miracles; the question is, how *many* do you believe in? He looked like a ghost in spring training. Manager Jurges warned us ahead of time that if Williams didn't come through he would be benched, just like anybody else. As it turned out, it was Jurges who was benched. Williams entered the 1960 season needing eight home runs to have a lifetime total of 500; after one time at bat in Washington, he needed seven. For a stretch, he was hitting a home run every second game that he played. He passed Lou Gehrig's lifetime total, then the number 500, then Mel Ott's total, and finished with 521, thirteen behind Jimmie Foxx, who alone stands between Williams and Babe Ruth's unapproachable 714. The summer was a statistician's picnic. His two thousandth walk came and went, his eighteen hundredth run batted in, his sixteenth All-Star Game. At one point, he hit a home run off a pitcher, Don Lee, off whose father, Thornton Lee, he had hit a home run a generation before. The only comparable season for a forty-two-year-old man was Ty Cobb's in 1928. Cobb batted .323 and hit one homer. Williams batted .316 but hit twenty-nine homers.

In sum, though generally conceded to be the greatest hitter of his era, he did not establish himself as "the greatest hitter who ever lived." Cobb, for average, and Ruth, for power, remain supreme. Cobb, Rogers Hornsby, Joe Jackson, and Lefty O'Doul, among players since 1900, have higher lifetime averages than Williams' .344. Unlike Foxx, Gehrig, Hack Wilson, Hank Greenberg, and Ralph Kiner, Williams never came close to matching Babe Ruth's season home-run total of sixty. In the list of major-league batting records, not one is held by Williams. He is second in walks drawn, third in home runs, fifth in lifetime averages, sixth in runs batted in, eighth in runs scored and in total bases, fourteenth in doubles, and thirtieth in hits. But if we allow him merely average seasons for the four-plus seasons he lost to two wars, and add another season for the months he lost to injuries, we get a man who in all the power totals would be second, and not a very distant second, to Ruth. And if we further allow that these years would have been not merely average but prime years, if we allow for all the months when Williams was playing in sub-par condition, if we permit his early and later years in baseball to be some sort of index of what the middle years could have been, if we give him a right-field fence that is not, like Fenway's, one of the most distant in the league, and if—the least excusable "if"—we imagine him condescending to outsmart the Williams Shift, we can defensibly assemble, like a colossus induced from the sizable fragments that do remain, a statistical figure not incommensurate with his grandiose ambition. From the statistics that are on the books, a good case can be made that in the *combination* of power and average Williams is first; nobody else ranks so high in both categories. Finally, there is the witness of the eyes; men whose memories go back to Shoeless Joe Jackson—another unlucky natural—rank him and Williams together as the best-looking hitters they have seen. It was for our last look that ten thousand of us had come.

Two girls, one of them with pert buckteeth and eyes as black as vest buttons, the other with white skin and flesh-colored hair, like an underdeveloped photograph of a redhead, came and sat on my right. On my other side was one of those frowning, chest-less young-old men who can frequently be seen, often wearing sailor hats, attending ball games alone. He did not once open his program but instead tapped it, rolled up, on his knee as he gave the game his disconsolate attention. A young lady, with freckles and a depressed, dainty nose that by an optical illusion seemed to thrust her lips forward for a kiss, sauntered down into the box seats and with striking aplomb took a seat right behind the roof of the Oriole dugout. She wore a blue coat with a Northeastern University emblem sewed to it. The girls beside me took it into their heads that this was Williams' daughter. She looked too old to me, and why would she be sitting behind the visitors' dugout? On the other hand, from the way she sat there, staring at the sky and French-inhaling, she clearly was *somebody*. Other fans came and eclipsed her from view. The crowd looked less like a weekday ballpark crowd than like the folks you might find in Yellowstone National Park, or emerging from automobiles at the top of scenic Mount Mansfield. There were a lot of competitively well-dressed couples of tourist age, and not a few babes in arms. A row of five seats in front of me was abruptly filled with a woman and four children, the youngest of them two years old, if that. Someday, presumably, he could tell his grandchildren that he saw Williams play. Along with these tots and second-honeymooners, there were Harvard freshmen, giving off that peculiar nervous glow created when a quantity of insouciance is saturated with insecurity; thick-necked Army officers with brass on their shoulders and lead in their voices; pepperings of priests; perfumed bouquets of Roxbury Fabian fans; shiny salesmen from Albany and Fall River; and those gray, hoarse men—taxi drivers, slaughterers, and bartenders—who will continue to click through the turnstiles long after everyone else has deserted to television and tramporamas. Behind me, two young male voices blossomed, cracking a joke about God's five proofs that Thomas Aquinas exists—typical Boston College levity.

The batting cage was trundled away. The Orioles fluttered to the sidelines. Diagonally across the field, by the Red Sox dugout, a cluster of men in overcoats were festering like maggots. I could see a splinter of white uniform, and Williams' head, held at a self-deprecating and evasive tilt. Williams' conversational stance is that of a six-foot-three-inch man under a six-foot ceil-

ing. He moved away to the patter of flashbulbs, and began playing catch with a young Negro outfielder named Willie Tasby. His
arm, never very powerful, had grown lax with the years, and his
throwing motion was a kind of muscular drawl. To catch the
ball, he flicked his glove hand onto his left shoulder (he batted
left but threw right, as every schoolboy ought to know) and let
the ball plop into it comically. This catch session with Tasby was
the only time all afternoon I saw him grin.

A tight little flock of human sparrows who, from the lambent
and pampered pink of their faces, could only have been Boston
politicians moved toward the plate. The loudspeakers mam-
mothly coughed as someone huffed on the microphone. The cer-
emonies began. Curt Gowdy, the Red Sox radio and television
announcer, who sounds like everybody's brother-in-law, delivered a brief sermon, taking the two words "pride" and "champion" as his text. It began, "Twenty-one years ago, a skinny kid
from San Diego, California . . . ," and ended, "I don't think we'll
ever see another like him." Robert Tibolt, chairman of the board
of the Greater Boston Chamber of Commerce, presented Williams with a big Paul Revere silver bowl. Harry Carlson, a member of the sports committee of the Boston Chamber, gave him a
plaque, whose inscription he did not read in its entirety, out of
deference to Williams' distaste for this sort of fuss. Mayor Col-
lins presented the Jimmy Fund with a thousand-dollar check.

Then the occasion himself stooped to the microphone, and
his voice sounded, after the others, very Californian; it seemed
to be coming, excellently amplified, from a great distance, ado-
lescently young and as smooth as a butternut. His thanks for the
gifts had not died from our ears before he glided, as if helplessly,
into "In spite of all the terrible things that have been said about
me by the maestros of the keyboard up there . . ." He glanced
up at the press rows suspended above home plate. The crowd tit-
tered, appalled. A frightful vision flashed upon me, of the press
gallery pelting Williams with erasers, of Williams clambering
up the foul screen to slug journalists, of a riot, of Mayor Col-
lins being crushed. ". . . And they *were* terrible things," Williams
insisted, with level melancholy, into the mike. "I'd like to forget
them, but I can't." He paused, swallowed his memories, and went

on, "I want to say that my years in Boston have been the greatest thing in my life." The crowd, like an immense sail going limp in a change of wind, sighed with relief. Taking all the parts himself, Williams then acted out a vivacious little morality drama in which an imaginary tempter came to him at the beginning of his career and said, "Ted, you can play anywhere you like." Leaping nimbly into the role of his younger self (who in biographical actuality had yearned to be a Yankee), Williams gallantly chose Boston over all the other cities, and told us that Tom Yawkey was the greatest owner in baseball and we were the greatest fans. We applauded ourselves heartily. The umpire came out and dusted the plate. The voice of doom announced over the loudspeakers that after Williams' retirement his uniform number, 9, would be permanently retired—the first time the Red Sox had so honored a player. We cheered. The national anthem was played. We cheered. The game began.

Williams was third in the batting order, so he came up in the bottom of the first inning, and Steve Barber, a young pitcher who was not yet born when Williams began playing for the Red Sox, offered him four pitches, at all of which he disdained to swing, since none of them were within the strike zone. This demonstrated simultaneously that Williams' eyes were razor-sharp and that Barber's control wasn't. Shortly, the bases were full, with Williams on second. "Oh, I hope he gets held up at third! That would be wonderful," the girl beside me moaned, and, sure enough, the man at bat walked and Williams was delivered into our foreground. He struck the pose of Donatello's David, the third-base bag being Goliath's head. Fiddling with his cap, swapping small talk with the Oriole third baseman (who seemed delighted to have him drop in), swinging his arms with a sort of prancing nervousness, he looked fine—flexible, hard, and not unbecomingly substantial through the middle. The long neck, the small head, the knickers whose cuffs were worn down near his ankles—all these points, often observed by caricaturists, were visible in the flesh.

With each pitch, Williams danced down the baseline, waving his arms and stirring dust, ponderous but menacing, like an attacking goose. It occurred to about a dozen humorists at once to shout "Steal home! Go, go!" Williams' speed afoot was never legendary. Lou Clinton, a young Sox outfielder, hit a fairly deep fly to center field. Williams tagged up and ran home. As he slid across the plate, the ball, thrown with unusual heft by Jackie Brandt, the Oriole center fielder, hit him on the back.

"Boy, he was really loafing, wasn't he?" one of the boys behind me said.

"It's cold," the other explained. "He doesn't play well when it's cold. He likes heat. He's a hedonist."

The run that Williams scored was the second and last of the inning. Gus Triandos, of the Orioles, quickly evened the score by plunking a home run over the handy left-field wall. Williams, who had had this wall at his back for twenty years, played the ball flawlessly. He didn't budge. He just stood there, in the center of the little patch of grass that his patient footsteps had worn brown, and, limp with lack of interest, watched the ball pass overhead. It was not a very interesting game. Mike Higgins, the Red Sox manager, with nothing to lose, had restricted his major-league players to the left-field line—along with Williams, Frank Malzone, a first-rate third baseman, played the game—and had peopled the rest of the terrain with unpredictable youngsters fresh, or not so fresh, off the farms. Other than Williams' recurrent appearances at the plate, the *maladresse* of the Sox infield was the sole focus of suspense; the second baseman turned every grounder into a juggling act, while the shortstop did a breath-taking impersonation of an open window. With this sort of assis-tance, the Orioles wheedled their way into a 4–2 lead. They had early replaced Barber with another young pitcher, Jack Fisher. Fortunately (as it turned out), Fisher is no cutie; he is willing to burn the ball through the strike zone, and inning after inning this tactic punctured Higgins' string of test balloons.

Whenever Williams appeared at the plate—pounding the dirt from his cleats, gouging a pit in the batter's box with his left foot, wringing resin out of the bat handle with his vehement grip, switching the stick at the pitcher with an electric ferocity—it was like having a familiar Leonardo appear in a shuffle of *Saturday*

Evening Post covers. This man, you realized—and here, perhaps, was the difference, greater than the difference in gifts—really intended to hit the ball. In the third inning, he hoisted a high fly to deep center. In the fifth, we thought he had it; he smacked the ball hard and high into the heart of his power zone, but the deep right field in Fenway and the heavy air and a casual east wind defeated him. The ball died. Al Pilarcik leaned his back against the big "380" painted on the right-field wall and caught it. On another day, in another park, it would have been gone. (After the game, Williams said, "I didn't think I could hit one any harder than that. The conditions weren't good.")

The afternoon grew so glowering that in the sixth inning the arc lights were turned on—always a wan sight in the daytime, like the burning headlights of a funeral procession. Aided by the gloom, Fisher was slicing through the Sox rookies, and Williams did not come to bat in the seventh. He was second up in the eighth. This was almost certainly his last time to come to the plate in Fenway Park, and instead of merely cheering, as we had at his three previous appearances, we stood, all of us— stood and applauded. Have you ever heard applause in a ballpark? Just applause—no calling, no whistling, just an ocean of handclaps, minute after minute, burst after burst, crowding and running together in continuous succession like the pushes of surf at the edge of the sand. It was a somber and considered tumult. There was not a boo in it. It seemed to renew itself out of a shifting set of memories as the kid, the Marine, the veteran of feuds and failures and injuries, the friend of children, and the enduring old pro evolved down the bright tunnel of twenty-one summers toward this moment. At last, the umpire signaled for Fisher to pitch; with the other players, he had been frozen in position. Only Williams had moved during the ovation, switching his hat impatiently, ignoring everything except his cherished task. Fisher wound up, and the applause sank into a hush.

Understand that we were a crowd of rational people. We knew that a home run cannot be produced at will; the right pitch must be perfectly met and luck must ride with the ball. Three innings before, we had seen a brave effort fail. The air was soggy; the season was exhausted. Nevertheless, there will always lurk, around a corner in a pocket of our knowledge of the odds, an indefensible hope, and this was one of the times, which you now and then find in sports, when a density of expectation hangs in the air and plucks an event out of the future.

Fisher, after his unsettling wait, was wide with the first pitch. He put the second one over, and Williams swung mightily and missed. The crowd grunted, seeing that classic swing, so long and smooth and quick, exposed, naked in its failure. Fisher threw the third time, Williams swung again, and there it was. The ball climbed on a diagonal line into the vast volume of air over center field. From my angle, behind third base, the ball seemed less an object in flight than the tip of a towering, motionless construct, like the Eiffel Tower or the Tappan Zee Bridge. It was in the books while it was still in the sky. Brandt ran back to the deepest corner of the outfield grass; the ball descended beyond his reach and struck in the crotch where the bullpen met the wall, bounced chunkily, and, as far as I could see, vanished.

Like a feather caught in a vortex, Williams ran around the square of bases at the center of our beseeching screaming. He ran as he always ran out home runs—hurriedly, unsmiling, head down, as if our praise were a storm of rain to get out of. He didn't tip his cap. Though we thumped, wept, and chanted "We want Ted" for minutes after he hid in the dugout, he did not come back. Our noise for some seconds passed beyond excitement into a kind of immense open anguish, a wailing, a cry to be saved. But immortality is nontransferable. The papers said that the other players, and even the umpires on the field, begged him to come out and acknowledge us in some way, but he never had and did not now. Gods do not answer letters.

Every true story has an anticlimax. The men on the field refused to disappear, as would have seemed decent, in the smoke of Williams' miracle. Fisher continued to pitch, and escaped further harm. At the end of the inning, Higgins sent Williams out to his left-field position, then instantly replaced him with Carroll Hardy, so we had a long last look at Williams as he ran out there and then back, his uniform jogging, his eyes steadfast on the ground. It was nice, and we were grateful, but it left a funny taste.

One of the scholasticists behind me said, "Let's go. We've seen everything. I don't want to spoil it." This seemed a sound aesthetic decision. Williams' last word had been so exquisitely chosen, such a perfect fusion of expectation, intention, and execution, that already it felt a little unreal in my head, and I wanted to get out before the castle collapsed. But the game, though played by clumsy midgets under the feeble glow of the arc lights, began to tug at my attention, and I loitered in the runway until it was over. Williams' homer had, quite incidentally, made the score 4–3. In the bottom of the ninth inning, with one out, Marlan Coughtry, the second-base juggler, singled. Vic Wertz, pinch-hitting, doubled off the left-field wall, Coughtry advancing to third. Pumpsie Green walked, to load the bases. Willie Tasby hit a double-play ball to the third baseman, but in making the pivot throw Billy Klaus, an ex–Red Sox infielder, reverted to form and threw the ball past the first baseman and into the Red Sox dugout. The Sox won, 5–4. On the car radio as I drove home I heard that Williams had decided not to accompany the team to New York. So he knew how to do even that, the hardest thing. Quit.

Randall Jarrell (1914–1965) was a superb poet (The Woman at the Washington Zoo, The Lost World) *and equally fine critic. In his essay collection* A Sad Heart at the Supermarket, *he despaired of the vulgarity of American consumer culture promoted by mass media. Jarrell's plight was that of an immensely cultivated intelligence in a society that seemed increasingly to devalue intellect; at the same time he felt a reluctant, amused affection for the brand-name world gathering around him.*

A SAD HEART AT THE SUPERMARKET

The emperor Augustus would sometimes say to his Senate: "Words fail me, my Lords; nothing I can say could possibly indicate the depth of my feelings in this matter." But in this matter of mass culture, the mass media, I am speaking not as an emperor but as a fool, a suffering, complaining, helplessly nonconforming poet-or-artist-of-a-sort, far off at the obsolescent rear of things; what I say will indicate the depth of my feelings and the shallowness and one-sidedness of my thoughts. If those English lyric poets who went mad during the eighteenth century had told you why the Age of Enlightenment was driving them crazy, it would have had a kind of documentary interest: what I say may have a kind of documentary interest. *The toad beneath the harrow knows / Exactly where each tooth-point goes*: if you tell me that the field is being harrowed to grow grain for bread, and to create a world in which there will be no more famines, or toads either, I will say: "I know"; but let me tell you where the tooth-points go, and what the harrow looks like from below.

Advertising men, businessmen speak continually of *media* or *the media* or *the mass media*. One of their trade journals is named, simply, *Media*. It is an impressive word: one imagines Mephistopheles offering Faust *media that no man has ever known*; one feels, while the word is in one's ear, that abstract, overmastering powers, of a scale and intensity unimagined yesterday, are being offered one by the technicians who discovered and control them—offered, and at a price. The word has the clear fatal ring of that new world whose space we occupy so luxuriously and precariously; the world that produces mink stoles, rockabilly records, and tactical nuclear weapons by the million; the world that Attila, Galileo, Hansel and Gretel never knew.

And yet, it's only the plural of *medium*. "*Medium*," says the dictionary, "that which lies in the middle; hence, middle condition or degree . . . A substance through which a force acts or an effect is transmitted . . . That through or by which anything is accomplished; as, an advertising *medium* . . . *Biol.* A nutritive mixture or substance, as broth, gelatin, agar, for cultivating bacteria, fungi, etc."

Let us name *our* trade journal *The Medium*. For all these media—television, radio, movies, newspapers, magazines, and the rest—are a single medium, in whose depths we are all being cultivated. This Medium is of middle condition or degree, mediocre; it lies in the middle of everything, between a man and his neighbor, his wife, his child, his self; it, more than anything else, is the substance through which the forces of our society act upon us, and make us into what our society needs.

And what does it need? For us to need.

Oh, it needs for us to do or be many things: workers, technicians, executives, soldiers, housewives. But first of all, last of all, it needs for us to be buyers; consumers; beings who want much and will want more—who want consistently and insatiably. Find some spell to make us turn away from the stoles, the records, and the weapons, and our world will change into something to us unimaginable. Find some spell to make us see that the product or service that yesterday was an unthinkable luxury today is an inexorable necessity, and our world will go on. It is the Medium which casts this spell—which is this spell. As we look at the television set, listen to the radio, read the magazines, the frontier of necessity is always being pushed forward. The Medium shows us what our new needs are—how often, without it, we should not have known!—and it shows us how they can be satisfied: they can be satisfied by buying something. The act of buying something is at the root of our world; if anyone wishes to paint the genesis of things in our society, he will paint a picture of God holding out to Adam a checkbook or credit card or Charge-a-Plate.

But how quickly our poor naked Adam is turned into a consumer, is linked to others by the great chain of buying!

> No outcast he, bewildered and depressed:
> Along his infant veins are interfused
> The gravitation and the filial bond
> Of nature that connect him with the world.

Children of three or four can ask for a brand of cereal, sing some soap's commercial; by the time that they are twelve or thirteen they are not children but teenage consumers, interviewed, graphed, analyzed. They are well on their way to becoming that ideal figure of our culture, the knowledgeable consumer. Let me define him: the knowledgeable consumer is someone who, when he comes to Weimar, knows how to buy a Weimaraner.

Daisy's voice sounded like money; everything about the knowledgeable consumer looks like or sounds like or feels like money, and informed money at that. To live is to consume, to understand life is to know what to consume: he has learned to understand this, so that his life is a series of choices—correct ones—among the products and services of the world. He is able to choose to consume something, of course, only because sometime, somewhere, he or someone else produced something—but just when or where or what no longer seems to us of as much interest. We may still go to Methodist or Baptist or Presbyterian churches on Sunday, but the Protestant ethic of frugal industry, of production for its own sake, is gone.

Production has come to seem to our society not much more than a condition prior to consumption. "The challenge of today," an advertising agency writes, "is to make the consumer raise his level of demand." This challenge has been met: the Medium has found it easy to make its people feel the continually increasing lacks, the many specialized dissatisfactions (merging into one great dissatisfaction, temporarily assuaged by new purchases) that it needs for them to feel. When in some magazine we see the Medium at its most nearly perfect, we hardly know which half is entertaining and distracting us, which half making us buy: some advertisement may be more ingeniously entertaining than the text beside it, but it is the text which has made us long for a product more passionately. When one finishes *Holiday* or *Harper's Bazaar* or *House and Garden* or *The New Yorker* or *High Fidelity* or *Road and Track* or—but make your own list—buying something, going somewhere seems a necessary completion to the act of reading the magazine.

Reader, isn't buying or fantasy-buying an important part of your and my emotional life? (If you reply, *No*, I'll think of you with bitter envy as more than merely human; as deeply un-American.) It is a standard joke that when a woman is bored or sad she buys something, to cheer herself up; but in this respect we are all women together, and can hear complacently the reminder of how feminine this consumer-world of ours has become. One imagines as a characteristic dialogue of our time an interview in which someone is asking of a vague gracious figure, a kind of Mrs. America: "But while you waited for the intercontinental ballistic missiles what did you *do*?" She answers: "I bought things."

She reminds one of the sentinel at Pompeii—a space among ashes, now, but at his post: she too did what she was supposed to do. Our society has delivered us—most of us—from the bonds of necessity, so that we no longer struggle to find food to keep from starving, clothing and shelter to keep from freezing; yet if the ends for which we work and of which we dream are only clothes and restaurants and houses, possessions, consumption, how have we escaped?—we have exchanged man's old bondage for a new voluntary one. It is more than a figure of speech to say that the consumer is trained for his job of consuming as the factory worker is trained for his job of producing; and the first can be a longer, more complicated training, since it is easier to teach a man to handle a tool, to read a dial, than it is to teach him to ask, always, for a name-brand aspirin—to want, someday, a standby generator.

What is that? You don't know? I used not to know, but the readers of *House Beautiful* all know, so that now I know. It is the electrical generator that stands in the basement of the suburban house owner, shining, silent, till at last one night the lights go out, the furnace stops, the freezer's food begins to—

Ah, but it's frozen for good, the lights are on forever; the owner has switched on the standby generator.

But you don't see that he really needs the generator, you'd rather have seen him buy a second car? He has two. A second bathroom? He has four. When the People of the Medium doubled everything, he doubled everything; and now that he's gone twice round he will have to wait three years, or four, till both are obsolescent—but while he waits there are so many new needs that he can satisfy, so many things a man can buy. "Man wants but little here below / Nor wants that little long," said the poet; what a lie! Man wants almost unlimited quantities of almost everything, and he wants it till the day he dies.

Sometimes in *Life* or *Look* we see a double-page photograph of some family standing on the lawn among its possessions: station wagon, swimming pool, power cruiser, sports car, tape recorder, television sets, radios, cameras, power lawn mower, garden tractor, lathe, barbecue set, sporting equipment, domestic appliances—all the gleaming, grotesquely imaginative paraphernalia of its existence. It was hard to get everything on two pages, soon it will need four. It is like a dream, a child's dream before Christmas; yet if the members of the family doubt that they are awake, they have only to reach out and pinch something. The family seems pale and small, a negligible appendage, beside its possessions; only a human being would need to ask: "Which owns which?" We are fond of saying that something is not just something but "a way of life"; this too is a way of life—our way, the way.

Emerson, in his spare stony New England, a few miles from Walden, could write: "Things are in the saddle / And ride mankind." He could say more now: that they are in the theater and studio, and entertain mankind; are in the pulpit and preach to mankind. The values of business, in a business society like our own, are reflected in every sphere: values which agree with them are reinforced, values which disagree are canceled out or have lip service paid to them. In business what sells is good, and that's the end of it—that is what *good* means; if the world doesn't beat a path to your door, your mousetrap wasn't better. The values of the Medium—which is both a popular business itself and the cause of popularity in other businesses—are business values: money, success, celebrity. If we are representative members of our society, the Medium's values are ours; and even if we are unrepresentative, non-conforming, our hands are—too often—subdued to the element they work in, and our unconscious expectations are all that we consciously reject. Darwin said that he always immediately wrote down evidence against a theory because otherwise, he'd noticed, he would forget it; in the same way, we keep forgetting the existence of those poor and unknown failures whom we might rebelliously love and admire.

If you're so smart why aren't you rich? is the ground-bass of our society, a grumbling and quite unanswerable criticism, since the society's non-monetary values *are* directly convertible into money. Celebrity turns into testimonials, lectures, directorships, presidencies, the capital gains of an autobiography *Told To* some professional ghost who photographs the man's life as Bachrach photographs his body. I read in the newspapers a lyric and perhaps exaggerated instance of this direct conversion of celebrity into money: his son accompanied Adlai Stevenson on a trip to Russia, took snapshots of his father, and sold them (to accompany his father's account of the trip) to *Look* for $20,000. When Liberace said that his critics' unfavorable reviews hurt him so much that he cried all the way to the bank, one had to admire the correctness and penetration of his press agent's wit—in another age, what might not such a man have become!

Our culture is essentially periodical: we believe that all that is deserves to perish and to have something else put in its place.

We speak of planned obsolescence, but it is more than planned, it is felt; is an assumption about the nature of the world. We feel that the present is better and more interesting, more real, than the past, and that the future will be better and more interesting, more real, than the present; but, consciously, we do not hold against the present its prospective obsolescence. Our standards have become to an astonishing degree the standards of what is called the world of fashion, where mere timeliness—being orange in orange's year, violet in violet's—is the value to which all other values are reducible. In our society the word *old-fashioned* is so final a condemnation that someone like Norman Vincent Peale can say about atheism or agnosticism simply that it is old-fashioned; the homely recommendation of the phrase *Give me that good old-time religion* has become, after a few decades, the conclusive rejection of the phrase *old-fashioned atheism.*

All this is, at bottom, the opposite of the world of the arts, where commercial and scientific progress do not exist; where the bone of Homer and Mozart and Donatello is there, always, under the mere blush of fashion; where the past—the remote past, even—is responsible for the way that we understand, value, and act in, the present. (When one reads an abstract expressionist's remark that Washington studios are "eighteen months behind" those of his colleagues in New York, one realizes something of the terrible power of business and fashion over those most overtly hostile to them.) An artist's work and life presuppose continuing standards, values extended over centuries or millennia, a future that is the continuation and modification of the past, not its contradiction or irrelevant replacement. He is working for the time that wants the best that he can do: the present, he hopes—but if not that, the future. If he sees that fewer and fewer people are any real audience for the serious artists of the past, he will feel that still fewer are going to be an audience for the serious artists of the present: for those who, willingly or unwillingly, sacrifice extrinsic values to intrinsic ones, immediate effectiveness to that steady attraction which, the artist hopes, true excellence will always exert.

The past's relation to the artist or man of culture is almost the opposite of its relation to the rest of our society. To him the present is no more than the last ring on the trunk, understandable and valuable only in terms of all the earlier rings. The rest of our society sees only that great last ring, the enveloping surface of the trunk; what's underneath is a disregarded, almost mythical foundation. When Northrop Frye writes that "the preoccupation of the humanities with the past is sometimes made a reproach against them by those who forget that we face the past: it may be shadowy, but it is all that is there," he is saying what for the artist or man of culture is self-evidently true. Yet for the Medium and the People of the Medium it is as self-evidently false: for them the present—or a past so recent, so quick-changing, so soon-disappearing, that it might be called the specious present—is all that is there.

In the past our culture's body of common knowledge—its frame of reference, its possibility of comprehensible allusion—changed slowly and superficially; the amount added to it or taken away from it, in any ten years, was surprisingly small. Now in any ten years a surprisingly large proportion of the whole is replaced. Most of the information people have in common is something that four or five years from now they will not even remember having known. A newspaper story remarks in astonishment that television quiz programs "have proved that ordinary citizens can be conversant with such esoterica as jazz, opera, the Bible, Shakespeare, poetry, and fisticuffs." You may exclaim: "Esoterica! If the Bible and Shakespeare are esoterica, what is there that's common knowledge?" The answer, I suppose, is that Elfrida von Nardroff and Teddy Nadler—the ordinary citizens on the quiz programs—are common knowledge; though not for long. Songs disappear in two or three months, celebrities in two or three years; most of the Medium is little felt and soon forgotten. Nothing is as dead as day-before-yesterday's newspaper, the next-to-the-last number on the roulette wheel; but most of the knowledge people have in common and lose in common is knowledge of such newspapers, such numbers. Yet the novelist or poet or dramatist, when he moves a great audience, depends upon the deep feelings, the living knowledge, that the people of that audience share; if so much has become contingent, superficial, ephemeral, it is disastrous for him.

New products and fashions replace the old, and the fact that they replace them is proof enough of their superiority. Similarly, the Medium does not need to show that the subjects which fill it are interesting or timely or important; the fact that they are its subjects makes them so. If *Time*, *Life*, and the television shows are full of Tom Fool this month, he's no fool. And when he has been gone from them a while, we do not think him a fool—we do not think of him at all. He no longer exists, in the fullest sense of the word *exist*: to be is to be perceived, to be a part of the Medium of our perception. Our celebrities are not kings, romantic in exile, but Representatives who, defeated, are forgotten; they had, always, only the qualities that we delegated to them.

After driving for four or five minutes along the road outside my door, I come to a row of one-room shacks about the size of kitchens, made out of used boards, metal signs, old tin roofs. To the people who live in them an electric dishwasher of one's own is as much a fantasy as an ocean liner of one's own. But since the Medium (and those whose thought is molded by it) does not perceive them, these people are themselves a fantasy. No matter how many millions of such exceptions to the general rule there are, they do not really exist, but have a kind of anomalous, statistical subsistence; our moral and imaginative view of the world is no more affected by them than by the occupants of some home for the mentally deficient a little farther along the road. If some night one of these outmoded, economically deficient ghosts should scratch at my window, I could say only: "Come back twenty or thirty years ago." And if I myself, as an old-fashioned, one-room poet, a friend of "quiet culture," a "meek lover of the good," should go out some night to scratch at another window, shouldn't I hear someone's indifferent or regretful: "Come back a century or two ago"?

When those whose existence the Medium recognizes ring the chimes of the writer's doorbell, fall through his letter slot, float out onto his television screen, what is he to say to them? A man's unsuccessful struggle to get his family food is material for a work of art—for tragedy, almost; his unsuccessful struggle to get his family a standby generator is material for what? Comedy? Farce? Comedy on such a scale, at such a level, that our society and its standards seem, almost, farce? And yet it is the People of the Medium—those who struggle for and get, or struggle for and don't get, the generator—whom our society finds representative: they are there, there primarily, there to be treated first of all. How shall the artist treat them? And the Medium itself—an end of life and a means of life, something essential to people's understanding and valuing of their existence, something many of their waking hours are spent listening to or looking at—how is it to be treated as subject matter for art? The artist cannot merely reproduce it; should he satirize or parody it? But by the time the artist's work reaches its audience, the portion of the Medium which it satirized will already have been forgotten; and parody is impossible, often, when so much of the Medium is already an unintentional parody. (Our age might be defined as the age in which real parody became impossible, since any parody had already been duplicated, or parodied, in earnest.) Yet the Medium, by now, is an essential part of its watchers. How can you explain those whom Mohammedans call the People of the Book in any terms that omit the Book? We are people of the television set, the magazine, the radio, and are inexplicable in any terms that omit them.

Oscar Wilde said that Nature imitates Art, that before Whistler painted them there were no fogs along the Thames. If his statement were not false, it would not be witty. But to say that Nature imitates Art, when the Nature is human nature and the Art that of television, radio, motion pictures, magazines, is literally true. The Medium shows its People what life is, what people are, and its People believe it: expect people to be that, try themselves to be that. Seeing is believing; and if what you see in *Life* is different from what you see in life, which of the two are you to believe? For many people it is what you see in *Life* (and in the movies, over television, on the radio) that is real life; and everyday existence, mere local or personal variation, is not real in the same sense.

The Medium mediates between us and raw reality, and the mediation more and more replaces reality for us. Many radio stations have a news broadcast every hour, and many people like and need to hear it. In many houses either the television set or the radio is turned on during most of the hours the family is awake. It is as if they longed to be established in reality, to be reminded continually of the "real," "objective" world—the created world of the Medium—rather than to be left at the mercy of actuality, of the helpless contingency of the world in which the radio receiver or television set is sitting. And surely we can sympathize: which of us hasn't found a similar refuge in the "real," created world of Cézanne or Goethe or Verdi? Yet Dostoevsky's world is too different from Wordsworth's, Piero della Francesca's from Goya's, Bach's from Wolf's, for us to be able to substitute one homogeneous mediated reality for everyday reality in the belief that it is everyday reality. For many watchers, listeners, readers, the world of events and celebrities and performers—the Great World—has become the world of primary reality: how many times they have sighed at the colorless unreality of their own lives and families, and sighed for the bright reality of, say, Elizabeth Taylor's. The watchers call the celebrities by their first names, approve or disapprove of "who they're dating," handle them with a mixture of love, identification, envy, and contempt. But however they handle them, they *handle* them: the Medium has given everyone so terrible a familiarity with everyone that it takes great magnanimity of spirit not to be affected by it. These celebrities are not heroes to us, their valets.

Better to have these real ones play themselves, and not sacrifice too much of their reality to art; better to have the watcher play himself, and not lose too much of himself in art. Usually the watcher is halfway between two worlds, paying full attention to neither: half distracted from, half distracted by, this distraction; and able for the moment not to be too greatly affected, have too great demands made upon him, by either world. For in the Medium, which we escape to from work, nothing is ever *work*, makes intellectual or emotional or imaginative demands which we might find it difficult to satisfy. Here in the half-world everything is homogeneous—is, as much as possible, the same as everything else: each familiar novelty, novel familiarity has the same treatment on top and the same attitude and conclusion at bottom; only the middle, the particular subject of the particular program or article, is different. If it *is* different: everyone is given the same automatic "human interest" treatment, so that it is hard for us to remember, unnecessary for us to remember, which particular celebrity we're reading about this time—often it's the same one, we've just moved on to a different magazine.

Francesco Caracciolo said that the English have a hundred religions and one sauce; so do we; and we are so accustomed to this sauce or dye or style of presentation, the aesthetic equivalent of Standard Brands, that a very simple thing can seem obscure or perverse without it. And, too, we find it hard to have to shift from one genre to another, to vary our attitudes and expectations, to use our unexercised imaginations. Poetry disappeared long ago, even for most intellectuals; each year fiction is a little less important. Our age is the age of articles: we buy articles in stores, read articles in magazines, exist among the interstices of articles: of columns, interviews, photographic essays, documentaries; of facts condensed into headlines or expanded into nonfiction bestsellers; of real facts about real people.

Art lies to us to tell us the (sometimes disquieting) truth. The Medium tells us truths, facts, in order to make us believe some reassuring or entertaining lie or half-truth. These actually existing celebrities, of universally admitted importance, about whom we are told directly authoritative facts—how can fictional characters compete with these? These *are* our fictional characters, our Lears and Clytemnestras. (This is ironically appropriate, since many of their doings and sayings are fictional, made up by public relations officers, columnists, agents, or other affable familiar ghosts.) And the Medium gives us such facts, such tape recordings, such clinical reports not only about the great but also about (representative samples of) the small. When we have been shown so much about so many—*can* be shown, we feel, anything about anybody—does fiction seem so essential as it once seemed? Shakespeare or Tolstoy can show us all about someone, but so can *Life*; and when *Life* does, it's someone real.

The Medium is half life and half art, and competes with both life and art. It spoils its audience for both; spoils both for its audience. For the People of the Medium life isn't sufficiently a matter of success and glamour and celebrity, isn't entertaining enough, distracting enough, *mediated* enough; and art is too dif-

ficult or individual or novel, too much a matter of tradition and
the past, too much a matter of special attitudes and aptitudes—
its mediation sometimes is queer or excessive, and sometimes is
not even recognizable as mediation. The Medium's mixture of
rhetoric and reality, in which people are given what they know
they want to be given in the form in which they know they want
to be given it, is something more efficient and irresistible than
any real art. If a man has all his life been fed a combination of
marzipan and ethyl alcohol—if eating, to him, is a matter of
being knocked unconscious by an ice-cream soda—can he, by
taking thought, come to prefer a diet of bread and wine, apples
and well water? Will a man who has spent his life watching gladiatorial games come to prefer listening to chamber music? And
those who produce the bread and the wine and the quartets for
him—won't they be tempted either to give up producing them,
or else to produce a bread that's half sugar and half alcohol, a
quartet that ends with the cellist at the violist's bleeding throat?

Any outsider who has worked for the Medium will have
observed that the one thing which seems to its managers most
unnatural is for someone to do something naturally, to speak or
write as an individual speaking or writing to other individuals,
and not as a subcontractor supplying a standardized product to
the Medium. It is as if producers and editors and supervisors—
middlemen—were particles forming a screen between maker and
public, one which will let through only particles of their own size
and weight (or as they say, the public's). As you look into their
strained pureed faces, their big horn-rimmed eyes, you despair
of Creation itself, which seems for the instant made in their own
owl-eyed image. There are so many extrinsic considerations
involved in the presentation of his work, the maker finds, that
by the time it is presented almost any intrinsic consideration has
come to seem secondary. No wonder that the professional who
writes the ordinary commercial success—the ordinary script,
scenario, or bestseller—resembles imaginative writers less than
he resembles editors, producers, executives. The supplier has
come to resemble those he supplies, and what he supplies them
resembles both. With an artist you never know what you will get;
with him you know what you will get. He is a reliable source

for a standard product. He is almost exactly the opposite of the imaginative artist: instead of stubbornly or helplessly sticking to what he sees and feels—to what is right for him, true to his reality, regardless of what the others think and want—he gives the others what they think and want, regardless of what he himself sees and feels.

The Medium represents, to the artist, all that he has learned not to do: its surefire stereotypes seem to him what any true art, true spirit, has had to struggle past on its way to the truth. The artist sees the values and textures of this art-substitute replacing those of his art, so far as most of society is concerned; conditioning the expectations of what audience his art has kept. Mass culture either corrupts or isolates the writer. His old feeling of oneness—of speaking naturally to an audience with essentially similar standards—is gone; and writers no longer have much of the consolatory feeling that took its place, the feeling of writing for the happy few, the kindred spirits whose standards are those of the future. (Today they feel: the future, should there be one, will be worse.) True works of art are more and more produced away from or in opposition to society. And yet the artist needs society as much as society needs him: as our cultural enclaves get smaller and drier, more hysterical or academic, one mourns for the artists inside and the public outside. An incomparable historian of mass culture, Ernest van den Haag, has expressed this with laconic force: "The artist who, by refusing to work for the mass market, becomes marginal, cannot create what he might have created had there been no mass market. One may prefer a monologue to addressing a mass meeting. But it is still not a conversation."

Even if the rebellious artist's rebellion is wholehearted, it can never be whole-stomach'd, whole-unconscious'd. Part of him wants to be like his kind, is like his kind; longs to be loved and admired and successful. Our society—and the artist, in so far as he is truly a part of it—has no place set aside for the different and poor and obscure, the fools for Christ's sake: they all go willy-nilly into Limbo. The artist is tempted, consciously, to give his society what it wants—or if he won't or can't, to give it nothing at all; is tempted, unconsciously, to give it superficially independent or contradictory works which are at heart works of the Medium. But it is hard for him to go on serving both God and Mammon when God is so really ill-, Mammon so really well-organized.

"Shakespeare wrote for the Medium of his day; if Shakespeare were alive now he'd be writing *My Fair Lady*; isn't *My Fair Lady*, then, our *Hamlet*? Shouldn't you be writing *Hamlet* instead of sitting there worrying about your superego? I need my *Hamlet*!" So society speaks to the artist, reasons with the artist; and after he has written it its *Hamlet* it is satisfied, and tries to make sure that he will never do it again. There are many more urgent needs that it wants him to satisfy: to lecture to it; to be interviewed; to appear on television programs; to give testimonials; to attend book luncheons; to make trips abroad for the State Department; to judge books for Book Clubs; to read for publishers, judge for publishers, be a publisher for publishers; to edit magazines; to teach writing at colleges or conferences; to write scenarios or scripts or articles—articles about his hometown for *Holiday*, about cats or clothes or Christmas for *Vogue*, about "How I Wrote *Hamlet*" for anything; to—

But why go on? I once heard a composer, lecturing, say to a poet, lecturing: "They'll pay us to do *anything*, so long as it isn't writing music or writing poems." I knew the reply that as a member of my society I should have made: "As long as they pay you, what do you care?" But I didn't make it: it was plain that they cared . . . But how many more learn not to care, to love what they once endured! It is a whole so comprehensive that any alternative seems impossible, any opposition irrelevant; in the end a man says in a small voice: "I accept the Medium." The Enemy of the People winds up as the People—but where there is no enemy, the people perish.

The climate of our culture is changing. Under these new rains, new suns, small things grow great, and what was great grows small; whole species disappear and are replaced. The American present is very different from the American past: so different that our awareness of the extent of the changes has been repressed, and we regard as ordinary what is extraordinary—ominous perhaps—both for us and for the rest of the world. The Ameri-

can present is many other peoples' future: our cultural and economic example is to much of the world mesmeric, and it is only
its weakness and poverty that prevent it from hurrying with us
into the Roman future. But at this moment of our power and
success, our thought and art are full of a troubled sadness, of
the conviction of our own decline. When the president of Yale
University writes that "the ideal of the good life has faded from
the educational process, leaving only miscellaneous prospects
of jobs and joyless hedonism," are we likely to find it unfaded
among our entertainers and executives? Is the influence of what
I have called the Medium likely to lead us to any good life? to
make us love and try to attain any real excellence, beauty, magnanimity? or to make us understand these as obligatory but transparent rationalizations behind which the realities of money and
power are waiting?

The tourist Matthew Arnold once spoke about our green
culture in terms that have an altered relevance—but are not yet
irrelevant—to our ripe one. He said: "What really dissatisfies in
American civilization is the want of the *interesting*, a want due
chiefly to the want of those two great elements of the interesting,
which are elevation and beauty." This use of *interesting*—and,
perhaps, this tone of a curator pointing out what is plain and
culpable—shows how far along in the decline of the West Arnold
came: it is only in the latter days that we ask to be interested.
He had found the word, he tells us, in Carlyle. Carlyle is writing to a friend to persuade him not to emigrate to the United
States; he asks: "Could you banish yourself from all that is interesting to your mind, forget the history, the glorious institutions,
the noble principles of old Scotland—that you might eat a better dinner, perhaps?" We smile, and feel like reminding Carlyle
of the history, the glorious institutions, the noble principles of
new America—of that New World which is, after all, the heir of
the Old.

And yet . . . Can we smile as comfortably, today, as we could
have smiled yesterday? Nor could we listen as unconcernedly, if
on taking leave of us some other tourist should conclude, with
the penetration and obtuseness of his kind:

"I remember reading somewhere: that which you inherit from

your fathers you must earn in order to possess. I have been so much impressed with your power and your possessions that I have neglected, perhaps, your principles. The elevation or beauty of your spirit did not equal, always, that of your mountains and skyscrapers: it seems to me that your society provides you with 'all that is interesting to the mind' only exceptionally, at odd hours, in little reservations like those of your Indians. But as for your dinners, I've never seen anything like them: your daily bread comes *flambé*. And yet—wouldn't you say—the more dinners a man eats, the more comforts he possesses, the hungrier and more uncomfortable some part of him becomes: inside every fat man there is a man who is starving. Part of you is being starved to death, and the rest of you is being stuffed to death. But this will change: no one goes on being stuffed to death or starved to death forever.

"This is a gloomy, an equivocal conclusion? Oh yes, I come from an older culture, where things are accustomed to coming to such conclusions; where there is no last-paragraph fairy to bring one, always, a happy ending—or that happiest of all endings, no ending at all. And have I no advice to give you as I go? None. You are too successful to need advice, or to be able to take it if it were offered; but if ever you should fail, it is there waiting for you, the advice or consolation of all the other failures."

Clement Greenberg (1909–1994) was an influential art critic who established a theoretical context for the Abstract Expressionist painting of Jackson Pollock, Willem de Kooning, Franz Kline, and others who were shaking up the postwar art world. He argued in his famous 1939 essay "Avant-Garde and Kitsch" that commercial considerations and social forces inevitably affected artists hoping to break new ground. From then on, he refined a formalist aesthetic, which favored the deft application of paint to a flat canvas over considerations of subject matter. In essays written for Partisan Review, The Nation, *and* Commentary, *he also argued that the center of art had shifted from Europe to America.*

MODERNIST PAINTING

Modernism includes more than art and literature. By now it covers almost the whole of what is truly alive in our culture. It happens, however, to be very much of a historical novelty. Western civilization is not the first civilization to turn around and question its own foundations, but it is the one that has gone furthest in doing so. I identify Modernism with the intensification, almost the exacerbation, of this self-critical tendency that began with the philosopher Kant. Because he was the first to criticize the means itself of criticism, I conceive of Kant as the first real Modernist.

The essence of Modernism lies, as I see it, in the use of characteristic methods of a discipline to criticize the discipline itself, not in order to subvert it but in order to entrench it more firmly in its area of competence. Kant used logic to establish the limits of logic, and while he withdrew much from its old jurisdiction, logic was left all the more secure in what there remained to it.

The self-criticism of Modernism grows out of, but is not the same thing as, the criticism of the Enlightenment. The Enlightenment criticized from the outside, the way criticism in its accepted sense does; Modernism criticizes from the inside, through the procedures themselves of that which is being criticized. It seems natural that this new kind of criticism should have appeared first in philosophy, which is critical by definition, but as the eighteenth century wore on, it entered many other fields. A more rational justification had begun to be demanded of every formal social activity, and Kantian self-criticism, which had arisen in philosophy in answer to this demand in the first place, was called on eventually to meet and interpret it in areas that lay far from philosophy.

We know what has happened to an activity like religion, which could not avail itself of Kantian, immanent, criticism in order to justify itself. At first glance the arts might seem to have been in a situation like religion's. Having been denied by the Enlightenment all tasks they could take seriously, they looked as though they were going to be assimilated to entertainment pure and simple, and entertainment itself looked as though it were going to be assimilated, like religion, to therapy. The arts could save themselves from this leveling down only by demonstrating that the kind of experience they provided was valuable in its own right and not to be obtained from any other kind of activity.

Each art, it turned out, had to perform this demonstration on its own account. What had to be exhibited was not only that which was unique and irreducible in art in general, but also that which was unique and irreducible in each particular art. Each art had to determine, through its own operations and works, the effects exclusive to itself. By doing so it would, to be sure, narrow its area of competence, but at the same time it would make its possession of that area all the more certain.

It quickly emerged that the unique and proper area of competence of each art coincided with all that was unique in the nature of its medium. The task of self-criticism became to eliminate from the specific effects of each art any and every effect that might conceivably be borrowed from or by the medium of any other art. Thus would each art be rendered "pure," and in its "purity" find the guarantee of its standards of quality as well as of its independence. "Purity" meant self-definition, and the enterprise of self-criticism in the arts became one of self-definition with a vengeance.

Realistic, naturalistic art had dissembled the medium, using art to conceal art; Modernism used art to call attention to art. The limitations that constitute the medium of painting—the flat surface, the shape of the support, the properties of the pigment—were treated by the Old Masters as negative factors that could be acknowledged only implicitly or indirectly. Under Modernism these same limitations came to be regarded as positive factors, and were acknowledged openly. Manet's became the first Modernist pictures by virtue of the frankness with which they declared the flat surfaces on which they were painted. The Impressionists, in Manet's wake, abjured underpainting and glazes, to leave the eye under no doubt as to the fact that the colors they used were made of paint that came from tubes or pots. Cézanne sacrificed verisimilitude, or correctness, in order to fit his drawing and design more explicitly to the rectangular shape of the canvas.

It was the stressing of the ineluctable flatness of the surface that remained, however, more fundamental than anything else to the processes by which pictorial art criticized and defined itself under Modernism. For flatness alone was unique and exclusive to pictorial art. The enclosing shape of the picture was a limiting condition, or norm, that was shared with the art of the theater; color was a norm and a means shared not only with the theater, but also with sculpture. Because flatness was the only condition painting shared with no other art, Modernist painting oriented itself to flatness as it did to nothing else.

The Old Masters had sensed that it was necessary to preserve what is called the integrity of the picture plane: that is, to signify the enduring presence of flatness underneath and above the most vivid illusion of three-dimensional space. The apparent contradiction involved was essential to the success of their art, as it is indeed to the success of all pictorial art. The Modernists have neither avoided nor resolved this contradiction; rather, they have reversed its terms. One is made aware of the flatness of their pictures before, instead of after, being made aware of what the flatness contains. Whereas one tends to see what is in an Old Master before one sees the picture itself, one sees a Modernist picture as a picture first. This is, of course, the best way of seeing any kind of picture, Old Master or Modernist, but Modernism imposes it as the only and necessary way, and Modernism's success in doing so is a success of self-criticism.

Modernist painting in its latest phase has not abandoned the representation of recognizable objects in principle. What it has abandoned in principle is the representation of the kind of space that recognizable objects can inhabit. Abstractness, or the nonfigurative, has in itself still not proved to be an altogether necessary moment in the self-criticism of pictorial art, even though artists as eminent as Kandinsky and Mondrian have thought so. As such, representation, or illustration, does not attain the uniqueness of pictorial art; what does do so is the associations of things represented. All recognizable entities (including pictures themselves) exist in three-dimensional space, and the barest suggestion of a recognizable entity suffices to call up associations of that kind of space. The fragmentary silhouette of a human figure, or of a teacup, will do so, and by doing so alienate pictorial space from the literal two-dimensionality which is the guarantee of painting's independence as an art. For, as has already been said, three-dimensionality is the province of sculpture. To achieve autonomy, painting has had above all to divest itself of everything it might share with sculpture, and it is in its effort to do this, and not so much—I repeat—to exclude the representational or literary, that painting has made itself abstract.

At the same time, however, Modernist painting shows, precisely by its resistance to the sculptural, how firmly attached it remains to tradition beneath and beyond all appearances to the contrary. For the resistance to the sculptural dates far back before the advent of Modernism. Western painting, in so far as it is naturalistic, owes a great debt to sculpture, which taught it in the beginning how to shade and model for the illusion of relief, and even how to dispose that illusion in a complementary illusion of deep space. Yet some of the greatest feats of Western painting are due to the effort it has made over the last four centuries to rid itself of the sculptural. Starting in Venice in the sixteenth century and continuing in Spain, Belgium, and Holland in the seventeenth, that effort was carried on at first in the name of color. When David, in the eighteenth century, tried to revive sculptural painting, it was, in part, to save pictorial art from the decorative flattening-out that the emphasis on color seemed to induce. Yet the strength of David's own best pictures, which are predominantly his informal ones, lies as much in their color as in anything else. And Ingres, his faithful pupil, though he subordinated color far more consistently than did David, executed portraits that were among the flattest, least sculptural paintings done in the West by a sophisticated artist since the fourteenth century. Thus, by the middle of the nineteenth century, all ambitious tendencies in painting had converged amid their differences, in an anti-sculptural direction.

Modernism, as well as continuing this direction, has made it more conscious of itself. With Manet and the Impressionists the question stopped being defined as one of color versus drawing, and became one of purely optical experience against optical experience as revised or modified by tactile associations. It was in the name of the purely and literally optical, not in the name of color, that the Impressionists set themselves to undermining shading and modeling and everything else in painting that seemed to connote the sculptural. It was, once again, in the name of the sculptural, with its shading and modeling, that Cézanne, and the Cubists after him, reacted against Impressionism, as David had reacted against Fragonard. But once more, just as David's and Ingres' reaction had culminated, paradoxically, in a kind of painting even less sculptural than before, so the Cubist counterrevolution eventuated in a kind of painting flatter than anything in Western art since before Giotto and Cimabue—so flat indeed that it could hardly contain recognizable images.

In the meantime the other cardinal norms of the art of painting had begun, with the onset of Modernism, to undergo a revision that was equally thorough if not as spectacular. It would take me more time than is at my disposal to show how the norm of

the picture's enclosing shape, or frame, was loosened, then tightened, then loosened once again, and isolated, and then tightened
once more, by successive generations of Modernist painters. Or
how the norms of finish and paint texture, and of value and color
contrast, were revised and rerevised. New risks have been taken
with all these norms, not only in the interests of expression but
also in order to exhibit them more clearly as norms. By being
exhibited, they are tested for their indispensability. That testing
is by no means finished, and the fact that it becomes deeper as it
proceeds accounts for the radical simplifications that are also to
be seen in the very latest abstract painting, as well as for the radical complications that are also seen in it.

Neither extreme is a matter of caprice or arbitrariness. On
the contrary, the more closely the norms of a discipline become
defined, the less freedom they are apt to permit in many directions. The essential norms or conventions of painting are at the
same time the limiting conditions with which a picture must
comply in order to be experienced as a picture. Modernism has
found that these limits can be pushed back indefinitely—before
a picture stops being a picture and turns into an arbitrary object;
but it has also found that the further back these limits are pushed
the more explicitly they have to be observed and indicated. The
crisscrossing black lines and colored rectangles of a Mondrian
painting seem hardly enough to make a picture out of, yet they
impose the picture's framing shape as a regulating norm with a
new force and completeness by echoing that shape so closely. Far
from incurring the danger of arbitrariness, Mondrian's art proves,
as time passes, almost too disciplined, almost too tradition- and
convention-bound in certain respects; once we have gotten used
to its utter abstractness, we realize that it is more conservative in
its color, for instance, as well as in its subservience to the frame,
than the last paintings of Monet.

It is understood, I hope, that in plotting out the rationale of
Modernist painting I have had to simplify and exaggerate. The
flatness towards which Modernist painting orients itself can never
be an absolute flatness. The heightened sensitivity of the picture
plane may no longer permit sculptural illusion, or *trompe-l'oeil*,
but it does and must permit optical illusion. The first mark made

on a canvas destroys its literal and utter flatness, and the result of the marks made on it by an artist like Mondrian is still a kind of illusion that suggests a kind of third dimension. Only now it is a strictly pictorial, strictly optical third dimension. The Old Masters created an illusion of space in depth that one could imagine oneself walking into, but the analogous illusion created by the Modernist painter can only be seen into; can be traveled through, literally or figuratively, only with the eye.

The latest abstract painting tries to fulfill the Impressionist insistence on the optical as the only sense that a completely and quintessentially pictorial art can invoke. Realizing this, one begins also to realize that the Impressionists, or at least the Neo-Impressionists, were not altogether misguided when they flirted with science. Kantian self-criticism, as it now turns out, has found its fullest expression in science rather than in philosophy, and when it began to be applied in art, the latter was brought closer in real spirit to scientific method than ever before—closer than it had been by Alberti, Uccello, Piero della Francesca, or Leonardo in the Renaissance. That visual art should confine itself exclusively to what is given in visual experience, and make no reference to anything given in any other order of experience, is a notion whose only justification lies in scientific consistency.

Scientific method alone asks, or might ask, that a situation be resolved in exactly the same terms as that in which it is presented. But this kind of consistency promises nothing in the way of aesthetic quality, and the fact that the best art of the last seventy or eighty years approaches closer and closer to such consistency does not show the contrary. From the point of view of art in itself, its convergence with science happens to be a mere accident, and neither art nor science really gives or assures the other of anything more than it ever did. What their convergence does show, however, is the profound degree to which Modernist art belongs to the same specific cultural tendency as modern science, and this is of the highest significance as a historical fact.

It should also be understood that self-criticism in Modernist art has never been carried on in any but a spontaneous and largely subliminal way. As I have already indicated, it has been altogether a question of practice, immanent to practice, and never a topic of theory. Much is heard about programs in connection with Modernist art, but there has actually been far less of the programmatic in Modernist than in Renaissance or Academic painting. With a few exceptions like Mondrian, the masters of Modernism have had no more fixed ideas about art than Corot did. Certain inclinations, certain affirmations and emphases, and certain refusals and abstinences as well, seem to become necessary simply because the way to stronger, more expressive art lies through them. The immediate aims of the Modernists were, and remain, personal before anything else, and the truth and success of their works remain personal before anything else. And it has taken the accumulation, over decades, of a good deal of personal painting to reveal the general self-critical tendency of Modernist painting. No artist was, or yet is, aware of it, nor could any artist ever work freely in awareness of it. To this extent—and it is a great extent—art gets carried on under Modernism in much the same way as before.

And I cannot insist enough that Modernism has never meant, and does not mean now, anything like a break with the past. It may mean a devolution, an unraveling, of tradition, but it also means its further evolution. Modernist art continues the past without gap or break, and wherever it may end up it will never cease being intelligible in terms of the past. The making of pictures has been controlled, since it first began, by all the norms I have mentioned. The Paleolithic painter or engraver could disregard the norm of the frame and treat the surface in a literally sculptural way only because he made images rather than pictures, and worked on a support—a rock wall, a bone, a horn, or a stone—whose limits and surface were arbitrarily given by nature. But the making of pictures means, among other things, the deliberate creating or choosing of a flat surface, and the deliberate circumscribing and limiting of it. This deliberateness is precisely what Modernist painting harps on: the fact, that is, that the limiting conditions of art are altogether human conditions.

But I want to repeat that Modernist art does not offer theoretical demonstrations. It can be said, rather, that it happens to convert theoretical possibilities into empirical ones, in doing which it tests many theories about art for their relevance to the actual practice and actual experience of art. In this respect alone can Modernism be considered subversive. Certain factors we used to think essential to the making and experiencing of art are shown not to be so by the fact that Modernist painting has been able to dispense with them and yet continue to offer the experience of art in all its essentials. The further fact that this demonstration has left most of our old value judgments intact only makes it the more conclusive. Modernism may have had something to do with the revival of the reputations of Uccello, Piero della Francesca, El Greco, Georges de La Tour, and even Vermeer; and Modernism certainly confirmed, if it did not start, the revival of Giotto's reputation; but it has not lowered thereby the standing of Leonardo, Raphael, Titian, Rubens, Rembrandt, or Watteau. What Modernism has shown is that, though the past did appreciate these masters justly, it often gave wrong or irrelevant reasons for doing so.

In some ways this situation is hardly changed today. Art criticism and art history lag behind Modernism as they lagged behind pre-Modernist art. Most of the things that get written about Modernist art still belong to journalism rather than to criticism or art history. It belongs to journalism—and to the millennial complex from which so many journalists and journalist intellectuals suffer in our day—that each new phase of Modernist art should be hailed as the start of a whole new epoch in art, marking a decisive break with all the customs and conventions of the past. Each time, a kind of art is expected so unlike all previous kinds of art, and so free from norms of practice or taste, that everybody, regardless of how informed or uninformed he happens to be, can have his say about it. And each time, this expectation has been disappointed, as the phase of Modernist art in question finally takes its place in the intelligible continuity of taste and tradition.

Nothing could be further from the authentic art of our time than the idea of a rupture of continuity. Art is—among other things—continuity, and unthinkable without it. Lacking the past of art, and the need and compulsion to maintain its standards of excellence, Modernist art would lack both substance and justification.

Rachel Carson (1907–1964) was a science writer and biologist with the U.S. Fish and Wildlife Service, whose first book, The Sea Around Us, *was universally praised for its lyrically precise language. But it was her bestselling fourth book,* Silent Spring, *that changed the world: in it she warned of the dangers of pesticides like DDT and other chemical pollutants affecting the environment. Carson drew on her scientific research and grasp of technical facts to construct a passionately eloquent argument—one that led to corrective legislation and that inspired a generation of environmental writers. "The Obligation to Endure," a chapter from* Silent Spring, *can function as a stand-alone essay.*

THE OBLIGATION TO ENDURE

The history of life on earth has been a history of interaction between living things and their surroundings. To a large extent, the physical form and the habits of the earth's vegetation and its animal life have been molded by the environment. Considering the whole span of earthly time, the opposite effect, in which life actually modifies its surroundings, has been relatively slight. Only within the moment of time represented by the present century has one species—man—acquired significant power to alter the nature of his world.

During the past quarter century this power has not only increased to one of disturbing magnitude but it has changed in character. The most alarming of all man's assaults upon the environment is the contamination of air, earth, rivers, and sea with dangerous and even lethal materials. This pollution is for the most part irrecoverable; the chain of evil it initiates not only in the world that must support life but in living tissues is for the most part irreversible. In this now universal contamination of the environment, chemicals are the sinister and little-recognized partners of radiation in changing the very nature of the world— the very nature of its life. Strontium 90, released through nuclear explosions into the air, comes to earth in rain or drifts down as fallout, lodges in soil, enters into the grass or corn or wheat grown there, and in time takes up its abode in the bones of a human being, there to remain until his death. Similarly, chemicals sprayed on croplands or forests or gardens lie long in soil, entering into living organisms, passing from one to another in a chain of poisoning and death. Or they pass mysteriously by underground streams until they emerge and, through the alchemy of air and sunlight, combine into new forms that kill vegetation, sicken cattle, and work unknown harm on those who drink from once pure wells. As Albert Schweitzer has said, "Man can hardly even recognize the devils of his own creation."

It took hundreds of millions of years to produce the life that now inhabits the earth—eons of time in which that developing and evolving and diversifying life reached a state of adjustment and balance with its surroundings. The environment, rigorously shaping and directing the life it supported, contained elements that were hostile as well as supporting. Certain rocks gave out dangerous radiation; even within the light of the sun, from which all life draws its energy, there were short-wave radiations with power to injure. Given time—time not in years but in millennia— life adjusts, and a balance has been reached. For time is the essential ingredient; but in the modern world there is no time.

The rapidity of change and the speed with which new situations are created follow the impetuous and heedless pace of man rather than the deliberate pace of nature. Radiation is no longer merely the background radiation of rocks, the bombardment of cosmic rays, the ultraviolet of the sun that have existed before there was any life on earth; radiation is now the unnatural creation of man's tampering with the atom. The chemicals to which life is asked to make its adjustment are no longer merely the calcium and silica and copper and all the rest of the minerals washed out of the rocks and carried in rivers to the sea; they are the synthetic creations of man's inventive mind, brewed in his laboratories, and having no counterparts in nature.

To adjust to these chemicals would require time on the scale that is nature's; it would require not merely the years of a man's life but the life of generations. And even this, were it by some miracle possible, would be futile, for the new chemicals come from our laboratories in an endless stream; almost five hundred annually find their way into actual use in the United States alone. The figure is staggering and its implications are not easily grasped— five hundred new chemicals to which the bodies of men and animals are required somehow to adapt each year, chemicals totally outside the limits of biologic experience.

Among them are many that are used in man's war against nature. Since the mid-1940s over two hundred basic chemicals have been created for use in killing insects, weeds, rodents, and other organisms described in the modern vernacular as "pests"; and they are sold under several thousand different brand names.

These sprays, dusts, and aerosols are now applied almost universally to farms, gardens, forests, and homes—nonselective chemicals that have the power to kill every insect, the "good" and the "bad," to still the song of birds and the leaping of fish in the streams, to coat the leaves with a deadly film, and to linger on in soil—all this though the intended target may be only a few weeds or insects. Can anyone believe it is possible to lay down such a barrage of poisons on the surface of the earth without making it unfit for all life? They should not be called "insecticides," but "biocides."

The whole process of spraying seems caught up in an endless spiral. Since DDT was released for civilian use, a process of escalation has been going on in which ever more toxic materials must be found. This has happened because insects, in a triumphant vindication of Darwin's principle of the survival of the fittest, have evolved super-races immune to the particular insecticide used, hence a deadlier one has always to be developed—and then a deadlier one than that. It has happened also because, for reasons to be described later, destructive insects often undergo a "flareback," or resurgence, after spraying, in numbers greater than before. Thus the chemical war is never won, and all life is caught in its violent crossfire.

Along with the possibility of the extinction of mankind by nuclear war, the central problem of our age has therefore become the contamination of man's total environment with such substances of incredible potential for harm—substances that accumulate in the tissues of plants and animals and even penetrate the germ cells to shatter or alter the very material of heredity upon which the shape of the future depends.

Some would-be architects of our future look toward a time when it will be possible to alter the human germ plasm by design. But we may easily be doing so now by inadvertence, for many chemicals, like radiation, bring about gene mutations. It is ironic to think that man might determine his own future by something so seemingly trivial as the choice of an insect spray.

All this has been risked—for what? Future historians may well be amazed by our distorted sense of proportion. How could intelligent beings seek to control a few unwanted species by a method that contaminated the entire environment and brought the threat of disease and death even to their own kind? Yet this is precisely what we have done. We have done it, moreover, for reasons that collapse the moment we examine them. We are told that the enormous and expanding use of pesticides is necessary to maintain farm production. Yet is our real problem not one of *overproduction*? Our farms, despite measures to remove acreages from production and to pay farmers *not* to produce, have yielded such a staggering excess of crops that the American taxpayer in 1962 is paying out more than one billion dollars a year as the total carrying cost of the surplus-food storage program. And is the situation helped when one branch of the Agriculture Department tries to reduce production while another states, as it did in 1958, "It is believed generally that reduction of crop acreages under provisions of the Soil Bank will stimulate interest in use of chemicals to obtain maximum production on the land retained in crops"?

All this is not to say there is no insect problem and no need of control. I am saying, rather, that control must be geared to realities, not to mythical situations, and that the methods employed must be such that they do not destroy us along with the insects.

The problem whose attempted solution has brought such a train of disaster in its wake is an accompaniment of our modern way of life. Long before the age of man, insects inhabited the earth—a group of extraordinarily varied and adaptable beings. Over the course of time since man's advent, a small percentage of the more than half a million species of insects have come into conflict with human welfare in two principal ways: as competitors for the food supply and as carriers of human disease.

Disease-carrying insects become important where human beings are crowded together, especially under conditions where sanitation is poor, as in time of natural disaster or war or in situations of extreme poverty and deprivation. Then control of some sort becomes necessary. It is a sobering fact, however, as we shall presently see, that the method of massive chemical control has had only limited success, and also threatens to worsen the very conditions it is intended to curb.

Under primitive agricultural conditions the farmer had few insect problems. These arose with the intensification of agriculture—the devotion of immense acreages to a single crop. Such a system set the stage for explosive increases in specific insect populations. Single-crop farming does not take advantage of the principles by which nature works; it is agriculture as an engineer might conceive it to be. Nature has introduced great variety into the landscape, but man has displayed a passion for simplifying it. Thus he undoes the built-in checks and balances by which nature holds the species within bounds. One important natural check is a limit on the amount of suitable habitat for each species. Obviously then, an insect that lives on wheat can build up its population to much higher levels on a farm devoted to wheat than on one in which wheat is intermingled with other crops to which the insect is not adapted.

The same thing happens in other situations. A generation or more ago, the towns of large areas of the United States lined their streets with the noble elm tree. Now the beauty they hopefully created is threatened with complete destruction as disease sweeps through the elms, carried by a beetle that would have only limited chance to build up large populations and to spread from tree to tree if the elms were only occasional trees in a richly diversified planting.

Another factor in the modern insect problem is one that must be viewed against a background of geologic and human history: the spreading of thousands of different kinds of organisms from their native homes to invade new territories. This worldwide migration has been studied and graphically described by the British ecologist Charles Elton in his recent book *The Ecology of Invasions*. During the Cretaceous Period, some hundred million years ago, flooding seas cut many land bridges between continents and living things found themselves confined in what Elton calls "colossal separate nature reserves." There, isolated from others of their kind, they developed many new species. When some of the landmasses were joined again, about fifteen million years ago, these species began to move out into new territories— a movement that is not only still in progress but is now receiving considerable assistance from man.

The importation of plants is the primary agent in the modern spread of species, for animals have almost invariably gone along with the plants, quarantine being a comparatively recent and not completely effective innovation. The United States Office of Plant Introduction alone has introduced almost 100,000 species and varieties of plants from all over the world. Nearly half of the 180 or so major insect enemies of plants in the United States are accidental imports from abroad, and most of them have come as hitchhikers on plants.

In new territory, out of reach of the restraining hand of the natural enemies that kept down its numbers in its native land, an invading plant or animal is able to become enormously abundant. Thus it is no accident that our most troublesome insects are introduced species.

These invasions, both the naturally occurring and those dependent on human assistance, are likely to continue indefinitely. Quarantine and massive chemical campaigns are only extremely expensive ways of buying time. We are faced, according to

Dr. Elton, "with a life-and-death need not just to find new technological means of suppressing this plant or that animal"; instead we need the basic knowledge of animal populations and their relations to their surroundings that will "promote an even balance and damp down the explosive power of outbreaks and new invasions."

Much of the necessary knowledge is now available but we do not use it. We train ecologists in our universities and even employ them in our governmental agencies but we seldom take their advice. We allow the chemical death rain to fall as though there were no alternative, whereas in fact there are many, and our ingenuity could soon discover many more if given opportunity.

Have we fallen into a mesmerized state that makes us accept as inevitable that which is inferior or detrimental, as though having lost the will or the vision to demand that which is good? Such thinking, in the words of the ecologist Paul Shepard, "idealizes life with only its head out of water, inches above the limits of toleration of the corruption of its own environment . . . Why should we tolerate a diet of weak poisons, a home in insipid surroundings, a circle of acquaintances who are not quite our enemies, the noise of motors with just enough relief to prevent insanity? Who would want to live in a world which is just not quite fatal?"

Yet such a world is pressed upon us. The crusade to create a chemically sterile, insect-free world seems to have engendered a fanatic zeal on the part of many specialists and most of the so-called control agencies. On every hand there is evidence that those engaged in spraying operations exercise a ruthless power. "The regulatory entomologists . . . function as prosecutor, judge and jury, tax assessor and collector and sheriff to enforce their own orders," said Connecticut entomologist Neely Turner. The most flagrant abuses go unchecked in both state and federal agencies.

It is not my contention that chemical insecticides must never be used. I do contend that we have put poisonous and biologically potent chemicals indiscriminately into the hands of persons largely or wholly ignorant of their potentials for harm. We have subjected enormous numbers of people to contact with these poisons, without their consent and often without their knowledge. If the Bill of Rights contains no guarantee that a citizen shall be secure against lethal poisons distributed either by private individuals or by public officials, it is surely only because our forefathers, despite their considerable wisdom and foresight, could conceive of no such problem.

I contend, furthermore, that we have allowed these chemicals to be used with little or no advance investigation of their effect on soil, water, wildlife, and man himself. Future generations are unlikely to condone our lack of prudent concern for the integrity of the natural world that supports all life.

There is still very limited awareness of the nature of the threat. This is an era of specialists, each of whom sees his own problem and is unaware of or intolerant of the larger frame into which it fits. It is also an era dominated by industry, in which the right to make a dollar at whatever cost is seldom challenged. When the public protests, confronted with some obvious evidence of damaging results of pesticide applications, it is fed little tranquilizing pills of half truth. We urgently need an end to these false assurances, to the sugarcoating of unpalatable facts. It is the public that is being asked to assume the risks that the insect controllers calculate. The public must decide whether it wishes to continue on the present road, and it can do so only when in full possession of the facts. In the words of Jean Rostand, "The obligation to endure gives us the right to know."

Norman Mailer (1923–2007), a larger-than-life figure, was a force who dominated American letters for decades, from the postwar era to his death. His main subject was himself, but a self that engaged with open curiosity an impressive range of subjects (politics, war, gender, graffiti, Marilyn Monroe, boxing, murderers and executioners, moon landings, ancient Egypt). Prodigiously brilliant if uneven in his novels, he showed greatest control in his nonfiction masterpieces Advertisements for Myself *and* The Armies of the Night. *He positioned himself in the midst of public discourse and was fiercely, ambivalently attracted to power and celebrity. "Norman Mailer was a writer who never met a corner he didn't wish to paint himself into," wrote Jonathan Lethem, and we can see that in this edgy, self-mocking double portrait of Jackie Kennedy and himself, in which reporting gives way to essayistic speculation.*

AN EVENING WITH
JACKIE KENNEDY

A few of you may remember that on February 14, last winter, our First Lady gave us a tour of the White House on television. For reasons to be explained in a while, I was in no charitable mood that night and gave Mrs. Kennedy a close scrutiny. Like anybody else, I have a bit of tolerance for my vices, at least those which do not get into the newspapers, but I take no pride in giving a hard look at a lady when she is on television. Ladies are created for an encounter face-to-face. No man can decide a lady is trivial until he has spent some minutes alone with her. Now while I have been in the same room with Jackie Kennedy twice, for a few minutes each time, it was never very much alone, and for that matter I do not think anyone's heart was particularly calm. The weather was too hectic. It was the summer of 1960, after the Democratic Convention, before the presidential campaign had formally begun, at Hyannis Port, site of the Summer White House—those of you who know Hyannis ("High-anus," as the natives say) will know how funny is the title—all those motels and a Summer White House too: the Kennedy compound, an enclosure of three summer homes belonging to Joe Kennedy, Sr., RFK, and JFK, with a modest amount of lawn and beach to share among them. In those historic days the lawn was overrun with journalists, cameramen, magazine writers, politicians, delegations, friends and neighboring gentry, government intellectuals, family, a prince, some Massachusetts state troopers, and red-necked hard-nosed tourists patrolling outside the fence for a glimpse of the boy. He was much in evidence, a bit of everywhere that morning, including the lawn, and particularly handsome at times as one has described elsewhere (*Esquire*, November 1960), looking like a good version of Charles Lindbergh at noon on a hot August day. Well, Jackie Kennedy was inside in her living room sitting around talking with a few of us, Arthur Schlesinger, Jr., and his wife Marian, Prince Radziwill, Peter Maas the writer, Jacques Lowe the photographer, and Pierre Salinger. We were a curious assortment indeed, as oddly assembled in our way as some of the do-gooders and real baddies on the lawn outside. It would have taken a hostess of broad and perhaps dubious gifts, Perle Mesta, no doubt, or Ethel Merman, or Elsa Maxwell, to have woven some mood into this occasion, because pop! were going the flashbulbs out in the crazy August sun on the sun-drenched terrace just beyond the bay window at our back, a politician— a stocky machine type sweating in a dark suit with a white shirt and white silk tie—was having his son, seventeen perhaps, short, chunky, dressed the same way, take a picture of him and his wife, a Mediterranean dish around sixty with a bright, happy, flowered dress. The boy took a picture of father and mother, father took a picture of mother and son—another heeler came along to take a picture of all three—it was a little like a rite surrounding droit du seigneur, as if afterward the family could press a locket in your hand and say, "Here, here are contained three hairs from the youth of the Count, discovered by me on my wife next morning." There was something low and greedy about this picture-taking, perhaps the popping of the flashbulbs in the sunlight, as if everything monstrous and overreaching in our insane public land were tamped together in the foolproof act of taking a sun-drenched picture at noon with no shadows and a flashbulb—do we sell insurance to protect our cadavers against the corrosion of the grave?

And I had the impression that Jackie Kennedy was almost suffering in the flesh from their invasion of her house, her terrace, her share of the lands, that if the popping of the flashbulbs went on until midnight on the terrace outside she would have a tic forever in the corner of her eye. Because that was the second impression of her, of a lady with delicate and exacerbated nerves. She was no broad hostess, not at all; broad hostesses are monumental animals turned mellow: hippopotami, rhinoceri, plump lion, sweet gorilla, warm bear. Jackie Kennedy was a cat, narrow and wild, and her fur was being rubbed every which way. This was the second impression. The first had been simpler. It had been merely of a college girl who was nice. Nice and clean and very merry. I had entered her house perspiring—talk of the politician, I was wearing a black suit myself, a washable, the only one in my closet not completely unpressed that morning, and I had been forced to pick a white shirt with button-down collar: all the white summer shirts were in the laundry. What a set-to I had had with Adele Mailer at breakfast. Food half-digested in anger, sweating like a goat, tense at the pit of my stomach for I would be interviewing Kennedy in a half hour, I was feeling not a little jangled when we were introduced, and we stumbled mutually over a few polite remarks, which was my fault I'm sure more than hers for I must have had a look in my eyes—I remember I felt like a drunk marine who knows in all clarity that if he doesn't have a fight soon it'll be good for his character but terrible for his constitution.

She offered me a cool drink—iced verbena tea with sprig of mint no doubt—but the expression in my face must have been rich because she added, still standing by the screen in the doorway, "We do have something harder of course," and something droll and hard came into her eyes as if she were a very naughty eight-year-old indeed. More than one photograph of Jackie Kennedy had put forward just this saucy regard—it was obviously the life of her charm. But I had not been prepared for another quality, of shyness conceivably. There was something quite remote in her. Not willed, not chilly, not directed at anyone in particular, but distant, detached as the psychologists say, moody and abstracted the novelists used to say. As we sat around the coffee table on summer couches, summer chairs, a pleasant living room in light colors, lemon, white and gold seeming to predominate, the sort of living room one might expect to find in Cleveland, may it be, at the home of a fairly important young executive whose wife had taste, sitting there, watching people go by, the group I mentioned earlier kept a kind of conversation going. Its center, if it had one, was obviously Jackie Kennedy. There was a natural tendency to look at her and see if she were amused. She did not sit there like a movie star with a ripe olive in each eye for the brain, but in fact gave conversation back, made some of it, laughed often. We had one short conversation about Provincetown, which was pleasant. She remarked that she had been staying no more than fifty miles away for all these summers but had never seen it. She must, I assured her. It was one of the few fishing villages in America which still had beauty. Besides it was the Wild West of the East. The local police were the Indians and the beatniks were the poor hardworking settlers. Her eyes turned merry. "Oh, I'd love to see it," she said. But how did one go? In three black limousines and fifty police for escort, or in a sports car at four a.m. with dark glasses? "I suppose now I'll never get to see it," she said wistfully.

She had a keen sense of laughter, but it revolved around the absurdities of the world. She was probably not altogether unlike a soldier who has been up at the front for two weeks. There was a hint of gone laughter. Soldiers who have had it bad enough can laugh at the fact some trooper got killed crossing an open area because he wanted to change his socks from khaki to green. The front lawn of this house must have been, I suppose, a kind of no-man's-land for a lady. The story I remember her telling was about Stash, Prince Radziwill, her brother-in-law, who had gone into the second-story bathroom that morning to take a shave and discovered, to his lack of complete pleasure, that a crush of tourists was watching him from across the road. Yes, the house had been besieged, and one knew she thought of the sightseers as a mob, a motley of gargoyles, like the horde who riot through the last pages in *The Day of the Locust*.

Since there was an air of self-indulgence about her, subtle but precise, one was certain she liked time to compose herself. While we sat there she must have gotten up a half-dozen times, to go away for two minutes, come back for three. She had the exasperated impatience of a college girl. One expected her to swear mildly. "Oh, Christ!" or "Sugar!" or "Fudge!" And each time she got up, there was a glimpse of her calves, surprisingly thin, not unfeverish. I was reminded of the legs on those adolescent Southern girls who used to go out together and walk up and down the streets of Fayetteville, North Carolina, in the summer of 1944 at Fort Bragg. In the petulant Southern air of their boredom many of us had found something luminous that summer, a mixture of languor, heat, innocence and stupidity which was our cocktail vis-à-vis the knowledge we were going soon to Europe or the other war. One mentions this to underline the determinedly romantic aura in which one had chosen to behold Jackie Kennedy. There was a charm this other short summer of 1960 in the thought a young man with a young attractive wife might soon become president. It offered possibilities and vistas; it brought a touch of life to the monotonies of politics, those monotonies so profoundly entrenched into the hinges and mortar of the Eisenhower administration. It was thus more interesting to look at Jackie Kennedy as a woman than as a probable First Lady. Perhaps it was out of some such motive, such a desire for the clean air and tang of unexpected montage, that I spoke about her in just the way I did later that afternoon.

"Do you think she's happy?" asked a lady, an old friend, on the beach at Wellfleet.

"I guess she would rather spend her life on the Riviera."

"What would she do there?"

"End up as the mystery woman, maybe, in a good murder case."

"Wow," said the lady, giving me my reward.

It had been my way of saying I liked Jackie Kennedy, that she was not at all stuffy, that she had perhaps a touch of that artful madness which suggests future drama.

My interview the first day had been a little short, and I was invited back for another one the following day. Rather nicely, Senator Kennedy invited me to bring anyone I wanted. About a week later I realized this was part of his acumen. You can tell a lot about a man by whom he invites in such a circumstance. Will it be a political expert or the wife? I invited my wife. The presence of this second lady is not unimportant, because this time she had the conversation with Jackie Kennedy. While I was busy somewhere or other, they were introduced. Down by the Kennedy family wharf. The senator was about to take Jackie for a sail. The two women had a certain small general resemblance. They were something like the same height, they both had dark hair, and they had each been wearing it in a similar style for many years. Perhaps this was enough to create a quick political intimacy. "I wish," said Jackie Kennedy, "that I didn't have to go on this corny sail, because I would like very much to talk to you, Mrs. Mailer." A stroke. Mrs. M. did not like many people quickly, but Jackie now had a champion. It must have been a pleasant sight. Two attractive witches by the water's edge.

II

Jimmy Baldwin once entertained the readers of *Esquire* with a sweet and generously written piece called "The Black Boy Looks at the White Boy" in which he talked a great deal about himself and a little bit about me, a proportion I thought well-taken since he is on the best of terms with Baldwin and digs next to nothing about this white boy. As a method, I think it has its merits.

After I saw the Kennedys I added a few paragraphs to my piece about the convention, secretly relieved to have liked them, for my piece was most favorable to the senator, and how would I have rewritten it if I had not liked him? With several mishaps it was printed three weeks before the election. Several days later, I received a letter from Jackie Kennedy. It was a nice letter, generous in its praise, accurate in its details. She remembered, for example, the color of the sweater my wife had been wearing, and mentioned she had one like it in the same purple. I answered with a letter which was out of measure. I was in a Napoleonic mood, I had decided to run for mayor of New York; in a few weeks, I was to zoom and crash—my sense of reality was extravagant. So in response to a modestly voiced notion by Mrs. Kennedy that she wondered if the "impressionistic" way in which I had treated the convention could be applied to the history of the past, I replied in the cadence of a Goethe that while I was now engaged in certain difficulties of writing about the present, I hoped one day when work was done to do a biography of the Marquis de Sade and the "odd strange honor of the man."

I suppose this is as close to the edge as I have ever come. At the time, it seemed reasonable that Mrs. Kennedy, with her publicized interest in France and the eighteenth century, might be fascinated by de Sade. The style of his thought was, after all, a fair climax to the Age of Reason.

Now sociology has few virtues, but one of them is sanity. In writing such a letter to Mrs. Kennedy I was losing my sociology. The Catholic wife of a Catholic candidate for president was not likely to find de Sade as familiar as a tea cozy. I received no reply. I had smashed the limits of such letter-writing. In politics a break in sociology is as clean as a break in etiquette.

At the time I saw it somewhat differently. The odds were against a reply, I decided, three-to-one against, or eight-to-one against. I did not glean they were eight-hundred-to-one against. It is the small inability to handicap odds which is family to the romantic, the desperate and the insane. "That man is going to kill me," someone thinks with fear, sensing a stranger. At this moment, they put the odds at even money, they may even be ready to die for their bet, when, if the fact could be measured, there is one chance in a thousand the danger is true. Exceptional leverage upon the unconscious life in other people is the strength of the artist and the torment of the madman.

Now if I have bothered to show my absence of proportion, it is because I want to put forward a notion which will seem criminal to some of you, but was believed in by me, is still believed in by me, and so affects what I write about the Kennedys.

Jack Kennedy won the election by one hundred thousand votes. A lot of people could claim therefore to be the mind behind his victory. Jake Arvey could say the photo-finish would have gone the other way if not for the track near his Chicago machine. J. Edgar Hoover might say he saved the victory because he did not investigate the track. Lyndon Johnson could point to LBJ Ranch, and the vote in Texas. *Time* magazine could tell you that the abstract intrepidity of their support for Nixon gave the duke to Kennedy. Sinatra would not be surprised if the late ones who glommed onto Kennedy were not more numerous than the early-risers he scattered. And one does not even need to speak of the corporations, the Mob, the money they delivered by messenger, the credit they would use later. So if I came to the cool conclusion I had won the election for Kennedy with my piece in *Esquire*, the thought might be high presumption, but it was not unique. I had done something curious but indispensable for the campaign—succeeded in making it dramatic. I had not shifted one hundred thousand votes directly, I had not. But a million people might have read my piece and some of them talked to other people. The cadres of Stevenson Democrats whose morale was low might now revive with an argument that Kennedy was different in substance from Nixon. Dramatically different. The piece titled "Superman Comes to the Supermarket" affected volunteer work for Kennedy, enough to make a clean critical difference through the country. But such counting is a quibble. At bottom I had the feeling that if there were a power which made presidents, a power which might be termed Wall Street or Capitalism or The Establishment, a Mind or Collective Mind of some Spirit, some Master, or indeed *the* Master, no less, that then perhaps my article had turned that intelligence a fine hair in its circuits. This was what I thought. Right or wrong, I thought it, still do, and tell it now not to convince others (the act of stating such a claim is not happy), but to underline the proprietary tone I took when Kennedy invaded Cuba.

"You've cut . . ." I wrote in *The Village Voice*, April 27, 1961:
". . . the shape of your plan for history, and it smells . . . rich

and smug and scared of the power of the worst, dullest and most oppressive men of our land."

There was more. A good deal more. I want to quote more. Nothing could ever convince me the invasion of Cuba was not one of the meanest blunders in our history:

> "You are a virtuoso in political management but you will never understand the revolutionary passion which comes to those who were one way or another too poor to learn how good they might have been; the greediness of the rich had already crippled their youth.
>
> "Without this understanding you will never know what to do about Castro and Cuba. You will never understand that the man is the country, revolutionary, tyrannical . . . hysterical . . . brave as the best of animals, doomed perhaps to end in tragedy, but one of the great figures of the twentieth century, at the present moment a far greater figure than yourself."

Later, through the grapevine which runs from Washington to New York, it could be heard that Jackie Kennedy was indignant at this piece, and one had the opportunity to speculate if her annoyance came from the postscript:

> "I was in a demonstration the other day . . . five literary magazines (so help me) which marched in a small circle of protest against our intervention in Cuba. One of the pickets was a very tall poetess with black hair which reached near to her waist. She was dressed like a medieval varlet, and she carried a sign addressed to your wife:
>
> > Jacqueline, *vous avez*
> > *perdu vos artistes*
> > 'Tin soldier, you are depriving us of the Muse.'"

Months later, when the anger cooled, one could ask oneself what one did make of Washington now, for it was not an easy place to understand. It was intelligent, yes, but it was not original; there was wit in the detail and ponderousness in the program; vivacity, and dullness to equal it; tactical brilliance, political timidity; facts were still superior to the depths, criticism was less to be admired than the ability to be amusing—or so said the losers; equality and justice meandered; bureaucratic canals and locks; slums were replaced with buildings which looked like prisons; success was to be admired again, self-awareness dubious; television was attacked, but for its violence, not its mendacity, for its lack of educational programs, not its dearth of grace. There seemed no art, no real art in the new administration, and all the while the new administration proclaimed its eagerness to mother the arts. Or as Mr. Collingwood said to Mrs. Kennedy, "This Administration has shown a particular affinity for artists, musicians, writers, poets. Is this because you and your husband just feel that way or do you think that there's a relationship between the Government and the arts?"

"That's so complicated," answered Mrs. Kennedy with good sense. "I don't know. I just think that everything in the White House should be the best."

Stravinsky had been invited of course and Robert Frost. Pablo Casals, Leonard Bernstein, Arthur Miller, Tennessee.

"But what about us?" growled the apes. Why did one know that Richard Wilbur would walk through the door before Allen Ginsberg; or Saul Bellow and J. D. Salinger long before William Burroughs or Norman Mailer. What special good would it do to found an Establishment if the few who gave intimations of high talent were instinctively excluded? I wanted a chance to preach to the president and to the First Lady. "Speak to the people a little more," I would have liked to say, "talk on television about the things you do not understand. Use your popularity to be difficult and intellectually dangerous. There is more to greatness than liberal legislation." And to her I would have liked to go on about what the real meaning of an artist might be, of how the marrow of a nation was contained in his art, and one deadened artists at one's peril, because artists were not so much gifted as endowed; they had been given what was secret and best in their parents and in all the other people about them who had been generous or influenced them or made them, and so artists embodied the essence of what was best in the nation, embodied it in their talent rather than in their character, which could be small, but their talent—this fruit of all that was rich and nourishing in their lives—was related directly to the dreams and the ambitions of the most imaginative part of the nation. So the destiny of a nation was not separate at all from the fate of its artists. I would have liked to tell her that every time an artist failed to complete the full mansion, jungle, garden, armory, or city of his work the nation was subtly but permanently poorer, which is why we return so obsessively to the death of Tom Wolfe, the broken air of Scott Fitzgerald, and the gloomy smell of the vault which collects already about the horror of Hemingway's departure. I would have liked to say to her that a war for the right to express oneself had been going on in this country for fifty years, and that there were counterattacks massing because there were many who hated the artist now, that as the world dipped into the totalitarian trough of the twentieth century there was a mania of abhorrence for whatever was unpredictable. For all too many, security was the only bulwark against emptiness, eternity and death. The void was what America feared. Communism was one name they gave this void. The unknown was Communist. The girls who wore dungarees were Communist, and the boys who grew beards, the people who walked their dog off the leash. It was comic, but it was virulent, and there was a fanatic rage in much too much of the population. Detestation of the beatnik seethed like rabies on the mouths of small-town police officers.

Oh, there was much I wanted to tell her, even—exit sociology, enter insanity—that the obscene had a right to exist in the novel. For every fifteen-year-old who would be hurt by premature exposure, somewhere another, or two or three, would emerge from sexual experience which had been too full of moral funk onto the harder terrain of sex made alive by culture, that it was the purpose of culture finally to enrich all of the psyche, not just part of us, and damage to particular people in passing was a price we must pay. Thirty thousand Americans were killed each year by automobile crashes. No one talked of giving up the automobile: it was necessary to civilization. As necessary, I wanted to say, was art. Art in all its manifestations. Including the rude, the obscene, and the unsayable. Art was as essential to the nation as technology. I would tell her these things out of romantic abundance, because I liked her and thought she would understand what one was talking about, because as First Lady she was queen of the arts, she was our Muse if she chose to be. Perhaps it would not be altogether a disaster if America had a Muse.

Now it is not of much interest to most of you who read this that a small but distinct feud between the editors of *Esquire* and the writer was made up around the New Year. What is not as much off the matter was the suggestion, made at the time by one of these editors, that a story be done about Jackie Kennedy.

One liked the idea. What has been written already is curious prose if it is not obvious how much one liked the idea. Pierre Salinger was approached by the magazine, and agreed to present the same idea to Mrs. Kennedy. I saw Salinger in his office for a few minutes. He told me: not yet a chance to talk to the Lady, but might that evening. I was leaving Washington. A few days later, one of the editors spoke to him. Mrs. Kennedy's answer: negative.

One didn't know. One didn't know how the idea had been presented, one didn't know just when it had been presented. It did not matter all that much. Whatever the details, the answer had come from the core. One's presence was not required. Which irritated the vanity. The vanity was no doubt outsize, but one thought of oneself as one of the few writers in the country. There was a right to interview Mrs. Kennedy. She was not only a woman looking for privacy, but an institution being put together before our eyes. If the people of America were to have a symbol, one had the right to read more about the creation. The country would stay alive by becoming more extraordinary, not more predictable.

III

Not with a kind eye then did I watch Mrs. Kennedy give the nation a tour. One would be fair. Fair to her and fair to the truth of one's reactions. There was now an advantage in not having had the interview.

I turned on the program a minute after the hour. The image on the screen was not of Mrs. Kennedy, but the White House. For some minutes she talked, reading from a prepared script while the camera was turned upon old prints, old plans, and present views of the building. Since Jackie Kennedy was not visible during this time, there was an opportunity to listen to her voice. It produced a small continuing shock. At first, before the picture emerged from the set, I thought I was turned to the wrong station, because the voice was a quiet parody of the sort of voice one hears on the radio late at night, dropped softly into the ear by girls who sell soft mattresses, depilatories, or creams to brighten the skin.

Now I had heard the First Lady occasionally on newsreels and in brief interviews on television, and thought she showed an odd public voice, but never paid attention, because the first time to hear her was in the living room at Hyannis Port and there she had been clear, merry and near excellent. So I discounted the public voice, concluded it was muffled by shyness perhaps or was too urgent in its desire to sound like other voices, to sound, let us say, like an attractive small-town salesgirl, or like Jackie Kennedy's version of one: the gentry in America have a dim ear for the nuances of accent in the rough, the poor, and the ready. I had decided it was probably some mockery of her husband's political ambitions, a sport upon whatever advisers had been trying for years to guide her to erase whatever was too patrician or cultivated in her speech. But the voice I was hearing now, the public voice, the voice after a year in the White House had grown undeniably worse, had nourished itself on its faults. Do some of you remember the girl with the magnificent sweater who used to give the weather reports on television in a swarmy singsong tone? It was a self-conscious parody, very funny for a little while: "Temperature—forty-eight. Humidity—twenty-eight. Prevailing winds." It had the style of the pinup magazine, it caught their prose: "Sandra Sharilee is 37-25-37, and likes to stay in at night." The girl who gave the weather report captured the voice of those pinup magazines, dreamy, narcissistic, visions of sex on the moon. And Jackie Kennedy's voice, her public voice, might as well have been influenced by the weather girl. What madness is loose in our public communication. And what self-ridicule that consciously or unconsciously, wittingly, willy-nilly, by the aid of speech teachers or all on her stubborn own, this was the manufactured voice Jackie Kennedy chose to arrive at. One had heard better ones at Christmastime in Macy's selling gadgets to the grim.

The introduction having ended, the camera moved onto Jackie Kennedy. We were shown the broad planes of the First Lady's most agreeable face. Out of the deep woods now. One could return to them by closing one's eyes and listening to the voice again, but the image was reasonable, reassuringly stiff. As the eye followed Mrs. Kennedy and her interlocutor, Charles Collingwood, through the halls, galleries and rooms of the White House, through the Blue Room, the Green Room, the East Room, the State Dining Room, the Red Room; as the listeners were offered a reference to Dolley Madison's favorite sofa, or President Monroe's Minerva clock, Nelly Custis's sofa, Mrs. Lincoln's later poverty, Daniel Webster's sofa, Julia Grant's desk, Andrew Jackson's broken mirror, the chest President Van Buren gave to his grandson; as the paintings were shown to us, paintings entitled *Niagara Falls*, *Grapes and Apples*, *Naval Battle of 1812*, *Indian Guides*, *A Mountain Glimpse*, *Mouth of the Delaware*; as one contemplated the life of this offering, the presentation began to take on the undernourished, overdone air of a charity show, a telethon for a new disease. It was not Mrs. Kennedy's fault—she strove honorably. What an agony it must have been to establish the sequence of all these names, all these objects. Probably she knew them well, perhaps she was interested in her subject—although the detached quality of her presence on this program made it not easy to believe—but whether or not she had taken a day-to-day interest in the booty now within the White House, still she had had a script partially written for her, by a television writer with black horn-rimmed glasses no doubt, she had been obliged to memorize portions of this script, she had trained for the part. Somehow it was sympathetic that she walked through it like a starlet who is utterly without talent. Mrs. Kennedy moved like a wooden horse. A marvelous horse, perhaps even a live horse, its feet hobbled, its head unready to turn for fear of a flick from the crop. She had that intense wooden lack of rest, that lack of comprehension for each word offered up which one finds only in a few of those curious movie stars who are huge box office. Jane Russell comes to mind, and Rita Hayworth when she was sadly cast, Jayne Mansfield in deep water, Brigitte Bardot before she learned to act. Marilyn Monroe. But one may be too kind. Jackie Kennedy was more like a starlet who will never learn to act because the extraordinary livid unreality of her life away from the camera has so beclouded her brain and seduced her attention that she is incapable of the simplest and most essential demand, which is to live and breathe easily with the meaning of the words one speaks.

This program was the sort of thing Eleanor Roosevelt could have done, and done well. She had grown up among objects like this—these stuffed armchairs, these candelabra—no doubt they lived for her with some charm of the past. But Jackie Kennedy was unconvincing. One did not feel she particularly loved the past of America—not all of us do for that matter, it may not even be a crime—but one never had the impression for a moment that the White House fitted her style. As one watched this tame, lackluster and halting show, one wanted to take the actress by the near shoulder. Because names, dates and objects were boring down into the very secrets of her being—or so one would lay the bet—and this encouraged a fraud which could only sicken her. By extension it would deaden us. What we needed and what she could offer us was much more complex than this public image of a pompadour, a tea-dance dress, and a Colonial window welded together in committee: Would the Kennedys be no more intelligent than the near past, had they not learned America was not to be saved by Madison Avenue, that no method could work which induced nausea faster than the pills we push to carry it away?

Afterward one could ask what it was one wanted of her, and the answer was that she show herself to us as she is. Because what we suffer from in America, in that rootless moral wilderness of our expanding life, is the unadmitted terror in each of us that bit by bit, year by year, we are going mad. Very few of us know really where we have come from and to where we are going, why we do it, and if it is ever worthwhile. For better or for worse we have lost our past, we live in that airless no-man's-land of the perpetual present, and so suffer doubly as we strike into the future because we have no roots by which to project ourselves forward, or judge our trip.

And this tour of the White House gave us precisely no sense of the past. To the contrary, it inflicted the past upon us, pummeled us with it, depressed us with facts. I counted the names, the proper names, and the dates in the transcript. More than two hundred items were dumped upon us during that hour. If one counts repetitions, the number is closer to four hundred. One was not being offered education, but anxiety.

We are in the Green Room—I quote from the transcript:

Mr. Collingwood: What other objects of special interest are there in the room now?

Mrs. Kennedy: Well, there's this sofa which belonged to Daniel Webster and is really one of the finest pieces here in this room. And then there's this mirror. It was George Washington's and he had it in the Executive Mansion in Philadelphia, then he gave it to a friend and it was bought for Mount Vernon in 1891. And it was there until Mount Vernon lent it to us this fall. And I must say I appreciate that more than I can say, because when Mount Vernon, which is probably the most revered house in this country, lends something to the White House, you know they have confidence it will be taken care of.

A neurotic may suffer agonies returning to his past; so may a nation which is not well. The neurotic recites endless lists of his activities and offers no reaction to any of it. So do we teach with empty content and by rigid manner where there is anxiety in the lore. American history disgorges this anxiety. Where, in the pleasant versions of it we are furnished, can we find an explanation for the disease which encourages us to scourge our countryside, stifle our cities, kill the physical sense of our past, and throw up excruciatingly totalitarian new office buildings everywhere to burden the vista of our end? This disease, is it hidden in the evasions, the injustices, and the prevarications of the past, or does it come to us from a terror of what is yet to come? Whatever, however, we do not create a better nation by teaching schoolchildren the catalogs of the White House. Nor do we use the First Lady decently if she is flattered in this, for catalogs are imprisonment to the delicate, muted sensitivity one feels passing across Jackie Kennedy from time to time like a small summer wind on a good garden.

Yes, before the tour was over, one had to feel compassion. Because silly, ill-advised, pointless, empty, dull, and obsequious to the most slavish tastes in American life as was this show, still she was trying so hard, she wanted to please, she had given herself to this work, and it was hopeless there was no one about to tell her how very hopeless it was, how utterly without offering to the tormented adventurous spirit of American life. At times, in her eyes, there was a blank, full look which one could recognize. One had seen this look on a nineteen-year-old who was sweet and on the town and pushed too far. She slashed her wrists one night and tried to scar her cheeks and her breast. I had visited the girl in the hospital. She had blank eyes, a wide warm smile, a deadness in her voice. It did not matter about what she spoke—only her mouth followed the words, never her eyes. So I did not care to see that look in Jackie Kennedy's face, and I hoped by half—for more would be untrue—that the sense one got of her in newspaper photographs, of a ladygirl healthy and on the bounce, might come into her presence before our deadening sets. America needed a lady's humor to leaven the solemnities of our toneless power: finally we will send a man to Mars and the Martians will say, "God, he is dull."

Yes, it is to be hoped that Jackie Kennedy will come alive. Because I think finally she is one of us. By which I mean that she has not one face but many, not a true voice but accents, not a past so much as memories which cannot speak to one another. She attracts compassion. Somewhere in her mute vitality is a wash of our fatigue, of existential fatigue, of the great fatigue which comes from being adventurous in a world where most of the bets are covered cold and statisticians prosper. I liked her, I liked her still, but she was a phony—it was the crudest thing one could say, she was a royal phony. There was something very difficult and very dangerous she was trying from deep within herself to do, dangerous not to her safety but to her soul. She was trying, I suppose, to be a proper First Lady and it was her mistake. Because there was no need to copy the Ladies who had come before her. Suppose America had not yet had a First Lady who was even remotely warm enough for our needs? Or sufficiently imaginative? But who could there be to advise her in all that company of organized men, weaned on the handbook of past precedent? If she would be any use to the nation she must first regain the freedom to look us in the eye. And offer the hard drink. For then three times three hurrah, and hats, our hats, in the air. If she were really interested in her White House, we would grant it to her, we would not begrudge her the tour, not if we could believe she was beginning to learn the difference between the arts and the safe old crafts. And indeed there was a way she could show us she was beginning to learn, it was the way of the hostess: one would offer her one's sword when Henry Miller was asked to the White House as often as Robert Frost and Beat poetry's own Andy Hardy—good Gregory Corso—could do an Indian dance in the East Room with Archibald MacLeish. America would be as great as the royal rajah of her arts when the Academy ceased to be happy as a cherrystone clam, and the weakest of the Beats returned to form. Because our tragedy is that we diverge as countrymen further and further away from one another, like a spaceship broken apart in flight which now drifts mournfully in isolated orbits, satellites to each other, planets none, communication faint.

Martin Luther King, Jr. (1929–1968), minister, civil rights leader, Nobel Peace Prize winner, martyred visionary, wrote "Letter from Birmingham Jail" in April 1963, when he was incarcerated after participating in a march protesting racial segregation. It was written on scraps of paper in response to a public letter by white moderate clergymen, which deplored the nonviolent sit-ins and marches as breaking Alabama law. Perhaps all essays are, in a sense, letters to the reader, but this one literally took advantage of the direct conversational address of the epistolary form. It also displayed King's sweeping command of rhetorical devices: metaphor, quotation, irony, exhortation, and syntactical variety (like that long rolling sentence about the injustices suffered by African Americans).

LETTER FROM BIRMINGHAM JAIL

My Dear Fellow Clergymen:

While confined here in the Birmingham city jail, I came across your recent statement calling my present activities "unwise and untimely." Seldom do I pause to answer criticism of my work and ideas. If I sought to answer all the criticisms that cross my desk, my secretaries would have little time for anything other than such correspondence in the course of the day, and I would have no time for constructive work. But since I feel that you are men of genuine good will and that your criticisms are sincerely set forth,

I want to try to answer your statement in what I hope will be patient and reasonable terms.

I think I should indicate why I am here in Birmingham, since you have been influenced by the view which argues against "outsiders coming in." I have the honor of serving as president of the Southern Christian Leadership Conference, an organization operating in every southern state, with headquarters in Atlanta, Georgia. We have some eighty-five affiliated organizations across the South, and one of them is the Alabama Christian Movement for Human Rights. Frequently we share staff, educational and financial resources with our affiliates. Several months ago the affiliate here in Birmingham asked us to be on call to engage in a nonviolent direct action program if such were deemed necessary. We readily consented, and when the hour came we lived up to our promise. So I, along with several members of my staff, am here because I was invited here. I am here because I have organizational ties here.

But more basically, I am in Birmingham because injustice is here. Just as the prophets of the eighth century B.C. left their villages and carried their "thus saith the Lord" far beyond the boundaries of their home towns, and just as the Apostle Paul left his village of Tarsus and carried the gospel of Jesus Christ to the far corners of the Greco-Roman world, so am I compelled to carry the gospel of freedom beyond my own home town. Like Paul, I must constantly respond to the Macedonian call for aid.

Moreover, I am cognizant of the interrelatedness of all communities and states. I cannot sit idly by in Atlanta and not be concerned about what happens in Birmingham. Injustice anywhere is a threat to justice everywhere. We are caught in an inescapable network of mutuality, tied in a single garment of destiny. Whatever affects one directly, affects all indirectly. Never again can we afford to live with the narrow, provincial "outside agitator" idea. Anyone who lives inside the United States can never be considered an outsider anywhere within its bounds.

You deplore the demonstrations taking place in Birmingham. But your statement, I am sorry to say, fails to express a similar concern for the conditions that brought about the demonstrations. I am sure that none of you would want to rest content with the superficial kind of social analysis that deals merely with effects and does not grapple with underlying causes. It is unfortunate that demonstrations are taking place in Birmingham, but it is even more unfortunate that the city's white power structure left the Negro community with no alternative.

In any nonviolent campaign there are four basic steps: collection of the facts to determine whether injustices exist; negotiation; self-purification; and direct action. We have gone through all these steps in Birmingham. There can be no gainsaying the fact that racial injustice engulfs this community. Birmingham is probably the most thoroughly segregated city in the United States. Its ugly record of brutality is widely known. Negroes have experienced grossly unjust treatment in the courts. There have been more unsolved bombings of Negro homes and churches in Birmingham than in any other city in the nation. These are the hard, brutal facts of the case. On the basis of these conditions, Negro leaders sought to negotiate with the city fathers. But the latter consistently refused to engage in good-faith negotiation.

Then, last September, came the opportunity to talk with leaders of Birmingham's economic community. In the course of the negotiations, certain promises were made by the merchants—for example, to remove the stores' humiliating racial signs. On the basis of these promises, the Reverend Fred Shuttlesworth and the leaders of the Alabama Christian Movement for Human Rights agreed to a moratorium on all demonstrations. As the weeks and months went by, we realized that we were the victims of a broken promise. A few signs, briefly removed, returned; the others remained. As in so many past experiences, our hopes had been blasted, and the shadow of deep disappointment settled upon us. We had no alternative except to prepare for direct action, whereby we would present our very bodies as a means of laying our case before the conscience of the local and the national community. Mindful of the difficulties involved, we decided to undertake a process of self-purification. We began a series of workshops on nonviolence, and we repeatedly asked ourselves: "Are you able to accept blows without retaliating?" "Are you able to endure the ordeal of jail?" We decided to schedule our direct action program for the Easter season, realizing that except for

Christmas, this is the main shopping period of the year. Knowing that a strong economic-withdrawal program would be the by-product of direct action, we felt that this would be the best time to bring pressure to bear on the merchants for the needed change.

Then it occurred to us that Birmingham's mayoral election was coming up in March, and we speedily decided to postpone action until after election day. When we discovered that the Commissioner of Public Safety, Eugene "Bull" Connor, had piled up enough votes to be in the run-off, we decided again to postpone action until the day after the run-off so that the demonstrations could not be used to cloud the issues. Like many others, we waited to see Mr. Connor defeated, and to this end we endured postponement after postponement. Having aided in this community need, we felt that our direct action program could be delayed no longer.

You may well ask: "Why direct action? Why sit-ins, marches and so forth? Isn't negotiation a better path?" You are quite right in calling for negotiation. Indeed, this is the very purpose of direct action. Nonviolent direct action seeks to create such a crisis and foster such a tension that a community which has constantly refused to negotiate is forced to confront the issue. It seeks so to dramatize the issue that it can no longer be ignored. My citing the creation of tension as part of the work of the nonviolent resister may sound rather shocking. But I must confess that I am not afraid of the word "tension." I have earnestly opposed violent tension, but there is a type of constructive, nonviolent tension which is necessary for growth. Just as Socrates felt that it was necessary to create a tension in the mind so that individuals could rise from the bondage of myths and half truths to the unfettered realm of creative analysis and objective appraisal, so must we see the need for nonviolent gadflies to create the kind of tension in society that will help men rise from the dark depths of prejudice and racism to the majestic heights of understanding and brotherhood. The purpose of our direct action program is to create a situation so crisis packed that it will inevitably open the door to negotiation. I therefore concur with you in your call for negotiation. Too long has our beloved Southland been bogged down in a tragic effort to live in monologue rather than dialogue.

One of the basic points in your statement is that the action that I and my associates have taken in Birmingham is untimely. Some have asked: "Why didn't you give the new city administration time to act?" The only answer that I can give to this query is that the new Birmingham administration must be prodded about as much as the outgoing one, before it will act. We are sadly mistaken if we feel that the election of Albert Boutwell as mayor will bring the millennium to Birmingham. While Mr. Boutwell is a much more gentle person than Mr. Connor, they are both segregationists, dedicated to maintenance of the status quo. I have hope that Mr. Boutwell will be reasonable enough to see the futility of massive resistance to desegregation. But he will not see this without pressure from devotees of civil rights. My friends, I must say to you that we have not made a single gain in civil rights without determined legal and nonviolent pressure. Lamentably, it is an historical fact that privileged groups seldom give up their privileges voluntarily. Individuals may see the moral light and voluntarily give up their unjust posture; but, as Reinhold Niebuhr has reminded us, groups tend to be more immoral than individuals.

We know through painful experience that freedom is never voluntarily given by the oppressor; it must be demanded by the oppressed. Frankly, I have yet to engage in a direct action campaign that was "well timed" in the view of those who have not suffered unduly from the disease of segregation. For years now I have heard the word "Wait!" It rings in the ear of every Negro with piercing familiarity. This "Wait" has almost always meant "Never." We must come to see, with one of our distinguished jurists, that "justice too long delayed is justice denied."

We have waited for more than 340 years for our constitutional and God-given rights. The nations of Asia and Africa are moving with jetlike speed toward gaining political independence, but we still creep at horse and buggy pace toward gaining a cup of coffee at a lunch counter. Perhaps it is easy for those who have never felt the stinging darts of segregation to say, "Wait." But when you have seen vicious mobs lynch your mothers and fathers at will and drown your sisters and brothers at whim; when you have seen hate-filled policemen curse, kick and even kill your black brothers and sisters; when you see the vast majority of your twenty million Negro brothers smothering in an airtight cage of poverty in the midst of an affluent society; when you suddenly find your tongue twisted and your speech stammering as you seek to explain to your six-year-old daughter why she can't go to the public amusement park that has just been advertised on television, and see tears welling up in her eyes when she is told that Funtown is closed to colored children, and see ominous clouds of inferiority beginning to form in her little mental sky, and see her beginning to distort her personality by developing an unconscious bitterness toward white people; when you have to concoct an answer for a five-year-old son who is asking: "Daddy, why do white people treat colored people so mean?"; when you take a cross-country drive and find it necessary to sleep night after night in the uncomfortable corners of your automobile because no motel will accept you; when you are humiliated day in and day out by nagging signs reading "white" and "colored"; when your first name becomes "nigger," your middle name becomes "boy" (however old you are) and your last name becomes "John," and your wife and mother are never given the respected title "Mrs."; when you are harried by day and haunted by night by the fact that you are a Negro, living constantly at tiptoe stance, never quite knowing what to expect next, and are plagued with inner fears and outer resentments; when you are forever fighting a degenerating sense of "nobodiness"—then you will understand why we find it difficult to wait. There comes a time when the cup of endurance runs over, and men are no longer willing to be plunged into the abyss of despair. I hope, sirs, you can understand our legitimate and unavoidable impatience. You express a great deal of anxiety over our willingness to break laws. This is certainly a legitimate concern. Since we so diligently urge people to obey the Supreme Court's decision of 1954 outlawing segregation in the public schools, at first glance it may seem rather paradoxical for us consciously to break laws. One may well ask: "How can you advocate breaking some laws and obeying others?" The answer lies in the fact that there are two types of laws: just and unjust. I would be the first to advocate obeying just laws. One has not only a legal but a moral responsibility to obey just laws. Conversely, one has a moral responsibility to disobey unjust laws. I would agree with St. Augustine that "an unjust law is no law at all."

Now, what is the difference between the two? How does one determine whether a law is just or unjust? A just law is a man-made code that squares with the moral law or the law of God. An unjust law is a code that is out of harmony with the moral law. To put it in the terms of St. Thomas Aquinas: An unjust law is a human law that is not rooted in eternal law and natural law. Any law that uplifts human personality is just. Any law that degrades human personality is unjust. All segregation statutes are unjust because segregation distorts the soul and damages the personality. It gives the segregator a false sense of superiority and the segregated a false sense of inferiority. Segregation, to use the terminology of the Jewish philosopher Martin Buber, substitutes an "I it" relationship for an "I thou" relationship and ends up relegating persons to the status of things. Hence segregation is not only politically, economically and sociologically unsound, it is morally wrong and sinful. Paul Tillich has said that sin is separation. Is not segregation an existential expression of man's tragic separation, his awful estrangement, his terrible sinfulness? Thus it is that I can urge men to obey the 1954 decision of the Supreme Court, for it is morally right; and I can urge them to disobey segregation ordinances, for they are morally wrong.

Let us consider a more concrete example of just and unjust laws. An unjust law is a code that a numerical or power majority group compels a minority group to obey but does not make binding on itself. This is difference made legal. By the same token, a just law is a code that a majority compels a minority to follow and that it is willing to follow itself. This is sameness made legal. Let me give another explanation. A law is unjust if it is inflicted on a minority that, as a result of being denied the right to vote, had no part in enacting or devising the law. Who can say that the legislature of Alabama which set up that state's segregation laws was democratically elected? Throughout Alabama all sorts of devious methods are used to prevent Negroes from becoming registered voters, and there are some counties in which, even though Negroes constitute a majority of the population, not a

single Negro is registered. Can any law enacted under such circumstances be considered democratically structured?

Sometimes a law is just on its face and unjust in its application. For instance, I have been arrested on a charge of parading
without a permit. Now, there is nothing wrong in having an ordi-
nance which requires a permit for a parade. But such an ordi-
nance becomes unjust when it is used to maintain segregation
and to deny citizens the First Amendment privilege of peaceful
assembly and protest.

I hope you are able to see the distinction I am trying to point
out. In no sense do I advocate evading or defying the law, as
would the rabid segregationist. That would lead to anarchy. One
who breaks an unjust law must do so openly, lovingly, and with
a willingness to accept the penalty. I submit that an individual
who breaks a law that conscience tells him is unjust, and who
willingly accepts the penalty of imprisonment in order to arouse
the conscience of the community over its injustice, is in reality
expressing the highest respect for law.

Of course, there is nothing new about this kind of civil disobedience. It was evidenced sublimely in the refusal of Shadrach,
Meshach and Abednego to obey the laws of Nebuchadnezzar, on
the ground that a higher moral law was at stake. It was practiced
superbly by the early Christians, who were willing to face hungry
lions and the excruciating pain of chopping blocks rather than
submit to certain unjust laws of the Roman Empire. To a degree,
academic freedom is a reality today because Socrates practiced
civil disobedience. In our own nation, the Boston Tea Party represented a massive act of civil disobedience.

We should never forget that everything Adolf Hitler did in
Germany was "legal" and everything the Hungarian freedom
fighters did in Hungary was "illegal." It was "illegal" to aid
and comfort a Jew in Hitler's Germany. Even so, I am sure that,
had I lived in Germany at the time, I would have aided and
comforted my Jewish brothers. If today I lived in a Communist
country where certain principles dear to the Christian faith are
suppressed, I would openly advocate disobeying that country's
antireligious laws.

I must make two honest confessions to you, my Christian and

Jewish brothers. First, I must confess that over the past few years I have been gravely disappointed with the white moderate. I have almost reached the regrettable conclusion that the Negro's great stumbling block in his stride toward freedom is not the White Citizen's Counciler or the Ku Klux Klanner, but the white moderate, who is more devoted to "order" than to justice; who prefers a negative peace which is the absence of tension to a positive peace which is the presence of justice; who constantly says: "I agree with you in the goal you seek, but I cannot agree with your methods of direct action"; who paternalistically believes he can set the timetable for another man's freedom; who lives by a mythical concept of time and who constantly advises the Negro to wait for a "more convenient season." Shallow understanding from people of good will is more frustrating than absolute misunderstanding from people of ill will. Lukewarm acceptance is much more bewildering than outright rejection.

I had hoped that the white moderate would understand that law and order exist for the purpose of establishing justice and that when they fail in this purpose they become the dangerously structured dams that block the flow of social progress. I had hoped that the white moderate would understand that the present tension in the South is a necessary phase of the transition from an obnoxious negative peace, in which the Negro passively accepted his unjust plight, to a substantive and positive peace, in which all men will respect the dignity and worth of human personality. Actually, we who engage in nonviolent direct action are not the creators of tension. We merely bring to the surface the hidden tension that is already alive. We bring it out in the open, where it can be seen and dealt with. Like a boil that can never be cured so long as it is covered up but must be opened with all its ugliness to the natural medicines of air and light, injustice must be exposed, with all the tension its exposure creates, to the light of human conscience and the air of national opinion before it can be cured.

In your statement you assert that our actions, even though peaceful, must be condemned because they precipitate violence. But is this a logical assertion? Isn't this like condemning a robbed man because his possession of money precipitated the evil act of robbery? Isn't this like condemning Socrates because his unswerving commitment to truth and his philosophical inquiries precipitated the act by the misguided populace in which they made him drink hemlock? Isn't this like condemning Jesus because his unique God consciousness and never ceasing devotion to God's will precipitated the evil act of crucifixion? We must come to see that, as the federal courts have consistently affirmed, it is wrong to urge an individual to cease his efforts to gain his basic constitutional rights because the quest may precipitate violence. Society must protect the robbed and punish the robber. I had also hoped that the white moderate would reject the myth concerning time in relation to the struggle for freedom. I have just received a letter from a white brother in Texas. He writes: "All Christians know that the colored people will receive equal rights eventually, but it is possible that you are in too great a religious hurry. It has taken Christianity almost two thousand years to accomplish what it has. The teachings of Christ take time to come to earth." Such an attitude stems from a tragic misconception of time, from the strangely irrational notion that there is something in the very flow of time that will inevitably cure all ills. Actually, time itself is neutral; it can be used either destructively or constructively. More and more I feel that the people of ill will have used time much more effectively than have the people of good will. We will have to repent in this generation not merely for the hateful words and actions of the bad people but for the appalling silence of the good people. Human progress never rolls in on wheels of inevitability; it comes through the tireless efforts of men willing to be co-workers with God, and without this hard work, time itself becomes an ally of the forces of social stagnation. We must use time creatively, in the knowledge that the time is always ripe to do right. Now is the time to make real the promise of democracy and transform our pending national elegy into a creative psalm of brotherhood. Now is the time to lift our national policy from the quicksand of racial injustice to the solid rock of human dignity.

You speak of our activity in Birmingham as extreme. At first I was rather disappointed that fellow clergymen would see my nonviolent efforts as those of an extremist. I began thinking about the fact that I stand in the middle of two opposing forces in the Negro community. One is a force of complacency, made up in part of Negroes who, as a result of long years of oppression, are so drained of self-respect and a sense of "somebodiness" that they have adjusted to segregation; and in part of a few middle-class Negroes who, because of a degree of academic and economic security and because in some ways they profit by segregation, have become insensitive to the problems of the masses. The other force is one of bitterness and hatred, and it comes perilously close to advocating violence. It is expressed in the various black nationalist groups that are springing up across the nation, the largest and best known being Elijah Muhammad's Muslim movement. Nourished by the Negro's frustration over the continued existence of racial discrimination, this movement is made up of people who have lost faith in America, who have absolutely repudiated Christianity, and who have concluded that the white man is an incorrigible "devil."

I have tried to stand between these two forces, saying that we need emulate neither the "do nothingism" of the complacent nor the hatred and despair of the black nationalist. For there is the more excellent way of love and nonviolent protest. I am grateful to God that, through the influence of the Negro church, the way of nonviolence became an integral part of our struggle. If this philosophy had not emerged, by now many streets of the South would, I am convinced, be flowing with blood. And I am further convinced that if our white brothers dismiss as "rabble rousers" and "outside agitators" those of us who employ nonviolent direct action, and if they refuse to support our nonviolent efforts, millions of Negroes will, out of frustration and despair, seek solace and security in black nationalist ideologies—a development that would inevitably lead to a frightening racial nightmare.

Oppressed people cannot remain oppressed forever. The yearning for freedom eventually manifests itself, and that is what has happened to the American Negro. Something within has reminded him of his birthright of freedom, and something without has reminded him that it can be gained. Consciously or unconsciously, he has been caught up by the Zeitgeist, and with his black brothers of Africa and his brown and yellow brothers of Asia, South America and the Caribbean, the United States Negro is moving with a sense of great urgency toward the promised land of racial justice. If one recognizes this vital urge that has engulfed the Negro community, one should readily understand why public demonstrations are taking place. The Negro has many pent-up resentments and latent frustrations, and he must release them. So let him march; let him make prayer pilgrimages to the city hall; let him go on freedom rides—and try to understand why he must do so. If his repressed emotions are not released in nonviolent ways, they will seek expression through violence; this is not a threat but a fact of history. So I have not said to my people: "Get rid of your discontent." Rather, I have tried to say that this normal and healthy discontent can be channeled into the creative outlet of nonviolent direct action. And now this approach is being termed extremist. But though I was initially disappointed at being categorized as an extremist, as I continued to think about the matter I gradually gained a measure of satisfaction from the label. Was not Jesus an extremist for love: "Love your enemies, bless them that curse you, do good to them that hate you, and pray for them which despitefully use you, and persecute you." Was not Amos an extremist for justice: "Let justice roll down like waters and righteousness like an ever flowing stream." Was not Paul an extremist for the Christian gospel: "I bear in my body the marks of the Lord Jesus." Was not Martin Luther an extremist: "Here I stand; I cannot do otherwise, so help me God." And John Bunyan: "I will stay in jail to the end of my days before I make a butchery of my conscience." And Abraham Lincoln: "This nation cannot survive half slave and half free." And Thomas Jefferson: "We hold these truths to be self evident, that all men are created equal . . ." So the question is not whether we will be extremists, but what kind of extremists we will be. Will we be extremists for hate or for love? Will we be extremists for the preservation of injustice or for the extension of justice? In that dramatic scene on Calvary's hill three men were crucified. We must never forget that all three were crucified for the same crime—the crime of extremism. Two were extremists for immorality, and thus fell below their environment. The other, Jesus Christ, was an extremist for love, truth and goodness, and thereby rose above his environment. Perhaps the South, the nation and the world are in dire need of creative extremists.

I had hoped that the white moderate would see this need. Perhaps I was too optimistic; perhaps I expected too much. I suppose I should have realized that few members of the oppressor race can understand the deep groans and passionate yearnings of the oppressed race, and still fewer have the vision to see that injustice must be rooted out by strong, persistent and determined action. I am thankful, however, that some of our white brothers in the South have grasped the meaning of this social revolution and committed themselves to it. They are still all too few in quantity, but they are big in quality. Some—such as Ralph McGill, Lillian Smith, Harry Golden, James McBride Dabbs, Ann Braden and Sarah Patton Boyle—have written about our struggle in eloquent and prophetic terms. Others have marched with us down nameless streets of the South. They have languished in filthy, roach-infested jails, suffering the abuse and brutality of policemen who view them as "dirty nigger-lovers." Unlike so many of their moderate brothers and sisters, they have recognized the urgency of the moment and sensed the need for powerful "action" antidotes to combat the disease of segregation. Let me take note of my other major disappointment. I have been so greatly disappointed with the white church and its leadership. Of course, there are some notable exceptions. I am not unmindful of the fact that each of you has taken some significant stands on this issue. I commend you, Reverend Stallings, for your Christian stand on this past Sunday, in welcoming Negroes to your worship service on a nonsegregated basis. I commend the Catholic leaders of this state for integrating Spring Hill College several years ago.

But despite these notable exceptions, I must honestly reiterate that I have been disappointed with the church. I do not say this as one of those negative critics who can always find something wrong with the church. I say this as a minister of the gospel, who loves the church; who was nurtured in its bosom; who has been sustained by its spiritual blessings and who will remain true to it as long as the cord of life shall lengthen.

When I was suddenly catapulted into the leadership of the bus protest in Montgomery, Alabama, a few years ago, I felt we would be supported by the white church. I felt that the white ministers, priests and rabbis of the South would be among our strongest allies. Instead, some have been outright opponents, refusing to understand the freedom movement and misrepresenting its leaders; all too many others have been more cautious than courageous and have remained silent behind the anesthetizing security of stained glass windows.

In spite of my shattered dreams, I came to Birmingham with the hope that the white religious leadership of this community would see the justice of our cause and, with deep moral concern, would serve as the channel through which our just grievances could reach the power structure. I had hoped that each of you would understand. But again I have been disappointed.

I have heard numerous southern religious leaders admonish their worshipers to comply with a desegregation decision because it is the law, but I have longed to hear white ministers declare: "Follow this decree because integration is morally right and because the Negro is your brother." In the midst of blatant injustices inflicted upon the Negro, I have watched white churchmen stand on the sideline and mouth pious irrelevancies and sanctimonious trivialities. In the midst of a mighty struggle to rid our nation of racial and economic injustice, I have heard many ministers say: "Those are social issues, with which the gospel has no real concern." And I have watched many churches commit themselves to a completely otherworldly religion which makes a strange, un-Biblical distinction between body and soul, between the sacred and the secular.

I have traveled the length and breadth of Alabama, Mississippi and all the other southern states. On sweltering summer days and crisp autumn mornings I have looked at the South's beautiful churches with their lofty spires pointing heavenward. I have beheld the impressive outlines of her massive religious education buildings. Over and over I have found myself asking: "What kind of people worship here? Who is their God? Where were their voices when the lips of Governor Barnett dripped with words of interposition and nullification? Where were they when Governor Wallace gave a clarion call for defiance and hatred? Where were their voices of support when bruised and weary Negro men and women decided to rise from the dark dungeons of complacency to the bright hills of creative protest?"

Yes, these questions are still in my mind. In deep disappointment I have wept over the laxity of the church. But be assured that my tears have been tears of love. There can be no deep disappointment where there is not deep love. Yes, I love the church. How could I do otherwise? I am in the rather unique position of being the son, the grandson and the great-grandson of preachers. Yes, I see the church as the body of Christ. But, oh! How we have blemished and scarred that body through social neglect and through fear of being nonconformists.

There was a time when the church was very powerful—in the time when the early Christians rejoiced at being deemed worthy to suffer for what they believed. In those days the church was not merely a thermometer that recorded the ideas and principles of popular opinion; it was a thermostat that transformed the mores of society. Whenever the early Christians entered a town, the people in power became disturbed and immediately sought to convict the Christians for being "disturbers of the peace" and "outside agitators." But the Christians pressed on, in the conviction that they were "a colony of heaven," called to obey God rather than man. Small in number, they were big in commitment. They were too God-intoxicated to be "astronomically intimidated." By their effort and example they brought an end to such ancient evils as infanticide and gladiatorial contests. Things are different now. So often the contemporary church is a weak, ineffectual voice with an uncertain sound. So often it is an archdefender of the status quo. Far from being disturbed by the presence of the church, the power structure of the average community is consoled by the church's silent—and often even vocal—sanction of things as they are.

But the judgment of God is upon the church as never before. If today's church does not recapture the sacrificial spirit of the early church, it will lose its authenticity, forfeit the loyalty of millions, and be dismissed as an irrelevant social club with no meaning for the twentieth century. Every day I meet young people whose disappointment with the church has turned into outright disgust.

Perhaps I have once again been too optimistic. Is organized

religion too inextricably bound to the status quo to save our nation and the world? Perhaps I must turn my faith to the inner spiritual church, the church within the church, as the true ekklesia and the hope of the world. But again I am thankful to God that some noble souls from the ranks of organized religion have broken loose from the paralyzing chains of conformity and joined us as active partners in the struggle for freedom. They have left their secure congregations and walked the streets of Albany, Georgia, with us. They have gone down the highways of the South on tortuous rides for freedom. Yes, they have gone to jail with us. Some have been dismissed from their churches, have lost the support of their bishops and fellow ministers. But they have acted in the faith that right defeated is stronger than evil triumphant. Their witness has been the spiritual salt that has preserved the true meaning of the gospel in these troubled times. They have carved a tunnel of hope through the dark mountain of disappointment. I hope the church as a whole will meet the challenge of this decisive hour. But even if the church does not come to the aid of justice, I have no despair about the future. I have no fear about the outcome of our struggle in Birmingham, even if our motives are at present misunderstood. We will reach the goal of freedom in Birmingham and all over the nation, because the goal of America is freedom. Abused and scorned though we may be, our destiny is tied up with America's destiny. Before the pilgrims landed at Plymouth, we were here. Before the pen of Jefferson etched the majestic words of the Declaration of Independence across the pages of history, we were here. For more than two centuries our forebears labored in this country without wages; they made cotton king; they built the homes of their masters while suffering gross injustice and shameful humiliation—and yet out of a bottomless vitality they continued to thrive and develop. If the inexpressible cruelties of slavery could not stop us, the opposition we now face will surely fail. We will win our freedom because the sacred heritage of our nation and the eternal will of God are embodied in our echoing demands. Before closing I feel impelled to mention one other point in your statement that has troubled me profoundly. You warmly commended the Birmingham police force for keeping "order" and "preventing violence." I doubt that you would have so warmly commended the police force if you had seen its dogs sinking their teeth into unarmed, nonviolent Negroes. I doubt that you would so quickly commend the policemen if you were to observe their ugly and inhumane treatment of Negroes here in the city jail; if you were to watch them push and curse old Negro women and young Negro girls; if you were to see them slap and kick old Negro men and young boys; if you were to observe them, as they did on two occasions, refuse to give us food because we wanted to sing our grace together. I cannot join you in your praise of the Birmingham police department.

It is true that the police have exercised a degree of discipline in handling the demonstrators. In this sense they have conducted themselves rather "nonviolently" in public. But for what purpose? To preserve the evil system of segregation. Over the past few years I have consistently preached that nonviolence demands that the means we use must be as pure as the ends we seek. I have tried to make clear that it is wrong to use immoral means to attain moral ends. But now I must affirm that it is just as wrong, or perhaps even more so, to use moral means to preserve immoral ends. Perhaps Mr. Connor and his policemen have been rather nonviolent in public, as was Chief Pritchett in Albany, Georgia, but they have used the moral means of nonviolence to maintain the immoral end of racial injustice. As T. S. Eliot has said: "The last temptation is the greatest treason: To do the right deed for the wrong reason."

I wish you had commended the Negro sit-inners and demonstrators of Birmingham for their sublime courage, their willingness to suffer and their amazing discipline in the midst of great provocation. One day the South will recognize its real heroes. They will be the James Merediths, with the noble sense of purpose that enables them to face jeering and hostile mobs, and with the agonizing loneliness that characterizes the life of the pioneer. They will be old, oppressed, battered Negro women, symbolized in a seventy-two-year-old woman in Montgomery, Alabama, who rose up with a sense of dignity and with her people decided not to ride segregated buses, and who responded with ungrammatical profundity to one who inquired about her weariness: "My feets is tired, but my soul is at rest." They will be the young high school and college students, the young ministers of the gospel and a host of their elders, courageously and nonviolently sitting in at lunch counters and willingly going to jail for conscience's sake. One day the South will know that when these disinherited children of God sat down at lunch counters, they were in reality standing up for what is best in the American dream and for the most sacred values in our Judaeo-Christian heritage, thereby bringing our nation back to those great wells of democracy which were dug deep by the founding fathers in their formulation of the Constitution and the Declaration of Independence.

Never before have I written so long a letter. I'm afraid it is much too long to take your precious time. I can assure you that it would have been much shorter if I had been writing from a comfortable desk, but what else can one do when he is alone in a narrow jail cell, other than write long letters, think long thoughts and pray long prayers?

If I have said anything in this letter that overstates the truth and indicates an unreasonable impatience, I beg you to forgive me. If I have said anything that understates the truth and indicates my having a patience that allows me to settle for anything less than brotherhood, I beg God to forgive me.

I hope this letter finds you strong in the faith. I also hope that circumstances will soon make it possible for me to meet each of you, not as an integrationist or a civil-rights leader but as a fellow clergyman and a Christian brother. Let us all hope that the dark clouds of racial prejudice will soon pass away and the deep fog of misunderstanding will be lifted from our fear-drenched communities, and in some not too distant tomorrow the radiant stars of love and brotherhood will shine over our great nation with all their scintillating beauty.

*Philip Roth (1933–2018) was a great American novelist, celebrated for numerous masterpieces (*The Counterlife, American Pastoral, The Human Stain, Sabbath's Theater*). His novels, rooted in the Newark, New Jersey, world in which he grew up, dealt often with Jewish family life, male lust, American history, and the contrasting claims of fiction and reality. "Making fake biography, false history, concocting a half-imaginary existence out of the actual drama of my life is my life," he told an interviewer. It is noteworthy that one of his best books is a factual memoir,* Patrimony, *about his father, and that he wrote superb essays. The following one was an impassioned defense occasioned by criticisms from some in the Jewish community who had taken exception to his less than favorable portrayals of members of the tribe; Roth argued for the freedom of the fiction writer to tell his imaginative truths in his own way.*

WRITING ABOUT JEWS

I

Ever since some of my first stories were collected in 1959 in a volume called *Goodbye, Columbus*, my work has been attacked from certain pulpits and in certain periodicals as dangerous, dishonest, and irresponsible. I have read editorials and articles in Jewish community newspapers condemning these stories for ignoring the accomplishments of Jewish life, or, as Rabbi Emanuel Rackman recently told a convention of the Rabbinical Council of America, for creating a "distorted image of the basic

values of Orthodox Judaism," and even, he went on, for denying the non-Jewish world the opportunity of appreciating "the
overwhelming contributions which Orthodox Jews are making
in every avenue of modern endeavor. . . ." Among the letters I
receive from readers, there have been a number written by Jews
accusing me of being anti-Semitic and "self-hating," or, at the
least, tasteless; they argue or imply that the sufferings of the Jews
throughout history, culminating in the murder of six million by
the Nazis, have made certain criticisms of Jewish life insulting
and trivial. Furthermore, it is charged that such criticism as I
make of Jews—or apparent criticism—is taken by anti-Semites
as justification for their attitudes, as "fuel" for their fires, particularly as it is a Jew himself who seemingly admits to habits and
behavior that are not exemplary, or even normal and acceptable.
When I speak before Jewish audiences, invariably there have been
people who have come up to me afterward to ask, "Why don't
you leave us alone? Why don't you write about the Gentiles?"—
"Why must you be so critical?"—"Why do you disapprove of us
so?"—this last question asked as often with incredulity as with
anger; and often when asked by people a good deal older than
myself, asked as of an erring child by a loving but misunderstood
parent.

It is difficult, if not impossible, to explain to some of the people
claiming to have felt my teeth sinking in, that in many instances
they haven't been bitten at all. Not always, but frequently, what
readers have taken to be my disapproval of the lives lived by Jews
seems to have to do more with their own moral perspective than
with the one they would ascribe to me: at times they see wicked-
ness where I myself had seen energy or courage or spontaneity;
they are ashamed of what I see no reason to be ashamed of, and
defensive where there is no cause for defense.

Not only do they seem to me often to have cramped and unten-
able notions of right and wrong, but looking at fiction as they
do—in terms of "approval" and "disapproval" of Jews, "positive" and "negative" attitudes toward Jewish life—they are likely
not to see what it is that the story is really about.

To give an example. A story I wrote called "Epstein" tells of a sixty-year-old man who has an adulterous affair with the lady across the street. In the end, Epstein, who is the hero, is caught—caught by his family and caught and struck down by exhaustion, decay, and disappointment, against all of which he had set out to make a final struggle. There are Jewish readers, I know, who cannot figure out why I found it necessary to tell this story about a Jewish man: don't other people commit adultery, too? Why is it the Jew who must be shown cheating?

But there is more to adultery than cheating: for one thing, there is the adulterer himself. For all that some people may experience him as a cheat and nothing else, he usually experiences himself as something more. And generally speaking, what draws most readers and writers to literature is this "something more"—all that is beyond simple moral categorizing. It is not my purpose in writing a story of an adulterous man to make it clear how right we all are if we disapprove of the act and are disappointed in the man. Fiction is not written to affirm the principles and beliefs that everybody seems to hold, nor does it seek to guarantee us of the appropriateness of our feelings. The world of fiction, in fact, frees us from the circumscriptions that the society places upon feeling; one of the greatnesses of the art is that it allows both the writer and the reader to respond to experience in ways not always available in day-to-day conduct; or if they are available, they are not possible, or manageable, or legal, or advisable, or even necessary to the business of living. We may not even know that we have such a range of feelings and responses *until* we have come into contact with the work of fiction. This does not mean that either reader or writer no longer brings any moral judgment to bear upon human action. Rather, we judge at a different level of our being, for not only are we judging with the aid of new feelings, but without the necessity of having to act upon judgment, or even to be judged for our judgment. Ceasing for a while to be upright citizens, we drop into another layer of consciousness. And this dropping, this expansion of moral consciousness, this exploration of moral fantasy, is of considerable value to a man and to society.

I do not care to go at length here into what a good many readers take for granted are the purposes and possibilities of fiction.

I do want to make clear, however, to those whose interests may not lead them to speculate much on the subject, a few of the assumptions a writer may hold—assumptions such as lead me to say that I do not write a story to make evident whatever disapproval I may feel for adulterous men. I write a story of a man who is adulterous to reveal the condition of such a man. If the adulterous man is a Jew, then I am revealing the condition of an adulterous man who is a Jew. Why tell that story? Because I seem to be interested in how—and why and when—a man acts counter to what he considers to be his "best self," or what others assume it to be, or would like for it to be. The subject is hardly "mine"; it interested readers and writers for a long time before it became my turn to be engaged by it, too.

One of my readers, a man in Detroit, was himself not too engaged and suggested in a letter to me that he could not figure out why I was. He posed several questions which I believe, in their very brevity, were intended to disarm me. I quote from his letter without his permission.

The first question. "Is it conceivable for a middle-aged man to neglect business and spend all day with a middle-aged woman?" The answer is yes.

Next he asks, "Is it a Jewish trait?" I take it he is referring to adultery and not facetiously to the neglecting of business. The answer is, "Who said it was?" Anna Karenina commits adultery with Vronsky, with consequences more disastrous than those that Epstein brings about. Who thinks to ask, "Is it a Russian trait?" It is a decidedly human possibility. Even though the most famous injunction against it is reported as being issued, for God's own reasons, to the Jews, adultery has been one of the ways by which people of *all* faiths have sought pleasure, or freedom, or vengeance, or power, or love, or humiliation. . . .

The next in the gentleman's series of questions to me is, "Why so much *shmutz*?" Is he asking, why is there dirt in the world? Why is there disappointment? Why is there hardship, ugliness, evil, death? It would be nice to think these were the questions the gentleman had in mind, when he asks "Why so much *shmutz*?" But all he is really asking is, "Why so much *shmutz* in that story?" This, apparently, is what the story adds up to for him. An old man discovers the fires of lust are still burning in him? *Shmutz!* Disgusting! Who wants to hear that kind of stuff! Struck as he is by nothing but the dirty aspects of Epstein's troubles, the gentleman from Detroit concludes that I am narrow-minded.

So do others. Narrow-mindedness, in fact, was the charge that a New York rabbi, David Seligson, was reported in the *New York Times* recently as having brought against myself and other Jewish writers who, he told his congregation, dedicated themselves "to the exclusive creation of a melancholy parade of caricatures." Rabbi Seligson also disapproved of *Goodbye, Columbus* because I described in it "a Jewish adulterer . . . and a host of other lopsided schizophrenic personalities." Of course, adultery is not a characteristic symptom of schizophrenia, but that the rabbi should see it this way, as a sign of a diseased personality, indicates to me that we have different notions as to what health is. After all, it may be that *life* produces a melancholy middle-aged businessman like Lou Epstein, who in Dr. Seligson's eyes looks like another in a parade of caricatures. I myself find Epstein's adultery an unlikely solution to his problems, a pathetic, even a doomed response, and a comic one, too, since it does not even square with the man's own conception of himself and what he wants; but none of this *unlikeliness* leads me to despair of his sanity, or humanity. I suppose it is tantamount to a confession from me of lopsided schizophrenia to admit that the character of Epstein happened to have been conceived with considerable affection and sympathy. As I see it, one of the rabbi's limitations is that he cannot recognize a bear hug when one is being administered right in front of his eyes.

The *Times* report continues: "The rabbi said he could only 'wonder about' gifted writers, 'Jewish by birth, who can see so little in the tremendous saga of Jewish history.'" But I don't imagine the rabbi "wonders" any more about me than I wonder about him: that wondering business is only the voice of wisdom that is supposed to be making itself heard, always willing to be shown the light, if, of course, there is light to be pointed out; but I can't buy it. Pulpit fair-mindedness only hides the issue—as it does here in the rabbi's conclusion, quoted by the *Times*: " 'That they [the Jewish writers in question] must be free to write, we would affirm most vehemently; but that they would know their own people and tradition, we would fervently wish.'"

However, the issue is not knowledge of one's "people." At least, it is not a question of who has more historical data at his fingertips, or is more familiar with Jewish tradition, or which of us observes more customs and rituals. It is even possible, needless to say, to "know" a good deal about tradition, and to misunderstand what it is that tradition signifies. The story of Lou Epstein stands or falls not on how much I "know" about tradition, but on how much I know and understand about Lou Epstein. Where the history of the Jewish people comes down in time and place to become the man whom I called Epstein, that is where my knowledge must be sound. But I get the feeling that Rabbi Seligson wants to rule Lou Epstein *out* of Jewish history. I find him too valuable to forget or dismiss, even if he is something of a *grubber yung* and probably more ignorant of history and tradition than the rabbi believes me to be.

Epstein is pictured not as a learned rabbi, after all, but the owner of a small paper-bag company; his wife is not learned either, and neither is his mistress; consequently, a reader should not expect to find in this story knowledge on my part, or the part of the characters, of the *Sayings of the Fathers*; he has every right to expect that I be close to the truth as to what might conceivably be the attitudes of a Jewish man of Epstein's style and history, toward marriage, family life, divorce, and fornication. The story is called "Epstein" because Epstein, not the Jews, is the subject; where the story is weak I think I know by this time; but the rabbi will never find out until he comes at the thing in terms of what *it* wants to be about rather than what he would like it to be about.

Obviously, though, his interest is not in the portrayal of character; what he wants in my fiction is, in his words, "a balanced portrayal of Jews as we know them." I even suspect that something called "balance" is what the rabbi would advertise as the most significant characteristic of Jewish life; what Jewish history comes down to is that at long last we have in our ranks one of everything. But his assumptions about the art of fiction are what

I should like to draw particular attention to. In his sermon Rabbi Seligson says of Myron Kaufmann's *Remember Me to God* that it can "hardly be said to be recognizable as a Jewish sociological study." But Mr. Kaufmann, as a novelist, probably had no intention of writing a sociological study, or—for this seems more like what the rabbi really yearns for in the way of reading— a nice positive sampling. *Madame Bovary* is hardly recognizable as a sociological study, either, having at its center only a single, dreamy, provincial Frenchwoman, and not one of every other kind of provincial Frenchwoman too; this does not, however, diminish its brilliance as a novel, as an exploration of Madame Bovary herself. Literary works do not take as their subjects characters and events which have impressed a writer primarily by the *frequency* of their appearance. For example, how many Jewish men, as we know them, have come nearly to the brink of plunging a knife into their only son because they believed God had commanded them to? The story of Abraham and Isaac derives its meaning from something other than its being a familiar, recognizable, everyday occurrence. The test of any literary work is not how broad is its range of representation—for all that breadth may be characteristic of a kind of narrative—but the depth with which the writer reveals whatever it may be that he has chosen to represent.

To confuse a "balanced portrayal" with a novel is finally to be led into absurdities. "Dear Fyodor Dostoevsky—All the students in our school, and most of the teachers, feel that you have been unfair to us. Do you call Raskolnikov a balanced portrayal of students as we know them? Of Russian students? Of poor students? What about those of us who have never murdered anyone, who do our school work every night?" "Dear Mark Twain—None of the slaves on our plantation has ever run away. We have a perfect record. But what will our owner think when he reads of Nigger Jim?" "Dear Vladimir Nabokov—The girls in our class . . . ," and so on. What fiction does and what the rabbi would like for it to do are two entirely different things. The concerns of fiction, let it be said, are not those of a statistician—or of a public-relations firm. The novelist asks himself, "What do people think?"; the PR man asks, "What *will* people think?" But I believe this is what is actually troubling the rabbi, when he calls for his "balanced portrayal of Jews." What will people think?

Or to be exact: what will the *goyim* think?

II

This was the question raised—and urgently—when another story of mine, "Defender of the Faith," appeared in *The New Yorker* in April 1959. The story is told by Nathan Marx, an Army sergeant just rotated back to Missouri from combat duty in Germany, where the war has ended. As soon as he arrives, he is made first sergeant in a training company, and immediately is latched on to by a young recruit who tries to use his attachment to the sergeant to receive kindnesses and favors. His attachment, as he sees it, is that they are both Jews. As the story progresses, what the recruit, Sheldon Grossbart, comes to demand are not mere considerations, but privileges to which Marx does not think he is entitled. The story is about one man who uses his own religion, and another's uncertain conscience, for selfish ends; but mostly it is about this other man, the narrator, who, because of the ambiguities of being a member of his particular religion, is involved in a taxing, if mistaken, conflict of loyalties.

I don't now, however, and didn't while writing, see Marx's problem as nothing more than "Jewish": confronting the limitations of charity and forgiveness in one's nature—having to draw a line between what is merciful and what is just—trying to distinguish between apparent evil and the real thing, in one's self and others—these are problems for most people, regardless of the level at which they are perceived or dealt with. Yet, though the moral complexities are not exclusively characteristic of the experience of being a Jew, I never for a moment considered that the characters in the story should be anything other than Jews. Someone else might have written a story embodying the same themes, and similar events perhaps, and had at its center Negroes or Irishmen; for me there was no choice. Nor was it a matter of making Grossbart a Jew and Marx a Gentile, or vice versa; telling half the truth would have been much the same here as telling a lie. Most of those jokes beginning, "Two Jews were walking down the street," lose a little of their punch if one of the Jews, or both, are disguised as Englishmen or Republicans. Similarly, to have made any serious alteration in the Jewish factuality of "Defender of the Faith," as it began to fill itself out in my imagination, would have so unsprung the tensions I felt in the story that I would no longer have had left a story that I wanted to tell, or one I believed myself able to.

Some of my critics must wish that this had happened, for in going ahead and writing this story about Jews, what else did I do but confirm an anti-Semitic stereotype? But to me the story confirms something different, if no less painful to its readers. To me Grossbart is not something we can dismiss solely as an anti-Semitic stereotype; he is a Jewish fact. If people of bad intention or weak judgment have converted certain facts of Jewish life into a stereotype of The Jew, that does not mean that such facts are no longer important in our lives, or that they are taboo for the writer of fiction. Literary investigation may even be a way to redeem the facts, to give them the weight and value that they should have in the world, rather than the disproportionate significance they probably have for some misguided or vicious people.

Sheldon Grossbart, the character I imagined as Marx's antagonist, has his seed in fact. He is not meant to represent The Jew, or Jewry, nor does the story indicate that it is the writer's intention that he be so understood by the reader. Grossbart is depicted as a single blundering human being, one with force, self-righteousness, cunning, and, on occasion, even a little disarming charm; he is depicted as a man whose lapses of integrity seem to him so necessary to his survival as to convince him that such lapses are actually committed in the name of integrity. He has been able to work out a system whereby his own sense of responsibility can suspend operation, what with the collective guilt of the others having become so immense as to have seriously altered the conditions of trust in the world. He is presented not as the stereotype of The Jew, but as a Jew who acts like the stereotype, offering back to his enemies their vision of him, answering the punishment with the crime. Given the particular kinds of denials, humiliations, and persecutions that the nations have practiced on their Jews, it argues for far too much nobility to deny not only that Jews like Grossbart exist, but to deny that the temptations to Grossbartism exist in many who perhaps have more grace, or will, or are perhaps only more cowed, than the simple frightened soul that I imagined weeping with fear and disappointment at the end of the story. Grossbart is not The Jew; but he is a fact of Jewish experience and well within the range of its moral possibilities.

And so is his adversary, Marx, who is, after all, the story's central character, its consciousness and its voice. He is a man who calls himself a Jew more tentatively than does Grossbart; he is not sure what it means—means for *him*—for he is not unintelligent or without conscience; he is dutiful, almost to a point of obsession, and confronted by what are represented to him as the needs of another Jew, he does not for a while know what to do. He moves back and forth from feelings of righteousness to feelings of betrayal, and only at the end, when he truly does betray the trust that Grossbart tries to place in him, does he commit what he has hoped to all along: an act he can believe to be honorable.

Marx does not strike me, nor any of the readers I heard from, as unlikely, incredible, "made-up"; the verisimilitude of the characters and their situation was not what was called into question. In fact, an air of convincingness that the story was believed to have, caused a number of people to write to me, and *The New Yorker*, and the Anti-Defamation League, protesting its publication.

Here is one of the letters I received after the story was published:

Mr. Roth:

With your one story, "Defender of the Faith," you have done as much harm as all the organized anti-Semitic organizations have done to make people believe that all Jews are cheats, liars, connivers. Your one story makes people—the general

public—forget all the great Jews who have lived, all the
Jewish boys who served well in the armed services, all the
Jews who live honest hard lives the world over. . . .

Here is one received by *The New Yorker*:

Dear Sir:

. . . We have discussed this story from every possible
angle and we cannot escape the conclusion that it will do
irreparable damage to the Jewish people. We feel that this
story presented a distorted picture of the average Jewish
soldier and are at a loss to understand why a magazine of
your fine reputation should publish such a work which lends
fuel to anti-Semitism.
      Clichés like "this being Art" will not be acceptable. A
reply will be appreciated.

Here is a letter received by the Anti-Defamation League, who
out of the pressure of the public response, telephoned to ask if I
wanted to talk to them. The strange emphasis of the invitation,
I thought, indicated the discomfort they felt at having to pass
on—or believing they had to pass on—messages such as this:

Dear ——,

What is being done to silence this man? Medieval Jews would
have known what to do with him. . . .

The first two letters I quoted were written by Jewish laymen,
the last by a rabbi and educator in New York City, a man of
prominence in the world of Jewish affairs.
      The rabbi was later to communicate directly with me. He did
not mention that he had already written the Anti-Defamation
League to express regret over the decline of medieval justice,
though he was careful to point out at the conclusion of his first
letter his reticence in another quarter. I believe I was supposed

to take it as an act of mercy: "I have not written to the editorial board of *The New Yorker*," he told me. "I do not want to compound the sin of informing. . . ."

Informing. There was the charge so many of the correspondents had made, even when they did not want to make it openly to me, or to themselves. I had informed on the Jews. I had told the Gentiles what apparently it would otherwise have been possible to keep secret from them: that the perils of human nature afflict the members of our minority. That I had also informed them it was possible for there to be such a Jew as Nathan Marx did not seem to bother anybody; if I said earlier that Marx did not strike my correspondents as unlikely, it is because he didn't strike them at all. He might as well not have been there. Of the letters that I read, only one even mentioned Marx, and only to point out that I was no less blameworthy for portraying the sergeant as "a white Jew," as he was described by my correspondent, a kind of Jewish Uncle Tom.

But even if Marx were that and only that, a white Jew, and Grossbart only a black one, did it in any way follow that because I had examined the relationship between them—another concern central to the story which drew barely a comment from my correspondents—that I had then advocated that Jews be denationalized, deported, persecuted, murdered? Well, no. Whatever the rabbi may believe privately, he did not indicate to me that he thought I was an anti-Semite. There was a suggestion, however, and a grave one, that I had acted like a fool. "You have earned the gratitude," he wrote, "of all who sustain their anti-Semitism on such conceptions of Jews as ultimately led to the murder of six million in our time."

Despite the sweep there at the end of the sentence, the charge made is actually up at the front: I "earned the gratitude . . ." But of whom? I would put it less dramatically, but maybe more exactly: of those who are predisposed to misread the story—out of bigotry, ignorance, malice, or even innocence. If I did earn their gratitude, it was because they failed to see, even to look for, what I was talking about. . . . Such conceptions of Jews as anti-Semites hold, then, and as they were able to confirm by misunderstanding my story, are the same, the rabbi goes on to say, as those which "ultimately led to the murder of six million in our time."

"Ultimately"? Is that not a gross simplification of the history of the Jews and the history of Hitler's Germany? People hold serious grudges against one another, vilify one another, deliberately misunderstand one another, and tell lies about one another, but they do not always, as a consequence, *murder* one another, as the Germans murdered the Jews, and as other Europeans allowed the Jews to be murdered, or even helped the slaughter along. Between prejudice and persecution there is usually, in civilized life, a barrier constructed by the individual's convictions and fears, and the community's laws, ideals, and values. What "ultimately" caused this barrier to disappear in Germany cannot be explained only in terms of anti-Semitic misconceptions; surely what must also be understood here is the intolerability of Jewry, on the one hand, and its usefulness, on the other, to the Nazi ideology and dream.

By simplifying the Nazi-Jewish relationship, by making *prejudice* appear to be the primary cause of annihilation, the rabbi is able to make the consequences of publishing "Defender of the Faith" in *The New Yorker* seem very grave indeed. He doesn't appear to be made at all anxious, however, by the consequences of his own position. For what he is suggesting is that some subjects must not be written about, or brought to public attention, because it is possible for them to be misunderstood by people with weak minds or malicious instincts. Thus he consents to put the malicious and weak-minded in a position of determining the level at which open communication on these subjects will take place. This is not fighting anti-Semitism, but submitting to it: that is, submitting to a restriction of consciousness as well as communication because being conscious and being candid is too risky.

In his letter the rabbi calls my attention to that famous madman who shouts "Fire!" in "a crowded theater." He leaves me to complete the analogy myself: by publishing "Defender of the Faith" in *The New Yorker*: (1) I am shouting; (2) I am shouting "Fire!"; (3) there is no fire; (4) all this is happening in the equivalent of "a crowded theater." The crowded theater: there is the risk. I should agree to sacrifice the freedom that is essential to my vocation, and even to the general well-being of the culture, because—because of what? "The crowded theater" has absolutely no relevance to the situation of the Jew in America today. It is a grandiose delusion. It is not a metaphor describing a cultural condition, but a revelation of the nightmarish visions that must plague people as demoralized as the rabbi appears to be: rows endless, seats packed, lights out, doors too few and too small, panic and hysteria just under the skin . . . No wonder he says to me finally, "Your story—in Hebrew—in an Israeli magazine or newspaper—would have been judged exclusively from a literary point of view." That is, ship it off to Israel. But please don't tell it here, now.

Why? So that "they" will not commence persecuting Jews again? If the barrier between prejudice and persecution collapsed in Germany, this is hardly reason to contend that no such barrier exists in our country. And if it should ever begin to appear to be crumbling, then we must do what is necessary to strengthen it. But not by putting on a good face; not by refusing to admit to the intricacies and impossibilities of Jewish lives; not by pretending that Jews have existences less in need of, less deserving of, honest attention than the lives of their neighbors; not by making Jews invisible. The solution is not to convince people to like Jews so as not to want to kill them; it is to let them know that they cannot kill them even if they despise them. And how to let them know? Surely repeating over and over to oneself, "It can happen here," does little to prevent "it" from happening. Moreover, ending persecution involves more than stamping out persecutors. It is necessary, too, to unlearn certain responses to them. All the tolerance of persecution that has seeped into the Jewish character— the adaptability, the patience, the resignation, the silence, the self-denial—must be squeezed out, until the only response there is to *any* restriction of liberties is "No, I refuse."

The chances are that there will always be some people who will despise Jews, just so long as they continue to call themselves Jews; and, of course, we must keep an eye on them. But if some Jews are dreaming of a time when they will be accepted

by Christians as Christians accept one another—if *this* is why
certain Jewish writers should be silent—it may be that they are
dreaming of a time that cannot be, and of a condition that does
not exist, this side of one's dreams. Perhaps even the Christians
don't accept one another as they are imagined to in that world
from which Jews may believe themselves excluded solely because
they are Jews. Nor are the Christians going to feel toward Jews
what one Jew may feel toward another. The upbringing of the
alien does not always alert him to the whole range of human
connections which exists between the liaisons that arise out of
clannishness, and those that arise—or fail to—out of deliberate
exclusion. Like those of most men, the lives of Jews no longer
take place in a world that is just *landsmen* and enemies. The cry
"Watch out for the *goyim!*" at times seems more the expression
of an unconscious wish than of a warning: Oh that they were out
there, so that we could be together in here! A rumor of persecution, a taste of exile, might even bring with it that old world of
feelings and habits—something to replace the new world of social
accessibility and moral indifference, the world which tempts all
our promiscuous instincts, and where one cannot always figure
out what a Jew is that a Christian is not.

   Jews are people who are not what anti-Semites say they are.
That was once a statement out of which a man might begin to
construct an identity for himself; now it does not work so well,
for it is difficult to act counter to the ways people expect you to
act when fewer and fewer people define you by such expectations.
The success of the struggle against the defamation of Jewish
character in this country has itself made more pressing the need
for a Jewish self-consciousness that is relevant to this time and
place, where neither defamation nor persecution are what they
were elsewhere in the past. Surely, for those Jews who choose to
continue to call themselves Jews, and find reason to do so, there
are courses to follow to prevent it from ever being 1933 again that
are more direct, reasonable, and dignified than beginning to act
as though it already is 1933—*or as though it always is.* But the
death of all those Jews seems to have taught my correspondent, a
rabbi and a teacher, little more than to be discreet, to be foxy, to
say this but not that. It has taught him nothing other than how to

remain a victim in a country where he does not have to live like one if he chooses. How pathetic. And what an insult to the dead. Imagine: sitting in New York in the 1960s and piously summoning up "the six million" to justify one's own timidity.

Timidity—and paranoia. It does not occur to the rabbi that there are Gentiles who will read the story intelligently. The only Gentiles the rabbi can imagine looking into *The New Yorker* are those who hate Jews and those who don't know how to read very well. If there are others, they can get along without reading about Jews. For to suggest that one translate one's stories into Hebrew and publish them in Israel, is to say, in effect: "There is nothing in our lives we need to tell the Gentiles about, unless it has to do with how well we manage. Beyond that, it's none of their business. We are important to no one but ourselves, which is as it should be (or better be) anyway." But to indicate that moral crisis is something to be hushed up, is not of course, to take the prophetic line; nor is it a rabbinical point of view that Jewish life is of no significance to the rest of mankind.

Even given his own kinds of goals, however, the rabbi is not very farsighted or imaginative. What he fails to see is that the stereotype as often arises from ignorance as from malice; deliberately keeping Jews out of the imagination of Gentiles, for fear of the bigots and their stereotyping minds, is really to invite the invention of stereotypical ideas. A book like Ralph Ellison's *Invisible Man*, for instance, seems to me to have helped many whites who are not anti-Negro, but who do hold Negro stereotypes, to surrender simple-minded notions about Negro life. I doubt, however, that Ellison, reporting as he does not just the squalid circumstances Negroes must put up with but certain bestial aspects of his Negro characters as well, has converted one Alabama redneck or one United States senator over to the cause of desegregation; nor could the novels of James Baldwin cause Governor Wallace to conclude anything more than that Negroes were just as hopeless a lot as he'd always known them to be. As novelists, neither Baldwin nor Ellison are (to quote Mr. Ellison on himself) "cogs in the machinery of civil rights legislation." Just as there are Jews who feel that my books do nothing for the Jewish cause, so there are Negroes, I am led to understand, who feel that Mr. Ellison's work has done little for the Negro cause and probably has harmed it. But that seems to place the Negro cause somewhat outside the cause of truth and justice. That many blind people are still blind does not mean that Mr. Ellison's book gives off no light. Certainly those of us who are willing to be taught, and who needed to be, have been made by *Invisible Man* less stupid than we were about Negro lives, including those lives that a bigot would point to as affirming his own half-baked, inviolable ideas.

III

But it is the treachery of the bigot that the rabbi appears to be worried about and that he presents to me, to himself, and probably to his congregation, as the major cause for concern. Frankly, I think those are just the old words coming out, when the right buttons are pushed. Can he actually believe that on the basis of my story anyone is going to start a pogrom, or keep a Jew out of medical school, or even call some Jewish schoolchild a kike? The rabbi is entombed in his nightmares and fears; but that is not the whole of it. He is also hiding something. Much of this disapproval of "Defender of the Faith" because of its effect upon Gentiles seems to me a cover-up for what is really objected to, what is immediately painful—and that is its direct effect upon certain Jews. "You have hurt a lot of people's feelings because you have revealed something they are ashamed of." That is the letter the rabbi did not write, but should have. I would have argued then that there are things of more importance—even to these Jews—than those feelings that have been hurt, but at any rate he would have confronted me with a genuine fact, with something I was actually responsible for, and which my conscience would have had to deal with, as it does.

For the record, all the letters that came in about "Defender of the Faith," and that I saw, were from Jews. Not one of those people whose gratitude the rabbi believes I earned wrote to say, "Thank you," nor was I invited to address any anti-Semitic organizations. When I did begin to receive speaking invitations, they were from Jewish ladies' groups, Jewish community centers, and from all sorts of Jewish organizations, large and small.

And I think this bothers the rabbi, too. On the one hand, some Jews are hurt by my work; but on the other, some are interested. At the rabbinical convention I mentioned earlier, Rabbi Emanuel Rackman, a professor of political science at Yeshiva University, reported to his colleagues that certain Jewish writers were "assuming the mantle of self-appointed spokesmen and leaders for Judaism." To support this remark he referred to a symposium held in Israel this last June, at which I was present; as far as I know, Rabbi Rackman was not. If he had been there, he would have heard me make it quite clear that I did not want to, did not intend to, and was not able to speak *for* American Jews; I surely did not deny, and no one questioned the fact, that I spoke *to* them, and hopefully to others as well. The competition that Rabbi Rackman imagines himself to be engaged in hasn't to do with who will presume to lead the Jews; it is really a matter of who, in addressing them, is going to take them more seriously—strange as that may sound—with who is going to see them as something more than part of the mob in a crowded theater, more than helpless and threatened and in need of reassurance that they are as "balanced" as anyone else. The question really is, who is going to address men and women like men and women, and who like children. If there are Jews who have begun to find the stories the novelists tell more provocative and pertinent than the sermons of some of the rabbis, perhaps it is because there are regions of feeling and consciousness in them which cannot be reached by the oratory of self-congratulation and self-pity.

*Susan Sontag (1933–2004) was a fearlessly intellectual essayist who brought a philosophical background to a wide range of topics, including literature, movies, sexuality, and politics. Her essay collections (*Against Interpretation, Styles of Radical Will, *and* Under the Sign of Saturn) *and her book-length ruminations (*On Photography, Illness as Metaphor*) were inflected with a love of European thinkers such as Walter Benjamin and Roland Barthes. Though Sontag claimed she had little use for first person, it is impossible to read her without deriving a vivid impression of the strong, complicated woman behind the authoritative pronouncements. In "Notes on 'Camp,' " one of her signature pieces, she tackles her subject in a mosaic essay, composed of fragments assembled into a highly evocative whole.*

NOTES ON "CAMP"

Many things in the world have not been named; and many things, even if they have been named, have never been described. One of these is the sensibility—unmistakably modern, a variant of sophistication but hardly identical with it—that goes by the cult name of "Camp."

A sensibility (as distinct from an idea) is one of the hardest things to talk about; but there are special reasons why Camp, in particular, has never been discussed. It is not a natural mode of sensibility, if there be any such. Indeed the essence of Camp is its love of the unnatural: of artifice and exaggeration. And Camp is esoteric—something of a private code, a badge of identity even, among small urban cliques. Apart from a lazy two-page sketch in Christopher Isherwood's novel *The World in the Evening* (1954), it has hardly broken into print. To talk about Camp is therefore to betray it. If the betrayal can be defended, it will be for the edification it provides, or the dignity of the conflict it resolves. For myself, I plead the goal of self-edification, and the goad of a sharp conflict in my own sensibility. I am strongly drawn to Camp, and almost as strongly offended by it. That is why I want to talk about it, and why I can. For no one who wholeheartedly shares in a given sensibility can analyze it; he can only, whatever his intention, exhibit it. To name a sensibility, to draw its contours and to recount its history, requires a deep sympathy modified by revulsion.

Though I am speaking about sensibility only—and about a sensibility that, among other things, converts the serious into the frivolous—these are grave matters. Most people think of sensibility or taste as the realm of purely subjective preferences, those mysterious attractions, mainly sensual, that have not been brought under the sovereignty of reason. They *allow* that considerations of taste play a part in their reactions to people and to works of art. But this attitude is naïve. And even worse. To patronize the faculty of taste is to patronize oneself. For taste governs every free—as opposed to rote—human response. Nothing is more decisive. There is taste in people, visual taste, taste in emotion—and there is taste in acts, taste in morality. Intelligence, as well, is really a kind of taste: taste in ideas. (One of the facts to be reckoned with is that taste tends to develop very unevenly. It's rare that the same person has good visual taste *and* good taste in people *and* taste in ideas.)

Taste has no system and no proofs. But there is something like a logic of taste: the consistent sensibility which underlies and gives rise to a certain taste. A sensibility is almost, but not quite, ineffable. Any sensibility which can be crammed into the mold of a system, or handled with the rough tools of proof, is no longer a sensibility at all. It has hardened into an idea . . .

To snare a sensibility in words, especially one that is alive and powerful,* one must be tentative and nimble. The form of jot-

---

* The sensibility of an era is not only its most decisive but also its most perishable aspect. One may capture the ideas (intellectual history) and

tings, rather than an essay (with its claim to a linear, consecutive argument), seemed more appropriate for getting down something of this particular fugitive sensibility. It's embarrassing to be solemn and treatise-like about Camp. One runs the risk of having, oneself, produced a very inferior piece of Camp.

These notes are for Oscar Wilde.

> One should either be a work of art, or wear a work of art.
> —*Phrases & Philosophies for the Use of the Young*

1. To start very generally: Camp is a certain mode of aestheticism. It is one way of seeing the world as an aesthetic phenomenon. That way, the way of Camp, is not in terms of beauty, but in terms of the degree of artifice, of stylization.

2. To emphasize style is to slight content, or to introduce an attitude which is neutral with respect to content. It goes without saying that the Camp sensibility is disengaged, depoliticized—or at least apolitical.

3. Not only is there a Camp vision, a Camp way of looking at things. Camp is as well a quality discoverable in objects and the behavior of persons. There are "campy" movies, clothes, furniture, popular songs, novels, people, buildings . . . This distinction is important. True, the Camp eye has the power to transform experience. But not everything can be seen as Camp. It's not all in the eye of the beholder.

4. Random examples of items which are part of the canon of Camp:

Zuleika Dobson

Tiffany lamps

---

the behavior (social history) of an epoch without ever touching upon the sensibility or taste which informed those ideas, that behavior. Rare are those historical studies—like Huizinga on the late Middle Ages, Febvre on sixteenth-century France—which do tell us something about the sensibility of the period.

Scopitone films

The Brown Derby restaurant on Sunset Boulevard in LA

The *Enquirer*, headlines and stories

Aubrey Beardsley drawings

Swan Lake

Bellini's operas

Visconti's direction of *Salome* and *'Tis Pity She's a Whore*

certain turn-of-the-century picture postcards

Schoedsack's *King Kong*

the Cuban pop singer La Lupe

Lynd Ward's novel in woodcuts, *Gods' Man*

the old Flash Gordon comics

women's clothes of the twenties (feather boas, fringed and beaded dresses, etc.)

the novels of Ronald Firbank and Ivy Compton-Burnett

stag movies seen without lust

5. Camp taste has an affinity for certain arts rather than others. Clothes, furniture, all the elements of visual décor, for instance, make up a large part of Camp. For Camp art is often decorative art, emphasizing texture, sensuous surface, and style at the expense of content. Concert music, though, because it is contentless, is rarely Camp. It offers no opportunity, say, for a contrast between silly or extravagant content and rich form . . . Sometimes whole art forms become saturated with Camp. Classical ballet, opera, movies have seemed so for a long time. In the last two years, popular music (post rock-'n'-roll,

what the French call yé-yé) has been annexed. And movie
criticism (like lists of "The 10 Best Bad Movies I Have
Seen") is probably the greatest popularizer of Camp
taste today, because most people still go to the movies in
a high-spirited and unpretentious way.

6. There is a sense in which it is correct to say: "It's too
good to be Camp." Or "too important," not marginal
enough. (More on this later.) Thus, the personality and
many of the works of Jean Cocteau are Camp, but not
those of André Gide; the operas of Richard Strauss, but
not those of Wagner; concoctions of Tin Pan Alley and
Liverpool, but not jazz. Many examples of Camp are
things which, from a "serious" point of view, are either
bad art or kitsch. Not all, though. Not only is Camp
not necessarily bad art, but some art which can be
approached as Camp (example: the major films of Louis
Feuillade) merits the most serious admiration and study.

The more we study Art, the less we care for Nature.
                                   —"The Decay of Lying"

7. All Camp objects, and persons, contain a large element
of artifice. Nothing in nature can be campy . . . Rural
Camp is still man-made, and most campy objects are
urban. (Yet, they often have a serenity—or a naïveté—
which is the equivalent of pastoral. A great deal of Camp
suggests Empson's phrase, "urban pastoral.")

8. Camp is a vision of the world in terms of style—but
a particular kind of style. It is the love of the exaggerated, the "off," of things-being-what-they-are-not. The
best example is in Art Nouveau, the most typical and
fully developed Camp style. Art Nouveau objects, typically, convert one thing into something else: the lighting
fixtures in the form of flowering plants, the living room
which is really a grotto. A remarkable example: the Paris
Métro entrances designed by Hector Guimard in the late
1890s in the shape of cast-iron orchid stalks.

9. As a taste in persons, Camp responds particularly to the markedly attenuated and to the strongly exaggerated. The androgyne is certainly one of the great images of Camp sensibility. Examples: the swooning, slim, sinuous figures of pre-Raphaelite painting and poetry; the thin, flowing, sexless bodies in Art Nouveau prints and posters, presented in relief on lamps and ashtrays; the haunting androgynous vacancy behind the perfect beauty of Greta Garbo. Here, Camp taste draws on a mostly unacknowledged truth of taste: the most refined form of sexual attractiveness (as well as the most refined form of sexual pleasure) consists in going against the grain of one's sex. What is most beautiful in virile men is something feminine; what is most beautiful in feminine women is something masculine . . . Allied to the Camp taste for the androgynous is something that seems quite different but isn't: a relish for the exaggeration of sexual characteristics and personality mannerisms. For obvious reasons, the best examples that can be cited are movie stars. The corny flamboyant female-ness of Jayne Mansfield, Gina Lollobrigida, Jane Russell, Virginia Mayo; the exaggerated he-man-ness of Steve Reeves, Victor Mature. The great stylists of temperament and mannerism, like Bette Davis, Barbara Stanwyck, Tallulah Bankhead, Edwige Feuillère.

10. Camp sees everything in quotation marks. It's not a lamp, but a "lamp"; not a woman, but a "woman." To perceive Camp in objects and persons is to understand Being-as-Playing-a-Role. It is the farthest extension, in sensibility, of the metaphor of life as theater.

11. Camp is the triumph of the epicene style. (The convertibility of "man" and "woman," "person" and "thing.") But all style, that is, artifice, is, ultimately, epicene. Life is not stylish. Neither is nature.

12. The question isn't, "Why travesty, impersonation, theatricality?" The question is, rather, "When does travesty, impersonation, theatricality acquire the special flavor of

Camp?" Why is the atmosphere of Shakespeare's com-
edies (*As You Like It*, etc.) not epicene, while that of *Der
Rosenkavalier* is?

13. The dividing line seems to fall in the eighteenth century;
there the origins of Camp taste are to be found (Gothic
novels, Chinoiserie, caricature, artificial ruins, and so
forth). But the relation to nature was quite different then.
In the eighteenth century, people of taste either patronized nature (Strawberry Hill) or attempted to remake it
into something artificial (Versailles). They also indefati-
gably patronized the past. Today's Camp taste effaces
nature, or else contradicts it outright. And the relation
of Camp taste to the past is extremely sentimental.

14. A pocket history of Camp might, of course, begin farther back—with the mannerist artists like Pontormo,
Rosso, and Caravaggio, or the extraordinarily theatrical painting of Georges de La Tour, or Euphuism (Lyly,
etc.) in literature. Still, the soundest starting point seems
to be the late seventeenth and early eighteenth century,
because of that period's extraordinary feeling for artifice,
for surface, for symmetry; its taste for the picturesque
and the thrilling, its elegant conventions for representing
instant feeling and the total presence of character—the
epigram and the rhymed couplet (in words), the flourish
(in gesture and in music). The late seventeenth and early
eighteenth century is the great period of Camp: Pope,
Congreve, Walpole, but not Swift; *les précieux* in France;
the rococo churches of Munich; Pergolesi. Somewhat
later: much of Mozart. But in the nineteenth century,
what had been distributed throughout all of high culture
now becomes a special taste; it takes on overtones of the
acute, the esoteric, the perverse. Confining the story to
England alone, we see Camp continuing wanly through
nineteenth-century aestheticism (Burne-Jones, Pater,
Ruskin, Tennyson), emerging full-blown with the Art
Nouveau movement in the visual and decorative arts,
and finding its conscious ideologists in such "wits" as
Wilde and Firbank.

15. Of course, to say all these things are Camp is not to argue they are simply that. A full analysis of Art Nouveau, for instance, would scarcely equate it with Camp. But such an analysis cannot ignore what in Art Nouveau allows it to be experienced as Camp. Art Nouveau is full of "content," even of a political-moral sort; it was a revolutionary movement in the arts, spurred on by a Utopian vision (somewhere between William Morris and the Bauhaus group) of an organic politics and taste. Yet there is also a feature of the Art Nouveau objects which suggests a disengaged, unserious, "aesthete's" vision. This tells us something important about Art Nouveau—and about what the lens of Camp, which blocks out content, is.

16. Thus, the Camp sensibility is one that is alive to a double sense in which some things can be taken. But this is not the familiar split-level construction of a literal meaning, on the one hand, and a symbolic meaning, on the other. It is the difference, rather, between the thing as meaning something, anything, and the thing as pure artifice.

17. This comes out clearly in the vulgar use of the word Camp as a verb, "to camp," something that people do. To camp is a mode of seduction—one which employs flamboyant mannerisms susceptible of a double interpretation; gestures full of duplicity, with a witty meaning for cognoscenti and another, more impersonal, for outsiders. Equally and by extension, when the word becomes a noun, when a person or a thing is "a camp," a duplicity is involved. Behind the "straight" public sense in which something can be taken, one has found a private zany experience of the thing.

To be natural is such a very difficult pose to keep up.
—*An Ideal Husband*

18. One must distinguish between naïve and deliberate Camp. Pure Camp is always naïve. Camp which knows itself to be Camp ("camping") is usually less satisfying.

19. The pure examples of Camp are unintentional; they are

dead serious. The Art Nouveau craftsman who makes a lamp with a snake coiled around it is not kidding, nor is he trying to be charming. He is saying, in all earnestness: Voilà! the Orient! Genuine Camp—for instance, the numbers devised for the Warner Brothers musicals of the early thirties (*42nd Street; The Gold Diggers of 1933; . . . of 1935; . . . of 1937*; etc.) by Busby Berkeley—does not mean to be funny. Camping—say, the plays of Noël Coward—does. It seems unlikely that much of the traditional opera repertoire could be such satisfying Camp if the melodramatic absurdities of most opera plots had not been taken seriously by their composers. One doesn't need to know the artist's private intentions. The work tells all. (Compare a typical nineteenth-century opera with Samuel Barber's *Vanessa*, a piece of manufactured, calculated Camp, and the difference is clear.)

20. Probably, intending to be campy is always harmful. The perfection of *Trouble in Paradise* and *The Maltese Falcon*, among the greatest Camp movies ever made, comes from the effortless smooth way in which tone is maintained. This is not so with such famous would-be Camp films of the fifties as *All About Eve* and *Beat the Devil*. These more recent movies have their fine moments, but the first is so slick and the second so hysterical; they want so badly to be campy that they're continually losing the beat . . . Perhaps, though, it is not so much a question of the unintended effect versus the conscious intention, as of the delicate relation between parody and self-parody in Camp. The films of Hitchcock are a showcase for this problem. When self-parody lacks ebullience but instead reveals (even sporadically) a contempt for one's themes and one's materials—as in *To Catch a Thief, Rear Window, North by Northwest*—the results are forced and heavy-handed, rarely Camp. Successful Camp—a movie like Carné's *Drôle de Drame*; the film performances of Mae West and Edward Everett Horton; portions of *The Goon Show*—even when it reveals self-parody, reeks of self-love.

21. So, again, Camp rests on innocence. That means Camp discloses innocence, but also, when it can, corrupts it. Objects, being objects, don't change when they are singled out by the Camp vision. Persons, however, respond to their audiences. Persons begin "camping": Mae West, Bea Lillie, La Lupe, Tallulah Bankhead in *Lifeboat*, Bette Davis in *All About Eve*. (Persons can even be induced to camp without their knowing it. Consider the way Fellini got Anita Ekberg to parody herself in *La Dolce Vita*.)

22. Considered a little less strictly, Camp is either completely naïve or else wholly conscious (when one plays at being campy). An example of the latter: Wilde's epigrams themselves.

It's absurd to divide people into good and bad. People are either charming or tedious.
                                                    —*Lady Windermere's Fan*

23. In naïve, or pure, Camp, the essential element is seriousness, a seriousness that fails. Of course, not all seriousness that fails can be redeemed as Camp. Only that which has the proper mixture of the exaggerated, the fantastic, the passionate, and the naïve.

24. When something is just bad (rather than Camp), it's often because it is too mediocre in its ambition. The artist hasn't attempted to do anything really outlandish. ("It's too much," "It's too fantastic," "It's not to be believed," are standard phrases of Camp enthusiasm.)

25. The hallmark of Camp is the spirit of extravagance. Camp is a woman walking around in a dress made of three million feathers. Camp is the paintings of Carlo Crivelli, with their real jewels and *trompe-l'oeil* insects and cracks in the masonry. Camp is the outrageous aestheticism of Sternberg's six American movies with Dietrich, all six, but especially the last, *The Devil Is a Woman* . . . In Camp there is often something *démesuré* in the quality of the ambition, not only in the style of the work itself. Gaudí's lurid and beautiful buildings in

Barcelona are Camp not only because of their style but
because they reveal—most notably in the Cathedral of
the Sagrada Familia—the ambition on the part of one
man to do what it takes a generation, a whole culture to
accomplish.

26. Camp is art that proposes itself seriously, but cannot be
taken altogether seriously because it is "too much." *Titus
Andronicus* and *Strange Interlude* are almost Camp, or
could be played as Camp. The public manner and rhetoric of de Gaulle, often, are pure Camp.

27. A work can come close to Camp, but not make it, because
it succeeds. Eisenstein's films are seldom Camp because,
despite all exaggeration, they do succeed (dramatically)
without surplus. If they were a little more "off," they
could be great Camp—particularly *Ivan the Terrible I
& II*. The same for Blake's drawings and paintings, weird
and mannered as they are. They aren't Camp; though
Art Nouveau, influenced by Blake, is.

What is extravagant in an inconsistent or an unpas-
sionate way is not Camp. Neither can anything be Camp
that does not seem to spring from an irrepressible, a
virtually uncontrolled sensibility. Without passion, one
gets pseudo-Camp—what is merely decorative, safe, in
a word, chic. On the barren edge of Camp lie a number of attractive things: the sleek fantasies of Dalí,
the haute couture preciosity of Albicocco's *The Girl
with the Golden Eyes*. But the two things—Camp and
preciosity—must not be confused.

28. Again, Camp is the attempt to do something extraordinary. But extraordinary in the sense, often, of being
special, glamorous. (The curved line, the extravagant
gesture.) Not extraordinary merely in the sense of effort.
Ripley's Believe-It-Or-Not items are rarely campy. These
items, either natural oddities (the two-headed rooster,
the eggplant in the shape of a cross) or else the products of immense labor (the man who walked from here
to China on his hands, the woman who engraved the
New Testament on the head of a pin), lack the visual

reward—the glamour, the theatricality—that marks off certain extravagances as Camp.

29. The reason a movie like *On the Beach*, books like *Winesburg, Ohio* and *For Whom the Bell Tolls* are bad to the point of being laughable, but not bad to the point of being enjoyable, is that they are too dogged and pretentious. They lack fantasy. There is Camp in such bad movies as *The Prodigal* and *Samson and Delilah*, the series of Italian color spectacles featuring the superhero Maciste, numerous Japanese science fiction films (*Rodan*, *The Mysterians*, *The H-Man*) because, in their relative unpretentiousness and vulgarity, they are more extreme and irresponsible in their fantasy—and therefore touching and quite enjoyable.

30. Of course, the canon of Camp can change. Time has a great deal to do with it. Time may enhance what seems simply dogged or lacking in fantasy now because we are too close to it, because it resembles too closely our own everyday fantasies, the fantastic nature of which we don't perceive. We are better able to enjoy a fantasy as fantasy when it is not our own.

31. This is why so many of the objects prized by Camp taste are old-fashioned, out-of-date, *démodé*. It's not a love of the old as such. It's simply that the process of aging or deterioration provides the necessary detachment—or arouses a necessary sympathy. When the theme is important, and contemporary, the failure of a work of art may make us indignant. Time can change that. Time liberates the work of art from moral relevance, delivering it over to the Camp sensibility . . . Another effect: time contracts the sphere of banality. (Banality is, strictly speaking, always a category of the contemporary.) What was banal can, with the passage of time, become fantastic. Many people who listen with delight to the style of Rudy Vallee revived by the English pop group the Temperance Seven would have been driven up the wall by Rudy Vallee in his heyday.

Thus, things are campy, not when they become

old—but when we become less involved in them, and can enjoy, instead of be frustrated by, the failure of the attempt. But the effect of time is unpredictable. Maybe Method acting (James Dean, Rod Steiger, Warren Beatty) will seem as Camp someday as Ruby Keeler's does now—or as Sarah Bernhardt's does, in the films she made at the end of her career. And maybe not.

32. Camp is the glorification of "character." The statement is of no importance—except, of course, to the person (Loie Fuller, Gaudí, Cecil B. DeMille, Crivelli, de Gaulle, etc.) who makes it. What the Camp eye appreciates is the unity, the force of the person. In every move the aging Martha Graham makes she's being Martha Graham, etc., etc. . . . This is clear in the case of the great serious idol of Camp taste, Greta Garbo. Garbo's incompetence (at the least, lack of depth) as an *actress* enhances her beauty. She's always herself.

33. What Camp taste responds to is "instant character" (this is, of course, very eighteenth century); and, conversely, what it is not stirred by is the sense of the development of character. Character is understood as a state of continual incandescence—a person being one, very intense thing. This attitude toward character is a key element of the theatricalization of experience embodied in the Camp sensibility. And it helps account for the fact that opera and ballet are experienced as such rich treasures of Camp, for neither of these forms can easily do justice to the complexity of human nature. Wherever there is development of character, Camp is reduced. Among operas, for example, *La Traviata* (which has some small development of character) is less campy than *Il Trovatore* (which has none).

Life is too important a thing ever to talk seriously about it.
                                          —*Vera, or The Nihilists*

34. Camp taste turns its back on the good-bad axis of ordinary aesthetic judgment. Camp doesn't reverse things. It

doesn't argue that the good is bad, or the bad is good. What it does is to offer for art (and life) a different—a supplementary—set of standards.

35. Ordinarily we value a work of art because of the seriousness and dignity of what it achieves. We value it because it succeeds—in being what it is and, presumably, in fulfilling the intention that lies behind it. We assume a proper, that is to say, straightforward relation between intention and performance. By such standards, we appraise *The Iliad*, Aristophanes' plays, the Art of the Fugue, *Middlemarch*, the paintings of Rembrandt, Chartres, the poetry of Donne, *The Divine Comedy*, Beethoven's quartets, and—among people—Socrates, Jesus, St. Francis, Napoleon, Savonarola. In short, the pantheon of high culture: truth, beauty, and seriousness.

36. But there are other creative sensibilities besides the seriousness (both tragic and comic) of high culture and of the high style of evaluating people. And one cheats oneself, as a human being, if one has respect only for the style of high culture, whatever else one may do or feel on the sly.

For instance, there is the kind of seriousness whose trademark is anguish, cruelty, derangement. Here we do accept a disparity between intention and result. I am speaking, obviously, of a style of personal existence as well as of a style in art; but the examples had best come from art. Think of Bosch, Sade, Rimbaud, Jarry, Kafka, Artaud, think of most of the important works of art of the twentieth century, that is, art whose goal is not that of creating harmonies but of overstraining the medium and introducing more and more violent, and unresolvable, subject-matter. This sensibility also insists on the principle that an *oeuvre* in the old sense (again, in art, but also in life) is not possible. Only "fragments" are possible . . . Clearly, different standards apply here than to traditional high culture. Something is good not because it is achieved, but because another kind of truth about the human situation, another experience of what it is to be human—in short, another valid sensibility—is being revealed.

And third among the great creative sensibilities is Camp: the sensibility of failed seriousness, of the theatricalization of experience. Camp refuses both the harmonies of traditional seriousness, and the risks of fully identifying with extreme states of feeling.

37. The first sensibility, that of high culture, is basically moralistic. The second sensibility, that of extreme states of feeling, represented in much contemporary "avant-garde" art, gains power by a tension between moral and aesthetic passion. The third, Camp, is wholly aesthetic.

38. Camp is the consistently aesthetic experience of the world. It incarnates a victory of "style" over "content," "aesthetics" over "morality," of irony over tragedy.

39. Camp and tragedy are antitheses. There is seriousness in Camp (seriousness in the degree of the artist's involvement) and, often, pathos. The excruciating is also one of the tonalities of Camp; it is the quality of excruciation in much of Henry James (for instance, *The Europeans*, *The Awkward Age*, *The Wings of the Dove*) that is responsible for the large element of Camp in his writings. But there is never, never tragedy.

40. Style is everything. Genet's ideas, for instance, are very Camp. Genet's statement that "the only criterion of an act is its elegance"* is virtually interchangeable, as a statement, with Wilde's "in matters of great importance, the vital element is not sincerity, but style." But what counts, finally, is the style in which ideas are held. The ideas about morality and politics in, say, *Lady Windermere's Fan* and in *Major Barbara* are Camp, but not just because of the nature of the ideas themselves. It is those ideas, held in a special playful way. The Camp ideas in *Our Lady of the Flowers* are maintained too grimly, and

---

* Sartre's gloss on this in *Saint Genet* is: "Elegance is the quality of conduct which transforms the greatest amount of being into appearing."

the writing itself is too successfully elevated and serious, for Genet's books to be Camp.

41. The whole point of Camp is to dethrone the serious. Camp is playful, anti-serious. More precisely, Camp involves a new, more complex relation to "the serious." One can be serious about the frivolous, frivolous about the serious.

42. One is drawn to Camp when one realizes that "sincerity" is not enough. Sincerity can be simple philistinism, intellectual narrowness.

43. The traditional means for going beyond straight seriousness—irony, satire—seem feeble today, inadequate to the culturally oversaturated medium in which contemporary sensibility is schooled. Camp introduces a new standard: artifice as an ideal, theatricality.

44. Camp proposes a comic vision of the world. But not a bitter or polemical comedy. If tragedy is an experience of hyperinvolvement, comedy is an experience of underinvolvement, of detachment.

I adore simple pleasures, they are the last refuge of the complex.

—*A Woman of No Importance*

45. Detachment is the prerogative of an elite; and as the dandy is the nineteenth century's surrogate for the aristocrat in matters of culture, so Camp is the modern dandyism. Camp is the answer to the problem: how to be a dandy in the age of mass culture.

46. The dandy was overbred. His posture was disdain, or else ennui. He sought rare sensations, undefiled by mass appreciation. (Models: Des Esseintes in Huysmans' *À Rebours*, *Marius the Epicurean*, Valéry's *Monsieur Teste*.) He was dedicated to "good taste."

     The connoisseur of Camp has found more ingenious pleasures. Not in Latin poetry and rare wines and velvet jackets, but in the coarsest, commonest pleasures, in the arts of the masses. Mere use does not defile the objects of his pleasure, since he learns to possess them in a rare way. Camp—Dandyism in the age of mass culture—makes no distinction between the unique object and the mass-produced object. Camp taste transcends the nausea of the replica.

47. Wilde himself is a transitional figure. The man who, when he first came to London, sported a velvet beret, lace shirts, velveteen knee-breeches and black silk stockings, could never depart too far in his life from the pleasures of the old-style dandy; this conservatism is reflected in *The Picture of Dorian Gray*. But many of his attitudes suggest something more modern. It was Wilde who formulated an important element of the Camp sensibility—the equivalence of all objects—when he announced his intention of "living up" to his blue-and-white china, or declared that a doorknob could be as admirable as a painting. When he proclaimed the importance of the necktie, the boutonniere, the chair, Wilde was anticipating the democratic *esprit* of Camp.

48. The old-style dandy hated vulgarity. The new-style dandy, the lover of Camp, appreciates vulgarity. Where the dandy would be continually offended or bored, the connoisseur of Camp is continually amused, delighted. The dandy held a perfumed handkerchief to his nostrils and was liable to swoon; the connoisseur of Camp sniffs the stink and prides himself on his strong nerves.

49. It is a feat, of course. A feat goaded on, in the last analysis, by the threat of boredom. The relation between boredom and Camp taste cannot be overestimated. Camp taste is by its nature possible only in affluent societies, in societies or circles capable of experiencing the psychopathology of affluence.

What is abnormal in Life stands in normal relations to Art. It is the only thing in Life that stands in normal relations to Art.
—*A Few Maxims for the Instruction of the Over-Educated*

50. Aristocracy is a position vis-à-vis culture (as well as vis-à-vis power), and the history of Camp taste is part of the history of snob taste. But since no authentic aristocrats in the old sense exist today to sponsor special tastes, who is the bearer of this taste? Answer: an improvised self-elected class, mainly homosexuals, who constitute themselves as aristocrats of taste.

51. The peculiar relation between Camp taste and homosexuality has to be explained. While it's not true that Camp taste *is* homosexual taste, there is no doubt a peculiar affinity and overlap. Not all liberals are Jews, but Jews have shown a peculiar affinity for liberal and reformist causes. So, not all homosexuals have Camp taste. But homosexuals, by and large, constitute the vanguard—and the most articulate audience—of Camp. (The analogy is not frivolously chosen. Jews and homosexuals are the outstanding creative minorities in contemporary urban culture. Creative, that is, in the truest sense: they are creators of sensibilities. The two pioneering forces of modern sensibility are Jewish moral seriousness and homosexual aestheticism and irony.)

52. The reason for the flourishing of the aristocratic posture among homosexuals also seems to parallel the Jewish case. For every sensibility is self-serving to the group that promotes it. Jewish liberalism is a gesture of self-legitimization. So is Camp taste, which definitely has something propagandistic about it. Needless to say, the propaganda operates in exactly the opposite direction. The Jews pinned their hopes for integrating into modern society on promoting the moral sense. Homosexuals have pinned their integration into society on promoting the aesthetic sense. Camp is a solvent of morality. It neutralizes moral indignation, sponsors playfulness.

53. Nevertheless, even though homosexuals have been its vanguard, Camp taste is much more than homosexual taste. Obviously, its metaphor of life as theater is peculiarly suited as a justification and projection of a certain

aspect of the situation of homosexuals. (The Camp insistence on not being "serious," on playing, also connects with the homosexual's desire to remain youthful.) Yet one feels that if homosexuals hadn't more or less invented Camp, someone else would. For the aristocratic posture with relation to culture cannot die, though it may persist only in increasingly arbitrary and ingenious ways. Camp is (to repeat) the relation to style in a time in which the adoption of style—as such—has become altogether questionable. (In the modern era, each new style, unless frankly anachronistic, has come on the scene as an anti-style.)

One must have a heart of stone to read the death of Little Nell without laughing.

—In Conversation

54. The experiences of Camp are based on the great discovery that the sensibility of high culture has no monopoly upon refinement. Camp asserts that good taste is not simply good taste; that there exists, indeed, a good taste of bad taste. (Genet talks about this in *Our Lady of the Flowers*.) The discovery of the good taste of bad taste can be very liberating. The man who insists on high and serious pleasures is depriving himself of pleasure; he continually restricts what he can enjoy; in the constant exercise of his good taste he will eventually price himself out of the market, so to speak. Here Camp taste supervenes upon good taste as a daring and witty hedonism. It makes the man of good taste cheerful, where before he ran the risk of being chronically frustrated. It is good for the digestion.

55. Camp taste is, above all, a mode of enjoyment, of appreciation—not judgment. Camp is generous. It wants to enjoy. It only seems like malice, cynicism. (Or, if it is cynicism, it's not a ruthless but a sweet cynicism.) Camp taste doesn't propose that it is in bad taste to be serious; it doesn't sneer at someone who succeeds in being

seriously dramatic. What it does is to find the success in certain passionate failures.

56. Camp taste is a kind of love, love for human nature. It relishes, rather than judges, the little triumphs and awkward intensities of "character" . . . Camp taste identifies with what it is enjoying. People who share this sensibility are not laughing at the thing they label as "a camp," they're enjoying it. Camp *is* a tender feeling.

(Here one may compare Camp with much of Pop Art, which—when it is not just Camp—embodies an attitude that is related, but still very different. Pop Art is more flat and more dry, more serious, more detached, ultimately nihilistic.)

57. Camp taste nourishes itself on the love that has gone into certain objects and personal styles. The absence of this love is the reason why such kitsch items as *Peyton Place* (the book) and the Tishman Building aren't Camp.

58. The ultimate Camp statement: it's good *because* it's awful . . . Of course, one can't always say that. Only under certain conditions, those which I've tried to sketch in these notes.

Richard Hofstadter (1916–1970) was a highly respected historian who served for many years on the Columbia University faculty, training and inspiring future historians. His graceful writing style in books such as the Pulitzer Prize–winning Age of Reform *and* Anti-Intellectualism in American Life *made him popular with a large reading public as well as within his academic discipline. In a key essay that originally appeared in* Harper's, *"The Paranoid Style in American Politics," he brought a balanced historical perspective to extremist, anti-liberal positions: this oft-cited text has, if anything, gained in pertinence.*

THE PARANOID STYLE IN AMERICAN POLITICS

American politics has often been an arena for angry minds. In recent years we have seen angry minds at work mainly among extreme right-wingers, who have now demonstrated in the Goldwater movement how much political leverage can be got out of the animosities and passions of a small minority. But behind this I believe there is a style of mind that is far from new and that is not necessarily right-wing. I call it the paranoid style simply because no other word adequately evokes the sense of heated exaggeration, suspiciousness, and conspiratorial fantasy that I have in mind. In using the expression "paranoid style" I am not speaking in a clinical sense, but borrowing a clinical term for other purposes. I have neither the competence nor the desire to classify any figures of the past or present as certifiable lunatics. In fact, the idea of the paranoid style as a force in politics would have little contemporary relevance or historical value if it were applied only to men with profoundly disturbed minds. It is the use of paranoid modes of expression by more or less normal people that makes the phenomenon significant.

Of course this term is pejorative, and it is meant to be; the paranoid style has a greater affinity for bad causes than good. But nothing really prevents a sound program or demand from being advocated in the paranoid style. Style has more to do with the way in which ideas are believed than with the truth or falsity of their content. I am interested here in getting at our political psychology through our political rhetoric. The paranoid style is an old and recurrent phenomenon in our public life which has been frequently linked with movements of suspicious discontent.

Here is Senator McCarthy, speaking in June 1951 about the parlous situation of the United States:

> How can we account for our present situation unless we believe that men high in this government are concerting to deliver us to disaster? This must be the product of a great conspiracy on a scale so immense as to dwarf any previous such venture in the history of man. A conspiracy of infamy so black that, when it is finally exposed, its principals shall be forever deserving of the maledictions of all honest men. . . . What can be made of this unbroken series of decisions and acts contributing to the strategy of defeat? They cannot be attributed to incompetence. . . . The laws of probability would dictate that part of . . . [the] decisions would serve the country's interest.

Now turn back fifty years to a manifesto signed in 1895 by a number of leaders of the Populist party:

> As early as 1865–66 a conspiracy was entered into between the gold gamblers of Europe and America. . . . For nearly thirty years these conspirators have kept the people quarreling over less important matters while they have pursued with unrelenting zeal their one central purpose. . . . Every device of treachery, every resource of statecraft, and every

artifice known to the secret cabals of the international gold ring are being used to deal a blow to the prosperity of the people and the financial and commercial independence of the country.

Next, a Texas newspaper article of 1855:

. . . It is a notorious fact that the Monarchs of Europe and the Pope of Rome are at this very moment plotting our destruction and threatening the extinction of our political, civil, and religious institutions. We have the best reasons for believing that corruption has found its way into our Executive Chamber, and that our Executive head is tainted with the infectious venom of Catholicism. . . . The Pope has recently sent his ambassador of state to this country on a secret commission, the effect of which is an extraordinary boldness of the Catholic church throughout the United States. . . . These minions of the Pope are boldly insulting our Senators; reprimanding our Statesmen; propagating the adulterous union of Church and State; abusing with foul calumny all governments but Catholic, and spewing out the bitterest execrations on all Protestantism. The Catholics in the United States receive from abroad more than $200,000 annually for the propagation of their creed. Add to this the vast revenues collected here. . . .

These quotations give the keynote of the style. In the history of the United States one finds it, for example, in the anti-Masonic movement, the nativist and anti-Catholic movement, in certain spokesmen of abolitionism who regarded the United States as being in the grip of a slaveholders' conspiracy, in many alarmists about the Mormons, in some Greenback and Populist writers who constructed a great conspiracy of international bankers, in the exposure of a munitions makers' conspiracy of World War I, in the popular left-wing press, in the contemporary American right wing, and on both sides of the race controversy today, among White Citizens' Councils and Black Muslims. I do not propose to try to trace the variations of the paranoid style that can be found in all these movements, but will confine myself to a few leading episodes in our past history in which the style emerged in full and archetypal splendor.

Illuminism and Masonry

I begin with a particularly revealing episode—the panic that broke out in some quarters at the end of the eighteenth century over the allegedly subversive activities of the Bavarian Illuminati. This panic was a part of the general reaction to the French Revolution. In the United States it was heightened by the response of certain men, mostly in New England and among the established clergy, to the rise of Jeffersonian democracy. Illuminism had been started in 1776 by Adam Weishaupt, a professor of law at the University of Ingolstadt. Its teachings today seem to be no more than another version of Enlightenment rationalism, spiced with the anticlerical atmosphere of eighteenth-century Bavaria. It was a somewhat naïve and utopian movement which aspired ultimately to bring the human race under the rules of reason. Its humanitarian rationalism appears to have acquired a fairly wide influence in Masonic lodges.

Americans first learned of Illuminism in 1797, from a volume published in Edinburgh (later reprinted in New York) under the title *Proofs of a Conspiracy Against All the Religions and Governments of Europe, Carried on in the Secret Meetings of Free Masons, Illuminati, and Reading Societies.* Its author was a well-known Scottish scientist, John Robison, who had himself been a somewhat casual adherent of Masonry in Britain, but whose imagination had been inflamed by what he considered to be the far less innocent Masonic movement on the Continent. Robison seems to have made his work as factual as he could, but when he came to estimating the moral character and the political influence of Illuminism, he made the characteristic paranoid leap into fantasy. The association, he thought, was formed "for the express purpose of ROOTING OUT ALL RELIGIOUS ESTABLISHMENTS,

AND OVERTURNING ALL THE EXISTING GOVERNMENTS OF EUROPE."
It had become "one great and wicked project fermenting and
working all over Europe." And to it he attributed a central role
in bringing about the French Revolution. He saw it as a libertine,
anti-Christian movement, given to the corruption of women,
the cultivation of sensual pleasures, and the violation of property rights. Its members had plans for making a tea that caused
abortion—a secret substance that "blinds or kills when spurted in
the face," and a device that sounds like a stench bomb—a "method
for filling a bedchamber with pestilential vapours."

These notions were quick to make themselves felt in America.
In May 1798, a minister of the Massachusetts Congregational
establishment in Boston, Jedidiah Morse, delivered a timely
sermon to the young country, which was then sharply divided
between Jeffersonians and Federalists, Francophiles and Anglo-
men. Having read Robison, Morse was convinced of a Jacobini-
cal plot touched off by Illuminism, and that the country should
be rallied to defend itself. His warnings were heeded throughout New England wherever Federalists brooded about the rising
tide of religious infidelity or Jeffersonian democracy. Timothy
Dwight, the president of Yale, followed Morse's sermon with a
Fourth of July discourse on *The Duty of Americans in the Present Crisis,* in which he held forth against the Antichrist in his own
glowing rhetoric. Soon the pulpits of New England were ringing
with denunciations of the Illuminati, as though the country were
swarming with them.

The anti-Masonic movement of the late 1820s and the 1830s
took up and extended the obsession with conspiracy. At first, this
movement may seem to be no more than an extension or repetition of the anti-Masonic theme sounded in the outcry against the
Bavarian Illuminati. But whereas the panic of the 1790s was confined mainly to New England and linked to an ultraconservative
point of view, the later anti-Masonic movement affected many
parts of the northern United States, and was intimately linked
with popular democracy and rural egalitarianism. Although
anti-Masonry happened to be anti-Jacksonian (Jackson was a
Mason), it manifested the same animus against the closure of
opportunity for the common man and against aristocratic insti-

tutions that one finds in the Jacksonian crusade against the Bank of the United States.

The anti-Masonic movement was a product not merely of natural enthusiasm but also of the vicissitudes of party politics. It was joined and used by a great many men who did not fully share its original anti-Masonic feelings. It attracted the support of several reputable statesmen who had only mild sympathy with its fundamental bias, but who as politicians could not afford to ignore it. Still, it was a folk movement of considerable power, and the rural enthusiasts who provided its real impetus believed in it wholeheartedly.

As a secret society, Masonry was considered to be a standing conspiracy against republican government. It was held to be particularly liable to treason—for example, Aaron Burr's famous conspiracy was alleged to have been conducted by Masons. Masonry was accused of constituting a separate system of loyalty, a separate imperium within the framework of federal and state governments, which was inconsistent with loyalty to them. Quite plausibly it was argued that the Masons had set up a jurisdiction of their own, with their own obligations and punishments, liable to enforcement even by the penalty of death. So basic was the conflict felt to be between secrecy and democracy that other, more innocent societies such as Phi Beta Kappa came under attack.

Since Masons were pledged to come to each other's aid under circumstances of distress, and to extend fraternal indulgence at all times, it was held that the order nullified the enforcement of regular law. Masonic constables, sheriffs, juries, and judges must all be in league with Masonic criminals and fugitives. The press was believed to have been so "muzzled" by Masonic editors and proprietors that news of Masonic malfeasance could be suppressed. At a moment when almost every alleged citadel of privilege in America was under democratic assault, Masonry was attacked as a fraternity of the privileged, closing business opportunities and nearly monopolizing political offices.

Certain elements of truth and reality there may have been in these views of Masonry. What must be emphasized here, however, is the apocalyptic and absolutistic framework in which this hostility was commonly expressed. Anti-Masons were not content simply to say that secret societies were rather a bad idea. The author of the standard exposition of anti-Masonry declared that Freemasonry was "not only the most abominable but also the most dangerous institution that ever was imposed on man. . . . It may truly be said to be HELL'S MASTER PIECE."

The Jesuit Threat

Fear of a Masonic plot had hardly been quieted when the rumors arose of a Catholic plot against American values. One meets here again the same frame of mind, but a different villain. The anti-Catholic movement converged with a growing nativism, and while they were not identical, together they cut such a wide swath in American life that they were bound to embrace many moderates to whom the paranoid style, in its full glory, did not appeal. Moreover, we need not dismiss out of hand as totally parochial or mean-spirited the desire of Yankee Americans to maintain an ethnically and religiously homogeneous society nor the particular Protestant commitments to individualism and freedom that were brought into play. But the movement had a large paranoid infusion, and the most influential anti-Catholic militants certainly had a strong affinity for the paranoid style.

Two books which appeared in 1835 described the new danger to the American way of life and may be taken as expressions of the anti-Catholic mentality. One, *Foreign Conspiracies Against the Liberties of the United States*, was from the hand of the celebrated painter and inventor of the telegraph, S. F. B. Morse. "A conspiracy exists," Morse proclaimed, and "its plans are already in operation . . . we are attacked in a vulnerable quarter which cannot be defended by our ships, our forts, or our armies." The main source of the conspiracy Morse found in Metternich's government: "*Austria is now acting in this country*. She has devised a grand scheme. She has organized a great plan for doing something here. . . . She has her Jesuit missionaries traveling through the land; she has supplied them with money, and has furnished a fountain for a regular supply." Were the plot successful, Morse said, some scion of the House of Hapsburg would soon be installed as emperor of the United States.

"It is an ascertained fact," wrote another Protestant militant,

> that Jesuits are prowling about all parts of the United States in every possible disguise, expressly to ascertain the advantageous situations and modes to disseminate Popery. A minister of the Gospel from Ohio has informed us that he discovered one carrying on his devices in his congregation; and he says that the western country swarms with them under the name of puppet show men, dancing masters, music teachers, peddlers of images and ornaments, barrel organ players, and similar practitioners.

Lyman Beecher, the elder of a famous family and the father of Harriet Beecher Stowe, wrote in the same year his *Plea for the West*, in which he considered the possibility that the Christian millennium might come in the American states. Everything depended, in his judgment, upon what influences dominated the great West, where the future of the country lay. There Protestantism was engaged in a life-or-death struggle with Catholicism. "Whatever we do, it must be done quickly. . . ." A great tide of immigration, hostile to free institutions, was sweeping in upon the country, subsidized and sent by "the potentates of Europe," multiplying tumult and violence, filling jails, crowding poorhouses, quadrupling taxation, and sending increasing thousands of voters to "lay their inexperienced hand upon the helm of our power."

Anti-Catholicism has always been the pornography of the Puritan. Whereas the anti-Masons had envisaged drinking bouts and had entertained themselves with sado-masochistic fantasies about the actual enforcement of grisly Masonic oaths,* the anti-Catholics invented an immense lore about libertine priests, the

---

* Many anti-Masons had been fascinated by the penalties involved if Masons failed to live up to their obligations. My own favorite is the oath attributed to a royal archmason who invited "having my skull smote off and my brains exposed to the scorching rays of the sun."

confessional as an opportunity for seduction, licentious convents and monasteries. Probably the most widely read contemporary book in the United States before *Uncle Tom's Cabin* was a work supposedly written by one Maria Monk, entitled *Awful Disclosures*, which appeared in 1836. The author, who purported to have escaped from the Hotel Dieu nunnery in Montreal after five years there as novice and nun, reported her convent life in elaborate and circumstantial detail. She reported having been told by the Mother Superior that she must "obey the priests in all things"; to her "utter astonishment and horror," she soon found what the nature of such obedience was. Infants born of convent liaisons were baptized and then killed, she said, so that they might ascend at once to heaven. Her book, hotly attacked and defended, continued to be read and believed even after her mother gave testimony that Maria had been somewhat addled ever since childhood after she had rammed a pencil into her head. Maria died in prison in 1849, after having been arrested in a brothel as a pickpocket.

Anti-Catholicism, like anti-Masonry, mixed its fortunes with American party politics, and it became an enduring factor in American politics. The American Protective Association of the 1890s revived it with ideological variations more suitable to the times—the depression of 1893, for example, was alleged to be an international creation of the Catholics who began it by starting a run on the banks. Some spokesmen of the movement circulated a bogus encyclical attributed to Leo XIII instructing American Catholics on a certain date in 1893 to exterminate all heretics, and a great many anti-Catholics daily expected a nationwide uprising. The myth of an impending Catholic war of mutilation and extermination of heretics persisted into the twentieth century.

Why They Feel Dispossessed

If, after our historically discontinuous examples of the paranoid style, we now take the long jump to the contemporary right wing, we find some rather important differences from the nineteenth-century movements. The spokesmen of those earlier movements felt that they stood for causes and personal types that were still in possession of their country—that they were fending off threats to a still established way of life. But the modern right wing, as Daniel Bell has put it, feels dispossessed: America has been largely taken away from them and their kind, though they are determined to try to repossess it and to prevent the final destructive act of subversion. The old American virtues have already been eaten away by cosmopolitans and intellectuals; the old competitive capitalism has been gradually undermined by socialistic and communistic schemers; the old national security and independence have been destroyed by treasonous plots, having as their most powerful agents not merely outsiders and foreigners as of old but major statesmen who are at the very centers of American power. Their predecessors had discovered conspiracies; the modern radical right finds conspiracy to be betrayal from on high.

Important changes may also be traced to the effects of the mass media. The villains of the modern right are much more vivid than those of their paranoid predecessors, much better known to the public; the literature of the paranoid style is by the same token richer and more circumstantial in personal description and personal invective. For the vaguely delineated villains of the anti-Masons, for the obscure and disguised Jesuit agents, the little-known papal delegates of the anti-Catholics, for the shadowy international bankers of the monetary conspiracies, we may now substitute eminent public figures like presidents Roosevelt, Truman, and Eisenhower, secretaries of state like Marshall, Acheson, and Dulles, justices of the Supreme Court like Frankfurter and Warren, and the whole battery of lesser but still famous and vivid alleged conspirators headed by Alger Hiss.

Events since 1939 have given the contemporary right-wing paranoid a vast theater for his imagination, full of rich and proliferating detail, replete with realistic cues and undeniable proofs of the validity of his suspicions. The theater of action is now the entire world, and he can draw not only on the events of World War II, but also on those of the Korean War and the Cold War.

Any historian of warfare knows it is in good part a comedy of errors and a museum of incompetence; but if for every error and every act of incompetence one can substitute an act of treason, many points of fascinating interpretation are open to the paranoid imagination. In the end, the real mystery, for one who reads the primary works of paranoid scholarship, is not how the United States has been brought to its present dangerous position but how it has managed to survive at all.

The basic elements of contemporary right-wing thought can be reduced to three: First, there has been the now-familiar sustained conspiracy, running over more than a generation, and reaching its climax in Roosevelt's New Deal, to undermine free capitalism, to bring the economy under the direction of the federal government, and to pave the way for socialism or communism. A great many right-wingers would agree with Frank Chodorov, the author of *The Income Tax: The Root of All Evil*, that this campaign began with the passage of the income-tax amendment to the Constitution in 1913.

The second contention is that top government officialdom has been so infiltrated by Communists that American policy, at least since the days leading up to Pearl Harbor, has been dominated by men who were shrewdly and consistently selling out American national interests.

Finally, the country is infused with a network of Communist agents, just as in the old days it was infiltrated by Jesuit agents, so that the whole apparatus of education, religion, the press, and the mass media is engaged in a common effort to paralyze the resistance of loyal Americans.

Perhaps the most representative document of the McCarthyist phase was a long indictment of Secretary of State George C. Marshall, delivered in 1951 in the Senate by Senator McCarthy, and later published in a somewhat different form. McCarthy pictured Marshall as the focal figure in a betrayal of American interests stretching in time from the strategic plans for World War II to the formulation of the Marshall Plan. Marshall was associated with practically every American failure or defeat, McCarthy insisted, and none of this was either accident or incompetence.

There was a "baffling pattern" of Marshall's interventions in the war, which always conduced to the well-being of the Kremlin. The sharp decline in America's relative strength from 1945 to 1951 did not "just happen"; it was "brought about, step by step, by will and intention," the consequence not of mistakes but of a treasonous conspiracy, "a conspiracy on a scale so immense as to dwarf any previous such venture in the history of man."

Today, the mantle of McCarthy has fallen on a retired candy manufacturer, Robert H. Welch, Jr., who is less strategically placed and has a much smaller but better organized following than the senator. A few years ago Welch proclaimed that "Communist influences are now in almost complete control of our government"—note the care and scrupulousness of that "almost." He has offered a full-scale interpretation of our recent history in which Communists figure at every turn: They started a run on American banks in 1933 that forced their closure; they contrived the recognition of the Soviet Union by the United States in the same year, just in time to save the Soviets from economic collapse; they have stirred up the fuss over segregation in the South; they have taken over the Supreme Court and made it "one of the most important agencies of Communism."

Close attention to history wins for Mr. Welch an insight into affairs that is given to few of us. "For many reasons and after a lot of study," he wrote some years ago, "I personally believe [John Foster] Dulles to be a Communist agent." The job of Professor Arthur F. Burns as head of Eisenhower's Council of Economic Advisors was "merely a cover-up for Burns's liaison work between Eisenhower and some of his Communist bosses." Eisenhower's brother Milton was "actually [his] superior and boss within the Communist party." As for Eisenhower himself, Welch characterized him, in words that have made the candy manufacturer famous, as "a dedicated, conscious agent of the Communist conspiracy"—a conclusion, he added, "based on an accumulation of detailed evidence so extensive and so palpable that it seems to put this conviction beyond any reasonable doubt."

Emulating the Enemy

The paranoid spokesman sees the fate of conspiracy in apocalyptic terms—he traffics in the birth and death of whole worlds, whole political orders, whole systems of human values. He is always manning the barricades of civilization. He constantly lives at a turning point. Like religious millennialists he expresses the anxiety of those who are living through the last days and he is sometimes disposed to set a date for the apocalypse. ("Time is running out," said Welch in 1951. "Evidence is piling up on many sides and from many sources that October 1952 is the fatal month when Stalin will attack.")

As a member of the avant-garde who is capable of perceiving the conspiracy before it is fully obvious to an as yet unaroused public, the paranoid is a militant leader. He does not see social conflict as something to be mediated and compromised, in the manner of the working politician. Since what is at stake is always a conflict between absolute good and absolute evil, what is necessary is not compromise but the will to fight things out to a finish. Since the enemy is thought of as being totally evil and totally unappeasable, he must be totally eliminated—if not from the world, at least from the theater of operations to which the paranoid directs his attention. This demand for total triumph leads to the formulation of hopelessly unrealistic goals, and since these goals are not even remotely attainable, failure constantly heightens the paranoid's sense of frustration. Even partial success leaves him with the same feeling of powerlessness with which he began, and this in turn only strengthens his awareness of the vast and terrifying quality of the enemy he opposes.

The enemy is clearly delineated: he is a perfect model of malice, a kind of amoral superman—sinister, ubiquitous, powerful, cruel, sensual, luxury-loving. Unlike the rest of us, the enemy is not caught in the toils of the vast mechanism of history, himself a victim of his past, his desires, his limitations. He wills, indeed he manufactures, the mechanism of history, or tries to deflect the normal course of history in an evil way. He makes crises, starts runs on banks, causes depressions, manufactures disasters, and then enjoys and profits from the misery he has produced. The paranoid's interpretation of history is distinctly personal: decisive events are not taken as part of the stream of history, but as the consequences of someone's will. Very often the enemy is held to possess some especially effective source of power: he controls the press; he has unlimited funds; he has a new secret for influencing the mind (brainwashing); he has a special technique for seduction (the Catholic confessional).

It is hard to resist the conclusion that this enemy is on many counts the projection of the self; both the ideal and the unacceptable aspects of the self are attributed to him. The enemy may be the cosmopolitan intellectual, but the paranoid will outdo him in the apparatus of scholarship, even of pedantry. Secret organizations set up to combat secret organizations give the same flattery. The Ku Klux Klan imitated Catholicism to the point of donning priestly vestments, developing an elaborate ritual and an equally elaborate hierarchy. The John Birch Society emulates Communist cells and quasi-secret operation through "front" groups, and preaches a ruthless prosecution of the ideological war along lines very similar to those it finds in the Communist enemy.[*] Spokesmen of the various fundamentalist anti-Communist "crusades" openly express their admiration for the dedication and discipline the Communist cause calls forth.

On the other hand, the sexual freedom often attributed to the enemy, his lack of moral inhibition, his possession of especially effective techniques for fulfilling his desires, give exponents of the paranoid style an opportunity to project and express unacknowledgeable aspects of their own psychological concerns. Catholics and Mormons—later, Negroes and Jews—have lent themselves to a preoccupation with illicit sex. Very often the fantasies of

---

[*] In his recent book, *How to Win an Election*, Stephen C. Shadegg cites a statement attributed to Mao Tse-tung: "Give me just two or three men in a village and I will take the village." Shadegg comments: "In the Goldwater campaigns of 1952 and 1958 and in all campaigns where I have served as consultant I have followed the advice of Mao Tse-tung." "I would suggest," writes Senator Goldwater in *Why Not Victory?* "that we analyze and copy the strategy of the enemy; theirs has worked and ours has not."

true believers reveal strong sado-masochistic outlets, vividly expressed, for example, in the delight of anti-Masons with the cruelty of Masonic punishments.

Renegades and Pedants

A special significance attaches to the figure of the renegade from the enemy cause. The anti-Masonic movement seemed at times to be the creation of ex-Masons; certainly the highest significance was attributed to their revelations, and every word they said was believed. Anti-Catholicism used the runaway nun and the apostate priest; the place of ex-Communists in the avant-garde anti-Communist movements of our time is well known. In some part, the special authority accorded the renegade derives from the obsession with secrecy so characteristic of such movements: the renegade is the man or woman who has been in the arcanum, and brings forth with him or her the final verification of suspicions which might otherwise have been doubted by a skeptical world. But I think there is a deeper eschatological significance that attaches to the person of the renegade: in the spiritual wrestling match between good and evil which is the paranoid's archetypal model of the world, the renegade is living proof that all the conversions are not made by the wrong side. He brings with him the promise of redemption and victory.

A final characteristic of the paranoid style is related to the quality of its pedantry. One of the impressive things about paranoid literature is the contrast between its fantasied conclusions and the almost touching concern with factuality it invariably shows. It produces heroic strivings for evidence to prove that the unbelievable is the only thing that can be believed. Of course, there are highbrow, lowbrow, and middlebrow paranoids, as there are likely to be in any political tendency. But respectable paranoid literature not only starts from certain moral commitments that can indeed be justified but also carefully and all but obsessively accumulates "evidence." The difference between this "evidence" and that commonly employed by others is that it seems less a means of entering into normal political controversy than a means of warding off the profane intrusion of the secular political world. The paranoid seems to have little expectation of actually convincing a hostile world, but he can accumulate evidence in order to protect his cherished convictions from it.

Paranoid writing begins with certain broad defensible judgments. There *was* something to be said for the anti-Masons. After all, a secret society composed of influential men bound by special obligations could conceivably pose some kind of threat to the civil order in which they were suspended. There was also something to be said for the Protestant principles of individuality and freedom, as well as for the nativist desire to develop in North America a homogeneous civilization. Again, in our time an actual laxity in security allowed some Communists to find a place in governmental circles, and innumerable decisions of World War II and the Cold War could be faulted.

The higher paranoid scholarship is nothing if not coherent—in fact the paranoid mind is far more coherent than the real world. It is nothing if not scholarly in technique. McCarthy's 96-page pamphlet, *McCarthyism*, contains no less than 313 footnote references, and Mr. Welch's incredible assault on Eisenhower, *The Politician*, has one hundred pages of bibliography and notes. The entire right-wing movement of our time is a parade of experts, study groups, monographs, footnotes, and bibliographies. Sometimes the right-wing striving for scholarly depth and an inclusive worldview has startling consequences: Mr. Welch, for example, has charged that the popularity of Arnold Toynbee's historical work is the consequence of a plot on the part of Fabians, "Labour party bosses in England," and various members of the Anglo-American "liberal establishment" to overshadow the much more truthful and illuminating work of Oswald Spengler.

The Double Sufferer

The paranoid style is not confined to our own country and time; it is an international phenomenon. Studying the millennial sects of Europe from the eleventh to the sixteenth century, Norman Cohn believed he found a persistent psychic complex that corresponds broadly with what I have been considering—a style made up of certain preoccupations and fantasies: "the megalomaniac view of oneself as the Elect, wholly good, abominably persecuted, yet assured of ultimate triumph; the attribution of gigantic and demonic powers to the adversary; the refusal to accept the ineluctable limitations and imperfections of human existence, such as transience, dissention, conflict, fallibility whether intellectual or moral; the obsession with inerrable prophecies . . . systematized misinterpretations, always gross and often grotesque."

This glimpse across a long span of time emboldens me to make the conjecture—it is no more than that—that a mentality disposed to see the world in this way may be a persistent psychic phenomenon, more or less constantly affecting a modest minority of the population. But certain religious traditions, certain social structures and national inheritances, certain historical catastrophes or frustrations may be conducive to the release of such psychic energies, and to situations in which they can more readily be built into mass movements or political parties. In American experience ethnic and religious conflict have plainly been a major focus for militant and suspicious minds of this sort, but class conflicts also can mobilize such energies. Perhaps the central situation conducive to the diffusion of the paranoid tendency is a confrontation of opposed interests which are (or are felt to be) totally irreconcilable, and thus by nature not susceptible to the normal political processes of bargain and compromise. The situation becomes worse when the representatives of a particular social interest—perhaps because of the very unrealistic and unrealizable nature of its demands—are shut out of the political process. Having no access to political bargaining or the making of decisions, they find their original conception that the world of power is sinister and malicious fully confirmed. They see only the consequences of power—and this through distorting lenses—and have no chance to observe its actual machinery. A distinguished historian has said that one of the most valuable things about history is that it teaches us how things do *not* happen. It is precisely this kind of awareness that the paranoid fails to develop. He has a special resistance of his own, of course, to developing such awareness, but circumstances often deprive him of exposure to events that might enlighten him—and in any case he resists enlightenment.

We are all sufferers from history, but the paranoid is a double sufferer, since he is afflicted not only by the real world, with the rest of us, but by his fantasies as well.

Paul Goodman (1911–1972) was a poet, essayist, social critic, gadfly, and polymath. The last of the generalists, he wrote with conviction and prophetic originality on city planning, linguistics, Kafka, sexual freedom, and psychotherapy. Always inclined to think outside the box, his books on schooling in America, the bestselling Growing Up Absurd *and* Compulsory Miseducation, *challenged the educational establishment. Though inclined to think of himself as a lonely voice in the wilderness, at one point his influence on the sixties' rebellious counterculture was significant, and he remains a prophet with some honor in his own land.*

THE UNIVERSAL TRAP

A conference of experts on school dropouts will discuss the background of poverty, cultural deprivations, race prejudice, family and emotional troubles, neighborhood uprooting, urban mobility. It will explore ingenious expedients to counteract these conditions, though it will not much look to remedying them—that is not its business. And it will suggest propaganda—e.g., no school, no job—to get the youngsters back in school. It is axiomatic that they ought to be in school.

After a year, it proves necessary to call another conference to cope with the alarming fact that more than 75 percent of the dropouts who have been cajoled into returning, have dropped out again. They persist in failing; they still are not sufficiently motivated. What curricular changes must there be? How can the teachers learn the lifestyle of the underprivileged?

Curiously muffled in these conferences is the question that puts the burden of proof the other way: What are they dropouts from? Is the schooling really good for them, or much good for anybody? Since, for many, there are such difficulties with the present arrangements, might not some better arrangements be invented? Or bluntly, since schooling undertakes to be compulsory, must it not continually review its claim to be useful? Is it the only means of education? Isn't it unlikely that *any* single type of social institution could fit almost every youngster up to the age of sixteen and beyond? (It is predicted that by 1970, 50 percent will go to college.)

But conferences on dropouts are summoned by school professionals, so perhaps we cannot hope that such elementary questions will be raised, yet neither are they raised by laymen. There is a mass superstition, underwritten by additional billions every year, that adolescents must continue going to school. The middle class *know* that no professional competence—i.e., status and salary—can be attained without many diplomas; and poor people have allowed themselves to be convinced that the primary remedy for their increasing deprivation is to agitate for better schooling. Nevertheless, I doubt that, *at present or with any reforms that are conceivable under current school administration,* going to school is the best use for the time of life of the majority of youth.

Education is a natural community function and occurs inevitably, since the young grow up on the old, towards their activities, and into (or against) their institutions; and the old foster, teach, train, exploit and abuse the young. Even neglect of the young, except physical neglect, has an educational effect—not the worst possible.

Formal schooling is a reasonable auxiliary of the inevitable process, whenever an activity is best learned by singling it out or special attention with a special person to teach it. Yet it by no means follows that the complicated artifact of a school system has much to do with education, and certainly not with good education.

Let us bear in mind the way in which a big school system might have nothing to do with education at all. The New York system turns over $700 million annually, not including capital improvements. There are 750 schools, with perhaps fifteen annually being replaced at an extra cost of two to five million dollars each. There are 40,000 paid employees. This is a vast vested interest, and it is very probable that—like much of our economy and almost all of our political structure, of which the public schools are a part—it goes on for its own sake, keeping more than a million people busy, wasting wealth, and preempting time and space in which something else could be going on. It is a gigantic market for textbook manufacturers, building contractors and graduate schools of education.

The fundamental design of such a system is ancient, yet it has not been altered although the present operation is altogether different in scale from what it was, and therefore it must have a different meaning. For example, in 1900, 6 percent of the seventeen-year-olds graduated from high school, and less than 0.5 percent went to college; whereas in 1963, 65 percent graduated from high school and 35 percent went on to something called college. Likewise, there is a vast difference between schooling intermitted in life on a farm or in a city with plenty of small jobs, and schooling that is a child's only "serious" occupation and often his only adult contact. Thus, a perhaps outmoded institution has become almost the only allowable way of growing up. And with this preempting, there is an increasing intensification of the one narrow experience, e.g., in the shaping of the curriculum and testing according to the increasing requirements of graduate schools far off in time and place. Just as our American society as a whole is more and more tightly organized, so its school system is more and more regimented as part of that organization.

In the organizational plan, the schools play a non-educational and an educational role. The non-educational role is very important. In the tender grades, the schools are a babysitting service during a period of collapse of the old-type family and during a time of extreme urbanization and urban mobility. In the junior and senior high-school grades, they are an arm of the police, providing cops and concentration camps paid for in the budget under the heading "Board of Education." The educational role is, by and large, to provide—at public and parents' expense—

apprentice-training for corporations, government and the teaching profession itself, and also to train the young, as New York's commissioner of education has said (in the Morley case), "to handle constructively their problems of adjustment to authority."

The public schools of America have indeed been a powerful, and beneficent, force for the democratizing of a great mixed population. But we must be careful to keep reassessing them when, with changing conditions, they become a universal trap and democracy begins to look like regimentation.

Let me spend a page on the history of the compulsory nature of the school systems. In 1961, in *The Child, the Parent, and the State*, James Conant mentions a possible incompatibility between "individual development" and "national needs"; this, to my mind, is a watershed in American philosophy of education and puts us back to the ideology of Imperial Germany, or on a par with contemporary Russia.

When Jefferson and Madison conceived of compulsory schooling, such an incompatibility would have been unthinkable. They were in the climate of the Enlightenment, were strongly influenced by Congregational (town-meeting) ideas, and were of course makers of a revolution. To them, "citizen" meant society-maker, not one "participating in" or "adjusted to" society. It is clear that they regarded themselves and their friends as citizens existentially, so to speak; to make society was their breath of life. But obviously such conceptions are worlds removed from, and diametrically opposed to, our present political reality, where the ground rules and often the score are predetermined.

For Jefferson, people had to be taught in order to multiply the sources of citizenly initiative and to be vigilant for freedom. Everybody had to become literate and study history, in order to make constitutional innovations and be fired to defend free institutions, which was presumably the moral that history taught. And those of good parts were to study a technological natural philosophy, in order to make inventions and produce useful goods for the new country. By contrast, what are the citizenly reasons for which we compel everybody to be literate, etc.? To

keep the economy expanding, to understand the mass communications, to choose between indistinguishable Democrats and
Republicans. Planning and decision-making are lodged in top
managers; rarely, and at most, the electorate serves as a pressure
group. There is a new emphasis on teaching science—we will discuss this in another context—but the vast majority will never use
this knowledge and will forget it; they are consumers.

Another great impulse for compulsory education came from
the new industrialism and urbanism during the three or four
decades after the Civil War, a time also of maximum immigration. Here the curricular demands were more mundane: in the
grades, literacy and arithmetic; in the colleges, professional skills
to man the expanding economy. But again, no one would have
spoken of an incompatibility between "individual development"
and "national needs," for it was considered to be an open society, abounding in opportunity. Typically, the novels of Horatio
Alger, Jr., treat schooling as morally excellent as well as essential
for getting ahead; and there is no doubt that the immigrants saw
education-for-success as also a human value for their children.
Further, the school system was not a trap. The 94 percent who
in 1900 did not finish high school had other life opportunities,
including making a lot of money and rising in politics. But again,
by and large this is not our present situation. There is plenty of
social mobility, opportunity to rise—except precisely for the
ethnic minorities who are our main concern as dropouts—but
the statuses and channels are increasingly stratified, rigidified,
cut and dried. Most enterprise is parceled out by feudal corporations, or by the State; and these determine the requirements.
Ambition with average talent meets these rules or fails; those
without relevant talent, or with unfortunate backgrounds, cannot even survive in decent poverty. The requirements of survival
are importantly academic, attainable only in schools and universities; but such schooling is ceasing to have an initiating or moral
meaning.

We do not have an open economy; even when jobs are not
scarce, the corporations and State dictate the possibilities of
enterprise. General Electric swoops down on the high schools,

or IBM on the colleges, and skims off the youth who have been pre-trained for them at public or private expense. (Private college tuition runs upward of $6,000, and this is estimated as a third or less of the actual cost for education and educational administration.) Even a department store requires a diploma for its salespeople, not so much because of the skills they have learned as that it guarantees the right character: punctual and with a smooth record. And more generally, since our powers-that-be have opted for an expanding economy with a galloping standard of living, and since the powers of the world are in an arms and space race, there is a national need for many graduates specifically trained. Thus, even for those selected, the purpose is irrelevant to citizenly initiative, the progress of an open society, or personal happiness, and the others have spent time and effort in order to be progressively weeded out. Some drop out.

It is said that our schools are geared to "middle-class values," but this is a false and misleading use of terms. The schools less and less represent *any* human values, but simply adjustment to a mechanical system.

Because of the increasing failure of the schools with the poor urban mass, there has developed a line of criticism—e.g., Oscar Lewis, Patricia Sexton, Frank Riessman, and even Edgar Friedenberg—asserting that there is a "culture of poverty" which the "middle-class" schools do not fit, but which has its own virtues of spontaneity, sociality, animality. The implication is that the "middle class," for all its virtues, is obsessional, prejudiced, and prudish.

Pedagogically, this insight is indispensable. A teacher must try to teach each child in terms of what he brings, his background, his habits, the language he understands. But if taken to be more than technical, it is a disastrous conception. The philosophic aim of education must be to get each one out of his isolated class and into the one humanity. Prudence and responsibility are not middle-class virtues but human virtues; and spontaneity and sexuality are not powers of the simple but of human health. One has the impression that our social-psychologists are looking not to a human community but to a future in which the obsessionals will take care of the impulsives!

In fact, some of the most important strengths that have historically belonged to the middle class are flouted by the schools: independence, initiative, scrupulous honesty, earnestness, utility, respect for thorough scholarship. Rather than bourgeois, our schools have become petty bourgeois, bureaucratic, timeserving, gradgrind-practical, timid and nouveau riche climbing. In the upper grades and colleges, they often exude a cynicism that belongs to rotten aristocrats.

Naturally, however, the youth of the poor and of the middle class respond differently to the petty bourgeois atmosphere. For many poor children, school is orderly and has food, compared to chaotic and hungry homes, and it might even be interesting compared to total deprivation of toys and books. Besides, the wish to improve a child's lot, which on the part of a middle-class parent might be frantic status-seeking and pressuring, on the part of a poor parent is a loving aspiration. There is here a gloomy irony. The school that for a poor Negro child might be a great joy and opportunity is likely to be dreadful; whereas the middle-class child might be better off *not* in the "good" suburban school he has.

Other poor youths herded into a situation that does not suit their disposition, for which they are unprepared by their background, and which does not interest them, simply develop a reactive stupidity very different from their behavior on the street or ball field. They fall behind, play truant, and as soon as possible drop out. If the school situation is immediately useless and damaging to them, their response must be said to be life-preservative. They thereby somewhat diminish their chances of a decent living, but we shall see that the usual propaganda—that schooling is a road to high salaries—is for most poor youths a lie; and the increase in security is arguably not worth the torture involved.

The reasonable social policy would be not to have these youths in school, certainly not in high school, but to educate them otherwise and provide opportunity for a decent future in some other way. How? I shall venture some suggestions later; in my opinion, the wise thing would be to have our conferences on *this* issue, and omit the idea of dropout altogether. But the brute fact is that our society isn't really interested; the concern for the dropouts is mainly because they are a nuisance and a threat and can't be socialized by the existing machinery.

Numerically far more important than these dropouts at sixteen, however, are the children who conform to schooling between the ages of six to sixteen or twenty, but who drop out internally and daydream, their days wasted, their liberty caged and scheduled. And there are many such in the middle class, from backgrounds with plenty of food and some books and art, where the youth is seduced by the prospect of money and status, but even more where he is terrified to jeopardize the only pattern of life he knows.

It is in the schools and from the mass media, rather than at home or from their friends, that the mass of our citizens in all classes learn that life is inevitably routine, depersonalized, venally graded; that it is best to toe the mark and shut up; that there is no place for spontaneity, open sexuality, free spirit. Trained in the schools, they go on to the same quality of jobs, culture, and politics. This *is* education, miseducation, socializing to the national norms and regimenting to the national "needs."

John Dewey used to hope, naïvely, that the schools could be a community somewhat better than society and serve as a lever for social change. In fact, our schools reflect our society closely, except that they *emphasize* many of its worst features, as well as having the characteristic defects of academic institutions of all times and places.

Let us examine realistically half a dozen aspects of the school that is dropped out *from*.

1. There is widespread anxiety about the children not learning to read, and hot and defensive argument about the methods of

teaching reading. Indeed, reading deficiency is an accumulating scholastic disadvantage that results in painful feeling of inferiority, truancy and dropout. Reading is crucial for school success—all subjects depend on it—and therefore for the status success that the diploma is about. Yet in all the anxiety and argument, there is no longer any mention of the freedom and human cultivation that literacy is supposed to stand for.

In my opinion, there is something phony here. For a change, let us look at this "reading" coldly and ask if it is really such a big deal except precisely in the school that is supposed to teach it and is sometimes failing to do so.

With the movies, TV and radio that the illiterate also share, there is certainly no lack of "communications." We cannot say that as humanities or science, the reading-matter of the great majority is in any way superior to the content of these other media. And in the present stage of technology and economy, it is probably *less* true than it was in the late nineteenth century—the time of the great push to universal literacy and arithmetic—that the mass teaching of reading is indispensable to operate the production and clerical system. It is rather our kind of urbanism, politics and buying and selling that require literacy. These are not excellent.

Perhaps in the present dispensation we should be as well off if it were socially acceptable for large numbers not to read. It would be harder to regiment people if they were not so well "informed"; as Norbert Wiener used to point out, every repetition of a cliché only increases the noise and *prevents* communication. With less literacy, there would be more folk culture. Much suffering of inferiority would be avoided if youngsters did not have to meet a perhaps unnecessary standard. Serious letters could only benefit if society were less swamped by trash, lies and bland verbiage. Most important of all, *more* people might become genuinely literate if it were understood that reading is not a matter of course but a *special useful art with a proper subject matter, imagination and truth*, rather than a means of communicating top-down decisions and advertising. (The advertising is a typical instance: when the purpose of advertising was to give information—"New shipment of salt fish arrived, very good, foot of Barclay Street"—it was useful to be able to read; when the point of advertising is to create a synthetic demand, it is better not to be able to read.)

2. Given their present motives, the schools are not competent to teach authentic literacy, reading as a means of liberation and cultivation. And I doubt that most of us who seriously read and write the English language ever learned it by the route of *Run, Spot, Run* to *Silas Marner*. Rather, having picked up the rudiments either in cultured homes or in the first two grades, we really learned to read by our own will and free exploration, following our bent, generally among books that are considered inappropriate by school librarians!

A great neurologist tells me that the puzzle is not how to teach reading, but why some children fail to learn to read. Given the amount of exposure that any urban child gets, any normal animal should spontaneously catch on to the code. What prevents? It is almost demonstrable that, for many children, it is precisely going to school that prevents—because of the schools' alien style, banning of spontaneous interest, extrinsic rewards and punishments. (In many underprivileged schools, the IQ steadily falls the longer they go to school.) Many of the backward readers might have had a better chance on the streets.

But let me say something, too, about the "successful" teaching of reading and writing in the schools. Consider, by contrast, the method employed by Sylvia Ashton-Warner in teaching little Maoris. She gets them to ask for their *own* words, the particular gut-word of fear, lust or despair that is obsessing the child that day; this is written for him on strong cardboard; he learns it instantaneously and never forgets it; and soon he has an exciting, if odd, vocabulary. From the beginning, writing is by demand, practical, magical; and of course it is simply an extension of speech—it is the best and strongest speech, as writing should be. What is read is what somebody is importantly trying to tell. Now what do our schools do? We use tricks of mechanical conditioning. These do positive damage to spontaneous speech, meant expression, earnest understanding. Inevitably, they create *in the majority* the wooden attitude toward "writing," as entirely different from speech, that college teachers later try to cope with in Freshman Composition. And reading inevitably becomes a manipulation of signs, e.g., for test-passing, that has no relation to experience.

(Until recently, the same discouragement by schoolteachers plagued children's musical and plastic expression, but there have been attempts to get back to spontaneity—largely, I think, because of the general revolution in modern art and musical theory. In teaching science, there is just now a strong movement to encourage imagination rather than conditioned "answers." In teaching foreign languages, the emphasis is now strongly on vital engagement and need to speak. Yet in teaching reading and writing, the direction has been the contrary; even progressive education has gone back to teaching spelling. These arts are regarded merely as "tools.")

3. The young rightly resist animal constraint. But, at least in New York where I have been a school-board visitor, most teachers—and the principals who supervise their classes—operate as if progressive education had not proved the case for noise and freedom of bodily motion. (Dewey stresses the salutary alternation of boisterousness and tranquility.) The seats are no longer bolted to the floor, but they still face front. Of course, the classes are too large to cope with without "discipline." Then make them smaller, or don't wonder if children escape out of the cage; either into truancy or baffled daydream. Here is a typical case: an architect replacing a Harlem school is forbidden by the board to spend money on soundproofing the classrooms, even though the principal has called it a necessity for the therapy of pent-up and resentful children. The resentment, pent-up hostility, is a major cause of reactive stupidity; yet there is usually an absolute ban on even expression of hostility, or even of normal anger and aggression.

Again, one has to be blind not to see that, from the onset of puberty, the dissidence from school is importantly sexual. Theoretically, the junior high school was introduced to fit this change of life; yet astoundingly, it is sexless. My own view, for what it's worth, is that sexuality is lovely, there cannot be too much of it, it is self-limiting if it is satisfactory, and satisfaction diminishes tension and clears the mind for attention and learning. Therefore, sexual expression should be approved in and out of season, also in school, and where necessary made the subject of instruction. But whether or not this view is correct, it certainly is more practical than the apparent attempt of the schools to operate as if sexual drives simply did not exist. When, on so crucial an issue, the schools act a hundred years out of date, they are crucially irrelevant.

But the following *is* something new:

Trenton, 24 May (AP)—A state health official believes some over-anxious New Jersey parents are dosing their children with tranquilizers before sending them to school . . . the Health Department pediatrician assigned to the State Education Department said the parents apparently are trying to protect the children from cracking under pressure for good grades.

4. Terrible damage is done to children simply by the size and standardization of the big system. Suppose a class size of twenty is good for average purposes, it does *not* follow that thirty-five is better than nothing. Rather, it is likely to be positively harmful, because the children have ceased to be persons and the teacher is destroyed as a teacher. A teacher with a ten-year-old class reading at seven-year level will have to use the content as well as the vocabulary of *Dick and Jane* since that is the textbook bought by the hundred thousands. The experience of a wise principal is that the most essential part of his job is to know every child's name and be an available "good father," so he wants a school for four hundred. Yet the city will build the school for two thousand, because only that is practical, even though the essence is entirely dissipated. The chief part of learning is in the community of scholars, where class work and social life may cohere; yet social engineers like Dr. Conant will, for putative efficiencies, centralize the high schools—the "enriched" curriculum with equipment is necessary for the national needs.

A program—e.g., to prevent dropout—will be, by an attentive teacher, exquisitely tailored to the children he works with; he will have a success. Therefore his program must be standardized, watered down, for seventy-five schools—otherwise it cannot be financed—although now it is worthless. But here is an unbearable anecdote: An architect is employed to replace a dilapidated school but is forbidden to consult the principal and teachers of the school about their needs, since his building must conform to uniform plans at headquarters, the plans being two generations out of date. As a functionalist, the architect demurs, and it requires an ad hoc assembly of all the superintendents to give him special permission.

Presumably all this is administratively necessary, but then it is also necessary for bruised children to quit. Our society makes a persistent error in metaphysics. We are so mesmerized by the operation of a system with the appropriate name, for instance "Education," that we assume that it *must* be working somewhat, though admittedly not perfectly, when perhaps it has ceased to fulfill its function altogether and might even be preventing the function, for instance education.

5. Especially today, when the hours of work will sharply diminish, the schools are supposed to educate for the satisfaction of life and for the worthwhile use of leisure. Again, let us try to be realistic, as a youngster is. For most people, I think, a candid self-examination will show that their most absorbing, long and satisfactory hours are spent in activities like friendly competitive sports, gambling, looking for love and love-making, earnest or argumentative conversation, political action with signs and sit-ins, solitary study and reading, contemplation of nature and cosmos, arts and crafts, music and religion. Now none of these requires much money. Indeed, elaborate equipment takes the heart out of them. Friends use one another as resources. God, nature and creativity are free. The media of the fine arts are cheap stuff. Health, luck and affection are the only requirements for good sex. Good food requires taking pains more than spending money.

What is the moral for our purposes? Can it be denied that in some respects the dropouts make a wiser choice than many who go to school, not to get real goods but to get money? Their choice of the "immediate"—their notorious "inability to tolerate delay"—is not altogether impulsive and neurotic. The bother is that in our present culture, which puts its entire emphasis on the consumption of expensive commodities, they are so nagged by inferiority, exclusion and despair of the future that they cannot employ their leisure with a good conscience. Because they know little, they are deprived of many profound simple satisfactions and they never know what to do with themselves. Being afraid of exposing themselves to awkwardness and ridicule, they just hang around. And our urban social arrangements—e.g., high rent—have made it impossible for anybody to be decently poor on a "low" standard. One is either in the rat race or has dropped out of society altogether.

6. As a loyal academic, I must make a further observation. Mainly to provide Ph.D.s, there is at present an overwhelming pressure to gear the "better" elementary schools to the graduate-universities. This is the great current reform, genre of Rickover. But what if the top of the ladder is corrupt and corrupts the lower grades? On visits to seventy colleges everywhere in the country, I have been appalled at how rarely the subjects are studied in a right academic spirit, for their truth and beauty and as part of humane international culture. The students are given, and seek, a narrow expertise, "mastery," aimed at licenses and salary. They are indoctrinated with a national thoughtlessness that is not even chauvinistic. Administrators sacrifice the community of scholars to aggrandizement and extramurally sponsored research.

Conversely, there is almost never conveyed the sense in which learning is truly practical, to enlighten experience, give courage to initiate and change, reform the state, deepen personal and social peace. On the contrary, the entire educational system itself creates professional cynicism or the resigned conviction that Nothing Can Be Done. If this is the university, how can we hope for aspiring scholarship in the elementary schools? On the con-

trary, everything will be grades and conforming, getting ahead
not in the subject of interest but up the ladder. Students "do"
Bronx Science in order to "make" MIT and they "do" MIT in
order to "make" Westinghouse; some of them have "done" Westinghouse in order to "make" jail.

What then? The compulsory system has become a universal trap,
and it is no good. Very many of the youth, both poor and middle
class, might be better off if the system simply did not exist, even
if they then had no formal schooling at all. (I am extremely curious for a philosophic study of Prince Edward County in Virginia,
where for some years schooling did not exist for Negro children.)

But what would become of these children? For very many,
both poor and middle class, their homes are worse than the
schools, and the city streets are worse in another way. Our urban
and suburban environments are precisely not cities or communities where adults naturally attend to the young and educate to a
viable life. Also, perhaps especially in the case of the overt dropouts, the state of their body and soul is such that we must give
them refuge and remedy, whether it be called school, settlement
house, youth worker or work camp.

There are thinkable alternatives. Throughout this little book,
as occasion arises, I shall offer alternative proposals that I as a
single individual have heard of or thought up. Here are half a
dozen directly relevant to the subject we have been discussing,
the system as compulsory trap. In principle, when a law begins to
do more harm than good, the best policy is to alleviate it or try
doing without it.

1. Have "no school at all" for a few classes. These children should
be selected from tolerable, though not necessarily cultured,
homes. They should be neighbors and numerous enough to be
a society for one another so that they do not feel merely "different." Will they learn the rudiments anyway? This experiment
cannot do the children any academic harm, since there is good

evidence that normal children will make up the first seven years' schoolwork with four to seven months of good teaching.

2. Dispense with the school building for a few classes; provide teachers and use the city itself as the school—its streets, cafeterias, stores, movies, museums, parks and factories. Where feasible, it certainly makes more sense to teach using the real subject matter than to bring an abstraction of the subject matter into the school building as "curriculum." Such a class should probably not exceed ten children for one pedagogue. The idea—it is the model of Athenian education—is not dissimilar to youth-gang work, but not applied to delinquents and not playing to the gang ideology.

3. Along the same lines, but both outside and inside the school building, use appropriate *unlicensed* adults of the community— the druggist, the storekeeper, and the mechanic—as the proper educators of the young into the grown-up world. By this means we can try to overcome the separation of the young from the grown-up world so characteristic in modern urban life, and to diminish the omnivorous authority of the professional school-people. Certainly it would be a useful and animating experience for the adults. (There is the beginning of such a volunteer program in the New York and some other systems.)

4. Make class attendance not compulsory, in the manner of A. S. Neill's Summerhill. If the teachers are good, absence would tend to be eliminated; if they are bad, let them know it. The compulsory law is useful to get the children away from the parents, but it must not result in trapping the children. A fine modification of this suggestion is the rule used by Frank Brown in Florida: he permits the children to be absent for a week or a month to engage in any worthwhile enterprise or visit any new environment.

---

5. Decentralize an urban school (or do not build a new big building) into small units, twenty to fifty, in available storefronts or clubhouses. These tiny schools, equipped with record player and pinball machine, could combine play, serializing, discussion and formal teaching. For special events, the small units can be brought together into a common auditorium or gymnasium, so as to give the sense of the greater community. Correspondingly, I think it would be worthwhile to give the Little Red Schoolhouse a spin under modern urban conditions, and see how it works out: that is, to combine all the ages in a little room for twenty-five to thirty, rather than to grade by age.

6. Use a pro rata part of the school money to send children to economically marginal farms for a couple of months of the year, perhaps six children from mixed backgrounds to a farmer. The only requirement is that the farmer feed them and not beat them; best, of course, if they take part in the farm work. This will give the farmer cash, as part of the generally desirable program to redress the urban-rural ratio to something nearer to 70 percent to 30 percent. (At present, less than 8 percent of families are rural.) Conceivably, some of the urban children will take to the other way of life, and we might generate a new kind of rural culture.

I frequently suggest these and similar proposals at teachers' colleges, and I am looked at with an eerie look—do I really mean to *diminish* the state-aid grant for each student-day? But mostly the objective is that such proposals entail intolerable administrative difficulties.

Above all, we must apply these or any other proposals to particular individuals and small groups, without the obligation of uniformity. There is a case for uniform standards of achievement, lodged in the Regents, but they *cannot* be reached by uniform techniques. The claim that standardization of procedure is more efficient, less costly, or alone administratively practical, is often false. Particular inventiveness requires thought, but thought does not cost money.

*Tom Wolfe (1930–2018), before settling down into novel-writing, was one of the main proponents and stars of the New Journalism, which incorporated fictional techniques of scene and subjective voice into reportage. His sharp-edged dives into pop culture, drug culture, modern architecture, and radical politics showed a willingness to take on whatever fashions the zeitgeist had to offer, in books whose titles alone suggested his playful, satirically pop outlook (*The Kandy-Kolored Tangerine-Flake Streamline Baby, The Electric Kool-Aid Acid Test, Radical Chic and Mau-Mauing the Flak Catchers*). A virtuoso prose stylist, irresistibly readable, he so neared his subjects' consciousness that the line between embracing and eviscerating them tended to blur. In the essay below, he profiled a lionized example of someone "famous for being famous."*

THE GIRL OF THE YEAR

Bangs manes bouffants beehives Beatle caps butter faces brush-on lashes decal eyes puffy sweaters French thrust bras flailing leather blue jeans stretch pants stretch jeans honeydew bottoms eclair shanks elf boots ballerinas Knight slippers, hundreds of them, these flaming little buds, bobbing and screaming, rocketing around inside the Academy of Music Theater underneath that vast old moldering cherub dome up there—aren't they super-marvelous!

"Aren't they super-marvelous!" says Baby Jane, and then: "Hi, Isabel! Isabel! You want to sit backstage—with the Stones!"

The show hasn't even started yet, the Rolling Stones aren't

even on the stage, the place is full of a great shabby moldering dimness, and these flaming little buds.

Girls are reeling this way and that way in the aisle and through their huge black decal eyes, sagging with Tiger Tongue Lick Me brush-on eyelashes and black appliqués, sagging like display window Christmas trees, they keep staring at—her—Baby Jane—on the aisle. What the hell is this? She is gorgeous in the most outrageous way. Her hair rises up from her head in a huge hairy corona, a huge tan mane around a narrow face and two eyes opened—swock!—like umbrellas, with all that hair flowing down over a coat made of . . . zebra! Those motherless stripes! Oh, damn! Here she is with her friends, looking like some kind of queen bee for all flaming little buds everywhere. She twists around to shout to one of her friends and that incredible mane swings around on her shoulders, over the zebra coat.

"Isabel!" says Baby Jane, "Isabel, hi! I just saw the Stones! They look super-divine!"

That girl on the aisle, Baby Jane, is a fabulous girl. She comprehends what the Rolling Stones *mean*. Any columnist in New York could tell them who she is . . . a celebrity of New York's new era of Wog Hip . . . Baby Jane Holzer. Jane Holzer in *Vogue*, Jane Holzer in *Life*, Jane Holzer in Andy Warhol's underground movies, Jane Holzer in the world of High Camp, Jane Holzer at the rock and roll, Jane Holzer is—well, how can one put it into words? Jane Holzer is This Year's Girl, at least, the New Celebrity, none of your old idea of sexpots, prima donnas, romantic tragediennes, she is the girl who knows . . . The Stones, East End vitality . . .

"Isabel!" says Jane Holzer in the small, high, excited voice of hers, her Baby Jane voice. "Hi, Isabel! Hi!"

Down the row, Isabel, Isabel Eberstadt, the beautiful socialite who is Ogden Nash's daughter, has just come in. She doesn't seem to hear Jane. But she is down the row a ways. Next to Jane is some fellow in a chocolate-colored Borsalino hat, and next there is Andy Warhol, the famous pop artist.

"Isabel!" says Jane.

"What?" says Isabel.

"Hi, Isabel!" says Jane.

"Hello, Jane," says Isabel.

"You want to go backstage?" says Jane, who has to speak across everybody.

"Backstage?" says Isabel.

"With the Stones!" says Jane. "I was backstage with the Stones. They look di*vine*! You know what Mick said to me? He said, 'Koom on, love, give us a kiss!'"

But Isabel has turned away to say something to somebody.

"Isabel!" says Jane.

And all around, the little buds are batting around in the rococo gloom of the Academy of Arts Theater, trying to crash into good seats or just sit in the aisle near the stage, shrieking. And in the rear the Voice of Fifteen-year-old America cries out in a post-pubertal contralto, apropos of nothing, into the moldering void: "Yaaaagh! Yuh dirty fag!"

Well, so what; Jane laughs. Then she leans over and says to the fellow in the Borsalino hat:

"Wait'll you see the Stones! They're so sexy! They're pure sex. They're di*vine*! The Beatles, well, you know, Paul McCartney—*sweet* Paul McCartney. You know what I mean. He's such a *sweet person*. I mean, the Stones are *bitter*"—the words seem to spring from her lungs like some kind of wonderful lavender-yellow Charles Kingsley bubbles—"they're all from the working class, you know? the East End. Mick Jagger—well, it's all Mick. You know what they say about his lips? They say his lips are *diabolical*. That was in one of the magazines.

"When Mick comes into the Ad Lib in London—I mean, there's nothing like the Ad Lib in New York. You can go into the Ad Lib and everybody is there. They're all young, and they're taking over, it's like a whole revolution. I mean, it's *exciting*, they're all from the lower classes, East-End-sort-of-thing. There's nobody exciting from the upper classes anymore, except for Nicole and Alec Londonderry, Alec is a British marquis, the Marquis of Londonderry, and, OK, Nicole has to put in an appearance at this country fair or something, well, OK, she does it, but that doesn't mean—you know what I mean? Alec is so—you should see the way he walks, I could just watch him walk—*Undoes-one-ship!* They're *young*. They're all young, it's a whole new thing. It's not

the Beatles. Bailey says the Beatles are *passé*, because now everybody's mum pats the Beatles on the head. The Beatles are getting
fat. The Beatles—well, John Lennon's still thin, but Paul McCartney is getting a big bottom. That's all right, but I don't particularly care for that. The Stones are thin. I mean, that's why they're
beautiful, they're so thin. Mick Jagger—wait'll you see Mick."

Then the show begins. An electronic blast begins, electric guitars, electric bass, enormous speakers up there on a vast yellow-
gray stage. Murray the K, the DJ and MC, OK?, comes out from
the wings, doing a kind of twist soft shoe, wiggling around, a
stocky chap, thirty-eight years old, wearing Italian pants and a
Sun Valley snow lodge sweater and a Stingy Brim straw hat. Murray the K! Girls throw balls of paper at him, and as they arc onto
the stage, the stage lights explode off them and they look like
falling balls of flame.

And, finally, the Stones, now—how can one express it? the
Stones come onstage—

"Oh, God, Andy, aren't they di*vine*!"

—and spread out over the stage, the five Rolling Stones, from
England, who are modeled after the Beatles, only more lower-
class-deformed. One, Brian Jones, has an enormous blond Beatle
bouffant.

"Oh, Andy, look at Mick! Isn't he *beauti*ful! Mick! Mick!"

In the center of the stage a short thin boy with a sweatshirt on,
the neck of the sweatshirt almost falling over his shoulders, they
are so narrow, all surmounted by this . . . enormous head . . . with
the hair puffing down over the forehead and ears, this boy has
exceptional lips. He has two peculiarly gross and extraordinary
red lips. They hang off his face like giblets. Slowly his eyes pour
over the flaming bud horde soft as Karo syrup and then close and
then the lips start spreading into the most languid, most confi-
dential, the wettest, most labial, most concupiscent grin imagin-
able. Nirvana! The buds start shrieking, pawing toward the stage.

The girls have Their Experience. They stand up on their seats.
They begin to ululate, even between songs. The looks on their
faces! Rapturous agony! There, right up there, under the sulfur
lights, that is *them*. God, they're right there! Mick Jagger takes
the microphone with his tabescent hands and puts his huge head

against it, opens his giblet lips and begins to sing . . . with the voice of a bull Negro. Bo Diddley. You movung boo meb bee-uh-tul, bah-bee, oh vona breemb you' honey snurks oh crim pulzy yo' mim down, and, camping again, then turning toward the shrieking girls with his wet giblet lips dissolving . . .

And, occasionally, breaking through the ululation:

"Get off the stage, you finks!"

"Maybe we ought to scream," says Jane. Then she says to the fellow in the hat: "Tell me when it's five o'clock, will you, pussy-cat? I have to get dressed and go see Sam Spiegel." And then Baby Jane goes: "Eeeeeeeeeeeeeeeeeeeeee

Eeeeeeeeeeeeeeeeeyes!" says Diana Vreeland, the editor of *Vogue*. "Jane Holzer is the most contemporary girl I know."

Jane Holzer at the rock and roll—

Jane Holzer in the underground movies—in Andy's studio, Andy Warhol, the famous Pop artist, experiencing the rare world of Jonas and Adolph Mekas, truth and culture in a new holy medium, underground movie-making on the Lower East Side. And Jane is wearing a Jax shirt, strung like a Christmas tree with Diamonds, and they are making *Dracula*, or *Thirteen Beautiful Women* or *Soap Opera* or *Kiss*—in which Jane's lips . . . but how can one describe an underground movie? It is . . . avant-garde. "Andy calls everything super," says Jane. "I'm a super star, he's a super-director, we make super epics—and I mean, it's a completely new and natural way of acting. You can't imagine what really beautiful things can happen!"

Jane Holzer—with The New Artists, photographers like Jerry Schatzberg, David Bailey and Brian Duffy, and Nicky Haslam, the art director of *Show*. Bailey, Duffy and Haslam are English. Schatzberg says the photographers are the modern-day equivalents of the Impressionists in Paris around 1910, the men with a sense of New Art, the excitement of the salon, the excitement of the artistic style of life, while all the painters, the old artists, have moved uptown to West End Avenue and live in apartment buildings with Kwik-Fiks parquet floors and run around the corner to get a new cover for the ironing board before the stores close.

Jane in the world of High Camp—a world of thin young men in an environment, a decor, an atmosphere so—how can one say it?—so indefinably Yellow Book. Jane in the world of Teen Savage—Jane modeling here and there—wearing Jean Harlow dresses for *Life* and Italian fashions for *Vogue* and doing the most fabulous cover for Nicky at *Show*, David took the photograph, showing Jane barebacked wearing a little yacht cap and a pair of "World's Fair" sunglasses and holding an American flag in her teeth, so—so Beyond Pop Art, if you comprehend.

Jane Holzer at the LBJ Discotheque—where they were handing out aprons with a target design on them, and Jane Holzer put it on backward so that the target was behind and *then* did The Swim, a new dance.

Jane Holzer—well, there is no easy term available, Baby Jane has appeared constantly this year in just about every society and show business column in New York. The magazines have used her as a kind of combination of model, celebrity and socialite. And yet none of them have been able to do much more than, in effect, set down her name, Baby Jane Holzer, and surround it with a few asterisks and exploding stars, as if to say, well, here we have . . . What's Happening.

She is a socialite in the sense that she lives in a twelve-room apartment on Park Avenue with a wealthy husband, Leonard Holzer, heir to a real estate fortune, amid a lot of old Dutch and Flemish paintings, and she goes to a great many exciting parties. And yet she is not in Society the way the Good Book, the *Social Register*, thinks of Society, and the list of hostesses who have not thought of inviting Jane Holzer would be impressive. Furthermore, her stance is that she doesn't care, and she would rather be known as a friend of the Stones, anyway—and here she is at the April in Paris Ball, $150 per ticket, amid the heaving white and gold swag of the Astor Hotel ballroom, yelling to somebody: "If you aren't nice to me, I'll tell everybody you were here!"

Jane Holzer—the sum of it is glamor, of a sort very specific to New York. With her enormous corona of hair and her long straight nose, Jane Holzer can be quite beautiful, but she never comes on as A Beauty. "Some people look at my pictures and say I look very mature and sophisticated," Jane says. "Some people say I look like a child, you know, Baby Jane. And, I mean, I don't know what I look like, I guess it's just 1964 Jewish." She does not attempt to come on sexy. Her excitement is something else. It is almost pure excitement. It is the excitement of the New Style, the New Chic. The press watches Jane Holzer as if she were an exquisite piece of . . . radar. It is as if that entire ciliate corona of hers were spread out as an antenna for new waves of style. To the magazine editors, the newspaper columnists, the photographers and art directors, suddenly here is a single flamboyant girl who sums up everything new and chic in the way of fashion in the Girl of the Year.

How can one explain the Girl of the Year? The Girl of the Year is a symbolic figure the press has looked for annually in New York since World War I because of the breakdown of conventional High Society. The old establishment still holds forth, it still has its clubs, cotillions and coming-out balls, it is still basically Protestant and it still rules two enormously powerful areas of New York, finance and corporate law. But alongside it, all the while, there has existed a large and ever more dazzling society, Café Society it was called in the twenties and thirties, made up of people whose status rests not on property and ancestry but on various brilliant ephemera, show business, advertising, public relations, the arts, journalism or simply new money of various sorts, people with a great deal of ambition who have congregated in New York to satisfy it and who look for styles to symbolize it.

The establishment's own styles—well, for one thing they were too dull. And those understated clothes, dark woods, high ceilings, silver-smithery, respectable nannies, and so forth and so on. For centuries their kind of power created styles—Palladian buildings, starched cravats—but with the thickening democratic facade of American life, it has degenerated to various esoteric understatements, often cryptic—Topsiders instead of tennis sneakers, calling cards with "Mr." preceding the name, the right fork.

The magazines and newspapers began looking for heroines to symbolize the Other Society, Café Society, or whatever it should be called. At first, in the twenties, they chose the more flamboyant debutantes, girls with social credentials who also moved in Café Society. But the Other Society's styles began to shift and change at a madder and madder rate, and the Flaming Deb idea no longer worked. The last of the Flaming Debs, the kind of Deb who made The Cover of *Life*, was Brenda Frazier, and Brenda Frazier and Brenda Frazierism went out with the thirties. More recently the Girl of the Year has had to be more and more exotic . . . and extraordinary. Christina Paolozzi! Her exploits! Christina Paolozzi threw a twenty-first-birthday party for herself at a Puerto Rican pachanga palace, the Palladium, and after that the spinning got faster and faster until with one last grand centripetal gesture she appeared in the nude, face on, in *Harper's Bazaar*. Some became Girls of the Year because their fame suddenly shed a light on their style of life, and their style of life could be easily exhibited, such as Jackie Kennedy and Barbra Streisand.

But Baby Jane Holzer is a purer manifestation. Her style of life has created her fame—rock and roll, underground movies, decaying lofts, models, photographers, Living Pop Art, the twist, the frug, the mashed potatoes, stretch pants, pre-Raphaelite hair, Le Style Camp. All of it has a common denominator. Once it was power that created high style. But now high styles come from low places, from people who have no power, who slink away from it, in fact, who are marginal, who carve out worlds for themselves in the nether depths, in tainted "undergrounds." The Rolling Stones, like rock and roll itself and the twist—they come out of the netherworld of modern teenage life, out of what was for years the marginal outcast corner of the world of art, photography, populated by poor boys, pretenders. "Underground" movies— a mixture of camp and Artistic Alienation, with Jonas Mekas crying out like some foggy echo from Harold Stearns's last boat for Le Havre in 1921: "You filthy bourgeois pseudo-culturati! You say you love art—then why don't you give us money to buy the film to make our masterpieces and stop blubbering about the naked asses we show?—you mucky pseuds." Teenagers, bohos, camp culturati, photographers—they have won by default, because, after all, they *do* create styles. And now the Other Society goes to them for styles, like the decadenti of another age going down to the wharves in Rio to find those raw-vital devils, damn their potent hides, those proles, doing the tango. Yes! Oh my God, those raw-vital proles!

The ice floe is breaking, and can't one see, as Jane Holzer sees, that all these people—well, they *feel*, they are alive, and what does it mean simply to be sitting up in her Park Avenue apartment in the room with the two Rubenses on the wall, worth half a million dollars, if they are firmly authenticated? It means almost nothing. One doesn't feel it.

Jane has on a "Poor" sweater, clinging to the ribs, a new fashion, with short sleeves. Her hair is up in rollers. She is wearing tight slacks. Her hips are very small. She has a boyish body. She has thin arms and long, long fingers. She sits twisted about on a couch, up in her apartment on Park Avenue, talking on the telephone.

"Oh, I know what you mean," she says, "but, I mean, couldn't you wait just two weeks? I'm expecting something to jell, it's a movie, and then you'd have a real story. You know what I mean? I mean you would have something to write about and not just Baby Jane, sitting up in her Park Avenue apartment with her gotrocks. You know what I mean? . . . well, all right, but I think you'll have more of a story— . . . well, all right . . . bye, pussycat."

Then she hangs up and swings around and says, "That makes me mad. That was ———. He wants to do a story about me and do you know what he told me? 'We want to do a story about you,' he told me, 'because you're very big this year.' Do you know what that made me feel like? That made me feel like, All right, Baby Jane, we'll let you play this year, so get out there and dance, but next year, well, it's all over for you next year, Baby Jane. I mean,—! You know? I mean, I felt like telling him, 'Well, pussycat, you're the Editor of the Minute, and you know what? Your minute's up.'"

The thought leaves Jane looking excited but worried. Usually she looks excited about things but open, happy, her eyes wide open and taking it all in. Now she looks worried, as if the world could be such a simple and exhilarating place if there weren't so many old and arteriosclerotic people around to muck it up. There are two dogs on the floor at her feet, a toy poodle and a Yorkshire terrier, who rise up from time to time in some kind of secret needle-toothed fury, barking coloratura.

"Oh,———," says Jane, and then, "You know, if you have any-

thing at all, there are so many bitchy people just *waiting* to carve
you up. I mean, I went to the opening of the Met and I wore a
white mink coat, and do you know what a woman did? A woman
called up a columnist and said, 'Ha, ha, Baby Jane rented that
coat she went to the Met in. Baby Jane rents her clothes.' That's
how bitchy they are. Well, that coat happens to be a coat my
mother gave me two years ago when I was married. I mean, I
don't care if somebody thinks I rent clothes. OK——! Who
cares?"

Inez, the maid, brings in lunch on a tray, one rare hamburger,
one cheeseburger and a glass of tomato juice. Jane tastes the
tomato juice.

"Oh,——!" she says. "It's diet."

The Girl of the Year. It is as though nobody wants to give anyone credit for anything. They're only a *phenomenon*. Well, Jane
Holzer did a great deal of modeling before she got married and
still models, for that matter, and now some very wonderful things
may be about to happen in the movies. Some of it, well, she cannot go into it exactly, because it is at that precarious stage—you
know? But she has one of the best managers, a woman who manages the McGuire Sisters. And there has been talk about Baby
Jane for *Who's Afraid of Virginia Woolf* the movie, and Candy—

"Well, I haven't heard anything about it—but I'd *love* to play
Candy."

And this afternoon, later on, she is going over to see Sam Spiegel, the producer.

"He's wonderful. He's, you know, sort of advising me on
things at this point."

And somewhere out there in the apartment the dogs are loose
in a midget coloratura rage amid patina-green walls and paintings by old Lowland masters. There is a great atmosphere in the
apartment, an atmosphere of patina-green, faded plush and the
ashy light of Park Avenue reflecting on the great black and umber
slicks of the paintings. All that stretches on for twelve rooms.
The apartment belongs to the Holzers, who have built a lot of
New York's new apartment houses. Jane's husband, Leonard,
is a slim, good-looking young man. He went to Princeton. He
and Jane were married two years ago. Jane came from Florida,

where her father, Carl Brukenfeld, also made a lot of money in real estate. But in a way they were from New York, too, because they were always coming to New York and her father had a place here. There was something so stimulating, so flamboyant, about New York, you know? Fine men with anointed blue jowls combed their hair straight back and had their shirts made at Sulka's or Nica-Rattner's, and their wives had copper-gold hair, real chignons and things, and heavy apricot voices that said the funniest things—"Honey, I've got news for you, you're crazy!"—things like that, and they went to El Morocco. Jane went to Cherry Lawn School in Darien, Connecticut. It was a progressive school.

And then she went to Finch Junior College:

"Oh, that was just ghastly. I wanted to flunk out and go to work. If you miss too many classes, they campus you, if you have a messy room, they campus you, they were always campusing me, and I always sneaked out. The last spring term I didn't spend one night there. I was supposed to be campused and I'd be out dancing at El Morocco. I didn't take my exams because I wanted to flunk out, but do you know what they did? They just said I was out, period. I didn't care about that, because I wanted to flunk out and go to work anyway—but the way they did it. I have a lot of good paintings to give away, and it's too bad, they're not getting any. They were not *educators*. They could have at least kept the door open. They could have said, 'You're not ready to be a serious student, but when you decide to settle down and be a serious student, the door will be open.' I mean, I had already paid for the whole term, they *had* the money. I always wanted to go there and tell them, well, ha ha, too bad, you're not getting any of the paintings. So henceforth, Princeton, which was super-marvelous, will get all the paintings."

Jane's spirits pick up over that. Princeton! Well, Jane left Finch and then she did quite a bit of modeling. Then she married Lennie, and she still did some modeling, but the real break—well, the whole *thing* started in summer in London, the summer of 1963.

"Bailey is fantastic," says Jane. "Bailey created four girls that summer. He created Jean Shrimpton, he created me, he created Angela Howard and Susan Murray. There's no photographer like that in America. Avedon hasn't done that for a girl, Penn hasn't, and Bailey created four girls in one summer. He did some pictures of me for the English *Vogue*, and that was all it took."

But how does one really explain about the Stones, about Bailey, Shrimp and Mick—well, it's not so much what they *do*, that's such an old idea, what people *do*—it's what they *are*, it's a revolution, and it's the kids from the East End, Cockneys, if you want, who are making it.

"I mean today Drexel Duke sits next to Weinstein, and why shouldn't he? They both made their money the same way, you know? The furniture king sits next to the catsup king, and why shouldn't he-sort-of-thing. I mean, that's the way it was at the opening of the Met. A friend of mine was going to write an article about it.

"I mean, we don't lie to ourselves. Our mothers taught us to be pure and you'll fall in love and get married and stay in love with one man all your life. OK. But we know it doesn't happen that way and we don't lie to ourselves about it. Maybe you won't ever find anybody you love. Or maybe you find somebody you love four minutes, maybe ten minutes. But I mean, why lie to yourself? We know we're not going to love one man all our lives. Maybe it's the Bomb—we know it could all be over tomorrow, so why try to fool yourself today. Shrimp was talking about that last night. She's here now, she'll be at the party tonight—"

The two dogs, the toy poodle and the Yorkshire terrier, are yapping, in the patina-green. Inez is looking for something besides diet. The two Rubenses hang up on the walls. A couple of horns come up through the ashy light of Park Avenue. The high wind of East End London is in the air—whhhooooooooo

ooooooooooooosh! Baby Jane blows out all the candles. It is her twenty-fourth birthday. She and everybody, Shrimp, Nicky, Jerry, everybody but Bailey, who is off in Egypt or something, they are all up in Jerry Schatzberg's . . . *pad* . . . his lavish apartment at 333 Park Avenue South, up above his studio. There is a skylight. The cook brings out the cake and Jane blows out the candles. Twenty-four! Jerry and Nicky are giving a huge party, a dance, in honor of the Stones, and already the people are coming into the studio downstairs. But it is also Jane's birthday. She is wearing a black velvet jumpsuit by Luis Estevez, the designer. It has huge bell-bottom pants. She puts her legs together . . . it looks like an evening dress. But she can also spread them apart, like so, and strike very Jane-like poses. This is like the Upper Room or something. Downstairs, they're all coming in for the party, all those people one sees at parties, everybody who goes to the parties in New York, but up here it is like a tableau, like a tableau of . . . Us. Shrimp is sitting there with her glorious pout and her textured white stockings, Barbara Steele, who was so terrific in *8½*, with thin black lips and wrought-iron eyelashes. Nicky Haslam is there with his Byron shirt on and his tiger skin vest and blue jeans and boots. Jerry is there with his hair flowing back in curls. Lennie, Jane's husband, is there in a British suit and a dark blue shirt he bought on Forty-Second Street for this party, because this is a party for the Rolling Stones. The Stones are not here yet, but here in the upper room are Goldie and the Gingerbreads, four girls in gold lamé tights who will play the rock and roll for the party. Nicky discovered them at the Wagon Wheel. Gold lamé, can you imagine? Goldie, the leader, is a young girl with a husky voice and nice kind of slightly thick—you know—glorious sort of *East End* features, only she is from New York—ah, the delicacy of minor grossness, unabashed. The Stones' music is playing over the hi-fi.

Finally the Stones come in, in blue jeans, sweatshirts, the usual, and people get up and Mick Jagger comes in with his mouth open and his eyes down, faintly weary with success, and everybody goes downstairs to the studio, where people are now piling in, hundreds of them. Goldie and the Gingerbreads are on a stand at one end of the studio, all electric, electric guitars, electric bass, drums, loudspeakers, and a couple of spotlights exploding off the gold lamé. *Baby baby baby where did our love go.* The music suddenly fills up the room like a giant egg slicer. Sally Kirkland, Jr., a young actress, is out on the studio floor in a leopard print dress with her vast mane flying, doing the frug with Jerry Schatzberg. And then the other Girl of the Year, Caterine Milinaire, is out there in a black dress, and then Baby Jane is out

there with her incredible mane and her Luis Estevez jumpsuit,
frugging, and then everybody is out there. Suddenly it is very
odd. Suddenly everybody is out there in the gloaming, bobbing
up and down with the music plugged into *Baby baby baby*. The
whole floor of the studio begins to bounce up and down, like
a trampoline, the whole floor, some people are afraid and edge
off to the side, but most keep bobbing in the gloaming, and—
pow!—glasses begin to hit the floor, but every one keeps bouncing up and down, crushing the glass underfoot, while the brown
whiskey slicks around. So many heads bobbing, so many bodies
jiggling, so many giblets jiggling, so much anointed flesh shaking
and jiggling this way and that, so many faces one wanted so desperately to see, and here they are, red the color of dried peppers
in the gloaming, bouncing up and down with just a few fights,
wrenching in the gloaming, until five a.m.—gleeeang—Goldie
pulls all the electric cords out and the studio is suddenly just a
dim ochre studio with broken glass all over the floor, crushed
underfoot, and the sweet high smell of brown whiskey rising
from the floor.

Monday's papers will record it as the Mods and Rockers Ball,
as the Party of the Year, but that is Monday, a long way off. So
they all decide they should go to the Brasserie. It is the only place
in town where anybody would still be around. So they all get into
cabs and go up to the Brasserie, up on Fifty-Third Street between
Park and Lexington. The Brasserie is the right place, all right.
The Brasserie has a great entrance, elevated over the tables like a
fashion show almost. There are, what?, thirty-five people in the
Brasserie. They all look up, and as the first salmon light of dawn
comes through the front window, here come . . . four teenage girls
in gold lamé tights, and a chap in a tiger skin vest and blue jeans
and a gentleman in an English suit who seems to be wearing a
Forty-Second Street hood shirt and a fellow in a sweater who has
flowing curly hair . . . and then, a girl with an incredible mane,
a vast tawny corona, wearing a black velvet jumpsuit. One never
knows who is in the Brasserie at this hour—but are there any
so dead in here that they do not get the point? Girl of the Year?
Listen, they will never forget.

Edwin Denby (1903–1983) is considered the dean of American dance criticism. A poet associated through friendship with the New York School (John Ashbery, Frank O'Hara, Kenneth Koch), he brought a nuanced, precise, tender feeling for language to his critical explications of a nonverbal art form, no easy feat (see his collections Looking at the Dance *and* Dancers, Buildings and People in the Streets*). Writing in an era when choreographers such as George Balanchine, Merce Cunningham, Paul Taylor, and Yvonne Rainer were drawing inspiration from everyday movements, Denby similarly demystified the arcana of dance by linking it to the urban environment and daily life, as in this essay, which began as a talk.*

DANCERS, BUILDINGS AND PEOPLE IN THE STREETS

On the subject of dance criticism, I should like to make clear a distinction that I believe is very valuable, to keep the question from getting confused. And that is that there are two quite different aspects to it. One part of dance criticism is seeing what is happening onstage. The other is describing clearly what it is you saw. Seeing something happen is always fun for everybody, until they get exhausted. It is very exhausting to keep looking, of course, just as it is to keep doing anything else; and from an instinct of self-preservation many people look only a little. One can get along in life perfectly well without looking much. You all know how very little one is likely to see happening on the street—a familiar street at a familiar time of day while one is using the street to get somewhere. So much is happening inside one, one's private excitements and responsibilities, one can't find the energy to watch the strangers passing by, or the architecture or the weather around; one feels there is a use in getting to the place one is headed for and doing something or other there, getting a book or succeeding in a job or discussing a situation with a friend, all that has a use, but what use is there in looking at the momentary look of the street, of 106th and Broadway. No use at all. Looking at a dance performance has some use, presumably. And certainly it is a great deal less exhausting than looking at the disjointed fragments of impression that one can see in traffic. Not only that the performance is arranged so that it is convenient to look at, easy to pay continuous attention to, and attractive, but also that the excitement in it seems to have points of contact with the excitement of one's own personal life, with the curiosity that makes one want to go get a special book, or the exciting self-importance that makes one want to succeed, or even the absorbing drama of talking and listening to someone of one's own age with whom one is on the verge of being in love. When you feel that the emotion that is coming toward you from the performance is like a part of your own at some moment when you were very excited, it is easy to be interested. And of course if you feel the audience thrilled all around you just when you are thrilled too, that is very peculiar and agreeable. Instead of those people and houses on the street that are only vaguely related to you in the sense that they are Americans and contemporary, here in the theater, you are almost like in some imaginary family, where everybody is talking about something that concerns you intimately and everybody is interested and to a certain extent understands your own viewpoint and the irrational convictions you have that are even more urgent than your viewpoint. The amplitude that you feel you see with at your most intelligent moments, this amplitude seems in the theater to be naturally understood onstage and in the audience, in a way it isn't often appreciated while you are with the people you know outside the theater. At a show you can tell perfectly well when it is happening to you, this experience of an enlarged view of what is really so and true, or when it isn't happening to you. When you talk to your friends about it after the curtain goes down, they sometimes agree, and sometimes they don't. And it is strange how whether they do or don't, it is very hard usually to specify what the excitement was about, or the precise point at which it gave you the feeling of being really beautiful. Brilliant, magnificent, stupendous, no doubt all these things are true of the performance, but even if you and your friends agree that it was all those things, it is likely that there was some particular moment that made a special impression which you are not talking about. Maybe you are afraid that that particular moment wasn't really the most important, that it didn't express the idea or that it didn't get special applause or wasn't the climax. You were really excited by the performance and now you are afraid you can't show you understand it. Meanwhile while you hesitate to talk about it, a friend in the crowd who talks more readily is delivering a brilliant criticism specifying technical dance details, moral implications, musicological or iconographic finesses; or else maybe he is sailing off into a wild nonsensical camp that has nothing to do with the piece but which is fun to listen to, even though it's a familiar trick of his. So the evening slips out of your awareness like many others. Did you really see anything? Did you see any more than you saw in the morning on the street? Was it a real excitement you felt? What is left over of the wonderful moment you had, or didn't you really have any wonderful moment at all, where you actually saw onstage a real person moving and you felt the relation to your real private life with a sudden poignancy as if for that second you were drunk. Dance criticism has two different aspects: one is being made drunk for a second by seeing something happen; the other is expressing lucidly what you saw when you were drunk. I suppose I should add quite stuffily that it is the performance you should get drunk on, not anything else. But I am sure you have understood me anyway.

Now the second part of criticism, that of expressing lucidly what happened, is of course what makes criticism criticism. If you are going in for criticism you must have the gift in the first place, and in the second place you must cultivate it, you must practice and try. Writing criticism is a subject of interest to those who do it, but it is a separate process from that of seeing what happens. And seeing what happens is of course of much more general interest. This is what you presumably have a gift for, since you have chosen dancing as a subject of special study, and no doubt you have already cultivated this gift. I am sure you would all of you have something interesting and personal to say about what one can see and perhaps too about what one can't see.

Seeing is at any rate the subject I would like to talk about today, I can well imagine that for some of you this is not a subject of prime interest. Some of you are much more occupied with creating or inventing dances, than with seeing them; when you look at them you look at them from the point of view of an artist who is concerned with his own, with her own, creating. Creating, of course, is very exciting, and it is very exciting whether you are good at it or not; you must have noticed that already in watching other people create, whose work looks silly to you, but whose excitement, even if you think it ought not to be, is just as serious to them as that of a creator whose creating isn't silly. But creating dancing and seeing dancing are not the same excitement. And it is not about creating that I mean to speak; I am telling you this, so you won't sit here unless you can spare the time for considering in a disinterested way what seeing is like; please don't feel embarrassed about leaving now, though I agree it would be rude of you to leave later. And it is not very likely either that I shall tell you any facts that you had better write down. I rather think you know all the same facts I do about dancing, and certainly you know some I don't; I have forgotten some I used to know. About facts, too, what interests me just now is how differently they can look, one sees them one way and one sees them another way another time, and yet one is still seeing the same fact. Facts have a way of dancing about, now performing a solo then reappearing in the chorus, linking themselves now with facts of one kind, now with facts of another, and quite changing their style as they do. Of course you have to know the facts so you can recognize them, or you can't appreciate how they move, how they keep dancing. We are supposed to discuss dance history sometime in this seminar and I hope we will. But not today.

At the beginning of what I said today I talked about one sort of seeing, namely a kind that leads to recognizing onstage and inside yourself an echo of some personal, original excitement you already know. I call it an echo because I am supposing that the event which originally caused the excitement in one's self is not literally the same as the event you see happen onstage. I myself, for instance, have never been a prince or fallen in love with a creature that was half girl and half swan, nor have I myself been an enchanted swan princess, but I have been really moved, and transported by some performances of *Swan Lake*, and by both sides of that story. In fact, it is much more exciting if I can feel both sides happening to me, and not just one. But I am sure you have already jumped ahead of me to the next step of the argument, and you can see that not only have I never been such people or been in their situation, but besides that I don't look like either of them, nor could I, even if I were inspired, dance the steps the way they do. Nor even the steps of the other dancers, the soloists or the chorus.

You don't seem to have taken these remarks of mine as a joke. But I hope you realized that I was pointing out that the kind of identification one feels at a dance performance with the performers is not a literal kind. On the other hand, it is very probable that you yourselves watch a dance performance with a certain professional awareness of what is going on.

A professional sees quite clearly "I could do that better, I couldn't do that nearly so well." A professional sees the finesse or the awkwardness of a performer very distinctly, at least in a field of dance execution he or she is accustomed to working in; and a choreographer sees similarly how a piece is put together, or as the phrase is, how the material has been handled. But this is evidently a very special way of looking at a performance. One may go further and say that a theater performance is not intended to be seen from this special viewpoint. Craftsmanship is a matter of professional ethics; a surgeon is not bound to explain to you what he is doing while he is operating on you, and similarly no art form, no theater form is meant to succeed in creating its magic with the professionals scattered in the audience. Other doctors seeing a cure, may say, your doctor was a quack but he was lucky;

and similarly professionals may say after a performance, Yes, the
ballerina was stupendous, she didn't fake a thing—or else say,
she may not have thrilled you, but there aren't four girls in the
world who can do a something or other the way she did—and
this is all to the good, it is honorable and it is real seeing. But
I am interested just now to bring to your attention or recall to
your experience not that professional way of seeing, but a more
general way. I am interested at the moment in recalling to you
how it looks when one sees dancing as non-professionals do, in
the way you yourselves I suppose look at pictures, at buildings, at
political history or at landscapes or at strangers you pass on the
street. Or as you read poetry.

In other words the way you look at daily life or at art for the
mere pleasure of seeing, without trying to put yourself actively in
it, without meaning to do anything about it. I am talking about
seeing what happens when people are dancing, seeing how they
look. Watching them and appreciating the beauty they show.
Appreciating the ugliness they show if that's what you see. Seeing this is beautiful, this ugly, this is nothing as far as I can see.
As long as you pay attention there is always something going
on, either attractive or unattractive, but nobody can always pay
attention, so sometimes there is nothing as far as you can see,
because you have really had enough of seeing; and quite often
there is very little, but anyway you are looking at people dancing,
and you are seeing them while they dance.

Speaking personally, I think there is quite a difference between
seeing people dance as part of daily life, and seeing them dance
in a theater performance. Seeing them dance as part of daily
life is seeing people dance in a living room or a ballroom or a
nightclub, or seeing them dance folk dances either naturally or
artificially in a folk dance group. For that matter classroom dancing and even rehearsal dancing seems to me a part of daily life,
though it is as special as seeing a surgeon operate, or hearing the
boss blow up in his office. Dancing in daily life is also seeing the
pretty movements and gestures people make. In the Caribbean,
for instance, the walk of Negroes is often, well, miraculous. Both
the feminine stroll and the masculine one, each entirely different. In Italy you see another beautiful way of strolling, that of

shorter muscles, more complex in their plasticity, with girls deliciously turning their breast very slightly, deliciously pointing their feet. You should see how harmoniously the young men can loll. American young men loll quite differently, resting on a peripheral point, Italians loll resting on a more central one. Italians on the street, boys and girls, both have an extraordinary sense of the space they really occupy, and of filling that space harmoniously as they rest or move; Americans occupy a much larger space than their actual bodies do; I mean, to follow the harmony of their movement or of their lolling you have to include a much larger area in space than they are actually occupying. This annoys many Europeans; it annoys their instinct of modesty. But it has a beauty of its own, that a few of them appreciate. It has so to speak an intellectual appeal; it has because it refers to an imaginary space, an imaginary volume, not to a real and visible one. Europeans sense the intellectual volume but they fail to see how it is filled by intellectual concepts—so they suppose that the American they see lolling and assuming to himself too much space, more space than he actually needs, is a kind of a conqueror, is a kind of non-intellectual or merely material occupying power. In Italy I have watched American sailors, soldiers and tourists, all with the same expansive instinct in their movements and their repose, looking like people from another planet among Italians with their self-contained and traditionally centered movements. To me these Americans looked quite uncomfortable, and embarrassed, quite willing to look smaller if they only knew how. Here in New York where everybody expects them to look the way they do, Americans look unself-conscious and modest despite their traditional expansivity of movement. There is room enough. Not because there is actually more—there isn't in New York— but because people expect it, they like it if people move that way. Europeans who arrive here look peculiarly circumspect and tight to us. Foreign sailors in Times Square look completely swamped in the big imaginary masses surging around and over them.

Well, this is what I mean by dancing in daily life. For myself I think the walk of New Yorkers is amazingly beautiful, so large and clear. But when I go inland, or out west, it is much sweeter. On the other hand, it has very little either of Caribbean luscious-

ness or of Italian *contraposto*. It hasn't much savor, to roll on
your tongue, that it hasn't. Or at least you have to be quite subtle,
or very much in love to distinguish so delicate a perfume.

That, of course, is supposed to be another joke, but naturally
you would rather travel yourself than hear about it. I can't expect
you to see my point without having been to countries where the
way of walking is quite different from what ours is here. However, if you were observant, and you ought to be as dance majors,
you would have long ago enjoyed the many kinds of walking you
can see right in this city, boys and girls, Negro and white, Puerto
Rican and Western American and Eastern, foreigners, professors
and dancers, mechanics and businessmen, ladies entering a theater with half a drink too much, and shoppers at Macy's. You
can see everything in the world here in isolated examples at least,
peculiar characters or people who are for the moment you see
them peculiar. And everybody is quite peculiar now and then.
Not to mention how peculiar anybody can be at home.

Daily life is wonderfully full of things to see. Not only people's
movements, but the objects around them, the shape of the rooms
they live in, the ornaments architects make around windows and
doors, the peculiar ways buildings end in the air, the water tanks,
the fantastic differences in their street façades on the first floor.
A French composer who was here said to me, "I had expected the
streets of New York to be monotonous, after looking at a map
of all those rectangles; but now I see the differences in height
between buildings, I find I have never seen streets so diverse one
from another." But if you start looking at New York architecture,
you will notice not only the sometimes extraordinary delicacy
of the window framings, but also the standpipes, the grandiose
plaques of granite and marble on ground floors of office buildings, the windowless side walls, the careful, though senseless,
marble ornaments. And then the masses, the way the office and
factory buildings pile up together in perspective. And under them
the drive of traffic, those brilliantly colored trucks with their fan-
ciful lettering, the violent paint on cars, signs, houses, as well as
lips. Sunsets turn the red-painted houses in the cross-streets to
the flush of live rose petals. And the summer sky of New York
for that matter is as magnificent as the sky of Venice. Do you see

all this? Do you see what a forty- or sixty-story building looks like from straight below? And do you see how it comes up from the sidewalk as if it intended to go up no more than five stories? Do you see the bluish haze on the city as if you were in a forest? As for myself, I wouldn't have seen such things if I hadn't seen them first in the photographs of Rudolph Burckhardt. But after seeing them in his photographs, I went out to look if it were true. And it was. There is no excuse for you as dance majors not to discover them for yourselves. Go and see them. There is no point in living here, if you don't see the city you are living in. And after you have seen Manhattan, you can discover other grandeurs out in Queens, in Brooklyn, and in those stinking marshes of Jersey.

All that is here. And it is worth seeing. When you get to Rome, or to Fez in Morocco, or to Paris, or to Constantinople, or to Peking, I hope you will get there, I have always wanted to, you will see other things beautiful in another way, but meanwhile since you are dance majors and are interested and gifted in seeing, look around here. If you cut my talks and bring me instead a report of what you saw in the city, I will certainly mark you present, and if you can report something interesting I will give you a good mark. It is absurd to sit here in four walls while all that extraordinary interest is going on around us. But then education is a lazy, a dull way of learning, and you seem to have chosen it; forget it.

However, if you will insist on listening to me instead of going out and looking for yourselves, I will have to go on with this nonsense. Since you are here I have to go on talking and you listening, instead of you and me walking around and seeing things. And I have to go on logically, which we both realize is nonsense. Logically having talked about what you can see in daily life, I have to go on that very different way of seeing, which you use in seeing art.

For myself, I make a distinction between seeing daily life and seeing art. Not that seeing is different. Seeing is the same. But seeing art is seeing an ordered and imaginary world, subjective, and concentrated. Seeing in the theater is seeing what you don't see quite that way in life. In fact, it's nothing like that way. You sit all evening in one place and look at an illuminated stage, and music is going on, and people are performing who have been trained in some peculiar way for years, and since we are talking about a dance performance, nobody is expected to say a word, either onstage or in the house. It is all very peculiar. But there are quite a lot of people, ordinary enough citizens watching the stage along with you. All these people in the audience are used to having information conveyed to them by words spoken or written, but here they are just looking at young people dancing to music. And they expect to have something interesting conveyed to them. It is certainly peculiar.

But then, art is peculiar. I won't speak of concert music, which is obviously peculiar, and which thousands every evening listen to, and evidently get satisfaction out of. But even painting is a strange thing. That people will look at some dirt on a canvas, just a little rectangle on a wall, and get all sorts of exalted feelings and ideas from it is not at all natural, it is not at all obvious. Why do they prefer one picture so much to another one? They will tell you and get very eloquent, but it does seem unreasonable. It seems unreasonable if you don't see it. And for all the other arts it's the same. The difference between the "Ode on a Grecian Urn" and a letter on the editorial page of the *Daily News* isn't so great if you look at both of them without reading them. Art is certainly even more mysterious and nonsensical than daily life. But what a pleasure it can be. A pleasure much more extraordinary than a hydrogen bomb is extraordinary.

There is nothing everyday about art. There is nothing everyday about dancing as an art. And that is the extraordinary pleasure of seeing it. I think that is enough for today.

N. Scott Momaday (born 1934) is an essayist, poet, memoirist, and fiction writer, who has drawn inspiration from the landscape and folklore of his Kiowa Indian ancestry. His novel House Made of Dawn, *which won the Pulitzer Prize in 1969, is credited with having launched the Native American literary movement. Momaday's essays, collected initially in* The Way to Rainy Mountain, *are sustained by a musicality and eye for haunting detail, as well as a deep appreciation for the enduring qualities of his people—their traditions and spiritual wisdom.*

THE WAY TO RAINY MOUNTAIN

A single knoll rises out of the plain in Oklahoma, north and west of the Wichita Range. For my people, the Kiowas, it is an old landmark, and they gave it the name Rainy Mountain. The hardest weather in the world is there. Winter brings blizzards, hot tornadic winds arise in the spring, and in summer the prairie is an anvil's edge. The grass turns brittle and brown, and it cracks beneath your feet. There are green belts along the rivers and creeks, linear groves of hickory and pecan, willow and witch hazel. At a distance in July or August the steaming foliage seems almost to writhe in fire. Great green and yellow grasshoppers are everywhere in the tall grass, popping up like corn to sting the flesh, and tortoises crawl about on the red earth, going nowhere in the plenty of time. Loneliness is an aspect of the land. All things in the plain are isolate; there is no confusion of objects in the eye, but *one* hill or *one* tree or *one* man. To look upon that landscape in the early morning, with the sun at your back, is to lose the sense of proportion. Your imagination comes to life, and this, you think, is where Creation was begun.

I returned to Rainy Mountain in July. My grandmother had died in the spring, and I wanted to be at her grave. She had lived to be very old and at last infirm. Her only living daughter was with her when she died, and I was told that in death her face was that of a child.

I like to think of her as a child. When she was born, the Kiowas were living the last great moment of their history. For more than a hundred years they had controlled the open range from the Smoky Hill River to the Red, from the headwaters of the Canadian to the fork of the Arkansas and Cimarron. In alliance with the Comanches, they had ruled the whole of the southern Plains. War was their sacred business, and they were among the finest horsemen the world has ever known. But warfare for the Kiowas was preeminently a matter of disposition rather than of survival, and they never understood the grim, unrelenting advance of the U.S. Cavalry. When at last, divided and ill-provisioned, they were driven onto the Staked Plains in the cold rains of autumn, they fell into panic. In Palo Duro Canyon they abandoned their crucial stores to pillage and had nothing then but their lives. In order to save themselves, they surrendered to the soldiers at Fort Sill and were imprisoned in the old stone corral that now stands as a military museum. My grandmother was spared the humiliation of those high gray walls by eight or ten years, but she must have known from birth the affliction of defeat, the dark brooding of old warriors.

Her name was Aho, and she belonged to the last culture to evolve in North America. Her forebears came down from the high country in western Montana nearly three centuries ago. They were a mountain people, a mysterious tribe of hunters whose language has never been positively classified in any major group. In the late seventeenth century they began a long migration to the south and east. It was a journey toward the dawn, and it led to a golden age. Along the way the Kiowas were befriended by the Crows, who gave them the culture and religion of the Plains. They acquired horses, and their ancient nomadic spirit was suddenly free of the ground. They acquired Tai-me, the sacred Sun Dance doll, from that moment the object and symbol of their worship, and so shared in the divinity of the sun. Not least, they acquired the sense of destiny, therefore courage and pride. When they entered upon the southern Plains they had been transformed. No longer were they slaves to the simple necessity of survival; they were a lordly and dangerous society of fighters and thieves, hunters and priests of the sun. According to their origin myth, they entered the world through a hollow log. From one point of view, their migration was the fruit of an old prophecy, for indeed they emerged from a sunless world.

Although my grandmother lived out her long life in the shadow of Rainy Mountain, the immense landscape of the continental interior lay like memory in her blood. She could tell of the Crows, whom she had never seen, and of the Black Hills, where she had never been. I wanted to see in reality what she had seen more perfectly in the mind's eye, and traveled fifteen hundred miles to begin my pilgrimage.

Yellowstone, it seemed to me, was the top of the world, a region of deep lakes and dark timber, canyons and waterfalls. But, beautiful as it is, one might have the sense of confinement there. The skyline in all directions is close at hand, the high wall of the woods and deep cleavages of shade. There is a perfect freedom in the mountains, but it belongs to the eagle and the elk, the badger and the bear. The Kiowas reckoned their stature by the distance they could see, and they were bent and blind in the wilderness.

Descending eastward, the highland meadows are a stairway to the plain. In July the inland slope of the Rockies is luxuriant with flax and buckwheat, stonecrop and larkspur. The earth unfolds and the limit of the land recedes. Clusters of trees, and animals grazing far in the distance, cause the vision to reach away and wonder to build upon the mind. The sun follows a longer course in the day, and the sky is immense beyond all comparison. The great billowing clouds that sail upon it are shadows that move upon the grain like water, dividing light. Farther down, in the land of the Crows and Blackfeet, the plain is yellow. Sweet clover takes hold of the hills and bends upon itself to cover and seal the soil. There the Kiowas paused on their way; they had come to the place where they must change their lives. The sun is at home on the plains. Precisely there does it have the certain character of a god. When the Kiowas came to the land of the Crows, they could see the dark lees of the hills at dawn across the Bighorn River, the profusion of light on the grain shelves, the oldest deity ranging after the solstices. Not yet would they veer southward to the caldron of the land that lay below; they must wean their blood from the northern winter and hold the mountains a while longer in their view. They bore Tai-me in procession to the east.

A dark mist lay over the Black Hills, and the land was like iron. At the top of a ridge I caught sight of Devil's Tower upthrust against the gray sky as if in the birth of time the core of the earth had broken through its crust and the motion of the world was begun. There are things in nature that engender an awful quiet in the heart of man; Devil's Tower is one of them. Two centuries ago, because they could not do otherwise, the Kiowas made a legend at the base of the rock. My grandmother said:

> Eight children were there at play, seven sisters and their brother. Suddenly the boy was struck dumb; he trembled and began to run upon his hands and feet. His fingers became claws, and his body was covered with fur. Directly there was a bear where the boy had been. The sisters were terrified; they ran, and the bear after them. They came to the stump of a great tree, and the tree spoke to them. It bade them climb upon it, and as they did so it began to rise into the air. The bear came to kill them, but they were just beyond its reach. It reared against the tree and scored the bark all around with its claws. The seven sisters were borne into the sky, and they became the stars of the Big Dipper.

From that moment, and so long as the legend lives, the Kiowas have kinsmen in the night sky. Whatever they were in the mountains, they could be no more. However tenuous their well-being, however much they had suffered and would suffer again, they had found a way out of the wilderness.

My grandmother had a reverence for the sun, a holy regard that now is all but gone out of mankind. There was a wariness in her, and an ancient awe. She was a Christian in her later years, but she had come a long way about, and she never forgot her birthright. As a child she had been to the Sun Dances; she had taken part in those annual rites, and by them she had learned the restoration of her people in the presence of Tai-me. She was about seven when the last Kiowa Sun Dance was held in 1887 on the Washita River above Rainy Mountain Creek. The buffalo were gone. In order to consummate the ancient sacrifice—to impale the head of a buffalo bull upon the medicine tree—a delegation of old men journeyed into Texas, there to beg and barter for an animal from the Goodnight herd. She was ten when the Kiowas came together for the last time as a living Sun Dance culture. They could find no buffalo; they had to hang an old hide from the sacred tree. Before the dance could begin, a company of soldiers rode out from Fort Sill under orders to disperse the tribe. Forbidden without cause the essential act of their faith, having seen the wild herds slaughtered and left to rot upon the ground, the Kiowas backed away forever from the medicine tree. That was July 20, 1890, at the great bend of the Washita. My grandmother was there. Without bitterness, and for as long as she lived, she bore a vision of deicide.

Now that I can have her only in memory, I see my grandmother in the several postures that were peculiar to her: standing at the wood stove on a winter morning and turning meat in a great iron skillet; sitting at the south window, bent above her beadwork, and afterwards, when her vision failed, looking down for a long time into the fold of her hands; going out upon a cane, very slowly as she did when the weight of age came upon her; praying. I remember her most often at prayer. She made long, rambling prayers out of suffering and hope, having seen many things. I was never sure that I had the right to hear, so exclusive were they of all mere custom and company. The last time I saw her she prayed standing by the side of her bed at night, naked to the waist, the light of a kerosene lamp moving upon her dark skin. Her long, black hair, always drawn and braided in the day, lay upon her shoulders and against her breasts like a shawl. I do not speak Kiowa, and I never understood her prayers, but there was something inherently sad in the sound, some merest hesitation upon the syllables of sorrow. She began in a high and descending pitch, exhausting her breath to silence; then again and again—and always the same intensity of effort, of something that is, and is not, like urgency in the human voice. Transported so in the dancing light among the shadows of her room, she seemed beyond the reach of time. But that was illusion; I think I knew then that I should not see her again.

Houses are like sentinels in the plain, old keepers of the weather watch. There, in a very little while, wood takes on the appearance of great age. All colors wear soon away in the wind and rain, and then the wood is burned gray and the grain appears and the nails turn red with rust. The windowpanes are black and opaque; you imagine there is nothing within, and indeed there are many ghosts, bones given up to the land. They stand here and there against the sky, and you approach them for a longer time than you expect. They belong in the distance; it is their domain.

Once there was a lot of sound in my grandmother's house, a lot of coming and going, feasting and talk. The summers there were full of excitement and reunion. The Kiowas are a summer people; they abide the cold and keep to themselves, but when the season turns and the land becomes warm and vital they cannot hold still; an old love of going returns upon them. The aged visitors who came to my grandmother's house when I was a child were made of lean and leather, and they bore themselves upright. They wore great black hats and bright ample shirts that shook in the wind. They rubbed fat upon their hair and wound their braids with strips of colored cloth. Some of them painted their faces and carried the scars of old and cherished enmities. They were an old council of warlords, come to remind and be reminded of who they were. Their wives and daughters served them well. The women might indulge themselves; gossip was at once the mark and compensation of their servitude. They made loud and elaborate talk among themselves, full of jest and gesture, fright and false alarm. They went abroad in fringed and flowered shawls, bright beadwork and German silver. They were at home in the kitchen, and they prepared meals that were banquets.

There were frequent prayer meetings, and great nocturnal feasts. When I was a child I played with my cousins outside, where the lamplight fell upon the ground and the singing of the old people rose up around us and carried away into the darkness. There were a lot of good things to eat, a lot of laughter and surprise. And afterwards, when the quiet returned, I lay down with my grandmother and could hear the frogs away by the river and feel the motion of the air.

Now there is a funeral silence in the rooms, the endless wake of some final word. The walls have closed in upon my grandmother's house. When I returned to it in mourning, I saw for the first time in my life how small it was. It was late at night, and there was a white moon, nearly full. I sat for a long time on the stone steps by the kitchen door. From there I could see out across the land; I could see the long row of trees by the creek, the low light upon the rolling plains, and the stars of the Big Dipper. Once I looked at the moon and caught sight of a strange thing. A cricket had perched upon the handrail, only a few inches away from me. My line of vision was such that the creature filled the moon like a fossil. It had gone there, I thought, to live and die, for there, of all places, was its small definition made whole and eternal. A warm wind rose up and purled like the longing within me.

The next morning I awoke at dawn and went out on the dirt road to Rainy Mountain. It was already hot, and the grasshoppers began to fill the air. Still, it was early in the morning, and the birds sang out of the shadows. The long yellow grass on the mountain shone in the bright light, and a scissortail hied above the land. There, where it ought to be, at the end of a long and legendary way, was my grandmother's grave. Here and there on the dark stones were ancestral names. Looking back once, I saw the mountain and came away.

THE TWENTY-NINTH REPUBLICAN CONVENTION

The dark blue curtains part. As delegates cheer, the nominee walks toward the lectern, arms loose, shoulders somewhat rigid like a man who . . . No, as Henry James once said in quite a different but no less dramatic context, it cannot be done. What is there to say about Richard M. Nixon that was not said eight years ago? What is there to say that he himself did not say at that memorable "last" press conference in Los Angeles six years ago? For some time he has ceased to figure in the conscious regions of the mind, a permanent resident, one had thought, of that limbo where reside the Stassens and the Deweys and all those other ambitious men whose failures seemed so entirely deserved. But now, thanks to two murders in five years, Richard Nixon is again a presidential candidate. No second acts to American careers? Nonsense. What is lacking are decent codas. At Miami Beach, we were reminded that no politician can ever be written off this side of Arlington.

The week before the convention began, various Republican leaders met at the Fontainebleau Hotel to write a platform, knowing that no matter what wisdom this document might contain it would be ignored by the candidate. Nevertheless, to the extent issues ever intrude upon the making of presidents, the platform hearings do give publicity to different points of view, and that is why Ronald Reagan took time from his busy schedule as governor of California to fly to Miami Beach in order to warn the platform committee of the dangers of crime in the streets. The governor also made himself available to the flower of the national and international press who sat restively in a window-less low-ceilinged dining room of the Fontainebleau from two o'clock to two thirty to "just a short wait, please, the governor is on his way," interviewing one another and trying to look alert as the television cameras, for want of a candidate, panned from face to face. At last, His Excellency, as Ivy Baker Priest would say, entered the room, flanked by six secret servicemen. As they spread out on either side of him, they cased us narrowly and I knew that simply by looking into my face they could see the imaginary gun in my pocket.

Ronald Reagan is a well-preserved not young man. Close-to, the painted face is webbed with delicate lines while the dyed hair, eyebrows, and eyelashes contrast oddly with the sagging muscle beneath the as yet unlifted chin, soft earnest of wattle soon-to-be. The effect, in repose, suggests the work of a skillful embalmer. Animated, the face is quite attractive and at a distance youthful; particularly engaging is the crooked smile full of large porcelain-capped teeth. The eyes are the only interesting feature: small, narrow, apparently dark, they glitter in the hot light, alert to every move, for this is enemy country—the liberal Eastern press who are so notoriously immune to that warm and folksy performance which Reagan quite deliberately projects over their heads to some legendary constituency at the far end of the tube, some shining Carverville where good Lewis Stone forever lectures Andy Hardy on the virtues of thrift and the wisdom of the contract system at Metro-Goldwyn-Mayer.

The questions begin. Why don't you announce your candidacy? Are you a candidate? Why do people feel you will take votes away from George Wallace? Having answered these questions a hundred times before, the actor does not pause to consider his responses. He picks up each cue promptly, neatly, increasing the general frustration. Only once does the answer-machine jam. "Do you *want* to be president?" The room goes silent. The smile suddenly looks to have been drawn in clay, fit for baking in a Laguna kiln. Then the candidate finds the right button. He pushes it. We are told what an honor it is for any citizen to be considered for the highest office on earth. . . . We stop listening; he stops listening to himself.

"Governor, even though you're not a candidate, you must know that there is a good deal of support for you. . . ." The questioner's irony is suitably heavy. Reagan's lips purse—according to one biographer this is a sign he is displeased; there was a good deal of lip-pursing during the conference not to mention the days to come. "Well," he speaks through pursed lips, "I'd have to be unconscious not to know what was going on but . . ." As he continues his performance, his speech interlarded with "my lands" (for some reason Right Wingers invariably talk like Little Orphan Annie), I recalled my last glimpse of him, at the Cow Palace in San Francisco four years ago. The Reagans were seated in a box, listening to Eisenhower. While Mrs. Reagan darted angry looks about the hall (displeased at the press?) the star of *Death Valley Days* was staring intently at the speaker on the platform. Thus an actor prepares, I thought, and I suspected even then that Reagan would someday find himself up there on the platform. In any case, as the age of television progresses, the Reagans will be the rule, not the exception. "Thank you, Governor," said a journalist, and everyone withdrew, leaving Ronald Reagan with his six secret servicemen—one black, a ratio considerably better than that of the convention itself where only 2 percent could claim Africa as motherland.

Seventy-Second Street Beach is a gathering place for hustlers of all sexes. With some bewilderment, they watch one of their masters, the Chase Manhattan Bank made flesh—sweating flesh—display his wounds to the sandy and the dull, a Coriolanus but in reverse, one besotted with the vulgar. In shirtsleeves but firmly knotted tie, Nelson Aldrich Rockefeller stands on a platform crowded with officials and aides (most seriously crowded by the governor of Florida, Claude Kirk, who wears a bright orange sports jacket and a constant smile for his people, who regard him, the few who know who he is, with bright loathing). Ordinarily Rockefeller's face is veal-white, as though no blood courses beneath that thick skin. But now, responding to the lowering day, he has turned a delicate conch pink. What is he saying? "Well, let's face it, there's been some disagreement among the pollsters." The upper-class tough boy accent (most beautifully achieved by Montgomery Clift in *The Heiress*) proves effective even down here where consonants are disdained and vowels long. Laughter from the audience in clothes, bewildered looks from the hustlers in their bathing suits. "Like, man, who is it?"

"But now Harris and Gallup have agreed that I can beat . . ." Rockefeller quotes at length from those polls which are the oracles of our day, no, the very gods who speak to us of things to come. Over and over again, he says, "Let's face it," a phrase popular twenty years ago, particularly among girls inclined to alcoholism ("the governor drinks an occasional Dubonnet on the rocks before dinner," where did I read that?). Beside him stands his handsome wife, holding a large straw hat and looking as if she would like to be somewhere else, no loving Nancy Reagan or loyal Pat Nixon she. The convention is full of talk that there has been trouble between them. Apparently . . . one of the pleasures of American political life is that issues seldom intrude. Personalities are all that matter. Is he a nice man? Is she happy with him? What else should concern a sovereign people?

Rockefeller puts down the polls, takes off his glasses, and starts to attack the administration. "Look at what they're doing," he says with a nice vehemence. "They're *exhilarating* the war!" But although Rockefeller now sounds like a peace candidate, reprising Bobby Kennedy and Eugene McCarthy, he has always been devoted to the war in Vietnam and to the principle underlying it: American military intervention wherever "freedom is endangered." Consequently—and consistently—he has never found any defense budget adequate. Two years ago at a dinner in New York, he was more hawk than Johnson as he told us how the Viet Cong were coldbloodedly "shooting little mayors" (the phrase conjured up dead ponies); mournfully, he shook his head, "Why can't they learn to fight fair?" Nevertheless, compared to Nixon and Reagan, Rockefeller is positively Lincolnesque. All of us on Seventy-Second Street Beach liked him, except perhaps the hustlers wanting to score, and we wished him well, knowing that he had absolutely no chance of being nominated.

By adding the third character to tragedy, Sophocles changed the nature of drama. By exalting the chorus and diminishing the actors, television has changed entirely the nature of our continuing history. Watching things as they happen, the viewer is a part of events in a way new to man. And never is he so much a part of the whole as when things do not happen, for, as Andy Warhol so wisely observed, people will always prefer to look at something rather than nothing; between plain wall and flickering commercial, the eyes will have the second. As hearth and fire were once center to the home or lair so now the television set is the center of modern man's being, all points of the room converge upon its presence and the eye watches even as the mind dozes, much as our ancestors narcotized themselves with fire.

At Miami Beach television was everywhere: in the air, on the streets, in hotel lobbies, on the convention floor. "From gavel to gavel" the networks spared us nothing in the way of empty speeches and mindless interviews, but dull and uninformative as the events themselves were, something rather than nothing was being shown and the eye was diverted while the objects photographed (delegates et al.) reveled in the exposure even though it might be no more than a random shot of a nose being picked or a crotch rearranged. No matter: for that instant the one observed existed for all his countrymen. As a result the delegates were docile beyond belief, stepping this way and that as required by men with wired helmets and handmikes which, like magic wands, could confer for an instant total recognition.

The fact that television personalities so notoriously took precedence over the politicians at Miami Beach was noted with sour wonder by journalists who have begun to fear that their rendering of events that all can see into lines of linear type may prove to be as irrelevant an exercise as turning contemporary literature into Greek. The fact that in a hotel lobby it was Eric Sevareid not John Tower who collected a crowd was thought to be a sign of the essential light-mindedness of the electorate. Yet Sevareid belongs to the country in a way few politicians ever do. Certainly most people see more of David Brinkley than they do of their own relatives and it's no wonder that they are eager to observe him in the flesh since he has been so often a visitor in their house. Only Ronald Reagan among the politicians at Miami exerted the same spell, and for the same reason: he is a bona fide star of the Late Show, equally ubiquitous, equally mythic.

Miami Beach is a rich sandbar with a drawbridge, and in no sense part of the main. The televised convention made it even more remote than it is. So locked were we all in what we were doing that Miami's Negro riots on Wednesday went almost unnoticed. There are those who thought that the Republicans deliberately played down the riots, but that is too Machiavellian. The fact is no one was interested. For those involved in creating that formidable work of television art, the twenty-ninth Republican convention, there was only one important task, creating suspense where none was. Everyone pretended that Reagan and Rockefeller could stop Nixon on the first ballot and so persuasive is the medium that by continually acting as if there might be a surprise, all involved came to believe that there would be one.

Even Nixon who should have known better fell victim to the collective delusion. On Tuesday he made his deal with Thurmond: no candidate for vice president displeasing to the South. Yet there was never, we now know, any danger of the Southern delegations switching to Reagan, despite the actor's enormous appeal to them. After all, how could they not love a man who had campaigned for a segregationist Southern politician (Charlton Lyons of Louisiana), who had denounced the income tax as "Marxist," and federal aid to education as "a tool of tyranny," and welfare as an "encouragement to divorce and immorality," and who generally sounded as if he wouldn't mind nuking North Vietnam and maybe China, too? He was their man but Nixon was their leader.

By the time the balloting began on Wednesday night, it was all over. There were of course idle pleasures. Everett Dirksen prowling from camera to camera, playing the part of a senator with outrageous pleasure. Strom Thurmond, high constable of the South, staring coldly at the delegates with stone catfish face. John Lindsay of New York, slyly separating his elegant persona from any words that he might be called upon to say. The public liked Lindsay but the delegates did not. They regarded him with the same distaste that they regard the city of which he is mayor, that hellhole of niggers and kikes and commies, of dope and vice and smut. . . . So they talk among themselves, until an outsider approaches; then they shift gears swiftly and speak gravely of law and order and how this is a republic not a democracy.

A lady from Vermont read the roll of the states as though each state had somehow grievously offended her. Alabama was plainly a thorn to be plucked, while Alaska was a blot upon the Union. She did achieve a moment of ribald good humor when she asked one state chairman *which* Rockefeller his state was voting for. But long before the Yankee virago had got to Wisconsin it was plain that Nixon was indeed "the one" as the signs had proclaimed, and immediately the Medium began to look in on the hotel suites, to confront the losers, hoping for tears, and reveal the winner, hoping for . . . well, *what* do you hope for with Nixon?

The technician. Once nominated Nixon gravely explained how he had pulled it off. He talked about the logistics of campaigning. He took us backstage. It was a nice background briefing, but nothing more. No plans for the ghettos, no policy for Asia, just political maneuvering. He did assure us that he would select "a candidate for vice president who does not divide this country." Apparently he would have a free hand because "I won the nomination without paying any price or making any deals." The next day of course he revealed the nature of his deal with the Southerners and the price he must now pay for their support: Spiro Agnew of Maryland. Despite the howls of the party liberals and the total defection of the blacks, Nixon had probably done the wise thing.

Thursday was the big day. Agnew was proposed, opposed, nominated. A lumbering man who looks like a cross between Lyndon Johnson and Juan Perón, his acceptance speech was thin and ungrammatical; not surprisingly, he favored law and order. Adequate on civil rights when he became governor, Agnew behaved boorishly to the black establishment of Baltimore in the wake of riots last spring. This made him acceptable to Thurmond. Even so, all but the most benighted conservatives are somewhat concerned at Agnew's lack of experience. Should Nixon be elected and die, a man with only one year's experience as governor of a backward border state would become emperor of the West. Though firm with niggers, how would he be on other issues? No one knows, including the candidate himself whose great virtue, in his own eyes, "is that I try to be credible—I want to be believed. That's one of the most priceless assets." So it is. So it is.

Nixon is now onstage, ready to accept for a second time his party's nomination. He is leaner than in the past. In a thickly made-up face, the smile is not unappealing, upper lip slightly hooked over teeth in the Kennedy manner. With his jawline collapsing in a comforting way, the middle-aged Nixon resembles the average voter who, we are told, is forty-seven years old. The candidate swings neatly to left, hands raised, two forefingers of each hand making the victory salute. Arms drop. Slide step to right. Arms again extended above head as hands make salute. Then back to center stage and the lectern. The television camera zooms in on the speech: one can see lines crossed out, words added; the type is large, the speech mercifully short.

Nixon begins. The voice is deep and slightly toneless, with-

out regional accent, like a radio announcer's. We have been told
that he wrote his own script. It is possible. Certainly every line
was redolent of that strange uncharm characteristic of the man.
He spoke of Eisenhower ("one of the greatest Americans of our
time—or of any time") who was watching them from his hospital bed. "His heart is with us!" the candidate exclaimed, reminding us inadvertently that that poor organ was hardly the general's
strongest contribution to the moral crusade the times require.
No matter, "let's win this one for Ike!" (A rousing echo of *Knute
Rockne*, a film in which the youthful Ronald Reagan had been
most affecting.) Nixon next paid careful tribute to his Republican competitors, to the platform and, finally, to Spiro Agnew, "a
statesman of the first rank who will be a great campaigner." He
then drew a dark picture of today's America, ending with "did
we come all this way for this?" Despite the many hours of literary
labor, Nixon's style was seldom felicitous; he was particularly
afflicted by "thisness": "This I say is the real voice of America.
And in this year 1968 this is . . ." The real voice of America, needless to say, is Republican; "the forgotten Americans—the non-
shouters, the non-demonstrators"; in short, the non-protesting
white Protestants, who must, he enjoined, commit themselves to
the truth, "to see it like it is, and to tell it like it is," argot just
slightly wrong for now but to Nixon "tell it like it is" must sound
positively raunchy, the sort of thing had he been classy Jack Kennedy he might have heard at Vegas, sitting around with the Clan
and their back-scratchers.

Solemnly Nixon addressed himself to Vietnam. His administration would "bring to an honorable end the war." How? Well,
"after an era of confrontation, the time has come for an era of
negotiation." But in case that sounded like dangerous accommodation he quickly reminded us that since the American flag is spit
on almost daily around the world, it is now "time we started to
act like a great nation." But he did not tell us *how* a great nation
should act. Last January, he said that the war will end only when
the Communists are convinced that the U.S. "will use its immense
power and is not going to back down." In March he said, "There
is no alternative to the continuation of the war in Vietnam." It is
of course never easy to determine what if anything Nixon means.

When it was revealed that his recent support of public housing was not sincere but simply expedient (his secret remarks to a Southern caucus had been taped), no one was surprised. "He just had to say that," murmur his supporters whenever he contradicts himself, and they admire him for it. After all, his form of hypocrisy is deeply American: if you can't be good, be careful. Significantly, he was most loudly applauded when, inevitably, he struck this year's favorite Republican note: *Remember the* Pueblo. "The United States has fallen so low that a fourth-rate military power like North Korea [can] hijack a United States naval vessel. . . ." Quite forgotten were his conciliatory words of last spring: "If the captured American Intelligence spy ship violated North Korean waters, the United States has no choice but to admit it."

Nixon next praised the courts but then allowed that some of them have gone "too far in weakening the peace forces as against the criminal forces." Attacks on the judiciary are surefire with Republicans. Witness the old Nixon five years after the Supreme Court's 1954 decision on the integration of schools: "the Administration's position has not been, is not now, and should not be immediate total integration." Like Barry Goldwater he tends to the radical belief that the Supreme Court's decisions "are not, necessarily, the law of the land." Happily, once the present attorney general is replaced, it will be possible to "open a new front against the filth peddlers and the narcotics peddlers who are corrupting the lives of our children." As for the forty million poor, they can take heart from the example of past generations of Americans who were aided not by government "but because of what people did for themselves." Those small inequities that now exist in the American system can be easily taken care of by "the greatest engine of progress ever developed in the history of man—American private enterprise." The poor man who wants "a piece of the action" (Vegas again) is very apt to get it if the streets are orderly and enough tax cuts are given big business to encourage it to be helpful.

If Nixon's reputation as the litmus-paper man of American politics is deserved, his turning mauve instead of pink makes it plain that the affluent majority intend to do nothing at all in regard to the black and the poor and the aged, except repress with force their demonstrations, subscribing finally not so much to the bland hortatory generalities of the platform and the acceptance speech but to the past statements of the real Nixon who has said (1) "If the conviction rate was doubled in this country, it would do more to eliminate crime in the future than a quadrupling of the funds for any governmental war on poverty." (2) "I am opposed to pensions in any form, as it makes loafing more attractive to [*sic*] working." (3) To tie health care to social security "would set up a great state program which would inevitably head in the direction of herding the ill and elderly into institutions whether they desire this or not." Echo of those Republicans in 1935 who declared that once Social Security was law "you won't have a name any longer, only a number." Most ominous of all, the candidate of the military-industrial complex has no wish to decrease the military budget. Quite the contrary. As recently as last June he was warning us that "the United States has steadily fallen behind the Soviet Union in the leveling of its spending on research and development of advance systems to safeguard the nation." In short, there is no new Nixon, only the old Nixon experimenting with new campaigning techniques in response, as the Stalinists used to say, to new necessities. Nixon concluded his speech on a note of self-love. Most viewers thought it inappropriate: since no one loves him, why should he? To his credit, he sounded slightly embarrassed as he spoke of the boy from Whittier—a misfire but worth a try.

Friday. On the plane to New York. John Lindsay remarks, "Awful as it was, he made a vote-getting speech." He is probably right. Nixon has said in the past that no Republican can hope to get the Negro vote, so why try for it? Particularly when the principal danger to Nixon's candidacy is George Wallace, in the North as well as South. Nixon is also perfectly aware of a little-known statistic: the entire black vote plus the entire vote of whites under twenty-five is slightly less than one-fourth of the total electorate. Since Nixon has no chance of attracting either category, he has, by selecting Agnew, served notice that he is the candidate of that average forty-seven-year-old voter who tends to dislike and fear the young and the black and the liberal; in fact, the more open Nixon is in his disdain of this one-fourth of a nation, the more pleasing he will seem to the remaining three-fourths who want a change, any change, from Johnson-Humphrey as well as some assurance that the dissident forces at work in American life will be contained. The great technician has worked out a winning combination and, barring the (obligatory?) unexpected, it is quite likely that it will pay off and Richard Milhous Nixon will become the thirty-seventh president of the United States.

Albert Murray (1916–2013) wrote novels, literary criticism, and explications of jazz and the blues. In the introduction to his first, most popular work, The Omni-Americans, *he announced his desire to differentiate himself from "the polemics of moral outcry" as practiced, in his view, by Richard Wright and James Baldwin. Murray, who served in the United States Air Force and the Active Guard Reserve, was unwilling to make blanket denunciations of America or to dwell on black Americans' distress, preferring to celebrate their creative vitality and resilience. He was a close friend of Ralph Ellison, fellow Harlemite and jazz aficionado, and his essays have a jaunty sense of humor and a jazzy urbanity.*

THE BLUES IDIOM AND THE MAINSTREAM

The creation of an art style is, as most anthropologists would no doubt agree, a major cultural achievement. In fact, it is perhaps the highest as well as the most comprehensive fulfillment of culture; for an art style, after all, reflects nothing so much as the ultimate synthesis and refinement of a lifestyle.

Art is by definition a process of stylization; and what it stylizes is experience. What it objectifies, embodies, abstracts, expresses, and symbolizes is a sense of life. Accordingly, what is represented in the music, dance, painting, sculpture, literature, and architecture of a given group of people in a particular time, place, and circumstance is a conception of the essential nature and purpose of human existence itself. More specifically, an art style is the assimilation in terms of which a given community, folk, or communion of faith embodies its basic attitude toward experience.

That is not all. Of its very nature, an art style is also the essence of experience itself, in both the historical and sensory implications of the word. It is an attitude, description, and interpretation in action—or rather, perhaps most often, in reaction. For needless to say, action is seldom gratuitous or unmotivated. Not only does it take place *in* a situation, it also takes place *in response to a situation.*

Kenneth Burke has equated stylization with strategy. To extend the military metaphor, one can say stylization is the estimate become maneuver. In such a frame of reference, style is not only insight but disposition and gesture, not only do calculation and estimation become execution (as in engineering), but also motive and estimation become method and occupation. It is a way of sizing up the world, and so, ultimately, and beyond all else, a mode and medium of survival.

In the current social science usage, the concept of "survival technique" has somehow become confused with technology and restricted to matters of food, clothing, and shelter. Human survival, however, involves much more than biological prolongation. The human organism must be nourished and secured against destruction, to be sure, but what makes man human is style. Hence the crucial significance of art in the study of human behavior: *All human effort beyond the lowest level of struggle for animal subsistence is motivated by the need to live in style.*

Certainly the struggle for political and social liberty is nothing if not the quest for freedom to choose one's own way or style of life. Moreover, it should be equally as obvious that there can be no such thing as human dignity and nobility without a consummate, definitive style, pattern, or archetypal image. Economic interpretations of history notwithstanding, what activates revolutions is not destitution (which most often leads only to petty thievery and the like) but intolerable systems and methods—intolerable styles of life.

Most Americans know very well that the blues genre which in its most elaborate extensions includes elements of the spirituals, gospel music, folk song, chants, hollers, popular ditties, plus much of what goes into symphonic and even operatic composition, is the basic and definitive musical idiom of native-born U.S. Negroes. But few if any students of America seem either to understand or even to have a serious curiosity about the relationship of art style to Negro lifestyle. None seem to consider the blues idiom as a major cultural achievement. Not even those writers who have referred to it as being perhaps the only truly American innovation in contemporary artistic expression seem able to concede it any more significance than of some vague minor potential not unlike that of some exotic spice. The blues idiom sustains an un-excelled sense of human worth and possibility, what every other non-totalitarian culture seeks and elaborates: elastic individuality, esthetic receptivity and unique blends of warmth, sensitivity, nonsense, vitality and elegance.

As for the contemporary American social survey statistician, his interests seem never to extend beyond social pathology and the need for revolutionary political reform or community rehabilitation. Seldom do any of his all too comprehensive evaluations of Negro cultural phenomena reflect either anthropological insight into the dynamics of ritual or stylization, or even a rudimentary appreciation of the functional role of esthetics. What the blues represent in his view of things is a crude, simpleminded expression of frustration and despair. Thus, so far as he is concerned, swinging the blues achieves only an essentially pathetic therapeutic compensation for the bleak social and economic circumstances of black people in the United States.

Obviously most American social survey technicians see no connection at all in this context between swinging the blues and the fact that the pronounced emphasis on rhythm-oriented improvisation in U.S. Negro creative expression is derived from dance-oriented antecedents in African culture (although in other contexts, everyone is quick to talk about the African roots of this and that). But worse still they are thus also oblivious to the fact that the same basic improvisational stylization (with its special but unmistakable overtones of what Johan Huizinga, discussing

man as *homo ludens*, refers to as the play element in all cultures)
applies to positive as well as to negative situations. As a result,
they consistently misconstrue what is really the dynamics of confrontation for the mechanics of withdrawal, escape, and relief!

The blues ballad is a good example of what the blues are
about. Almost always relating a story of frustration, it could
hardly be described as a device for avoiding the unpleasant facts
of Negro life in America. On the contrary, it is a very specific
and highly effective vehicle, the obvious purpose of which is to
make Negroes acknowledge the essentially tenuous nature of all
human existence.

The sense of well-being that always goes with swinging the
blues is generated, as anyone familiar with Negro dance halls
knows, not by obscuring or denying the existence of the ugly
dimensions of human nature, circumstances, and conduct, but
rather through the full, sharp, and inescapable awareness of
them. One blues ballad after another informs and keeps reminding Negro dance couples (engaged, as are all dance couples, in
ritual courtship) of the complications and contradictions upon
which romances are contingent: *Now, don't be coming to me
with your head all knotty and your nose all snotty; if you don't
know what you doing you better ask somebody.*

As an art form, the blues idiom by its very nature goes beyond
the objective of making human existence bearable physically
or psychologically. The most elementary and hence the least
dispensable objective of all serious artistic expression, whether
aboriginal or sophisticated, is to make human existence *meaningful*. Man's primary concern with life is to make it as significant as possible, and the blues are part of this effort.

The definitive statement of the epistemological assumptions
that underlie the blues idiom may well be the colloquial title
and opening declaration of one of Duke Ellington's best-known
dance tunes from the midthirties: "It Don't Mean a Thing If It
Ain't Got That Swing." In any case, when the Negro musician
or dancer swings the blues, he is fulfilling the same fundamental
existential requirement that determines the mission of the poet,
the priest, and the medicine man. He is making an affirmative
and hence exemplary and heroic response to that which André

Malraux describes as *la condition humaine*. Extemporizing in response to the exigencies of the situation in which he finds himself, he is confronting, acknowledging, and contending with the infernal absurdities and ever-impending frustrations inherent in the nature of all existence *by playing with the possibilities that are also there*. Thus does man the player become man the stylizer and by the same token the humanizer of chaos; and thus does play become ritual, ceremony, and art; and thus also does the dance-beat improvisation of experience in the blues idiom become survival technique, esthetic equipment for living, and a central element in the dynamics of U.S. Negro lifestyle.

When the typical Negro dance orchestra plays the blues, it is also *playing with* the blues. When it swings, jumps, hops, stomps, bounces, drags, shuffles, rocks, and so on, its manner not only represents a swinging-the-blues attitude toward the "bad news" that comes with the facts of life, it also exemplifies and generates a riffing-the-blues disposition toward the "rough times" that beset all human existence.

The blues-idiom dancer like the solo instrumentalist turns disjunctures into continuities. He is not disconcerted by intrusions, lapses, shifts in rhythm, intensification of tempo, for instance; but is inspired by them to higher and richer levels of improvisation. As a matter of fact (and as the colloquial sense of the word suggests), the "break" in the blues idiom provides the dancer his greatest opportunity—which, at the same time, is also his most heroic challenge and his moment of greatest jeopardy.

But then, impromptu heroism such as is required only of the most agile of storybook protagonists, is precisely what the blues tradition has evolved to condition Negroes to regard as *normal procedure*! Nor is any other attitude toward experience more appropriate to the ever-shifting circumstances of all Americans or more consistent with the predicament of man in the contemporary world at large. Indeed, the blues idiom represents a major American innovation of universal significance and potential because it fulfills, among other things, precisely that fundamental function that Constance Rourke ascribes to the comedy, the irreverent wisdom, the sudden changes and adroit adaptations she found in the folk genre of the Yankee-backwoodsman-

Negro of the era of Andrew Jackson. It provides "emblems for a pioneer people who require resilience as a prime trait."

Obviously those who are conditioned by the folklore of white supremacy would have it otherwise. They insist that political powerlessness and economic exclusion can lead only to cultural deprivation. One unmistakable objective of white norm/black deviation survey data is to show how far outside the mainstream of American culture Negroes are. Another may well be to insinuate that they are unassimilable. The blues idiom, however, represents the most comprehensive and the most profound assimilation. It is the product of a sensibility that is completely compatible with the *human* imperatives of modern times and American life. Many white composers, unlike most white social technicians, are already aware of the ease with which the blues idiom soundtrack can be extended from the cotton fields and the railroad through megalopolis and into outer space.

So far, incredible as it may be, no Negro leader seems to have made any extensive political use of the so-called survival techniques and idiomatic equipment for living that the blues tradition has partly evolved in response to slavery and oppression. Even more incredible is the fact that most Negro leaders, spokesmen, and social technicians seem singularly unaware of the possibility of doing so. (There are many spokesmen whose fear of being stigmatized as primitive is so hysterical that they reject out of hand any suggestion that U.S. Negro lifestyle is geared to dance-beat improvisation. As far as they are concerned, such a conception is inseparable from the racism behind the old notion that all Negroes have natural rhythm.) In any case, the riff playing or vernacular inventiveness that is so fundamental to the way Negroes react otherwise is conspicuously absent from their political behavior. In other situations they play by ear, but for some curious reason they seem to think that political problems must be solved by the book, which in most instances only a few seem to have read and not that many have digested.

No self-respecting Negro musician would ever be guilty of following the stock arrangements of white songwriters as precisely as Negro leaders adhere to the Tin Pan Alley programs of white social technicians! Nor is bravado an adequate substitute for efficiency. Nor should riff-style be confused with the jive-time capers of second-rate con-men. White squares are always being "taken" by such small-time hustlers—but only for peanuts!

Part of the political failure of most Negro leaders, spokesmen, and even social technicians is that they really have been addressing themselves all these years to moral issues and not the actualities of local, state, and national power. Perhaps as more of them become more deeply and intimately involved with the practical requirements of government in action and hence more personally familiar with the chord structure and progression of official maneuvers, the extension of the riff-style into politics is inevitable. Perhaps when this happens even the young black radicals will move beyond their present academic reverence for radicalism per se and begin playing improvisations on the gospels of Marx, Mao, Guevara, and Fanon. Perhaps even they will begin to realize that when great Negro musicians like Armstrong, Basie, Ellington, Parker play by ear, they do so not because they cannot read the score but rather because in the very process of mastering it they have found it inadequate for their purposes. Nor should it be forgotten that they often find their own scores inadequate. (Harold Cruse's *The Crisis of the Negro Intellectual* represents a heroic attempt of one Negro writer to establish his own context and perspectives.)

As yet, however, most Negro social technicians seem unable to realize that the civil rights movement has now entered a stage that requires them to shift their primary emphasis from protest to practical politics. Such an obvious cultural lag may grow out of the fact that the most widely publicized black spokesmen are preachers, heads of organizations sponsored by white liberals, and student idealists, for all of whom a preference for moral outcry over the dirty business of wheeling and dealing with political machines is only natural.

Meanwhile, it is no less natural, or at least predictable, that Negroes in general continue to function in terms of extensions and elaborations that enabled their ancestors not only to endure slavery but also to sustain an unexcelled sense of human worth and possibility in the process. In spite of the restrictions and atrocities of the plantation system, the personal and social intercourse among slaves was so fabulous in the richness of its human fellowship, humor, esthetic inventiveness, and high spirits that the masters—who, ironically, lived in constant fear of black uprisings—could only pretend to shrug it off as childishness! It was not infantilism, however, that girded fugitive slaves for the ordeals of the Underground Railroad and conditioned so many of them to become productive and responsible citizens and men of their time as rapidly as the means became accessible and white resistance would allow.

Nor is it otherwise for contemporary Negroes. It is not cultural lag that creates the major obstacle for those who migrate from the farms and small towns of the South into the industrial and commercial web of the Northern metropolis. It is racism, much of it official, that prevents them from obtaining adequate employment, decent housing, and equal protection under the law. As for their ever so widely publicized lack of preparation in, for instance, specific job skills, such deficiencies, which are hardly greater than those of thousands of white immigrants, are more than offset by Negro eagerness to receive the technical training required. Nor are Negroes from the South any less teachable than any other erstwhile peasants. For the rest, sensibilities formed in the blues tradition seem uniquely equipped to withstand the dislocation traumas that usually result from such an abrupt and radical shift in environment and mode of existence.

Indeed, someday students of machine-age culture in the United States may find that Negro slaves in the cotton field had already begun confronting and evolving esthetic solutions to the problems of assembly line regimentation, depersonalization, and collectivization. After all, the so-called Industrial Revolution had as much to do with the way personnel was used as with machinery as such. In any event, Harlem and Detroit Negroes, for example, are neither terrified by the intricacies of contemporary technology nor overwhelmed by the magnitude of megalopolis. On the contrary, they seize every opportunity to get into the swing of things, almost always contributing vitality and new dimensions of elegance when they succeed.

It is also possible that the time will come when students of U.S. lifestyles will regard the so-called abnormal structure of the Negro family not as the national liability that the Moynihan Report depicts but as a positive force! They may find that it is an institution with a structure that has always been remarkably consistent and compatible with the structure of modern society, and produces personalities whose rugged flexibility is oriented to cope with the fragmented nature of contemporary experience. Further investigation may discover that the actual family of many contemporary Negroes, like that of plantation slaves, is the neighborhood. Much goes to show that among U.S. Negroes parental authority and responsibility have always been shared by neighborhood uncles and aunts of whom sometimes none are blood relatives. *White Southerners were not the only people who benefited from the magnanimity of the black mammy.* Nor have all Negroes been as inattentive to the worldly wit and wisdom of Uncle Remus as most of the current crop of civil rights spokesmen seem to have been.

The cultural deprivation from which Negroes in general suffer is not their own but rather the deprivation that makes for the incredible provincialism of those white social science technicians (and their Negro protégés), who when they report their observations and assessments of Negro life, invariably *celebrate* the very features of American life that the greatest artists and intellectuals have always found most highly questionable if not downright objectionable. But come to think of it, what usually seems to matter most in all findings and evaluations made by American social science survey technicians are indices of material affluence and power. In fact, sometimes it seems that even the most comprehensive social science assessments are predicated upon some indefinite but ruthlessly functional theology involving the worship of wealth and force. In any case, it almost always turns out that whoever has acquired money and power—by any means whatsoever—is assumed to be blessed with everything else, including the holiest moral disposition, the richest sense of humor, creative genius, and impeccable taste.

Of course the mechanics (or machinations) of white supremacy permit white Americans in general to presume themselves the natural heirs and assignees to a median legacy of such qualities. But for the rest, so barbarous is the anthropological value system to which contemporary American social science seems to be geared that so far as the technicians who survey Negro communities are concerned people without affluence and power are only creature-like beings whose humanity is measured in terms of their potential to accumulate material goods and exercise force with arrogance.

Alas, not even the most fundamental human value that democratic societies are specifically designed to guarantee seems to count for very much once such technicians become involved with Negroes. On the contrary, far from revealing any significant preoccupation with or even appreciation for personal freedom and self-realization in any intrinsic sense, the technicians now proceed in an alarming number of instances as if statistical measurements of central tendencies—for all that they may have been initiated in the interest of programming the greatest good for the greatest number—have become a means of justifying an ever increasing standardization, regimentation, and conformity. In doing so, they tend to condemn the very elements in U.S. Negro lifestyle that other non-totalitarian cultures seek and celebrate: its orientation to elastic individuality, for one, and its esthetic receptivity, and its unique blend of warmth, sensitivity, nonsense, vitality, and elegance.

There is, as no man of goodwill would ever dispute, everything to be said for the high priority that most Negro leaders and spokesmen have always placed on emergency measures to counteract poverty, exclusion, and injustice. But in giving so much emphasis to the moral aspects of the case, they often neglect the fundamental nature of the hardheaded pragmatism that underlies so much American behavior. Sometimes Americans are disposed to fair play and sometimes they are not. But they almost always invest their time, money, and enthusiasm in assets with promise, not liabilities. Even those who become involved in salvage operations have been sold on *inherent potential*.

There should never be any relaxation of the pressure for national fair play. But even so it may well be that more emphasis on the discovery, development, and assimilation of things that the so-called black community may contribute to the welfare of other Americans (who are not nearly so well off as advertised) may make the best sales pitch for the cause of black people precisely because it will offer investment possibilities that will best serve the immediate as well as the long-term interests of the entire Republic. The so-called population explosion does not alter the fact that there never has been a time when the United States did not need all of the human ingenuity it could muster.

Nor are the people who evolved the blues idiom likely to restrict their ingenuity to the proliferation of technological innovations. As would be entirely consistent with their tradition or lifestyle, they are far more likely to regard all mechanical devices as truly significant and useful only to the extent that such devices contribute to the art of living, the art, that is to say, of human enjoyment—without which there can be no such thing as human fulfillment no matter how rich the nation's natural resources or how refined its technology.

Loren Eiseley (1907–1977) was a paleontologist, a scientist, and a magnificent nonfiction writer. In literary masterpieces such as The Night Country *and* The Star Thrower, *he combined myriad facts about evolving species with personal musings about the immensity of the cosmos. A bestselling writer, his essays strike surprisingly dark, unreconciled, melancholy chords. The loneliness described in his insomnia essay, "One Night's Dying," may stem from an unhappy early life, growing up with a deaf mother and riding the rails as a hobo, superbly narrated in his memoir,* All the Strange Hours. *Eiseley's handling of time, shifting from a geological perspective of millions of years to "strange hours" plucked from memory, is a notable characteristic.*

ONE NIGHT'S DYING

There is always a soft radiance beyond the bedroom door from a night-light behind my chair. I have lived this way for many years now. I sleep or I do not sleep, and the light makes no difference except if I wake. Then, as I awaken, the dim forms of objects sustain my grip on reality. The familiar chair, the walls of the book-lined study reassert my own existence.

I do not lie and toss with doubt any longer, as I did in earlier years. I get up and write, as I am writing now, or I read in the old chair that is as worn as I am. I read philosophy, metaphysics, difficult works that sometime, soon or late, draw a veil over my eyes so that I drowse in my chair.

It is not that I fail to learn from these midnight examinations of the world. It is merely that I choose that examination to remain as remote and abstruse as possible. Even so, I cannot always prophesy the result. An obscure line may whirl me into a wide-awake, ferocious concentration in which ideas like animals leap at me out of the dark, in which sudden odd trains of thought drive me inexorably to my desk and paper. I am, in short, a victim of insomnia—sporadic, wearing, violent, and melancholic. In the words of Shakespeare, for me the world "does murder sleep." It has been so since my twentieth year.

In that year my father died—a man well loved, the mainstay of our small afflicted family. He died slowly in severe bodily torture. My mother was stone-deaf. I, his son, saw and heard him die. We lived in a place and time not free with the pain-alleviating drugs of later decades. When the episode of many weeks' duration was over, a curious thing happened: I could no longer bear the ticking of the alarm clock in my own bedroom.

At first I smothered it with an extra blanket in a box beside my cot, but the ticking persisted as though it came from my own head. I used to lie for hours staring into the dark of the sleeping house, feeling the loneliness that only the sleepless know when the queer feeling comes that it is the sleeping who are alive and those awake are disembodied ghosts. Finally, in desperation, I gave up the attempt to sleep and turned to reading, though it was difficult to concentrate.

It was then that human help appeared. My grandmother saw the light burning through the curtains of my door and came to sit with me. A few years later, when I touched her hair in farewell at the beginning of a journey from which I would not return to see her alive, I knew she had saved my sanity. Into that lonely room at midnight she had come, abandoning her own sleep, in order to sit with one in trouble. We had not talked much, but we had sat together by the lamp, reasserting our common humanity before the great empty dark that is the universe.

Grandmother knew nothing of psychiatry. She had not reestablished my sleep patterns, but she had done something more important. She had brought me out of a dark room and retied my thread of life to the living world. Henceforward, by night or day, though I have been subject to the moods of depression or gaiety which are a part of the lives of all of us, I have been able not merely to endure but to make the best of what many regard as an unbearable affliction.

It is true that as an educational administrator I can occasionally be caught nodding in lengthy committee meetings, but so, I have observed, can men who come from sound nights on their pillows. Strangely, I, who frequently grow round-eyed and alert as an owl at the stroke of midnight, find it pleasant to nap in daylight among friends. I can roll up on a couch and sleep peacefully while my wife and chatting friends who know my peculiarities keep the daytime universe safely under control. Or so it seems. For, deep-seated in my subconscious, is perhaps the idea that the black bedroom door is the gateway to the tomb.

I try in that bedroom to sleep high on two pillows, to have ears and eyes alert. Something shadowy has to be held in place and controlled. At night one has to sustain reality without help. One has to hear lest hearing be lost, see lest sight not return to follow moonbeams across the floor, touch lest the sense of objects vanish. Oh, sleeping, soundlessly sleeping ones, do you ever think who knits your universe together safely from one day's memory to the next? It is the insomniac, not the night policeman on his beat.

Many will challenge this point of view. They will say that electric power does the trick, that many a roisterer stumbles down the long street at dawn, after having served his purpose of holding the links of the mad world together. There are parts of the nighttime world, men say to me, that it is just as well I do not know. Go home and sleep, man. Others will keep your giddy world together. Let the thief pass quickly in the shadow, he is awake. Let the juvenile gangs which sidle like bands of evil crabs up from the dark waters of poverty into prosperous streets pass without finding you at midnight.

The advice is good, but in the city or the country small things important to our lives have no reporter except as he who does not sleep may observe them. And that man must be disencumbered of reality. He must have no commitments to the dark, as do the murderer and thief. Only he must see, though what he sees may come from the night side of the planet that no man knows well.

For even in the early dawn, while men lie unstirring in their sleep or stumble sleepy-eyed to work, some single episode may turn the whole world for a moment into the place of marvel that it is but that we grow too day-worn to accept.

For example, I call the place where I am writing now the bay of broken things. In the February storms, spume wraiths climb the hundred-foot cliff to fight and fall like bitter rain in the moon-light upon the cabin roof. The earth shakes from the drum roll of the surf. I lie awake and watch through the window beyond my bed. This is no ticking in my brain; this is the elemental night of chaos. This is the sea chewing its million-year way into the heart of the continent.

The caves beneath the cliff resound with thunder. Again those warring wraiths shoot high over the house. Impelled as though I were a part of all those leaping ghosts, I dress in the dark and come forth. With my back against the door, like an ancient nec-romancer, I hurl my mind into the white spray and try to sum-mon back, among those leaping forms, the faces and features of the dead I know. The shapes rise endlessly, but they pass inland before the wind, indifferent to my mortal voice.

I walk a half mile to a pathway that descends upon a little beach. Below me is a stretch of white sand. No shell is ever found unbroken, even on quiet days, upon that shore. Everything comes over the rocks to seaward. Wood is riven into splinters; the bones of seamen and of sea lions are pounded equally into white and shining sand. Throughout the night the long black rollers, like lines of frothing cavalry, form ranks, drum towering forward, and fall, fall till the mind is dizzy with the spume that fills it. I wait in the shelter of a rock for daybreak. At last the sea eases a trifle. The tide is going out.

I stroll shivering along the shore, and there, exposed in ines-capable nakedness, I see the elemental cruelty of the natural world. A broken-winged gull, hurled by the wind against the cliff, runs before me wearily along the beach. It will starve or, mercifully, the dogs will find it. I try not to hurry it, and walk on. A little later in a quieter bend of the shore, I see ahead of me a bleeding, bedraggled blot on the edge of the white surf. As I approach, it starts warily to its feet. We look at each other. It is a wild duck, also with a shattered wing. It does not run ahead of me like the longer-limbed gull. Before I can cut off its retreat it waddles painfully from its brief refuge into the water.

The sea continues to fall heavily. The duck dives awkwardly, but with long knowledge and instinctive skill, under the fall of the first two inshore waves. I see its head working seaward. A long green roller, far taller than my head, rises and crashes forward. The black head of the waterlogged duck disappears. This is the way wild things die, without question, without knowledge of mercy in the universe, knowing only themselves and their own pathway to the end. I wonder, walking farther up the beach, if the man who shot that bird will die as well.

This is the chaos before man came, before sages imbued with pity walked the earth. Indeed it is true, and in my faraway study my hands have often touched with affection the backs of the volumes which line my shelves. Nevertheless, I have endured the nights and mornings of the city. I have seen old homeless men who have slept for hours sitting upright on ledges along the outer hallway of one of the great Eastern stations straighten stiffly in the dawn and limp away with feigned businesslike aloofness before the approach of the policeman on his rounds. I know that on these cold winter mornings sometimes a man, like the pigeons I have seen roosting as closely as possible over warm hotel air vents, will fall stiffly and not awaken. It is true that there are shelters for the homeless, but some men, like their ice-age forebears, prefer their independence to the end.

The loneliness of the city was brought home to me one early sleepless morning, not by men like me tossing in lonely rooms, not by poverty and degradation, not by old men trying with desperate futility to be out among others in the great roaring hive, but by a single one of those same pigeons which I had seen from my hotel window, looking down at midnight upon the smoking air vents and chimneys.

The pigeon, *Columba livia*, is the city bird par excellence. He is a descendant of the rock pigeon that in the Old World lived among the cliffs and crevices above the caves that early man inhabited. He has been with us since our beginning and has adapted as readily as ourselves to the artificial cliffs of man's first cities. He has known the Roman palaces and the cities of Byzantium. His little flat feet, suited to high and precarious walking, have sauntered in the temples of vanished gods as readily as in New York's old Pennsylvania Station. In my dim morning strolls, waiting for the restaurants to open, I have seen him march quickly into the back end of a delivery truck while the driver was inside a store engaged in his orders with the proprietor. Yet for all its apparent tolerance of these highly adapted and often comic birds, New York also has a beach of broken things more merciless than the reefs and rollers of the ocean shore.

One morning, strolling sleepless as usual toward early breakfast time in Manhattan, I saw a sick pigeon huddled at an uncomfortable slant against a building wall on a street corner. I felt sorry for the bird, but I had no box, no instrument of help, and had learned long ago that pursuing wounded birds on city streets is a hopeless, dangerous activity. Pigeons, like men, die in scores every day in New York. As I hesitantly walked on, however, I wondered why the doomed bird was assuming such a desperately contorted position under the cornice that projected slightly over it.

At this moment I grew aware of something I had heard more loudly in European streets as the factory whistles blew, but never in such intensity as here, even though American shoes are built of softer materials. All around me the march of people was intensifying. It was New York on the way to work.

Space was shrinking before my eyes. The tread of innumerable feet passed from an echo to the steady murmuring of a stream, then to a drumming. A dreadful robot rhythm began to rack my head, a sound like the boots of Nazis in their heyday of power. I was carried along in an irresistible surge of bodies.

A block away, jamming myself between a waste-disposal basket and a light post, I managed to look back. No one hesitated at that corner. The human tide pressed on, joshing and pushing. My bird had vanished under that crunching, multifooted current as remorselessly as the wounded duck under the indifferent combers of the sea. I watched this human ocean, of which I was an unwilling droplet, rolling past, its individual faces like whitecaps passing on a night of storm, fixed, merciless, indifferent; man in the mass marching like the machinery of which he is already a replaceable part, toward desks, computers, missiles, and machines, marching like the waves toward his own death with a conscious ruthlessness no watery shore could ever duplicate. I have never returned to search in that particular street for the face of humanity. I prefer the endlessly rolling pebbles of the tide, the moonstones polished by the pulling moon.

And yet, plunged as I am in dire memories and midnight reading, I have said that it is the sufferer from insomnia who knits the torn edges of men's dreams together in the hour before dawn. It is he who from his hidden, winter vantage point sees the desperate high-hearted bird fly through the doorway of the grand hotel while the sleepy doorman nods, a deed equivalent in human terms to that of some starving wretch evading Peter at heaven's gate, and an act, I think, very likely to be forgiven.

It is a night more mystical, however, that haunts my memory. Around me I see again the parchment of old books and remember how, on one rare evening, I sat in the shadows while a firefly flew from volume to volume lighting its small flame, as if in literate curiosity. Choosing the last tide it had illuminated, I came immediately upon these words from St. Paul: "Beareth all things, believeth all things, hopeth all things, endureth all things." In this final episode I shall ask you to bear with me and also to believe.

I sat, once more in the late hours of darkness, in the airport of a foreign city. I was tired as only both the sufferer from insomnia and the traveler can be tired. I had missed a plane and had almost a whole night's wait before me. I could not sleep. The long corridor was deserted. Even the cleaning women had passed by.

In that white efficient glare I grew ever more depressed and weary. I was tired of the endless comings and goings of my profession; I was tired of customs officers and police. I was lonely for home. My eyes hurt. I was, unconsciously perhaps, looking for that warm stone, that hawthorn leaf, where, in the words of the poet, man trades in at last his wife and friend. I had an ocean to cross; the effort seemed unbearable. I rested my aching head upon my hand.

Later, beginning at the far end of that desolate corridor, I saw a man moving slowly toward me. In a small corner of my eye I merely noted him. He limped, painfully and grotesquely, upon a heavy cane. He was far away, and it was no matter to me. I shifted the unpleasant mote out of my eye.

But, after a time, I could still feel him approaching, and in one of those white moments of penetration which are so dreadful, my eyes were drawn back to him as he came on. With an anatomist's eye I saw this amazing conglomeration of sticks and broken, misshapen pulleys which make up the body of man. Here was an apt subject, and I flew to a raging mental dissection. How could anyone, I contended, trapped in this mechanical thing of joints and sliding wires expect the acts it performed to go other than awry?

The man limped on, relentlessly.

How, oh God, I entreated, did we become trapped within this substance out of which we stare so hopelessly upon our own eventual dissolution? How for a single minute could we dream or imagine that thought would save us, children deliver us, from the body of this death? Not in time, my mind rang with my despair; not in mortal time, not in this place, not anywhere in the world would blood be stanched, or the dark wrong be forever righted, or the parted be rejoined. Not in this time, not mortal time. The substance was too gross, our utopias bought with too much pain.

The man was almost upon me, breathing heavily, lunging and shuffling upon his cane. Though an odor emanated from him, I did not draw back. I had lived with death too many years. And then this strange thing happened, which I do not mean physically and cannot explain. The man entered me. From that moment I saw him no more. For a moment I was contorted within his shape, and then out of his body—our bodies, rather—there arose some inexplicable sweetness of union, some understanding between spirit and body which I had never before experienced. Was it I, the joints and pulleys only, who desired this peace so much?

I limped with growing age as I gathered up my luggage. Something of that terrible passer lingered in my bones, yet I was released, the very room had dilated. As I went toward my plane the words the firefly had found for me came automatically to my lips. "Beareth all things," believe, believe. It is thus that one day and the next are welded together, that one night's dying becomes tomorrow's birth. I, who do not sleep, can tell you this.

Edward Hoagland (born 1932) was dubbed by John Updike "the best essayist of my [Updike's] generation." As a young man he worked in the circus, taking care of the big cats, and afterward often went on the road, seeking wildlife adventures. Though esteemed as a nature writer, he is equally at home in the city—an unusual double allegiance. His rapport with animals is uncanny. Hoagland sees himself as a latter-day transcendentalist in the Thoreau mode, intuiting a rapturous connection among all living things. He was an intricate prose stylist, and his sentences torque through thickets of sensory description, before scurrying off in unexpected directions.

HOME IS TWO PLACES

Things are worse than many of us are admitting. I'm a brass-bound optimist by habit—I'm an optimist in the same way that I am right-handed, and will always be. It's simpler to be an optimist and it's a sensible defense against the uncertainties and abysses which otherwise confront us prematurely—we can die a dozen deaths and then usually we find that the outcome is not one we predicted, neither so "bad" nor so "good," but one we hadn't taken into consideration. In an election, though, for instance, where it's only a question of No. 1 or No. 2, I confidently assume that whoever seems to be the better fellow is going to win. When sometimes he doesn't, I begin to feel quite sure that perhaps the other man, now in a position of responsibility, will shift around to views much closer to my own. If this doesn't occur either, then I fall back on my fuzzy but rooted belief that people of opposed opinions at least do share the quality of good-heartedness, of wanting good things to happen, and so events finally will work out for the best.

The trouble is that they're not working out for the best. Even the cheerfully inveterate sardonicists, whose chirpy pessimism is an affirmation of sorts, are growing dispirited and alarmed. And it's not just the liberals; the unease emanates from everybody, Republicans and Christian Scientists—the lapel buttons and bumper stickers and decal figures imply a kind of general clamming-up, a sense of being beleaguered, maybe a panic at the great numbers of people we each pass in a single day—this with the hardening of sects of opinion which have despaired of conversing with one another but only holler out code words and threats. Many people think about finding some peaceful holing-up spot, which may be in the suburbs, or if the individual has already opted for the suburbs, may be up toward Mount Katahdin. As soon as he can afford it he starts wanting a second home, a place to recuperate from the place where he lives while he works, and though it used to be that such a home was frankly a luxury, now nearly everybody who makes a middle-class living starts to think about buying a cottage in the woods or a boat at the shore, if just for the sake of his health. The thirty-hour week, so heralded, may mean three hard ten-hour days of work in the city and then a fast retreat for everybody (in shifts) to what will pass for "the country" in twenty years, there to lead the leisure life, building canoes and greenhouses and picket fences.

I grew up in the suburbs. My father left for New York City every weekday morning and got home about seven p.m. The commuting was grueling and he liked a change of scene on his vacations in later years, but we didn't need to have a country cottage, since we saw deer in the evening and grew a Victory Garden during the war; there was a feed store in town, painted with checkerboards, where the local farmers talked about chicken diseases and trapping weasels. A man named Frank Weed trained pheasant dogs professionally, and my sister when she was growing up went across the road and watched a calf born every spring. Both she and I spent part of our childhoods developing a special sympathy for the animal personality. There was a magical fullness to my perceptions when I was with my dogs, a heat-lightning shiver and speed, quicker than words. Of course to rule is a pleasure, and yet as happiness, as intimacy, these interludes are not to be dismissed, and the experience of sensing other wavelengths in the world besides the human gabble needs woods and fields and isn't found as easily now.

The out-of-doors was everything to me. I spent the summer mornings on Miss Walker's big estate, vaulting the brooks, climbing the pines, creeping along the rabbit paths. Then I made lemonade for the afternoon heat wave and lay on the screen porch listening to Mel Allen broadcast the Yankee game. There'd be a thunderstorm and I would lie in the backyard for that, watching the black clouds brew, feeling the wind. Soaked, grinning, I'd go and sit inside the chicken coop for the clubbiness of the chickens, whose pecking order I knew all about. Later I traveled to prep school carrying my alligators wrapped in a blanket to protect them from the cold. But I loved Tommy Henrich too; I was a hero-worshipper. And at night, when I was jittery, I returned to the city, where I'd lived earlier; in the most frequent dream I jumped off the Empire State Building and flew with uneven success between the skyscrapers by flapping my arms. Winters were spent in galoshes, fooling on the school bus. Those bus rides were the best part of the day; we had no teacher accompanying us and the driver put up with anything. There was a boy who kept a Ford Model A to tinker with when he got home; another was the quarterback who won our football games; another the school mathematician or "brain." The mechanic has since turned into a clergyman, the quarterback works humbly for General Electric, the mathematician is mad. One nondescript goof-off has made a million dollars, and his chum of the period is a social worker with addicts. Of my own friends, the precocious radical has become a stockbroker and the knockabout juvenile delinquent journeys now in Africa. The same sea changes seem to have affected even the houses that I knew. Mrs. Holcomb's, where I took piano lessons, is now the Red Cross Headquarters; Dr. Ludlow's, where I went for inoculations, has become the town museum. Miss Walker's woodsy acres are the Nature Study Center, and the farm

where my sister watched the calves born—Mr. Hulendorf's—
has been subdivided into a deluxe set of hutches called Historic
Homes.

Wherever, whoever we were, we've been squeezed out of the
haunts of our childhood, and there is no reason why we shouldn't
have been. The question is only whether we are gradually being
squeezed out of all possible homes. To the fear of dying of the
ailments that killed our fathers, of angina or driving badly, we
have an added, overlying trepidation that life may be shortened
anyway for all of us. Old age seems not to exist as a possibility
culturally, and the generalized future seems incomprehensible—
exploding, crazily variant developments to be fitted together.
The more successful and propulsive a man of affairs is, the more
freckled and browned he usually looks, so that when he finally
folds up in exhaustion, he must correspond to a tree which has
turned to punk inside the bark invisibly and which suddenly
crumbles. Aging used to be a slow process involving wasting less
and less of one's energy as well as having less energy, and so,
for a long while at least, the pleasure in one's increased effectiveness just about balanced the sadness of winding down. And as
a man lost some of his youthful idealism, he lost, too, some of
the brutality that goes along with being young: a balance was
maintained there also. Now he's either young or on the shelf, and
if he's on the shelf he's savage.

When my father was dying I had a dream which amounts to a
first memory, brought up intact like some frozen fossil which the
ice has preserved. I was diapered, lying on my back in his hands,
well before I could talk. From comparing my size in his hands to
my daughter's size right now I would guess that I was about ten
months old. I was struggling, kicking, and he was dandling me,
blowing in my ear, a sensation too ticklish, too delicious to bear.
Squealing, powerless to prevent his doing it, I loved it, though at
the same time I was dependent upon him to stop before it became
excruciating—I was waving my arms in the air trying to protect
my ears. But the best, vividest piece of the memory is the whir-
ring, vital presence of my father, with deep eyes and a humming
voice, in the prime of life; I remember his strong hands. Even his
early baldness seemed to add to his vigor because it made for

more area of skin. He was several years younger than I am now, and so the continuity of seeing him then and myself now, and seeing him die, is startling.

This memory feeds on to the pinpoint events of a train wreck in Nebraska a year later, and to the familiar jumble of childhood. During the Depression we lived in the city; there were singers at the bottom of the air shaft whom the maid and I threw dimes down to, wrapped in toilet paper so that they wouldn't bounce too far. I pulled the bow of her apron twenty times a day to tease her, and she took me to Catholic church, whose mysteries I remember better than the inside of our church, though once recently when I was hurrying along Lexington Avenue I was brought up short by the sight of a mnemonic worn brick wall that shook me: Sunday school. My parents reappeared in youthful roles, and I could remember something about that whole extraordinary masquerade which one plays as a child—pretending to learn to read, as if we didn't know already, pretending to learn to tell the time, as if we hadn't known all about clocks for years and years.

My father was a financial lawyer. At first I went to an English-type school called St. Bernard's and to birthday parties at the St. Regis Hotel. I remember, too, watching King George pass in a cavalcade on Fifth Avenue from a dowager's wide windows. But Eisenhower, another wartime eminence whom I saw feted from those windows, represents much better my father's style. The side of Eisenhower that wasn't glamorous like Clark Gable resembled my father—the grin, the Kansas accent, the Middle-western forehead, the levelheaded calmness or caution, the sanguine and good-tempered informality. Each was a poor-boy democrat and a Republican; each stood out for rural, old-time values, though personally preferring to hang out at the golf club with industrialists; each was softer in manner than the average soldier or lawyer; and each had a Chinese face lurking behind the prosaic American bones which materialized inchmeal as he aged and died. My father worked in Eisenhower's administration, and Ike was the president he most approved of—an internationalist abroad, a gentle-minded conservative on the home front, who started, however, from the assumption that most people deserved to be liked.

Once when my father was leaving a Mario Lanza movie he stopped to hear one last aria again, and collapsed with emotion on the floor of the theater when it ended. And, if he hadn't much sense of humor (or it came hard to him), he laughed a lot, loudly, every chance he had. He thought that exercise, music and friends were the cure for mental illness: in other words, it terrified him. He thought homosexuality "sinister" on the occasions when he recognized it, and never drank much, and probably was sexually faithful, although I think he fooled himself about the nature of certain avuncular relationships he had; when one young woman married he tore her honeymoon picture in half. But his marriage wasn't unhappy. Quite often he ended his friendships with men who got divorced on what he considered frivolous grounds; he didn't swear or like swearing, although he liked vitality and a masculine air in his friends. He had the chest of a track man and may have read more passionately as a man of sixty than as a college boy, which is unusual—he was especially partial to trans-lated classics and to looking at Renaissance art. Mother married him partly because of his idealism, she says, though naturally I didn't think him idealistic at all. I even went to a different barber in town as a means of delineating the difference between us. Mine was the Town Barbershop, which had *Liberty* magazine beside the chairs and a proprietor nearly eighty years old, wonderfully wiry and tall, with black hair, knotted hands and a sharp nose. For the many years I went to him he knew me as "Peter"—in the beginning I'd been too shy to set him straight. The Colonial Barbershop, which my father patronized, did a smoother job, and the owner, who was a worldly man, tried at one point to break out into the wholesale barbering-supply business but went bank-rupt and soon was right back in the local shop. After that, he spent his weekends in New York, wandering reflectively among the skyscrapers, musing on the enigmas of fortune and wealth.

My father was battling for advancement at the same time, try-ing to rise from the position of a hired attorney to a directorship in the oil corporation he worked for. He wasn't an original type or a sparkplug—he seemed awfully meticulous—and so he lost. He went into retirement angry, though several offers came his way thereafter, such as to go to Hong Kong as consul or head a graduate school. Instead he drifted, wrote poetry, and went to Kyoto. When the World's Fair played on Long Island he drove out and roamed the cheerful pavilions, scanning the Midwestern faces, delighted by the accents, reminded of his boyhood; like the fair itself, he was hopeful. In manner, he was so deliberate some of the other commuters had called him Speed, and yet late in his life he traveled round the world, pulling my mother after him when her enthusiasm waned. He returned to Rome and Paris ten or twelve times, and he loved Florence—nothing that a thousand other men don't do but with as much intensity as any. Dutch Reform by background, he shifted towards agnosticism in middle age, joining the Episcopal Church as a form of neutralism. He liked to sail, sailed rather daringly, not with the caution that exasperated some business associates. He sent money to relatives who had hard rows to hoe and liked uninfluential people as well as the strong. For instance, when I was a boy he made me aware of a fellow at the oil company whose function was to meet transatlantic ships and speed the debarking of company bigwigs and guests—a tall, prudent, intelligent-looking man of mature years whom one would see standing among the crowd of passengers' relatives and friends as the ship docked. Noticeable for his banker's dress and for his height, he would step forward through the multitude and fix upon the personage he was supposed to meet (I suppose he studied photographs), bring over a Customs man, somehow accelerate the inspection, get porters, flag down a taxi, and see the mogul whisked away before most of the passengers were even off the boat. My father was touched by his plight.

When it was possible to procrastinate, my father did so, being a dreamy man, but he was decisive at the end. He went for a sail solo overnight in his little sloop before turning himself in, exhausted, to the doctor, with cancer signals, and while he was waiting to die, still ambulatory, he journeyed to Sarasota with my mother. She could scarcely get him to leave before it was too late for him to go under his own power, but then he settled into the house in Connecticut for the last siege with gallantry and gaiety, so that the big busty nurse, accustomed as she was to seeing men die, actually fell in love with him and became inconsolable. He enjoyed the ripening spring weather, the phonograph, the house he loved, and kept hold of his self-command (what, after all, can one do with one's time in those last weeks except to be friendly?). He talked on the telephone, blinked in the brightening sun—to overhear him in the final conversations he had with friends was piercing. And he did want the Church to fulfill its appointed duties, so when a cub minister was sent to visit him he wasn't satisfied with the small talk they were able to muster. Then an old senior minister, a tippler with a crumpled face, came and told him that he faced "a great adventure," which he accepted as being probably about as good a construction as anybody was going to be able to put on it. My mother saw horses with blowing manes climbing the sky for weeks after he died.

If we are to contrive to lead two lives now, one in the city and one near Katahdin, we can draw some quick assurance from the fact that our backgrounds individually are even more diverse than that. I've got millers, tailors, and outdoorsmen in mine, real out-doorsmen to whom the summer soldiers' Katahdin would be a tasty canapé. Though the two names, Morley and Hoagland, fit together neatly for me because I'm so used to them, the families—my mother's and father's—stretch back in complicated, quite disparate fashion, the Hoaglands to early Brooklyn; later they lived in New Jersey. They came out badly in the Revolutionary War—the branch of them I know about. A skirmish with the British a few minutes' walk from their farm put several of them out of commission for the rest of their lives. The ones who weren't too demoralized moved west and south shortly afterwards to Lexington, Kentucky, where they did fairly well, except that again my own ancestors after a generation or so migrated on by boat and wagon to the farming country of Bardolph, Illinois, where they spent the Civil War. One who had marched with Sherman creaked on from Bardolph by wagon to Hutchinson, Kansas, where he farmed a Soldier's Land Claim, kept a hotel, and worked with team and wagon on the construction of the Santa Fe Railroad, and wound up as the county agricultural agent and a Freemason. Though there were proud Eastern Hoaglands who belonged to the upper crust, and other Hoaglands who split away to seek lonelier, unknown destinies, most of my branch of the family were farmers consistently for two or three hundred years, right back to Brooklyn, and they appear to have filtered away into the soil finally, or else to have wound up in Los Angeles with the rest of the prairie farmers who scraped together a few thousand dollars, there joining the middling middle class.

One early pale fellow loyally fought cholera in the Kentucky epidemic of 1823, dying at his post, and my grandfather, who was a doctor too, died abruptly of meningitis in the 1930s after a bumpy career, mostly practicing obstetrics in Kansas City. He was a husky-faced, square-set man with a red complexion, certainly a kindly doctor, but he found it hard to make a living and for several interludes went down to the bayou lumber camps in Louisiana to work as a company physician. His oldest child died of a fever on one of these tours of duty; his youngest died in his arms after being hit by a trolley a little bit later. His wife, too, died young. I have the impression that his happiest years were while he was in the Medical Corps during the First World War. He and my father got along quite well, and my father, despite his successes and travels later on, would have gone to the state university and presumably stayed in Kansas City if at the last minute he hadn't noticed a scholarship competition for Yale on his school's bulletin board. Being a lawyer and the son of a doctor, he thought of us as a family of professionals and hoped that I would enter one of the professions—if not either of those, then what he called "the cloth"—rather than be a businessman. When I wound up a writer he was utterly taken by surprise.

The Morleys, by contrast, were merchants instead of farmers for as far back as I am aware. They arrived in the New World after the Hoaglands did, and whatever matters they applied themselves to when they first got off the boat, they were in upstate New York for a while before settling in Painesville, Ohio, in the nineteenth century. The Morley burial plot is still in Painesville, along with a rambling white house with long porches and a poppy and gentian field in the rear—a sort of family "seat," which the Hoaglands lack. It was partly the Morleys' clannishness that put me off them when I was a boy. By 1900 they were worthy people with fat family businesses, big family weddings—the marriages

were patriarchal; none of your warlike American ladies there—
and they kept right on flourishing, until by the time Franklin D.
Roosevelt campaigned through town, some of them wouldn't
even walk down to the railroad depot just to set eyes on the man.
Since I'd been brought up among the comforts my father's breadwinning had earned, these shrewd breadwinning businessmen
from Painesville, and Saginaw, Michigan, and Aberdeen, Washington, seemed like vaguely unsavory bores to me. The family
dinners, occurring whenever there was a visit, intimidated me;
the questioning was bluff, immediate and intimate, as if blood
were thicker than water. Yet I remember that when my great-
uncle Ralph came east for the last time, knowing he was soon
to die, he rented his suite at the Biltmore, invited my father up,
and spent that last interview with us reading aloud with relish
the notebook notations he kept in an inside pocket of what his
stock-market portfolio was. My father, who had nothing to do
with handling the Morleys' money, was astonished. This stingy
or mercenary quality afflicting many of the Morleys is in me also,
but they were a florid, varied crew whom a less Protestant person
than myself would have found fascinating from the start, and
next to whom we of the present tribe are insipid fellows. The
Morleys are following the Hoaglands into modest extinction,
part of the Johnny Carson family.

My mother's family's pride and principal vocation during the
time between the two world wars was Morley Bros., a department store and statewide hardware dealership located in Saginaw. Before opening that, her grandfather had had a saddlery
business in Chicago, after leaving Painesville as a young man.
While getting his Chicago operation going, he married a pack-
inghouse heiress, a Kelley (the family had sold out to Armour).
Later, in Saginaw, he founded a bank as a kind of a sideline.
Banking intrigued him, but during the 1929 boom he sold the
bank to a big Detroit bank that was looking for mergers. He happened to be in New York City on a business trip in October during the first black days of the Crash. Realizing the seriousness of
the situation, realizing that the Detroit bank was overcommitted
and might have to close, he hated to think of his own town's bank
collapsing along with it, and so he caught a Pullman home. The

panic was spreading west, the officers in Detroit already saw the handwriting on the wall, and hurrying to rally the help of a few other Saginaw citizens, he was able to buy back the bank and save it, in a fine hour. Banks were still a centerpiece in the post-Victorian era and banks do figure on this side of my family; this same ancestor's daughter-in-law, my grandmother, had grown up in Homer, New York, the child of the local bank president. But they'd had to sneak out of town in sudden disgrace during the 1893 Panic when their bank failed. Her father's health foundered in the aftermath; he died, and she weathered some very hard years.

At any rate, Morley Bros. prospered. My great-grandfather toured the world with his beautiful chestnut-haired Kelley, leaving Ralph in charge of the Saginaw business and A. J., my grandfather, based in Chicago running the older saddlery firm. There were two other brothers, Walter and Paul. Paul was a Peter Pan type who loved combing my mother's hair when she was a young girl (it was the Kelley hair). An aesthete and idealist, he hobnobbed with landscape painters and portrait artists and married a girl of nineteen who was so very demure and Alice-like that she proved to be feeble-minded. He died at only forty-six, welcoming death, so it is said, and leaving behind five blighted children who suffered from Saint Vitus' dance, and worse. Walter, a more earthly man, was a gambler and womanizer, a failed writer, and, later in life, a Presbyterian minister, who lived in relative poverty, exiled by his father to the Wisconsin woods after some early miscues. However, Walter was the first of the Morleys to venture out to the state of Washington. He got mixed up in some kind of woman scandal and went badly into debt to the sawmill promoters of Aberdeen, and A. J. was sent west to buy them off. After Walter had been extricated, though, A. J. went to work investing in timber himself. Bored with Chicago saddlery, he became a pioneer businessman in the Gray's Harbor woods. When his first wife died in childbirth, he married my grandmother, whom he met in a tiny town where she was schoolteaching and where he'd missed his train. Soon he had three trains of his own for hauling logs, and a house on the hill, a yacht, a mistress in downtown Aberdeen (also a schoolmarm, oddly enough), a burro for his children and a black manservant, Tom. Land that he bought for seven thousand dollars and logged was sold recently for three million dollars. He was a careful, decent man with no archenemies, although he fought the Wobblies, and he and Ralph had pleasing sons. Both he and Ralph partook of the Morleys' honest but griping conservatism about money, which ultimately prevented them from getting big-time. Back in Michigan, Ralph turned down a neighbor named Henry Ford who wanted him to invest in a motorcar company, while out in Aberdeen a decade or two later A. J. declined the chance to buy into a new corporation called Boeing. His eldest boy had been killed by a falling tree, but he and his other two sons put their resources into timberland in the Oregon Coast Range instead. One was a financial man, at ease with the business community in Portland; the other, silver-haired before his mid-thirties, could deal with the loggers and union men and drove around through the mountains all day in his pickup truck. Unfortunately, the financial son dropped dead in church in his early fifties. Immediately the hard-nosed investors in Saginaw got scared that my silver-haired uncle would not be able to manage the business alone, and they made him sell out. He did enlist the women in the family, who were also stockholders, to help him stave them off when it came to a vote until he'd delayed long enough to get the proper price.

There is much to the Morleys that I don't know about and much to be said for them. Two women of Northern persuasion wrote action-filled, observant diaries during the Civil War, for instance—all about guerrillas and the battlefronts along the Mississippi. But for a long time, certainly throughout my teens, it was my wish to start from scratch and make my own way in the world without the help of relatives. The Morleys were always boosting each other, some were slightly Babbitt-like, and they assumed, aggravatingly, that any relative was fair game for their gregariousness. Besides, my socialist sentiments leaned more toward the Hoaglands on their dirt farms—they were pleasingly faceless to me, the few I'd seen having just been the Los Angeles transplants. Of course I'd traveled through enough Kansas farming communities to know how little tolerance people there would show for an oddball like me if they perceived my true colors. So, glad to let them remain faceless, I simply liked to think of myself as anchored—in theory, at least—in the heartland, in the Wheat Belt.

Lately it's become the rage to ridicule young 1960s radicals from middle-class backgrounds who pretend to themselves that they are black or are blue-collar, when actually all they need to do if things get tough is reach a telephone to raise bail money or be invited home. The ridicule has been a political weapon because what most bothers people about these young persons is their accomplishment in challenging the nation's stance. I was in their shoes in the 1950s, and we weren't challenging anybody successfully; we kept our heads down, lived privately, and we were few and far between; perhaps the troubles of the present time may owe a little something to our ineffectuality. But like these activists, I'm sure, I was aware of the inconsistencies in my own position—being only too eager to give my parents' suburban address to officialdom if I edged into a jam instead of my grubby Lower East Side street number. Despite the inconsistencies, it seemed to me then that I had the choice of either going out in the world and seeing what was foreign and maybe wretched, having experiences which were not strictly necessary in my case, and *caring*, however uselessly, or else of spending my summer on the tennis courts and on the terrace at the country club, as some of my schoolmates were doing. The head start they supposed they had on people born into different surroundings has often proved illusory, and anyway the effort to make a beginning on independent lines, not piggyback on one's father's achievements, seemed admirable, even traditional, in America until recently. It's just lately, with the exasperated warfare between the generations, that attempting to make a new start for oneself is ridiculed.

Apart from the fuss of being political, the reasons why I was so agitated as a youngster, so angry at my parents that it amounted to a fury lasting for weeks on end, are difficult to reconstruct; I was a bunch of nerves. My mother, who besides being impulsive and generous was a strangely warm woman at times, would ask me to eat dinner without my glasses on so she could look at my

uncluttered face, and tried to insist that I move down from the
third floor to the room next to hers. Sometimes after my father
and I had had a conciliatory talk, she'd give me a quite opposite
report of what he thought, or thought of me, as though to revive
the quarrel. Later, in my twenties, looking back, my chief complaint against him was that he hadn't shielded me from some of
her eccentric whims and decisions; yet I'd fought with him rather
than her, especially when I was in earnest. She was my cohort,
guiding me most directly, and now, when I put first things first
and respond quickly to the moment, it's her influence. What I
learned from him was not the Boerlike sobriety and self-denial
he espoused but the qualities that I saw for myself: his gentleness
and slow-tempoed soft gaiety, his equanimity under pressure. I
liked the way he ate too; he ate like a gourmet whenever he could.

Although I would have been willing to ignore most facets of
the life of the town where I grew up, luckily it wasn't possible for
me to do that. So I have the many loose-leaf memories a hometown is supposed to provide—of the Kane children, whose father
was a gardener and who threw jackknives at trees whenever they
were mad, which, living as they did in other people's garages, was
a good deal of the time; of setter field trials and local football; of
woebegone neighbors and abrupt marital puzzles—a wife who
rejoiced when her husband died and buried him before his friends
knew there was going to be a funeral. There were some advertising people so rich that they lived in one large house by themselves and kept their children in another a hundred yards away.
There was a young architect struck into stone with polio, and a
lady who collected impoverished nobles in Italy after the war and
whose husband, left sick at home, made the maid disrobe at gun-
point when he finally got lonely. On the dark roads after supper
you'd see more than one commuter taking a determined-looking
constitutional, walking fast for miles, as if to get his emotions
under control.

After my father's death we sold our house and set about looking for new places to consider home, not an easy task. The memory was of twenty rooms, artesian water, a shady lawn, a little
orchard and many majestic maples and spruce, all situated where
an old crossroads stagecoach inn had stood. None of us came

up with an arrangement to equal that, but my mother has a trim pretty house on Martha's Vineyard. My sister married and, with her husband, found a farmhouse in Connecticut near his work with five or six acres on which she put ten horses, in order to start a riding stable. These were snake-necked, branded horses that they'd brought in a van from California, right off the range, with a long winter's growth of hair. The neighbors, who believed that life ought to have a dual, contemporary character, rushed to the zoning board to express dismay that in a fast-developing, year-round community the regulations hadn't yet been revised to bar such activities, which seemed more appropriate to a *summer* home. They were right to think it surprising, and yet the board was awfully reluctant to declare once and for all, officially, that the era of farms and barns had ended.

I married too and live in western Greenwich Village, which is an ungeometric district of architecture in a smorgasbord and little stores. There is a massive wholesale meat market in the neighborhood, a gypsy moving industry, many printing plants and bakeries, a trading center for antiques, a dozen ocean-oriented wharves, and four or five hundred mysterious-looking enterprises in lofts, each of which could either be a cover for the Federal Narcotics Bureau or house an inventor-at-work. I like the variety (the mounted police have a stable two blocks away, the spice industry's warehouses are not far south); I like the low nineteenth-century houses alongside bars with rock jukeboxes and all the swoosh of à la mode. The pull or the necessity of living in the city seems only to grow stronger as every sort of development is telescoped into a briefer span of time. We can either live in our own period or decline to, and to decline revokes many other choices we might have. Mostly what we try to do is live with one foot in the seventies and one foot in an earlier decade—the foot that doesn't mind going to sleep and maybe missing something.

I've just bought a house of my own in Vermont, eight rooms with a steel roof, all painted a witching green. It's two miles from the nearest light pole and it was cheap, but it's got forty acres, extending in a diamond shape, that back up to five thousand acres of state-owned land, and stands in a basin just underneath the western-style peak of a stiff little mountain, Wheeler

Mountain, that curves around in front. The Wheelers, our only neighbors, live next door on a three-hundred-acre farm, growing up in aspen, balsam, birch, and pine, just as our land is. Mr. Wheeler, who is in his eighties now, was a fireman on the Grand Trunk Railroad for much of his life but grew up here and returned during the Depression. His father had pioneered the land; the Butterfields pioneered mine. The Butterfields built a log house close to that of old Mr. Wheeler, for whom Mr. Butterfield worked. There was a sawmill, a sugar house, and even a granite quarry on Wheeler's place. The log house was really more like a root house than living quarters, to judge from the photograph we have, so in 1900 Mr. Butterfield and his three sons built this new home out of sawn spruce and big granite foundation blocks and plaster mixed from sand from the Boiling Spring over the hill. Their lame old horse did the hauling and pulled the scoop when they dug out the cellar hole, and young Wheeler, a schoolboy then, helped nail the laths.

Butterfield was a rough character, he says, "part Indian," as the phrase goes, but you could depend on him to do a job. His mother-in-law lived with the family, constantly fighting with him. She called him dumb and crude because he couldn't do sums, for instance; she wrote a column of numbers on the wall and watched him fail to add it. About 1909 he shot her, took his remaining relatives next door for refuge, and shot himself. There are bullet holes, stopped up with putty, and it is claimed that that nagging column of numbers on the parlor wall had finally been added correctly. Newspaper reporters buzzed around, the property soon passed to the Stanley family, and Burt Stanley, who was a stonemason, farmed it in his spare time until his death in the 1930s. Then a tax bill of thirteen dollars came due. His widow, Della, was unable to pay it (some say she paid it but got no receipt), so the town tax collector, a fellow named Byron Bundy, foreclosed and sold her home to a crony of his named Gray, who quickly reconveyed the place to Bundy himself. Bundy died, the house stood empty through World War II (the porcupines chewing away like carpenters at the corners and edges), and his heirs sold it to our predecessors at a joke of a price.

So I'm getting a grip on the ground, in other words—gathering the stories of what went on and poking in the woods. It's certainly not an onerous chore; I've explored so many wood lots which *weren't* mine. Up among the mountain ledges is a cave as big as a band concert shell, and a narrow unexpected swamp with pitcher plants growing in it, very lush, a spring that springs out of a rock, and a huge ash sheltered in a hollow which has disguised its height and kept the loggers and the lightning off. Not far away is a whetstone ledge where a little businesslike mining used to be done. And there are ravens, bats, barred owls, a hawk or two, phoebes under the eaves, and tales of big bears in the pasture and somebody being cornered by a bull. Delphiniums, mint, lemon lilies, catnip, wild roses, and marigolds grow next to the house. Storer's snakes live in the woodpile, as well as garter snakes, brick-colored and black. In the spring dogtooth violets come up, and trilliums, Dutchman's-breeches, boxflowers, foamflowers, and lady's slippers, and in the fall the fields fill up with goldenrod and brown-eyed Susans, aster, fireweed. Raspberries grow in masses; also blackberries, blueberries, wild cherries and wild plums. The apple orchard is complicated in its plotting, because these farmers wanted apples in late summer—Dutch apples, Yellow Transparents, and McIntosh—and then another set of trees which ripened in the autumn, perhaps Baldwins or Northern Spies, and lastly the hard winter apples, which weren't sweet and which they canned or cooked as applesauce or "sulphured" to keep till spring. An orchard was a man's bequest to his children, being something that they couldn't promptly create for themselves when the land passed to them. I've got more going on on that hill slope of apple trees than I know about, and when the fruit falls finally, the deer and bears eat it—the bears when they have grown impatient waiting have bashed down whole limbs.

In New York my home *is* New York; nothing less than the city itself is worth the abrasion of living there, and the alterations go on so fast that favorite hangouts go by the boards in a month's time; the stream of people and sensation is the thing. But in the country the one word is exactitude. If you don't like the barn behind the house and the slant of the land and the trees that you face, then you're not going to be happy. The Canadian cli-

mate of north Vermont makes for an ideal second home because
in four months three seasons can be witnessed. June is spring,
September already is autumn. The moonlight is wheat-colored
in August, and the mountain rises with protean gradualism to a
taciturn round peak. On the east face is a wall which, if you walk
around that way, can look to be nine thousand feet; the granite turns ice-white. The trees puff in the moonlight to swirling,
steeplish shapes, or look like ferns. During the day sometimes
a fog will effect the same exaggerated trick. High up, the wind
blows harder, gnarling the spruce and bringing clouds swiftly
across like those in the high Rockies; you seldom have a sense of
just what altitude you're at. Every winter the deer yard under the
cliffs in a cedar copse, and on the opposite side, the valley behind
the hill that lies behind the Wheelers' house and mine has never
been farmed and is so big it is called Big Valley. Vast and thick
with trees, it's like an inlet of the sea, sending off a sheen in mid-
summer as you look down on it.

Mr. Wheeler, the youngest in his family, went to school with
the Butterfield children in what is now the Wheelers' house,
remodeled and enlarged. He is a broad-shouldered, white-faced
man, a machinist at one point, until the dust bothered his lungs.
Now he tinkers with his tractor and the power mower, listening to the Red Sox games, although the only professional baseball he ever saw was when he lived in Montreal during the early
1920s. He's a serene, bold man who has survived heart trouble
and diabetes and says little but appears full of cheer even when
he's angry. Mrs. Wheeler is a dignified, straight-backed woman,
quite a reader, and formerly a psychiatric nurse. She once wrote
a column for the county newspaper, and used to brew a thousand pounds of cottage cheese during the summer and peddle
it among the vacationers, along with strawberries, butter, and
cream. She keeps a diary and a record of the visitors who come to
climb the mountain that we look at, and keeps a calorie count of
what her husband eats. She is his second wife, ten years younger.
They have a walkie-talkie for communication with the world
outside, and extra stocks of food, and a 280-gallon tank of kerosene for heating, so that the snows don't threaten them. The road
plugs up but eventually it's plowed; the snow in the fields gets five

feet deep and lasts so long "it mosses over—you always get six weeks of March." Being a vigorous walker still, Mrs. Wheeler is even less intimidated than her husband, and in the country style is reticently generous, as realistic as a nurse and farmer's wife combined.

In the old days there was a local man who could run down the deer and knife them, he had such endurance—he could keep up with their first dash, and as they porpoised through the woods, could keep going longer than they could. He hung the meat in a tree by his cabin to freeze, and liked raccoons particularly also, so that by midwinter the tree was strung with upwards of thirty raccoons, skinned and dressed, suspended like white pineapples. Another character, whose complexion was silver-colored, made a regular business out of bountying porcupines. The town paid fifty cents per pair of ears, and sometimes he brought in a hundred pairs. He claimed he had a super-hunting-dog, but actually he was cutting out triangular snips of stomach skin to make a dozen "porcupines" for every one he killed. He didn't do enough real work to break the Sabbath, as they say, and didn't lay in hay enough to last his cattle through the winter, so that by the end of February he would be dragging birch trees to the barn for them to scrape a living from. For spending money, he gave boxing lessons at night in the waiting room of the old railroad station at the foot of the hill. Roy Lord, who lives across from where the station was, learned to box from him. Lord has shot seventy-three deer in his lifetime. He lives with a sneezing parrot fifty-six years old, and a bull terrier who lost an eye in a fight in the driveway; he points out the spot where the eye fell. He can recite the details of the murders and suicides in the neighborhood going back forty years—all the fights with fenceposts, all the dirty cheating deals and sudden strange inheritances. He's learned the secrets of more than one suspicious death because he's made it a point over the years to get right to the scene, sometimes even before the police. Or they'd be gathering reinforcements, distributing riot guns, and radioing for instructions in front of the house, while Lord would sneak around to the back door and pop inside and see the way the brains were sprayed and where the body lay and where the gun was propped, and damn well *know* it wasn't sui-

cide. There was a family of Indians here, who'd murdered somebody in Canada and buried him in their cellar and moved across
the border. They slept on a pile of old buffalo robes laid on the
floor. The daughter, a half-breed, went back into the woods in
a fit of despondency and found a cliff and jumped. Then when
the men had died as well, the last of them, a white-haired old
woman, stretched out on the railroad tracks with her neck on a
rail and ended it that way. (Lord tells these stories while watching the TV—sheriffs slugging baddies and bouncers punching
drunks. His son was a sniper in the Pacific theater, stalking the
Japanese like deer; is now a quiet bachelor who works in Massachusetts, driving home weekends.)

I'm transplanting some spruce and beginning to clear my
upper field of striped maple and arctic birch. I'm also refashion-
ing a chicken coop to serve as a playhouse when our baby is four
or five. The barn is sturdy, moderate-sized, unpainted, built with
used planking fifteen years ago. Although the place where I grew
up probably had a better barn, I took that one for granted. Now
I stand in my own barn and look up at the joists and rafters, the
beams under the hayloft, the king posts, struts, and studding,
the slabs of wood nailed angularly for extra strength. It's all in
the same pattern as the other barns in town, and yet I marvel at
it. The junk inside consists of whiffle trees, neck yokes and har-
ness, a tractor and a harrow, neither functional, and painters'
ladders, milking stools, and broken stanchions. In the attic of the
house are smaller memorabilia, like fox and beaver traps, deer
antlers and tobacco cans of clean deer lard, an old grindstone,
an old bedpan, a pair of high green boots, a pile of *Reader's
Digest*s, which when matched with our assorted miscellany and
childhood books, stacked up, and different boxes of letters and
snapshots (snapshots of the prairie Hoaglands seventy years ago,
posed in jokey insouciance—Hoaglands who would have felt at
home here), will be the attic our daughter grows up to know.

Freight trains hoot through town; there is a busy blacksmith,
a Ben Franklin store, and a rest home called Poole's, whose telephone is the night number for all emergency facilities. People say
"the forenoon" and say a man whose wife has left him "keeps

bachelor's hall." Our predecessors in the house, the Basfords, ate groundhogs parboiled, and deer in season and out, and, though we're easier on the game, we cook on their wood stove and light with kerosene, and just as in the platitudes, it's a source of ease and peace. Nothing hokum-yokum, just a sense of competence and self-sufficiency. Everything takes time—when it's too dark to read we cook supper, hearing the calling of the owls; then maybe I take the dogs for a walk, playing the part of the blind god. Of course I wouldn't want to get along with wood and kerosene all *winter*; nor do I want to turn the clock back. It's simply doing what is necessary; there is one kind of necessity in the city and another here.

The Basfords only moved around the mountain when we bought their farm. The stove is one Mr. B.'s father bought in 1921—the salesman drove up with a team and wagon piled with iron stoves and told him that if he could break the lid of any of them he could have the whole stove free. The spring we pipe our water from Mr. B. found himself, using water-witching procedures. The first time that he dug a catch-hole he tried enlarging it with dynamite. One stick—detonated with the tractor engine— worked all right, but when he got greedy and wanted still a bigger source, he put in two more sticks and blew the spring away, tipping the base rock so that the water flowed by other routes. He had to go dowsing again, farther from the house, but found a new spot underground where three trickles joined together in front of a tree, and dug more modestly this time, although the overflow was sufficient for Mrs. B. to raise beds of celery there. She's English, once a war bride, now a giggly and seductive woman of about fifty. He is slow-speaking, sharp-witted, rather truculent and rather endearing. He doesn't vote, doesn't get along in town, doesn't work especially hard, doesn't look up to anyone, is an iconoclast. But she admires him. They seem to love each other in absolutely current terms. They're always having coffee, sipping wine, and talking endlessly.

Perhaps I might as well have begun this essay by saying that things are better than we think. In the public domain they're not, and we can't glance ahead with pleasure to the world our children will inhabit—more than us, they will have to swim for dear life. But middle age is the time when we give more than we get— give love, give work, seek sites. And sites can still be found, at least. You may discover you need two modest houses, but you can find your homes and set to work, living for the decade.

*Joan Didion (born 1934) is perhaps the most revered and influential nonfiction writer of today. Her essay collections and memoirs (*Slouching Towards Bethlehem, The White Album, After Henry, The Year of Magical Thinking) *chart the stresses and strains of America's cultural and political history from a perspective that combine coolly unblinking reportage with deeply personal, subjective inflections. Though she claimed to have fashioned her prose style initially by imitating Hemingway, she achieved a sublimely individual, poignantly suggestive way with sentences. Here she positions herself both inside and at a dispassionate distance from the era of the Sixties she had just passed through.*

ON THE MORNING AFTER THE SIXTIES

I am talking here about being a child of my time. When I think about the Sixties now I think about an afternoon not of the Sixties at all, an afternoon early in my sophomore year at Berkeley, a bright autumn Saturday in 1953. I was lying on a leather couch in a fraternity house (there had been a lunch for the alumni, my date had gone on to the game, I do not now recall why I had stayed behind), lying there alone reading a book by Lionel Trilling and listening to a middle-aged man pick out on a piano in need of tuning the melodic line to "Blue Room." All that afternoon, he sat at the piano, and all that afternoon he played "Blue Room" and he never got it right. I can hear and see it still, the wrong note in "We will thrive on / Keep alive on," the sunlight falling through the big windows, the man picking up his drink and beginning again and telling me, without ever saying a word, something I had not known before about bad marriages and wasted time and looking backward. That such an afternoon would now seem implausible in every detail—the idea of having had a "date" for a football lunch now seems to me so exotic as to be almost czarist—suggests the extent to which the narrative in which many of us grew up no longer applies.

The distance we have come from the world in which I went to college has been on my mind quite a bit during those seasons when not only Berkeley but dozens of other campuses were periodically shut down, incipient battlegrounds, their borders sealed. To think of Berkeley as it was in the Fifties was not to think of barricades and reconstituted classes. "Reconstitution" would have sounded to us then like Newspeak, and barricades are never personal. We were all very personal then, sometimes relentlessly so, and, at that point where we either act or do not act, most of us are still. I suppose I am talking about just that: the ambiguity of belonging to a generation distrustful of political highs, the historical irrelevancy of growing up convinced that the heart of darkness lay not in some error of social organization but in man's own blood. If man was bound to err, then any social organization was bound to be in error. It was a premise which still seems to me accurate enough, but one which robbed us early of a certain capacity for surprise.

At Berkeley in the Fifties no one was surprised by anything at all, a *donnée* which tended to render discourse less than spirited, and debate nonexistent. The world was by definition imperfect, and so of course was the university. There was some talk even then about IBM cards, but on balance the notion that free education for tens of thousands of people might involve automation did not seem unreasonable. We took it for granted that the Board of Regents would sometimes act wrongly. We simply avoided those students rumored to be FBI informers. We were that generation called "silent," but we were silent neither, as some thought, because we shared the period's official optimism nor, as others thought, because we feared its official repression. We were silent because the exhilaration of social action seemed to many of us just one more way of escaping the personal, of masking for a while that dread of the meaningless which was man's fate.

To have assumed that particular fate so early was the peculiarity of my generation. I think now that we were the last generation to identify with adults. That most of us have found adulthood just as morally ambiguous as we expected it to be falls perhaps into the category of prophecies self-fulfilled: I am simply not sure. I am telling you only how it was. The mood of Berkeley in those years was one of mild but chronic "depression," against which I remember certain small things that seemed to me somehow explications, dazzling in their clarity, of the world I was about to enter: I remember a woman picking daffodils in the rain one day when I was walking in the hills. I remember a teacher who drank too much one night and revealed his fright and bitterness. I remember my real joy at discovering for the first time how language worked, at discovering, for example, that the central line of *Heart of Darkness* was a postscript. All such images were personal, and the personal was all that most of us expected to find. We would make a separate peace. We would do graduate work in Middle English, we would go abroad. We would make some money and live on a ranch. We would survive outside history, in a kind of *idée fixe* referred to always, during the years I spent at Berkeley, as "some little town with a decent beach."

As it worked out I did not find or even look for the little town with a decent beach. I sat in a large bare apartment in which I lived my junior and senior years (I had lived awhile in a sorority, the Tri Delt house, and had left it, typically, not over any "issue" but because I, the implacable "I," did not like living with sixty people) and I read Camus and Henry James and I watched a flowering plum come in and out of blossom and at night, most nights, I walked outside and looked up to where the cyclotron and the bevatron glowed on the dark hillside, unspeakable mysteries which engaged me, in the style of my time, only personally. Later I got out of Berkeley and went to New York and later I got out of New York and came to Los Angeles. What I have made for myself is personal, but not exactly peace. Only one person I knew at Berkeley later discovered an ideology, dealt himself into history, cut himself loose from both his own dread and his own time. A few of the people I knew at Berkeley killed themselves not long after. Another attempted suicide in Mexico and then, in a recovery which seemed in many ways a more advanced derangement, came home and joined the Bank of America's three-year executive-training program. Most of us live less theatrically, but remain the survivors of a peculiar and inward time. If I could believe that going to a barricade would affect man's fate in the slightest I would go to that barricade, and quite often I wish that I could, but it would be less than honest to say that I expect to happen upon such a happy ending.

ACKNOWLEDGMENTS

I'm deeply beholden to the many friends and colleagues who came up with ideas for this anthology. Most crucially, I would like to thank Jennifer Ratner-Rosenhagen and the late Ned Stuckey-French for their copious suggestions. Others who contributed names include: Halbert Barton, Paul Berman, Robert Boyers, Adam Braver, Ian Buruma, Carmen Boullosa, Vivian Gornick, Eli Gottlieb, Michael Greenberg, Margo Jefferson, Randall Kennedy, Frances Kiernan, David Lazar, Richard Locke, David Mikics, Honor Moore, Max Nelson, Ross Posnock, Vijay Seshadri, Lee Siegal, Benjamin Taylor, Clifford Thompson, and Brenda Wineapple. Shifra Sharlin and Lisa Brennan Jobs read batches of pieces and gave invaluable advice. My Columbia graduate students, God bless them, allowed me to test-drive alternate texts on them. Hats off to the crew at Brooklyn Postal for their impeccable work. I'm supremely grateful to my editor, Diana Secker Tesdell, and to my agent, Gail Hochman, for making this volume happen in the first place and then seeing it through. I owe more than I can say to my capable assistant, Adam Schwartzman, for tracking down permissions. And lastly, a huge thank-you to my wife, Cheryl, and daughter, Lily, for keeping me sane (sort of) during the editing process.

PERMISSIONS